Havana

Havana

The Making of Cuban Culture

Antoni Kapcia

Oxford • New York

First published in 2005 by
Berg
Editorial offices:
1st Floor, Angel Court, 81 St Clements Street, Oxford, OX4 1AW, UK
175 Fifth Avenue, New York, NY 10010, USA

Berg is the imprint of Oxford International Publishers Ltd.

Library of Congress Cataloguing-in-Publication Data
Kapcia, Antoni.
Havana : the making of Cuban culture / Antoni Kapcia.
p. cm.
Includes bibliographical references and index.
ISBN 1-85973-837-0 (pbk.) — ISBN 1-85973-832-X (cloth)
1. Havana (Cuba)—Civilization. I. Title.
F1799.H35K37 2005
972.91'23—dc22   2005007951

British Library Cataloguing-in-Publication Data
A catalogue record for this book is available from the British Library.

ISBN-13 978 1 85973 832 0 (Cloth)
ISBN-10 1 85973 832 X (Cloth)

ISBN-13 978 1 85973 837 5 (Paper)
ISBN-10 1 85973 837 0 (Paper)

Typeset by Avocet Typeset, Chilton, Aylesbury, Bucks
Printed in the United Kingdom by Biddles Ltd, King's Lynn

www.bergpublishers.com

Contents

List of Figures   vii

Preface   ix

Glossary of Abbreviations Used   xi

Glossary of Spanish Terms   xiii

Introduction: The Havana Mosaic: Sweetness and Light   1
    Images of Havana   1
    Havana as Unique   2
    The Emergence of the City   4
    Theoretical Issues   5
    The Structure and Aim of the Book   21

1   The Colony (1550s–1902)   27
    Historical Overview   27
    Part I: The City in the Shadows – Pre-sugar Havana
        (1550s–1760s)   32
    Part II: The Boom City – Sugar and the Evolution of a
        Capital (1750s–1901)   36

2   The Republic (1902–1958)   61
    Historical Overview   61
    Part I: A Nation without a Capital and a Capital without a
        Nation (1902–33)   65
    Part II: Havana as the 'cultural problem' (1934–58) 88
    Part III: *Bohemia* Case Study   107
    Conclusions   116

3   **The Revolution from 1959 to 1990**   119
     Historical Overview   119
     Part I: Dark Days and Revolutionary Enlightenment
       (1959–71)   125
     Part II: The Grey Years – Conformity and Stagnation (the
       1970s and 1980s)   149
     Part III: Case Study – *Bohemia* and *Granma*   168

4   **The Revolution in a New Light?: Havana as a New Cultural**
     Space   179
     Historical Overview   179
     The Período Especial and Havana   182
     The Evolution and Rediscovery of a Havana Culture   189
     Case Study – the Casas de Cultura   200

Conclusion: Havana as Chiaroscuro   207

Bibliography   215

Index   227

List of Figures

1	Map of Havana	xvii
2	Map of Havana Region	xix
3	The Palacio de los Capitanes-Generales, the governor's palace in the central Plaza de Armas	39
4	The original building of the Sociedad Económica de Amigos del País	44
5	The Gran Teatro (built in 1915 as the Centro Gallego)	66
6	A synagogue in Vedado, one of the few remaining signs of a once significant Jewish (*polaco*) immigrant community	68
7	The Teatro Roldán (formerly the Teatro Auditorium), in Vedado, now the principal concert venue for classical music	82
8	The status of baseball revealed by this tomb to a Havana baseball association's members	88
9	The 1950s modernist façade of the Casa de las Américas building	129
10	The Gato Tuerto café, site of the Puente group's meetings	137
11	The statue to John Lennon in Vedado, a sign of shifting attitudes to a music disapproved in the 1960s but now enshrined as part of the canon	146
12	The restoration of Habana Vieja: the impressive Plaza Vieja	184
13	The Iglesia de San Francisco restored as a concert venue	185
14	*Gigantes* in Habana Vieja: the adaptation of the carnivalesque to tourist dollars	186
15	Street musicians in the restored Habana Vieja, by the Lonja del Comercio	187
16	The creation of green spaces as an integral part of the restoration of Habana Vieja	187
17	The restoration of Habana Vieja: the curious fusion of tourist-oriented manifestations of globalisation and socialism	188
18	*Azoteas* (flat roofs) in Havana: the ideal gathering site during the worst of the Special Period	190
19	Street booksellers in the Plaza de Armas	194
20	The power of baseball: a *peña* in full swing in its usual locale in the Parque Central	197
21	*Aficionado* paintings on display at a local Casa de Cultura (in Regla)	200
22	The entrance to a Casa de Cultura (Regla)	201

Preface

This book emerged, fundamentally, from an invitation by Berg Publishers, who published my previous book, but it clearly has roots in much of my earlier research. Indeed, when I was approached by them, my initial response was mixed. On the one hand, it offered me a fascinating opportunity to broaden my work into new areas, to examine the city I have come to know so well over the years, and to return to some of my research roots; for, having first studied literature at University College London (on what was then a pioneering multidisciplinary course on Iberia and Latin America) and then having undertaken doctoral research on Cuban literature, I discovered while completing that project my greater aptitude and preference for my 'other' root, the study of history, which thereafter became my discipline. Hence, the Berg invitation offered the chance to return to once familiar questions and take my historiography in new disciplinary directions.

Therein, however, also lay some caution. For I was aware that, by embarking on a cross-disciplinary work, I was entering an academic minefield, which, if genuinely interdisciplinary, could tread on toes, fall into unfamiliar theoretical traps and risk criticism for omitting or generalising about subjects on which specialists in the different fields could justifiably criticise the outcome, or for not paying sufficient attention to theoretical debates or frameworks within those areas. Hence, I decided from the outset that the best course was, firstly, to remind myself constantly that I am professionally a historian writing a history (and not *the* history) of a culture of a particular city and should stick to the methodology I know best (while being prepared to incorporate new approaches and perspectives where appropriate); secondly, to trust the subject matter itself to overcome any faults in the transdisciplinarity; and, lastly, to hope that the reader would be patient and understand the objectives, the approach and the omissions, on the grounds that, for all its pitfalls, crossing disciplines can be truly rewarding, at best casting new light on old subjects. The subject matter itself, of course, I assumed would be essentially fascinating.

As ever, of course, thanks must go where they are due (and apologies to those who have helped in the writing but whom space limitations prevent me from mentioning in person). Firstly, I must thank all those at Berg who not only gave this opportunity but who showed, throughout, great forbearance in the face of repeated extensions and delays (which made me much more sympathetic to my own students' failures to meet deadlines!). Secondly, I must give due thanks to my two UK institutions: to the University of Wolverhampton who gave me support, money and time (including valuable study leave) to embark on the project and then, since September 2003, to my new and current institution, the University of Nottingham, for their support, tolerance and interest while completing a project that I brought with me. Equally, thanks go to colleagues at the University of Havana and other friends in Cuba, who have, as ever, given me help, advice, introductions, criticism: in particular, I should name Rubén Zardoya, Hilda Torres, Carlos de la Icera, Rosa María de Lahaye Guerra, Jorge Ibarra Cuesta, Fernando Martínez Heredia, Pablo Pacheco López, Paquita López Civeira, Pepe Vázquez López and Paula Ortiz. In addition, I thank others I have met in Cuba without whose help this could not have taken shape as it did, including Alberto Granado, the staff of the Biblioteca Nacional José Martí and the Instituto de Literatura y Lingüística. I particularly need to thank Fernando Rojas (president of the Consejo Nacional de Casas de Cultura), Sara Lamerán Echevarría (former *instructora* and now official of the Consejo Nacional) and the staff of the Casa de Cultura 'Flora' in Marianao, for their invaluable information and help with the focus and research on the Casas de Cultura. In Britain, thanks should also go to academic colleagues who have con-tributed advice and materials, or from whose work, thoughts and research I have learned much of use (usually appearing here in some form or other, hopefully suit-ably acknowledged), including current and former postgraduate students I have been fortunate enough to work with: Par Kumaraswami, Kepa Artaraz, Anne Luke, Jill Ingham and Guy Baron, who have all helped me with aspects of the book.

Finally, of course, special thanks must go to those closest to me, to my sons Stefan and Jan, for their patience yet again over the months of this work, and to Jean, as ever the main source of inspiration for ideas, the main critic and the main support for the time, effort, and anguish which has gone into this work.

A few words of explanation might not go amiss here. The first is that I have chosen to use Spanish terms repeatedly in a few cases, most obviously when referring to the inhabitants of Havana, *habaneros* having no easy and concise translation, and Habana Vieja rather than Old Havana; most of the terms used, except where the meaning is obvious or an explanation given, are included in the Glossary. The second is that I have chosen to translate all the Spanish quotations myself.

Glossary of Abbreviations Used

CDR	Comité de Defensa de la Revolución (neighbourhood Defence Committee)
CNC	Consejo Nacional de Cultura (National Cultural Council)
CTC	Central de Trabadadores de Cuba (Cuban Workers' Confederation)
DEU	Directorio Estudiantil Universitario (University Students' Directorate)
DRE	Directorio Revolucionario Estudiantil (Revolutionary Student Directorate)
FAR	Fuerzas Armadas Revolucionarias (Revolutionary Armed Forces)
FEU	Federación Estudiantil Universitaria (University Students' Federation)
FMC	Federación de Mujeres Cubanas (Cuban Women's Federation)
ICAIC	Instituto Cubano de Artes e Industrias Cinematográficas (Cuban Film Institute)
INDER	Instituto Nacional de Deportes Educación Física y Recreación
INRA	Instituto Nacional de Reforma Agraria
INTUR	Instituto de Turismo
ISA	Instituto Superior de Artes
ORI	Organizaciones Revolucionarias Integradas
PSP	Partido Socialista Popular
PURS	Partido Unido de la Revolución Socialista
UJC	Unión de Jóvenes Comunistas (Young Communists' Union)
UMAP	Unidad Militar de Ayuda a la Producción (Military Unit to Aid Production)
UNEAC	Unión Nacional de Escritores y Artistas Cubanos (National Union of Cuban Writers and Artists)

Glossary of Spanish Terms

aficionado	fan; amateur performer
afrancesado	looking to French fashions, models etc.
agromercado	lit. agricultural market, i.e. food market
audiencia	(legal) court in the Empire
autocrítica	self-criticism, confession
azotea	flat roof
balsero	rafter (refugee on a raft, *balsa*)
barrio	city neighbourhood
batistato	Batista's period in office
batistiano	to do with (supporter of) Batista
bodega	food shop for ration-book supplies
bolero	romantic ballad
cabildo	(a) council (colonial period); (b) a black cultural society
campo	countryside
canario	from the Canaries
cartelera	noticeboard, billboard (for cultural events)
caso	(political) affair (as in *caso Padilla*)
colono	independent sugar-grower
comparsa	processional Afro-Cuban dance
criollo	(colonial period) a white born in Cuba
Cuba Libre	Free Cuba
cubanía	'Cuban-ness', and the belief in *cubanidad*
cubanidad	'Cuban-ness'
cuenta propia	lit. 'own account', i.e. self-employment (thus *cuentapropista*)
cuentista	storyteller, story-writer
chiquita	little
décima	traditional verse and song form
declamación	recital, learned and recited speech
encuentro	lit. meeting; usually concert, gathering, festival
escuela	school
finca	(coffee) farm
flota	fleet

friqui	'punk' (from 'freaky')
gallego	lit. Galician, but used for all Spaniards from 1902
guajiro	traditional term for (usually white, Spanish) peasant
guardia nocturna	night guard duty in the CDRs
habanero	inhabitant of Havana
ingenio	(traditional) sugar mill
inventar	lit. 'invent', but after 1990 meaning 'make do'
jineterismo	hustling (thus *jinetero* and *jinetera*)
junta	provisional government
latifundio	traditional large and powerful landholding
lectura	reading, but especially the public reading to tobacco workers
libreta	ration-book
machadato	Machado's period in office
mambí (pl. *mambises*)	(mostly black) rebel in the 1868–78 and 1895–98 wars
mestizo	mixed-race, usually in Latin America Amerindian and white (therefore also *mestizaje*, 'cultural fusion')
microbrigada	lit. micro-brigade, i.e. special construction unit
mulato	mulatto, mixed-race (black and white)
municipio	local authority unit of government ('township')
negrismo	the 1920s–1940s cultural movement using Afro-Cuban themes etc.
oriental	normally from Oriente province (now a region)
paladar	private restaurant
palenque	community of escaped slaves
parlamento obrero	workplace assembly
paseo	promenade (both as street and activity)
patria	lit. fatherland, i.e. nation, country
patrimonio	heritage
peninsular	(colonial period) a white born in Spain
peña	(culture) group, circle; (baseball) fan-club, supporters' gathering
permuta	the system of exchange (rather than sale) of housing
presentación	book launch
radionovela	radio soap opera
reconcentración	Weyler's policy of concentration camps in 1876–8 and 1895–8
resolver	lit. 'to resolve', but meaning 'get hold of' (often illegally)
roquero/rockero	rock-music fan

siboney	one of the pre-Columbian cultures in Cuba
solar	most typical kind of inner-city slum (tenement around a central courtyard)
taíno	one of the pre-Columbian cultures in Cuba
taller	workshop
telenovela	TV soap
tencén	pre-1959 corner-shop
tertulia	(a) (culture) regular cultural evening or gathering
	(b) (baseball) the equivalent of *peña*
timba	1990s Cuban variant of *salsa*
toma de conciencia	lit. examination of conscience, i.e. realisation, reassessment
trovador	lit. minstrel; balladeer
vega	tobacco-field
velada	*soirée* (*tertulia*)
volante	type of carriage
voluntario	voluntary (cf. *trabajo voluntario*: voluntary work) or volunteer
zafra	sugar harvest
zarzuela	traditional Spanish light opera

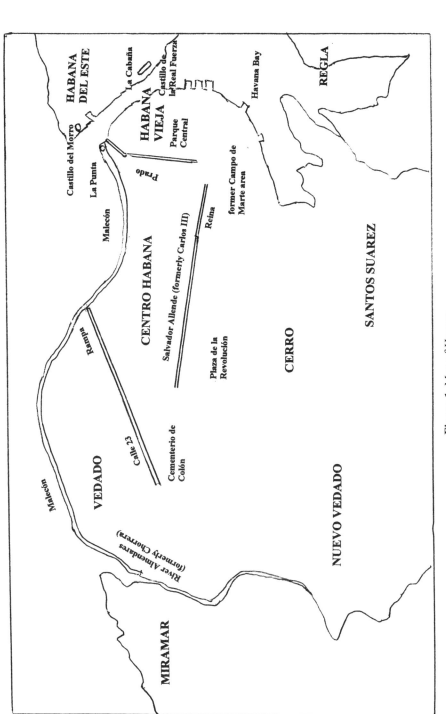

Figure 1 Map of Havana

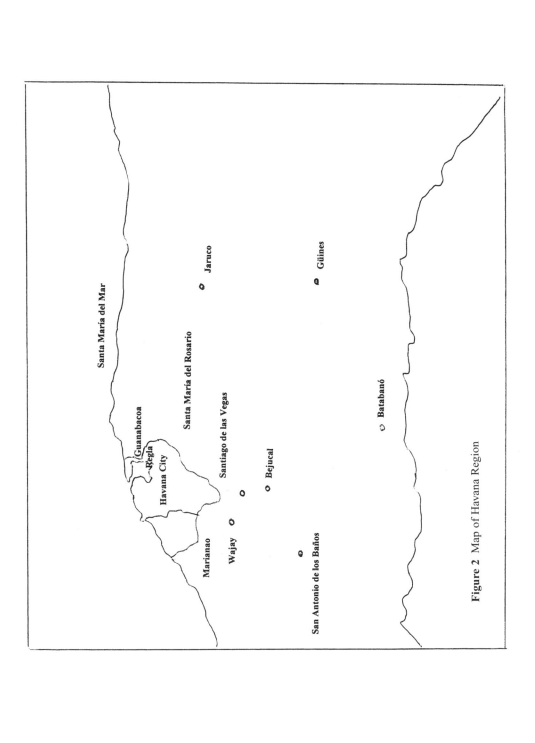

Figure 2 Map of Havana Region

Introduction
The Havana Mosaic: Sweetness and Light

Images of Havana

If it is true that most 'world cities have an instantly identifiable signature' (Dear and Flusty 1999: 64), the briefest encounter with Havana indicates how unusual that city is, visibly lacking a clearly identified architecture or urban pattern. Havana is not of course a 'world city' (as globalised megalopolis), but it has always been at the hub of world processes and one of the most internationalised sites for migration, trade and culture.

Even so, Havana is a city of few extremes, and, having emerged almost unplanned on one side of Havana Bay, it has a variegated feel and structure, 'the victory of medieval ideas held by the colonizers over the abstract theories of the Renaissance' (Segre, Coyula and Scarpaci 1997: 8). Indeed, Havana, with at least two possible 'centres' (Habana Vieja and the Rampa area), five historical 'nodes' and the newer 'political' foci (the Plaza de la Revolución and the Malecón) where *habaneros* are encouraged periodically to ritualise their 'belonging', really consists of a series of decentralised *barrios*, linked by infrastructure and an urban culture (Segre et al. 1997: 2).

Yet few visitors would deny that Havana has its own character and peculiarities of sound, sight and taste. Certainly one of its 'signatures' is its noise (the protagonist of Fernando Pérez's 2002 film *Suite Habana*); here it is not so much volume as the distinctive fusion of noises – of the relatively limited traffic, amplified by vehicles' age and dilapidation, of the distinctive loud music and of the cacophony of street noises of an essentially open-air culture. There are other sounds too: the trainee trumpeters rehearsing among the trees of Avenida Rancho Boyeros or the Quinta de los Molinos park, the regular television soap opera (*telenovela*), the schoolchildren's morning assembly incantations and the curious Sunday morning silence of a city without church bells.

1

Certainly that particular mix sets the scene for this study, music being fundamental to Havana's exaggerated culture, the open-air life reflecting traditional and new lifestyles and the material limitations signalling the circumstances of a capital of a dependent country isolated by the post–1960 US embargo and by the post–1990 economic crisis.

Havana's sights are equally characteristic in their fusion. This is the city of faded elegance, which, though the longest Spanish colony, lacks the grandiose imperial traces of other Latin American cities. Often described as beautiful, Havana is in fact beautiful in parts and potential, years of neglect and pragmatism having left a mess, with ruined areas, eyesores beyond restoration and a still dreadfully polluted Havana Bay. Yet, with restoration under way, Habana Vieja is a beautiful city in the re-making, 'uno de los más hermosos barrios del mundo entero' ('one of the most beautiful city areas in the whole world': Torrents 1989: 87), and its distinctive style lies in an often bemusing fusion of chaotically accumulated influences (Torrents 1989: 80). Most distinctive of all is the architectural mix of the ruined colonial, the fashionable twentieth-century American and the ugly modern functionalism, all unable to complete any real ostentation (Torrents 1989: 152).

Two other sights identify Havana. The first is the startling amount of vegetation, either in neat parks or growing out of ruins, much of it imported but flourishing in a striking metaphor (Torrents 1989: 75–6). The second is the constant conflict between the harsh tropical brightness of squares and modern streets and the often desperately sought shade of the narrow older streets, 'a charm of light and shade and colour' in 1915 (Robinson 1970: 56). Indeed, although light is immediately striking, Havana is often a dark city, 'hecha para la explotación de las sombras' ('constructed to make use of shade': Carpentier 1982: 13). Beyond the architectural, Havana's sights are unique: the shapeless but disciplined bus queues, the mid-street pedestrians fearlessly hailing lifts, the pavement booksellers, the white-clothed *santería* initiates, the innumerable busts of Martí and the street baseball.

The tastes of Havana are also particular, although Cuba has never shared its neighbours' gastronomic delights; this is the city of rum consumption, where the Catalan Constante invented 150 cocktails and, in 1820, converted the Piña de Plata restaurant into the Floridita, and where Hemingway enshrined the *mojito* (almost certainly created by the Spaniard, Angel Martínez, in the 1930s) in the Bodeguita del Medio.

Havana as Unique

Havana, therefore, is visibly distinct. Superficially, it shares many colonial or post-colonial characteristics. For long an *entrepôt* in a metropolitan-satellite relationship, where colonialism and neocolonialism imported goods, people and styles, and where the colony and neo-colony exported resources, it was also the administrative centre for colonial or neocolonial authority, susceptible to external political, cultural and intellectual influences and a focal point for struggles for national self-determination.

Hence, on the eve of the 1959 Revolution, Havana was an apparently typical example of primacy and macrocephalic development: six times larger than Santiago de Cuba, it accounted for a fifth of Cuba's population, half of its industrial output, 80 per cent of its imports and three quarters of its professional employment (Segre et al. 1997: 76–7). However, appearances misled, for Havana was set apart by Cuba's continuing Spanish colonialism after the 1820s and by its subsequent 'Americanisation', both affecting Havana more visibly than the rest of Cuba and other Latin American cities, making Havana, unusually for a capital, often peripheral to Cuban developments. Hence, at times of economic stagnation, Havana has often experienced ostentatious booms, and, after 1959, the customary centripetal trends were reversed, Havana stagnating compared to the rest of the island.

This leads to a fundamental theme in Havana's history: the ambivalent relationship between capital and interior. This reflects a long-standing Cuban dichotomy of competing discourses within an evolving national consciousness, where 'problem' and 'solution' were perceived as either endogenous or exogenous, explaining 'problems' either by endogenous defects (the 'solution' lying in external models) or by exogenous intrusion and distortion (the 'solution' lying in Cuba), a dichotomy often focusing on Havana as the channel for either 'solution' or 'problem' to enter exogenously, the 'other' Cuba being either a site for 'modernisation' or the essence of Cuba. This was, of course, simply a Cuban manifestation of a wider reality of dependency, where the primate city-port has a dual role, as the point where colony and metropolis encounter each other and establish hierarchies of power and influence, essential to hegemony and subordination, but also as the pole of attraction for 'colonials' seeking opportunities for development, employment, education and power, making the city a site of hegemonic contestation. Hence, Havana is now less Cuba's capital than a social, cultural and political entity in its own right.

This introduces another difference. For Cuba's traumatic experience of the 'Special Period', following the 1989–91 collapse of the Socialist Bloc, initially intensified the 'closed' features of the preceding decades of relative isolation, freezing Havana in time. Hence, if a 'postmodern urbanism' does exist in the wake of globalisation (Dear and Flusty 1999: 80), then post–1960 experiences have perhaps made this less applicable to Havana, which may be a Third World capital unusually protected from the worst distortions of globalisation.

Therefore, if Havana's uniqueness lies in chaotic fusions and a lack of homogeneity, then its 'style without style' (Carpentier 1982: 13) is still evident; if it was true that past fusions produced a uniqueness 'de lo abigarrado, de lo entremezclado, de lo encajado entre realidades distintas' ('of variegated and intermingled elements, interposed between different realities': Carpentier 1982: 13–14), then the same chaos, exaggerated by neglect since 1960, may be Havana's own signature. It is therefore a mosaic whose different fragments seemingly jar but whose overall image is instantly recognisable.

The Emergence of the City

This 'accidentalism' is, indeed, a metaphor for Havana's historical evolution. For some fifty years, the east was Cuba's centre of gravity, close to Hispaniola and to gold; governed administratively from Santiago and ecclesiastically from Baracoa, Havana offered little, its gold mine declining from the 1520s (Rey and García 1994: 90; Segre et al. 1997: 14). However, when westward imperialism incorporated Cuba into the overall conquest and colonisation, Diego Velazquez de Cuéllar's 1500–15 expedition saw Pánfilo de Narváez found the *villa* of San Cristóbal de La Habana on the south coast near Batabaná; from there, it moved in 1519 to escape swamps and poor mooring but also to catch the growing trade routes, first to Casiguagua on the north coast, by the Chorrera (now Almendares) river (Rey and García 1994: 85; Segre et al. 1997: 12), and then to the western shore of Havana Bay, at Puerto de Cárenas, already settled by Sebastián de Ocampo for its harbour (Torrents 1989: 23). Thus 'Havana' came into existence two decades after 'Cuba', almost as an afterthought. Even its name's origin is uncertain, explanations ranging from the indigenous chieftain Habaguanex, through a supposed Spanish transcription of the Taíno word for prairie (*sabana*) (Torrents 1989: 23), to the even more unlikely northern European 'haven' (Segre et al. 1997: 12).

Once established, Havana became a typical imperial town. Lacking artillery, munitions or reliable water (Pichardo 1977: 101) and following the centralising impulses of Spanish imperialism, which saw towns as 'principal agencies for the settlement of lands' (Elliott 1963: 56), Havana remained a subordinate *villa*, with a *cabildo* (council) under two *alcaldes* (mayors).

However, Diego Velázquez soon saw Havana's commercial, military and navigation potential (Torrents 1989: 23), as a base for continental expeditions: notably, by Cortés to Mexico (1520) and governor Hernando De Soto to Florida (1539), the latter's departure leaving his wife as Cuba's only female governor and depriving Havana of 600 of its able-bodied males (Rey and García 1994: 97). Indeed, Havana (like Cuba) lacked people, the indigenous inhabitants being rapidly wiped out, despite the 1500 prohibition of enslavement and the 1542 abolition of forced labour; between 1493 and 1544, the indigenous population fell from an estimated 60,000 to only 893 (Rey and García 1994: 91).

Moreover, the Amerindians were not replaced by either whites or African slaves. In 1520, Cuba only had 3,000 whites, declining with the Mexican conquest (Segre et al. 1997: 14) to 200 (Sorhegui and Fuente 1994a: 107). Equally, although *ladino* ('civilised') slaves were imported from 1513, from Iberia or other colonies (Segre et al. 1997: 15), by the mid–1500s, there were still only 1,000 (Sorhegui and Fuente 1994a: 110).

The cause of under-population was economic, for, with little gold and no indigenous population, Cuba offered little. After De Soto's neglect, successive governors tried to revive Cuba, Juanes Dávila importing African slaves and unsuccessfully encouraging sugar against livestock-based landowner resistance (Rey and García 1994: 97), and Antonio de Chávez ignoring the 1542 laws to allow forced labour. However, Havana was already dependent on one activity: the shipping following the *Carrera de las Indias* (the Indies route) to and from Spain, leading Chávez to move to Havana. Therefore, when, in 1561, the imperial fleet system was created, Havana, rather than Cuba, began to come into its own and develop a distinct identity, with a fundamental imperial role.

Theoretical Issues

This introduces two of the theoretical issues fundamental to this study. For, just as Havana's visible identity is one of fusion and confusion, so too can one trace a history based on the continuous fusion of cultural influences and manifestations, making a clear-cut identity as difficult to detect as the cityscape.

The first theoretical question to address is therefore, necessarily, national identity. For the Cuban search for identity has been a constant, evolving and almost obsessive theme of modern Cuban political life, culture and historiography, dating from the earliest notions in the mid-eighteenth century, through Cubans' identification of 'Cuba' and 'Cuban' preferences, to the twentieth century when it acquired new, dramatic, form as a theme and determinant of politics and culture.

However, what was meant by 'national identity' was never clear, being continually defined in a context where it was either denied or undermined by the pressures of neocolonialism and dependency. Even after 1959, the concept often became obscured by the evolving socialism, less able to accommodate nationalism and seeing 'nation' as a stage in a teleological process of historical evolution. Indeed, forty-five years of Revolution have, in one sense, been a process of definition, fusing 'nation' and 'socialism' in a new identity.

What is clear is that the formation of a national identity, 'un proceso sociopsicoantropológico de comunicación social' ('a socio-psycho-anthropological process of social communication': García Alonso 2002: 115), is customarily addressed through a process that 'involves establishing opposites and "others" whose actuality is always subject to the continuous interpretation and re-interpretation of their differences from "us"' (Said 1995: 332). For a collective identity (as group, nation or community) is about asserting 'we are this and not that', rejecting either a previous denial (by self or others) of being 'this', or, alternatively, a previous notion of a supposedly unreal 'us', as defined by others. This is because all efforts to define and defend an 'identity' imply 'authenticity', with previous supposed identities being 'unreal', since the search for identity implies the collective assertion 'this is how we see ourselves', either now or as a desired objective, seeking to assert a 'real' and organic identity.

What, however, is 'organic' is not clear, since identity is always subjective. Essentially, for an identity to be perceived as organic, by both subject and observer, it must be based on perceptions arising from (but not necessarily reflecting or representing) a shared lived experience. For an identity is about collective self-confidence, the sense that the subject group is speaking with its 'own voice', feeling good about itself, its members acknowledging a 'belonging' to a defined entity that 'counts', has discrete importance and credibility, and is acknowledged to exist separately rather than being an extension of another. Certainly 'belonging' is fundamental, since 'national identity' presupposes feelings of pride in belonging, and commitment and participation in social and cultural practices (Torre 1995: 112).

This is obviously the fundamental question, since, for the collective entity that a nation is or seeks to be, it is intrinsically more difficult to recognise the processes of rejection, assertion and self-identification. While, at one stage of 'the process of identification' (Bhabha 1998: 44), it is relatively easy to define what a nation is *not*, especially rejecting imposed or borrowed definitions, it is more difficult to define what the nation actually *is*, regarding the present or desired future, especially because a group identity will never be claimed by all, but, at best, by the majority, defined by one element on behalf of all, the process of 'identification' thus being a process of 'invention' rather than 'discovery'.

Hence, this calls into question 'authenticity', specifically questioning criteria that are at best imperfect measures of perception. However, one might reasonably posit that a greater sense of an 'authentic' national identity might imply the inclusion of all, since a 'nation' that needs to assert its identity has probably derived from a prior or existing colonialism, which denied identity to the colonised and fragmented in order to exercise hegemony.

The implication is that a national identity is, at one stage, an artificial construct, an 'invented tradition', i.e. 'a set of practices, normally governed by overtly or tacitly accepted rules, and of a ritual or symbolic nature, which seek to inculcate certain values and norms of behaviour by repetitions which automatically implies continuity with the past.' (Hobsbawm and Ranger 1995: 1). It is necessarily artificial precisely because the political need to define it implies a preceding negation or even non-existence. While a metropolis controls either by imposing a desired identity on key elements of the colonised society (a subaltern ruling or cultural elite) or by making a minority collective experience within the colony into the identity of all, the process of post-colonial identification must seek something called 'authenticity' in effective unity, since this state negates the previous explicit fragmentation. Certainly, any post-colonial state must seek to impose, discover, develop or assert a unity, however artificial or coerced in the first instance. Such a unity can either be imposed by the new previously counter-hegemonic elite (seeking necessary levels of conformity among the population as the new nation is shaped according to their 'blueprint') or can be imposed by a situation of isolation, especially if enforced. For one of the essential purposes of the common identity that accompanies nationality is 'cohesionar la sociedad' ('to make society cohere': Cristóbal 1995: 104), to prevent change from destroying a perhaps fragile unity.

National identity is also necessarily negative, defined as much by what it is not as by what it is; indeed, one problem is that where a national identity cannot be easily recognised, its absence is clearly noted. Hence, one defines such an identity not just by its distinctiveness but also by its relationship with other entities, in a process of 'interculturalidad' (García Alonso 2002: 115), since 'la identidad está siempre recreándose, enriqueciéndose por influencias que pueden venir incluso de lo que como referente externo constituye el otro frente al cual se dibuje' ('identity is always recreating itself, enriched by influences even from the external referent against which it defines itself': Torre 1995: 112). Moreover, such a flexible and movable concept can be defined according to different criteria at different times; thus, for example, recent Cuban scholarship has preferred an anthropological definition, as 'autoconciencia étnica cubana' ('Cuban ethnic self-consciousness': García Alonso and Baeza 1996: 49), taking its cue from the anthropologist Fernando Ortiz, updating his perspectives in the light of recent reassessments, stressing diversity and fusion (as Ortiz did) but also the constant process of development.

Yet, however fictive a national identity, it nonetheless possesses a reality as the subject of a viable political myth, in as much as, if enough members of a given a 'nation' believe in its existence and thus 'imagine' a community (Anderson 1991), then it exists, precisely because people wish it to, or imagine it into existence. Indeed, this is exactly where culture enters the process, for, if nation-building is the political realisation of an 'imagined community', then culture is the key to that imagining, since a sense of national identity implies a shared sense of cultural identity.

That, however, leads immediately to the need to establish the meaning of 'culture', since the term itself is in constant evolution and also contested, the subject of an academic, political and intellectual debate continually informed by inputs from different disciplines. It is thus important here to establish the parameters of the terms used in the following pages.

As Eagleton has observed, echoing Raymond Williams (Williams 1975: 16), the word 'culture' has tended in modern times to convey at least three different but interrelated meanings. The traditional meaning equated it with 'civilisation', an elitist interpretation reacting to the emergence of mass society and industrial capitalism and positing standards towards which all educated elites should aspire. The second is synonymous with 'the arts', but the third, by the mid-twentieth century, tended to mean 'way of life' (of thinking, being and recreating), linked, almost anthropologically, to such elements as religion, language, customs and what was increasingly being considered 'popular' culture (Eagleton 2000: 15). It is, of course, evident from any examination of culture in practice that there is no strict trichotomy, 'culture' often meaning all three at once. Certainly, Eagleton talks about more than one when identifying the four major points in a society when 'culture' matters: as the 'only apparent alternative to a degraded society', when lack of social change threatens the existence of 'culture', 'when it provides the terms in which a group or people seeks its political emancipation' and when a dominant power is 'forced to come to terms with the way of life of those it subjugates' (Eagleton 2000: 25). Any discussion of a given culture must, therefore, take into account all three meanings, with the emphasis varying according to the discussion's focus and purpose.

This is precisely the territory of 'cultural identity'. For, if the construction of a national identity is a real experience for those participating, then it follows that the creation of a cultural identity lies at the heart of that process of nation-building. This is because 'nation-denying' depends on non-communication, on the inability of those constituting the potential alternative to the colony to speak to each other recognisably (leading to classical linguistic or religious divide-and-rule strategies), and on the denial of the voice of the colonised, structurally, legally or through the weight of hegemony, leading to a necessary self-denial. Hence one key to the awakening of national consciousness and identity is the ability of accepted 'leaders' to speak with the 'authentic' voice of the colonised and the ability of the colonised to hear that discourse. For the leadership of the search for a national identity must include not only the political or military, but, necessarily, the cultural interpreters, whose education gives them the tools and the space to communicate, often as a minority uniquely protected precisely because of their potential usefulness to the hegemonic power, but, equally often, precisely because they have sought exile outside the colony's confines, thus acquiring external prestige on the hegemonic power's terms.

They are 'interpreters' because they are able to encode national myths, interpreting the basic story line integral to any historical-political myth (Kapcia 2000), especially when such myths have to become written, and thus relatively unchanging. Obviously, such interpreters often achieve this status, home and abroad, as intellectuals, thinkers and essayists, but it also follows that, as interpreters and encoders, they are likely to be poets, painters and musicians, since these three professions are able to find the necessary space and forms in ways less immediately comprehensible to the authorities.

Hence, if culture is also about thinking (about an individual adapting through education and a community finding its defining characteristics), then a national culture, however invented, is both a reality for the colonised denied their identity and an integral part of shaping a political identity. A political national identity can largely only be identified through the actions, declarations and public postures of those identified as political actors and thus has not always characterised the whole of a given society; that society's members may not necessarily have *lived* a political national identity, except at moments of relative consensus or when the system has been geared towards defining and shaping that goal. A *cultural* national identity, on the other hand, can, theoretically, be identified, felt and lived more commonly, and thus may be seen as the necessary precursor, or context, of the process of political identification.

This is because, while colonialism in underdeveloped countries inevitably divides to rule (economically through an informal sector, socially through migration, and politically by privileging key groups), it also imposes a cultural homogeneity, critical to cultural control, making the colonised conspire in their own subjugation. However, each effect of the processes of colonisation creates a new reality to which adaptation must be sought; economically, for example, the colonised tend to adapt individually, while political and social adaptation may mix individualism (survival and acceptance) with collective action (to resist or to construct a *favela* shanty). Hence, culture becomes a critical part of the process of adaptation, the search for cohesion and belonging; precisely because the processes of colonialism atomise societies, people need or use culture to adapt to a new belonging, having been deprived of the old. Hence, at the grass roots, culture is not necessarily about resistance but adaptation to an ever-changing reality; indeed, the process of cultural adaptation becomes a reality itself, the cultural equivalent of an organic *favela*.

This is because cultural identity necessarily has two distinct, but closely related, aspects. On the one hand it refers to the process whereby a people, increasingly consciously, identifies a common lived experience which achieves two purposes: to set them apart from other cultures (especially a dominant culture which denies their collective cultural autonomy) and to give them a set of behaviours, attitudes and preferences with which they can identify and to which they can feel they belong. Indeed, 'belonging' is one of the most fundamental determinants of a cultural identity, which means that it includes 'popular culture', popular and often traditional forms of music, dance or song, which lack formal recognition but are clearly shared, appreciated and understood, or even practised, by a sufficient proportion of the population as to make these forms be seen as organic to the desired identity.

The second meaning and purpose of cultural identity is the development, usually conscious, of an artistic and literary culture, which is more formal and widely recognised and which enjoys some prestige according to the established criteria of 'art' – produced or performed by identified and trained writers, composers and artists, whose role (or profession) is recognised in these terms. Clearly this refers to a conscious cultural elite, although 'cultural vanguard' is perhaps more appropriate when a national identity is being formed.

However, this again returns us to the meaning of 'culture', and especially to the vexed question of the perceived binarism inherent between 'high' culture' and 'non-high' manifestations, a minefield of loaded and subjective terms. Certainly, it was the subjectivism of preceding terms such as 'low culture' or the loaded concept of 'folk culture' that led, in the 1960s, to the use of the more expressive terms, 'mass culture' or 'popular culture', arising from the newer thinking of writers like Adorno (Adorno 1991) who posited 'popular culture', in an almost folkloric sense, as opposed not only to the hegemonic culture of social elites but also to the pressures of an essentially commercialised and capitalist 'mass culture', the product of the 'culture industry', commodified by an increasingly globalised capitalist system for 'the masses'. For all its benefits, this essentially pessimistic argument assumed two problematic elements: the essential passivity of the 'masses' (increased by the successful penetration of the mass culture) and an inherently one-way process whereby the 'masses' are influenced by the culture-sellers but never with any resistance or reverse influence (Rowe and Schelling 1996: 7).

Thus the term 'popular culture' has since become broader in scope and more active in its implications, transcending the folkloric to cover cultural manifestations as varied as sport, television, rock music and religious customs. This is especially so when cultural analysts examine the underdeveloped world and, in particular Latin America, where 'resistance' (to hegemony, imperialism or globalisation) has become a byword of studies of non-canonical cultural forms. For Latin America has indeed recently seen a curious juxtaposition. On the one hand, a social process has seen supposedly 'traditional' or 'marginal' social groups, cultural forms or political manifestations become interwoven with the supposedly 'modern' urban, externally oriented and externally generated forms of capitalism; however, on the other hand, successive generations of Latin American intellectuals, political leaders, artists and activists, challenging the hegemony of received perspectives, have explained and accorded prestige to 'their' cultural forms, and argued for a cultural perspective that recognises the Latin American people as subjects rather than objects and for a more empowering cultural environment. For example, the work of Jesús Martín-Barbero (Martín-Barbero 1998) has addressed the two-way process of any cultural encounter, arguing that the mass media have never been purely the instruments for hegemonic control but rather mediations for societies where the 'popular' (as traditional or rural-originating forms) is still felt, making the media sites for a complex process of influence, conflict, exchange and resistance.

Whether one accepts this formulation or not (and certainly it makes challenge-able assumptions about the 'popular' and about Latin America being still in some pre-industrial age), this approach does have the advantage of suggesting culture as a much more complex site for social interchange, conflict and adaptation, regard-less of whether it is uniformly about domination and resistance.

> The investigation of popular culture poses the rethinking of the whole cultural field, from the practice of everyday life to artistic production. Its proper documentation shakes up influential paradigms of cultural history (both folklore and media studies, for example), challenges discourses of identity (populist ones, for example), and under-mines literary and art-historical theories (magical-realist ones, for example). Inevitably a multi-disciplinary action, it requires taking the cultural sphere as neither merely derivative from the socio-economic, as a merely ideological phenomenon, nor as in some metaphysical sense preceding it. Rather, it is the decisive area where social con-flicts are expressed and evaluated. (Rowe and Schelling 1996: 12)

Thus we find that even 'popular culture' contains unhelpful preconceptions about 'the people' – seeking to defend their inherently 'good' culture, consciously self-defining and culturally resistant, and even relatively homogeneous. Hence, for the purposes of this study (seeking to trace a history of a whole urban community over a long period), we should reject not only the 'high–low' dichotomy but also the 'high–popular' one, since the latter still makes assumptions about the existence of two forms of culture (an 'us' and a 'them') which are not always reflected in reality.

Discussion of relationships between cultures leads, therefore, to the question of 'influence', since national identity's concern with 'authenticity' inevitably posits a notion of 'cultural imperialism' or 'cultural invasion' (Freire 1972: 121). Here again, recent trends now reject the concept of influence, talking of a perhaps more nuanced but still problematic 'hybridity', interculturalism or 'transculturation', each term bringing its own preconceptions and assumptions, and usually based on specific knowledge of specific circumstances.

Hence, to go beyond these debates, we should perhaps approach 'cultural influ-ence' from a different direction. What is suggested, in fact, is that we use explana-tions of the socio-economic relations between hegemonic and subaltern societies, since these have reflected and helped shape our perspectives of cultural influence, perspectives that have followed traditional developmentalist orthodoxy. This developmentalism (also called the 'diffusionist' model) viewed 'development' and 'modernisation' as diffusing from the historic 'core' to the 'periphery', often chan-nelled through 'enclaves' of externally generated 'modernisation' seeking to counter 'pre-modern' resistance – notions most notably represented by Rostow's 'growth theory' (Rostow 1962). From the 1960s, of course, that orthodoxy was challenged (from the 'periphery'), by those who questioned the assumed benefits of diffusion and who argued that the core–periphery relationship is essentially exploitative. This radical approach, inspired by Marxism and by the processes of decolonisation, then fostered a shift in cultural thinking, rejecting concepts of 'modernity' and seeing the 'popular' resisting modernisation to preserve identities. However, cultural thinking did not then take the same leap as economics. For, in the 1980s, micro-studies of urban Latin America began to discover that the 'conflictive' paradigm did not necessarily reflect the reality on the ground and that life 'on the margins' was more complex than the model suggested; in particular, it became clear that the Latin American city might not be simply the point where imperialism meets and exploits the periphery, but might also be a *sui generis* experience, a valid subject for study in and of itself.

Hence, one explanation of the complex nature of Latin American urban 'informality' may also help us to identify the complexities of intercultural relations: Milton Santos's 'dual circuits' model, elaborated in the 1970s for 'understanding the functioning of the city as a living organism' (Santos 1979: 17). According to this model, an 'upper circuit' represents the activity of the external capitalist and globalising world, integrated and clearly dominant, while a 'lower' circuit represents the economic and social activities of the 'host' underdeveloped city, also internally integrated but clearly dominated; where the 'circuits' meet is the site not necessarily of conflict but of fusion, interaction and gradual domination, with the city's daily functioning taking place in the 'overlap' between the two, where the 'informal sector' is formalised, where migration fuels urban development and where the external processes of capital accumulation extract the host city's resources.[1] However, this overlap is also a site of varying and fluctuating size and nature, which, over time, acquires a reality of its own, a site neither of influence nor conflict but of existence, where the processes of survival, adaptation and development are realised. In a sense this is the modern urban equivalent of Gruzinski's notion of *mestizaje*, originally perceived as a negative, as less than the sum of its component parts, but, over time, a separate reality in its own right (Gruzinski 2002).

While this model obviously risks being clumsily holistic, it does nonetheless offer us a model for new thinking about cultural exchanges between 'national' and 'international' cultures. For it is clear that, with ever-increasing growth, development, movement and communication, no one nation can survive in isolation and that there will always be areas where these communities overlap and affect each other, equally or unequally depending on the levels of internal cohesion, confidence or critical mass. For the cultural identity' of a dependent society, this overlap can be critical, as the site for domination, resistance, fusion, interchange and confusion, most probably the primate city-port, where 'imports' and models enter, 'exports' and resources leave (to be consumed abroad in the culturally defining 'markets'), and the external and internal hierarchies of prestige will encounter each other and interact.

For the overlap has its own reality and referents that enable it to sustain an autonomous cultural life, importing from above or below as necessary or appropriate, although importation is more likely to be of lower-circuit products, considered more relevant and meaningful, as confidence grows: 'Unlike the upper circuit, the lower circuit is well entrenched in the city and enjoys privileged relations with its environment' (Santos 1979: 9). However, before and during that moment of 'realisation', there are inevitable cultural tensions in the overlap, where elements aspire upwards, borrowing models and seeking to acquire prestige, while others look downwards, back to lost forms, seeking identity, belonging, distinction and inspiration.

This complexity of process introduces a further consideration. For one should remember that, rather than a simple pattern of one culture influencing another, the reality of cultural interaction is often more a case of contingency and rational choice, whereby cultural producers in a given society use whatever intellectual, philosophical or stylistic tools are available to them at a given moment.

In this sense, therefore, while it may well be right that 'the assumed uniformity of national cultures begins to be seen as a myth' (Featherstone and Lash 1999: 1) or that 'todas las culturas son de frontera' ('all cultures are frontier cultures': García Canclini 2001: 316), many such assertions arise from the perspective from 'the core', where 'nation' has become less relevant in the light of globalisation and where the denial of nation is an affordable luxury. In Latin America, however, where an indigenous idea of nation has historically been denied, the process of ensuring that the voice of the dispossessed is heard means the invention of nation. Therefore, a national culture may be a myth (as illusion), but it can very substantially be a myth as belief, if it is credible to enough members of a given society.

This discussion therefore leads us now towards an alternative paradigm for understanding and analysing influence and national culture. This is the notion of a 'cultural community'. What is meant by this concept is a grouping (probably, but not necessarily, larger than a cultural movement but smaller than a class) that defines itself by its perceived culture, by forms of self-expression that are either recreational or identifications of belief or belonging, that definition being determined by accepted or self-appointed 'cultural leaders' and with the purpose of identifying the group as distinct or unique. Hence, each such community must share a consensual view – real or imagined – of what its own preferred, organic or 'natural' culture actually is and a cultural community must have boundaries (geographical, linguistic, religious, educational, ability of access to cultural forms or to the means of communication) but also hierarchies of prestige (people, cultural forms). The advantage of talking of cultural communities rather than classes or movements is that they may well represent self-identifications within a given class, since membership of such a community is subjective, defined by self-definition and not by objective attribution. This is essentially because a cultural community, like any, is an 'imagined' one, the result of wishing to 'belong', and is by no means necessarily identifiable to outsiders by objective criteria.

Hence, the concept allows us to focus on self-identification, flexible definitions and notions of influence, but also to continue talking of 'elites' (as in an 'elite cultural community') in a more variegated sense. For the term can refer either to those who are placed in positions of cultural authority by the hegemonic social or political elites and thus given the task of defining, directing and sanctioning cultural forms and of establishing the canon, or to those who constitute a self-appointed group or 'community' of arbiters of cultural definition which is internally hegemonic. The latter, though not necessarily linked directly to the exercise of political, economic or social power, nonetheless exercise cultural and intellectual power by setting standards, bestowing authority and establishing hierarchies of people, genres and forms. Hence the term 'elite cultural community' can be appropriate if referring to a group that is in some sense hegemonic or to a 'counter-elite cultural community' (or 'vanguard cultural community') if, as a self-perceived community, it is challenging hegemony from a position within the elite; the latter can of course be countering that hegemony from any direction, for example advocating more socially aware definitions and forms, public as opposed to private artistic expressions, or politically committed definitions, or it can simply be challenging orthodoxy by proposing new aesthetic codes and values. Either way, these are essentially minority communities. However, although constituting a minority, they are invariably privileged through access to cultural power; this means that the boundaries of such a community are determined not at the edges but rather at the centre, membership being defined through participation in the community's authoritative institutions or through gatherings or publication in the community's allocated spaces and criteria being defined by 'leaders' (or patrons) who enact the necessary gate-keeping role.

This leads us on to those outside this community, where, because of the problems posed by the term 'popular culture', it may be more helpful to consider 'the people' or the 'masses' as constituting different and specific cultural communities (local, regional, ethnic, religious or social), all defined, and defining themselves, by some means that set them apart from the others but which are not necessarily easily recognisable to outsiders. Thus a cultural community can be real (where its members know and recognise each other and consciously share perspectives, preferences and criteria, supporting each other in their efforts, as in a cultural elite or movement) or it can be an imagined one where, as far as its members are concerned, it has a real enough existence. One might surmise that when several such communities coincide in their collective views, what emerges de facto is a larger cultural community with a wider cultural identity – which moves us into the realm of class-based or national cultural identities.

If we adopt this concept, therefore, we can approach the critical question of class with a different set of analytical tools. For, in Latin American societies in general and, certainly, pre–1959 Cuban society in particular, the 'middle class' is historically a critical subject for cultural investigation, often seen as mimicking the cultural elite or consuming 'mass culture' and lacking aesthetic taste, or alternatively as the social layer by definition estranged from the 'popular', *deraciné* and amorphous.

We perhaps need to consider the 'middle class' differently because, in any discussion of political history, the term should be treated cautiously if used at all, having acquired, over years of common, journalistic or political usage, many different meanings and preconceptions. Indeed, in pre–1959 Cuba, one should more accurately refer to bourgeoisie, petit bourgeoisie, national bourgeoisie and white-collar workers, defining a historically precise socio-economic class formation rather than a vague sociocultural grouping (which the term often means in modern Britain). However, it is suggested here that these more precise terms are not necessarily helpful when examining the cultural map or trajectory of a colonial or post-colonial society such as Havana, not least because the complicating effects of dependence and neocolonialism have created social groupings that, although they may not mirror their supposed European counterparts or models economically or politically, can often reflect a conscious or subconscious attempt to imitate those 'models' culturally or intellectually, making the socio-economic definitions difficult to fix. In the 1950s, this was evident to the American political scientist, John. J. Johnson, who coined the term 'middle sectors' to escape the preconceptions of 'middle class', when talking of groups who looked and behaved as a middle class in a sense recognisable to North Americans but who were plainly not so, economically or politically (Johnson, 1964: viii–ix). His essentially diffusionist perspective was countered, but curiously later reinforced, by André Gunder Frank's neologism, 'lumpenbourgeoisie', to describe a 'middle class' lacking a collective self-awareness or economic base and thus providing the raw material for forms of neocolonialism and populism (Frank 1972).

Here, we simply need to be precise, aware of the implications of accepted terms. Hence, when the term 'middle class' is used here it will have a precise and unique meaning – namely not an economic class but a cultural community, referring to that section of the (mostly Havana-based) bourgeoisie and petit bourgeoisie that self-consciously or unconsciously adopted a set of cultural aspirations and preferences following 'middle-class' models from Western Europe and, increasingly, the United States. In this sense, the Havana 'middle class' is essentially one of Anderson's 'imagined communities', since the 'class' mostly lacked an economic basis for self-definition and lacked political cohesion, will or representation, but did nonetheless see itself as different, as moving in a certain cultural direction, and as influential. Certainly when, in chapter 2, *Bohemia* is used to illustrate the evolution of Havana's cultural patterns, we will see that the target readership was constantly and increasingly offered images that posited middle-class aspirations and therefore came to see itself in those terms. In other words, the imagining of the 'imagined community' moved noticeably from a focus on, and aspiration towards, a European-influenced Cuban elite towards a North American middle class, with a range of significant implications for the question of identity.

However, it is within cultural communities and not class that we may find the answers we seek. For the formation of a national cultural identity is a process of fusing the micro-communities (localised, religious, adapting and lacking access to the powerful means of communication) into a larger unit, seen increasingly as coterminous with 'nation', and thus of fusing the new reality of the overlap with the cultures of the lower-circuit micro-communities, a process more likely when the 'upper circuit' is ruptured or damaged, or has lost national prestige or legitimacy for some reasons (for example, the political alienation or exile of its 'national' members); in this sense, cultural 'autarchy' is as possible (but as short-lived and dangerous) as its economic counterpart.

Of course within this question of cultural communities one of the critical notions is the valuation of the shared experience and culture, which leads us to the question of prestige; for, within any given cultural community, it is evident that some forms, expressions and ideas have a certain valuation above others. 'Prestige', of course, is usually associated with the canonically accepted norms that establish standards, but it seems logical that any such community can privilege a given cultural form with internal authority, valuing that form as belonging particularly or exclusively to the community and as helping define it and its members. Logically, the cultural elite or vanguard will usually be those with the means of communication or other resources to establish hierarchies that privilege their authority, enabling them to communicate their hegemony to other elites elsewhere who are seen to share their perspectives and tastes. Therefore, since it is inevitable that elite cultural communities will dominate our perspectives of 'prestige' but that any community must have its own hierarchy of authority as a basis for separate definition as a community, the concept of cultural authority rather than prestige will henceforth be used here when referring to internal valuation of cultural forms within a community, leaving 'prestige' to refer to externally imposed or imported valuations.

Equally, the notion of cultural community enables us to reconsider the reality of the cultural overlap in terms of imports and exports interacting in curious ways. One outstanding example is the story of the *mambo* which, originating in the traditional rural *rumba* and *son*, was commercialised in the United States for popular consumption (by US-based and occasionally non-Hispanic dance bands) and then, given American middle-class prestige, was in turn reimported to Cuba for a 'middle class' increasingly seeking to gear its tastes to North American models. Thus, a Cuban form, which hitherto enjoyed no authority within the Cuban middle-class cultural community, now became acceptable because of prestige bestowed by North American acceptance and conversion. This worked on two levels, convincing the Cuban community that it was following the tastes of its model, but also giving the Cuban middle class pride in the heritage that had created a form that now enjoyed prestige in the admired community. It thus contributed in complex ways to forming this middle community's developing sense of national cultural identity.

Of course, in tracing any community's cultural history, we should not focus principally, or at all, on the products of a culture (since that inevitably privileges forms that have been recorded and accorded prestige by those who control or dominate the means of communication and dissemination) but, rather, on the individual processes of creation and on the collective sites and communities for creation, authority-bestowing and change. Hence, this study will not attempt to provide an exhaustive inventory of publications, biographies or analyses of individual works, but, instead, will seek to identify, trace and judge the significance and processes of those sites where these acts and patterns of creation, gathering and change took place – sites that may be geographical (gathering sites), temporal (events shaping the community), institutional (bestowing internal authority), or indeed the media, which offered space in which the cultural forms could develop, gain authority and be recognised.

Talk of cultural overlap introduces another possible paradigm. In 1993, Anthony Pym usefully challenged conventional comparative literature approaches towards questions of influence and cultural transfer by borrowing from 'regime theory' in the study of international systems to posit that, instead of seeing 'centres' relating to each other via their points of peripheral contact, that point of contact should itself be seen as an 'a centre especially designed for the carrying out of transfers' (Pym 1993: 138). His approach offered the illuminating advantage of moving away from fruitless and loaded discussions of influence between either equal 'centres' or 'strong' and 'weak' centres, to a consideration of the 'frontier' as a place, a space in its own right, allowing us to focus less on the cultural producers (writers, artists or publishers) – who might, in conventional approaches, be the key players but who, in fact, may be unaware of any 'influence' they either exercise or imbibe – and more on the intermediaries.

In the context of Havana, this approach (although Eurocentrically downplaying colonialism's cultural impact) offers a new dimension in discussions of the city's cultural development, reminding us that to consider Havana as an intercultural frontier is to be one-dimensional and to miss the subtleties of the actual patterns of daily life. Instead, especially as Havana grew as a community, it was, always and increasingly, a centre in its own right, an urban space in which competing, contemporaneous, parallel or entirely separate communities shaped their cultural approaches to their life and their interactions. This approach confirms the previous suggestion that an examination of the cultural development of cities like Havana, with unique patterns and positioned between competing pressures, necessarily takes us away from the cultural product and producers to the cultural event, space, development and pattern, and above all to the cultural community.

However, against this we must set the reality that, however appealing Pym's paradigm, Havana was never a neutral site for contact and transfer, and thus could never be a neutral frontier and objective space. The cultural essence of colonialism and neocolonialism has always been the tension between unequal pressures, leading to patterns of domination, resistance, adaptation and survival in the interstices between the resulting conflicts.

In a very real sense, therefore, a national culture is simultaneously a fusion and a separate reality. Just as *mestizaje* has been both an inclusion and an exclusion, a process of privileging and marginalising (Gruzinski 2002), so too has the moment of 'identification' been the recognition that the supposed national culture is both the inheritance from the different cultural forebears and a *sui generis* culture in its own right, in other words a moment of sufficient confidence to neither reject nor copy but to assume both parentage and separate identity. Hence García Canclini's assertion about cultures' frontier nature needs to be tempered by the equal reality that the converse is also true: that all cultures are also characterised by a necessary stability, because in most cases sufficient members of a given 'national' society adhere to cultural forms that may adapt at the edges but whose essence changes slowly if at all, that stability being fundamental to the social cohesion whose purpose culture serves.

For an identity, if it exists, is not found in the obvious, the public statements and manifestos, but, rather, 'It is in the emergence of the interstices – the overlap and displacement of domains of difference – that the intersubjective and collective experiences of *nationness*, community interest, or cultural value are negotiated' (Bhabha 1998: 2). Logically, then, it is found in the mundane and the openly declared – 'the certainties of a nationalist pedagogy' (Bhabha 1998: 142) – in 'high culture' and in the hidden crevices of the popular, the 'patrimonio propio' (García Canclini 2001: 188), usually more representative of the local but less able to escalate to become a general patrimony. We find it in writing, in visual art and in music, especially song, which are 'performances, a form of ritualized practice in and through which meaning and significance is embedded' (Eyerman 1999: 119).

This finally leads us back to cultural identity, to the impulse to identify, shape and defend something called, here, a 'Cuban culture'. For, if we are to trace the evolution of a Cuban national identity, we have to identify and understand the underlying processes of cultural national identification, without which the identity lacks a context. The difficulty, of course, lies precisely in defining that process, in knowing what a given cultural identity is and how to recognise it.

Superficially, a Cuban cultural identity ought to be easily recognisable, having been the subject of much writing in and about Cuba. At its simplest, it might be taken as the notion of a culture generated in Cuba by Cubans and responding to a Cuban public and to Cuban references and stimuli, following patterns and models established in Cuba. However, the problem here is the historical Cuban reality that artists and writers have often had to leave Cuba to create their art, so production within Cuba cannot be a sine qua non of such a culture. Instead, one might talk of a culture produced *by* Cubans (born and largely raised in Cuba) responding to Cubans' demands, market, preferences, circumstances and the popular voice (i.e. informed by popular traditions, real or imagined). Here, one of the measures of 'Cuban-ness' is of course the readership or public at which the culture is, or has been, directed. Has it been seeking external recognition (and therefore more likely to respond to external criteria) or has it been trying to speak *to* Cubans? Or has it sought external recognition *for* Cuba by using Cuban themes and forms?

However, as we have seen, the problem here is the artificiality of any cultural identity at a certain stage, with cultural producers seeking to relate their creations explicitly to supposedly national themes or forms (as in the work of Smetana or Sibelius), from which a definable and recognisable identity must emerge organically to continue to be classified as separate – artists producing work on nation-specific themes or using nation-specific forms, because this has become the norm, is popular or reflects wider social and political concerns. Also, of course, all national identities need artificial stimulation at some stage, to boost collective self-confidence, to bestow prestige on popular nationalism and to gain external recognition. In this respect, the second meaning of 'national cultural identity' is relatively easy to identify and prove: the defined cultural vanguard or elite, whose products, statements and manifestos demonstrate their thinking, motivation and 'identity'. In Cuba, for example, one might take the work and declarations of *Cuba Contemporánea*, the Grupo Minorista or *Orígenes* (see chapter 2) to have a clear sense of the Cuban culture being consciously created by them.

What this of course means is that there are different definitions of cultural identity or different components of a single such identity, alongside which one should consider a likely or typical *process* of identity formation. Most obviously, a national cultural identity can be taken, and recognised, as the production and/or consumption of the country's own collective cultural expressions, in forms and about themes that are generally accepted and perceived as unique or especially pertinent to the cultural community that is the nation, or are seen to define that community culturally.

However, before a peripheral, colonised or subaltern community reaches that stage of self-confidence, one is more likely to find the emergence of a cultural identity in the consumption and conscious appreciation of the manifestations of other, more established, hegemonic and prestigious cultures, where the 'recipient' community is partly seeking self-confidence and recognition by other cultures and communities in the other cultures' terms, recognising the recipient community's cultural sophistication in those terms, and, indeed, thus partly becoming a part of a wider, prestigious, global cultural community, with its headquarters in, say, London, Paris or New York. Thus one key to this process of confidence-building and passive recognition is to be able to demonstrate that the recipient colonial community is au fait either with what we might call established 'classical' cultural forms – in other words, that it is 'cultured' – or, more adventurously and probably self-confidently, with metropolitan cultural fashions, being part of the latest avant-garde world and thus not just abreast of the 'developed' world but even ahead of it, in collaboration with those of that world who are challenging the accepted cultural mores and criteria.

A logical step along that process, therefore is the production of cultural manifestations that are recognised outside the country – by traditional or avant-garde standards and cultural communities – thus bringing the country's cultural producers (and the whole cultural community) fame, respect and prestige, putting the individuals and the country on the global cultural map, not just as consumers of others' cultures but, more importantly, as producers of widely accepted cultural expressions, on a par with, and thus essentially equal to, the accepted canon. Indeed, what this stage of the process means is that the country's cultural exponents have actually achieved canonical status themselves, thus bestowing prestige on the whole community.

What all this means is that, in seeking to trace the evolution of a Cuban cultural identity, we should watch for and seek to recognise certain critical stages: the importation of cultural forms, production according to the criteria of these consumed or imported models, the attainment of recognition by the standard-definers of the 'exporting' metropolis, the conscious incorporation of 'indigenous' elements (reflecting a search for 'roots' or a need to identify those products with distinctive 'authentic' elements, 'exoticising' their own culture). This latter process, when and if it occurs, should be identified by the prestige bestowed on essentially indigenous forms and the breakdown of distinctions between the canon and 'popular' forms, which, if recognised, should be a fertile ground for 'identity', found in the dynamism of the fusion of levels and forms and in the extent to which the 'colonised' producers have appropriated the forms, visions and criteria of the metropolis, adapted them and even re-exported them (perhaps as the 'voice' of the 'periphery' or the 'other'). Equally, one might look for a conscious intellectual decolonisation, the 'fighting phase', the expression being 'a harsh style, full of images ... a vigorous style, alive with rhythms, struck through and through with bursting life ... full of colour too, bronzed, sun-baked and violent' (Fanon 1970: 177–9).

Thus, we ought to know where to look for these manifestations. Firstly, one can look for the levels of cultural activity within the community (in this case, in Havana), by both producers and consumers, perhaps indicating and leading to a high level of cultural self-confidence. Secondly, one can look for evidence of external prestige, either in the inclusion of Cuban artists, composers or writers within the established canon or in the acceptance of popular Cuban forms by 'metropolitan' societies, although such evidence can be ambiguous, since a patronising adoption can distort the original form to a preferred, perhaps refined, form for metropolitan tastes. Thus, while the colonised cultural community may be celebrating the end of its 'marginality', it may well be confirming its 'subalternity'. Indeed, this raises again the question of exile, since such recognition may well involve a necessary physical separation from the potentially enclosed community but also a search for acceptance according to external criteria; in deciding whether to consider such producers as part of a 'Havana community', one probably has to look to factors such as regular links with and acceptance by that community. Thirdly, one can look for evidence of the Havana community appreciating its own cultural manifestations, 'high' or popular, and being willing to consume those even when given a choice between 'Cuban' and 'foreign', this perhaps being accompanied or followed by evidence of a willingness, and ability, not just to consume passively but to participate actively in the production and celebration of its 'own' culture, perhaps fusing imported and indigenous forms in a process of organic adaptation. Finally, of course, one might seek evidence that elites within the cultural community are also willing to acknowledge the authority of Cuban cultural forms, consuming and even practising them when given the choice and not automatically seeking external models, recognition and prestige.

The Structure and Aim of the Book

This leads naturally to an exposition of the approach and purpose of this study, which is first and foremost simply a cultural history of the city of Havana, with a focus on all three of Eagleton's definitions. For it is most obviously a study of a culture as 'art', but against the background of a culture as 'civilisation' and of culture as a 'way of being', the second meaning being fused, with increasing confidence and authenticity, with elements of the third. It is therefore a history of that process, of the evolving search for an acceptable definition of a national culture of which Havana was the site.

It is of course easy to expect this to become a 'catalogue' of the evolution of Havana's 'arts'; certainly, while histories of literature, music, dance or the visual arts in Cuba generally have been written, there has been limited attention to all together within the confines of the city alone, Lightfoot's study being an exception (Lightfoot 2002). However, out of context, such a catalogue would tell us little, informing but not explaining. Equally, an anthropological or ethnographic history of popular culture would provide rich material but would miss the tense, occasionally conflictive and increasingly symbiotic, relationship between the various forms, and would again lack a context.

One difficulty, of course, is 'the city'. Simply, what importance does Havana's city status have to this investigation? Inevitably, some of the recent theory on the city as cultural space is relevant, especially when offering explanations of the increasing cultural role of public spaces or, conversely, of the perceived increasing tendency for the postmodern city to atomise and individualise the collective experience, making the mass media the only collective cultural link between its inhabitants, who receive it passively rather than participate in it as subjects. To this extent, a significant part of the underlying perspective in this study has been informed by such considerations. However, it is perhaps important to reflect upon the extent to which Havana forces us away from these considerations as a major focus, the most obvious being the process since 1959 that transformed Havana's traditional character and function, neglecting it in favour of the countryside and that, through the US embargo and, much later, the enforced isolation after the 1989–91 crisis, cut off the city from many of its previous external links. Thus García Canclini's point about 'frontier cultures' simply applied much less to Havana after 1960, as Cuba – by default and by choice – turned in on itself in a kind of cultural autarky. This had a further effect, for one of the salient features of the development of Havana's arts was always the nature of the cultural elite, limited in social class and size, a feature which became exaggerated after 1960. Hence the increasingly self-referential nature of Cuban culture meant a potentially greater role for that vanguard or elite, especially as Cuba, after the Literacy Campaign of 1961, became a mass reading society for the first time; however, simultaneously, that vanguard was becoming isolated internationally and increasingly enclosed, and, in a world where everybody in the intellectual elite knew everyone else, the smallness of the vanguard was both a strength – increasing cohesion, mutual influence and self-sustenance – and a weakness, leading to claustrophobia and parochialism.

Therefore, while for long periods a cultural history of Havana would be simply a cultural history of Cuba, that is not generally so and occasionally far from the case. This is for two principal reasons. Firstly, after 1959 the Revolution took culture 'to the people' in a process of conscious democratisation that, inevitably, made Havana at times less relevant to Cuba's cultural development. Secondly, the critical question of exile has been a fundamental determining feature of Havana culture from early on. For any assessment of the nature, vibrancy and role of Havana culture within the overall national cultural trajectory must consider the absence rather than the presence of many leading exponents, spaces and movements. It can become problematic to ascribe to Havana a particular role, leading or following, when so many significant cultural figures and leaders have spent much of their productive life either outside Havana or outside Cuba. Hence, while these individuals' influence, stature or periodic visits may allow us to rightly consider them integral to the evolution of a *Cuban* culture and cultural identity, it is more difficult to see them as organic to any *Havana* cultural community.

Therefore, ultimately, this book is no more and no less than a study of the process by which Havana's different cultural communities have related to each other and to outside communities in the context of the search for a national cultural identity. Since that search has been largely defined by the elite/vanguard cultural community of Havana, this study necessarily focuses principally on the history of that community, especially as it is that community whose record over the span covered by this study is most accessible; the other cultural communities enter this history as they relate to the main one, either neglected by it or incorporated into its products if not its production processes.

It is thus the study of a necessarily chequered and contradictory process, where Havana was at one moment the spearhead of the upper circuit and at other times, the point where cultural resistance began, and where the overlap developed. It is thus a history of colonisation and decolonisation through the cultural spaces that Havana provided, and therefore focuses primarily on the twentieth century, the period when the processes of search and identification were most marked, most conflictive and clearest, and when the evidence is most readily available.

The book is thus structured chronologically. Conventional historiography on Cuba talks of accepted 'periods': the pre–1762 'pre-history', the period of sugar expansion under Spanish colonialism, the seminal US military occupation, the Republic (increasingly divided into 'First' and 'Second Republics'), and, finally, the Revolution. While historiographical instinct leads one naturally to question conventions, this division actually seems more or less useful for the book's purposes.

Hence the study is presented in four separate chapters, each chapter subdivided into parts. Chapter 1 simply deals with 'the Colony', from the 1550s to Independence, this being divided into 'before sugar' and 'after sugar'; this is because, while, until the 1760s, Havana had a relatively enclosed cultural existence, after that date, as with almost every other aspect of the colony, it blossomed and grew more recognisably. Equally, whatever arguments there might be for talking of an 'interregnum' in 1878–1902, when Spanish rule became less effective and Cuba gravitated increasingly towards the United States economically and politically, culturally this does not seem to have happened; hence, this book ends 'the Colony', conventionally, in 1902. Chapter 2 therefore largely follows convention in dealing with 'the Republic', subdivided into 1902–33 and 1934–58; again this is because, in terms of cultural and intellectual development, the 1933 revolution and the preceding Depression did indeed constitute a dividing line between one set of cultural characteristics (including the radicalisation of dissent and the integration of the popular) and another, notably the decline of commitment, the experience of exile and changes to the popularity of some cultural forms. Likewise, chapter 3 addresses one single phenomenon, the Revolution, but only until the 1990s; that is not because the Revolution ended then, but rather, that, culturally, the crisis that began in 1990 did indeed represent such a fundamental challenge to the existing system, criteria and familiar patterns of thinking that, henceforth, culture in Havana had to find new ways of approaching a new situation without abandoning the essence of the old. Hence chapter 4, from 1990 to the present, argues for a separate treatment of those ways discovered and chosen, creating and significantly changing the Havana we recognise today.

The four chapters, however, are not dealt with equally. Firstly, the evidence is unequal; secondly, the book's principal focus is the twentieth century, with 'the Colony' as a necessary background and with the present being a key element in the overall picture. Since the treatment is unequal, the evidence must also be; thus, the three chapters that argue the case most explicitly all end with a 'case study'. Chapter 2 uses *Bohemia*, which, more than any other medium, reflected the changing cultures and society of Havana and the changing attitudes of, and to, the cultural arbiters. Chapter 3 takes two organs, *Bohemia* (for the early years) and *Granma* (for the later period); this is because the explosion of writing and reading meant a constantly evolving multipolarity of cultural perspectives, best reflected through two different organs. Finally, chapter 4 departs from that kind of source and, instead, focuses on the Casas de la Cultura; partly that is because the early years of the Special Period saw a significant decrease in cultural activity and the print media, making that resource less useful, but mostly it is because the changes in culture after 1990 are best reflected in a close study of the phenomenon that was revived in the period and perhaps best expresses the new cultural manifestations and attitudes. Moreover, these institutions have not really been researched before outside Cuba, and thus the study breaks new ground.

Matthew Arnold wrote that culture was 'the pursuit of sweetness and light' (Arnold 1995: 78). If true, then that serves as an apposite introduction to this study, for two reasons. Firstly, the analysis of Havana's role within the evolution of a Cuban cultural identity inevitably links that to the evolution of Cuban sugar, which made Cuba's 'sweetness' often a 'bitter-sweet' reality, Secondly, light is something that immediately hits any visitor to Havana – the harsh light of the sun contrasted to the shade and to the universal gloom of badly lit streets.

Indeed, a walk around the newly refurbished Museo Nacional de Bellas Artes stresses the significance of this quotation as a metaphor for Cuba's cultural development. For, if one takes a chronological tour, one reality becomes abundantly clear: that the discovery of a Cuban cultural identity is actually about 'the pursuit of sweetness and light'. In the early, derivative, art there is almost no trace of 'Cuba'; instead we see white-skinned worthies against a dark, interior background or against landscapes that are darkly European, perhaps with the occasional palm tree. There is nowhere, early on, any hint of sugar, slavery, suffering or, indeed, of the island's characteristic light. Finally, by the end of the nineteenth century, both black Cubans and light begin to appear, the former invariably at first as picturesque peasants or comic characters, the latter as the artists moved out of the drawing-room and recognised the city and the countryside. By the twentieth century, that 'discovery' becomes more explicit (as chapters 2 and 3 will trace). More than any-thing else, this indicates eloquently that a Cuban 'cultural identity' is a matter of a culture with the self-confidence to be itself, to recognise that it is Cuba and not a colonial imitation of Europe, that it is, therefore, a culture of 'sweetness and light'.

Note

1. This use of 'circuits' should not be confused with Du Gay's notion of circuits of culture (Du Gay, Hall, Janes, Mackay, Negus 1997), referring to the process by which cultural practice or objects gain meaning through the process of encoding and dissemination generated in five identified stages.

–1–

The Colony (1550s–1902)

Historical Overview

Once the fleet system and imperial administration were established, Cuba's role for the next two centuries was determined, as a curious mixture of peripherality and centrality. While, on the one hand, it had a secondary role in providing the passing trade with supplies, recreation, harbour and protection, those same functions made Cuba central to the Empire's structures of power, administration and trade. This was reinforced by the unusually white (non-*mestizo*) and *peninsular* population, which remained transient for some time, with only a gradual importation of African slaves (perhaps 5,000 by 1609), principally for urban domestic, service, construction and artisan activity (Sorhegui and Fuente 1994b: 143).

Eventually, activities unrelated to Cuba's port function did emerge, especially coffee and tobacco, the latter primarily in the centre and west, cultivated by Spanish (*peninsular*) farmers but always hindered by Spanish controls. Hence, a recognisable elite, based on agriculture, administration and commerce, developed slowly, restricted by a rigid centralism and by poor opportunities for advancement. With little immigration until the nineteenth century, Cuba remained somewhat undeveloped as a colony, in comparison with Peru and Mexico.

Two developments of the late eighteenth century changed that. The first was the Spanish Bourbon monarchs' programme of administrative, commercial and military reforms, which, designed to reverse decades of steady imperial decline and of growing colonial autonomy, were especially effective in Cuba (Johnson 2001: 12–13), particularly the military reforms which, following a 1740–1 British blockade of Havana, produced a gradual 'Cubanisation'.

The second was the eleven-month British occupation of Havana in 1762. Most histories consider this event seminal: it introduced free trade and access to North American markets, it developed the hitherto small-scale sugar sector (also bringing technology and experience from Jamaica), and it imported some 5,000 slaves for plantations. One recent study (Johnson 2001) dissents from this, arguing that it was tobacco and the military reforms (rather than sugar) that changed Cuba, with the Cuban elite preferring diversification. Either way, the result was a rapid capital-based economic expansion and the rise of sugar to monocultural proportions, initially around Matanzas but soon expanding in all directions, eating up available land as both tobacco and coffee coincidentally declined. Significantly, the main sugar market was not Spain but, increasingly, the United States, taking some 40 per cent by the mid-century.

The boom was also based on the massive expansion of slave imports, reaching 636,465 by 1845 (Torres-Cuevas 1994a: 272–4), making over half of Cuba's population black by 1845 (Segre et al. 1997: 25), one third of them slaves (Torres-Cuevas 1994a: 268). However, one underlying weakness was the slave trade's increasingly contraband nature, which, in the face of British abolitionism and pressure, raised costs.

This all changed Cuban society rapidly. The putative elite of 1700 now became a powerful, interlocked oligarchy, dynamic but with internal *peninsular-criollo* tensions, the former with privileged access to capital and technology that enabled modernisation and the latter relying on an increasingly expensive slavery. Below them, the population was boosted by greater free immigration, mostly Spanish but including some 48,000 Chinese contract workers by 1860 (Segre et al. 1997: 24) and representing 15 per cent of the workforce (Barcía Zequeira and Torres-Cuevas 1994: 407), which saw the population rise from 171,620 (1774) to 1,396,530 by 1861 (Segre et al. 1997: 23–25). Further down the hierarchy was Cuba's black population, even free blacks' status being reduced.

In this context, pro-Spanish loyalism grew, strengthened by three influxes: of 30,000 conservative French settlers fleeing Haiti after 1791 (intensifying a white 'race fear'), of thousands more after the US purchase of Louisiana from France in 1803, and, finally, of thousands of loyal Spanish after Latin American independence (1810–26). However, *criollo* loyalism was mostly pragmatic, fearful of slave revolt and aware that colonialism perpetuated their wealth (by Madrid's tolerance of the slave trade) while independence would bring British abolitionist pressure, although intermarriage with the Spanish and military privileges did breed a more natural affinity for Spain (Johnson 2001: 122). Hence, when Napoleon's 1808 invasion of Spain presented Cubans with the opportunity of declaring a self-governing *junta* (as elsewhere in the colonies), the Cuban *criollos* rejected separatism, conspiracies being repressed easily, with the most vociferous separatists (notably Félix Varela and José Antonio Saco) being silenced or exiled. It was at this stage that the first stirrings of a search for a Cuban identity, in the emerging notion of *cubanidad* (Cuban-ness), began to be expressed and disseminated in intellectual circles, with Varela and Saco as its leading exponents; at that stage it tended largely to be a white notion, identified with *criollismo*, and referred more to a sense of local and putatively national identity than a clear-cut ideology.

In this context, overt loyalism only lasted about three decades. Squeezed between Spain's increasingly restrictive colonialism and growing commerce with the United States, many *criollos* realised that their future lay more with the latter, engendering a curious neo-separatism that advocated not Cuban 'nationhood' but 'statehood', as annexation by the United States, a sentiment uniting republican activists and conservative slavers and attracting southern US planters keen to add Cuba to their forces. The annexationist apogee was the 1840s, as Cuban rebels' efforts coincided with the United States' westward spread, victory in Mexico and the expansionist 'Manifest Destiny' idea; by the 1860s, however, the American Civil War made it irrelevant, although pro-American sentiments remained.

Meanwhile, Cuba's black population had evolved, status now being determined by its different African origins and levels of freedom. For Spanish rule was such that both slaves and free blacks (the latter more common in the west) 'learned how to use the domains in which Spanish authority was weak, such as religion and culture' (Helg 1995: 15), to protect their African traditions and fuse them together to create a new black syncretism, allowing the preservation of a 'reconstructed African world', adapting religion and tradition to the new context and creating 'community forms of self-help and mutual assistance that constituted a kind of alternative way of life', especially the tolerated black societies (*cabildos de nación*) (Helg 1995: 15). Hence, Cuba's black population eventually consisted of the majority Yoruba (or *lucumí*), the Bantu culture, the Benin-originating Arará and, by the 1830s, the most enclosed culture, the Niger delta-originating Abakuá tradition (incorporating the Carabalí Ibo and Efik cultures), founded by Cuban-born domestic slaves in Regla (Helg 1995: 29). By the 1840s, therefore, two patterns were discernible: adaptation and resistance. The former was evident in the emerging *sociedades de color*, mutual-aid societies for assistance, integration and entertainment, which helped develop an incipient consciousness among free blacks, but also in the emergence of *santería*, the increasingly syncretic religion or set of religious practices that evolved from the fusions of different African beliefs and of these with Christianity. The latter especially consisted of escape (to *palenque* maroon communities), strikes and rebellions, the most notable being the 1844 Escalera 'conspiracy' in Matanzas whose scale was exaggerated by the white authorities to play on race fears and to justify a widespread repression of free blacks and a massacre of some 3,000 supposedly rebellious slaves.

As the American option disappeared, as Spanish oscillations between promises of autonomy and sudden retrenchments frustrated, and as slave-dependent Cuban sugar holdings began to lose out to the Spanish, desperate *criollos* began to contemplate a break. In October 1868, Carlos Manuel de Céspedes, a white eastern planter, declared rebellion (the Grito de Yara) and freed his slaves, thus generating an irreversible de facto abolitionist process, as both sides followed suit. The following ten years of bitter warfare (the *Guerra Grande*) transformed Cuba, political rebellion soon becoming social revolution (as black *mambí* guerrillas fought a struggle for wider liberation, for a *Cuba Libre* that would include them) and the Spanish (led by the loyalist *voluntarios*) resisting with an increasing ferocity, displayed particularly in General Weyler's brutal concentrations of rural civilians and 'scorched earth' policies. Finally, the rebellion's white leaders, fearful of a perceived black threat and the imagined ambitions of the popular *mulato* leader, Antonio Maceo, surrendered in 1878, although Maceo resisted a while longer. During the war, a significant step had, however, been taken, the 1870 Moret Law acknowledging the momentum and abolishing slavery with effect from 1888. In 1879–80, eastern blacks then fought a second war, the *Guerra Chiquita*.

The aftermath was mixed. Firstly, devastation, abolition (ultimately brought forward to 1886), and punitive anti-*criollo* taxation and restrictions all combined to further weaken the Cuban-owned sugar sector; indeed, Cuban planters were now increasingly bought out by US corporate interests, whose more technological and concentrated approach brought a new boom but also fragmented cultivation, converting plantations into the more peasant-based *colono* sector, with greater unemployment and internal migration. Meantime, punitive US tariffs drove Cuban cigar producers to move production and the workforce to Florida, ending Cuba's major urban industrial sector.

Social change was inevitable, planter immiseration in the east being accompanied by increased Spanish immigration, which, more skilled than before (and mostly from the more developed regions), gravitated towards urban employment, trades and commerce, swelling the middle class. For Cuba's blacks, abolition created formal freedom but effective inequality, especially for thousands of urban migrants, with the old 'race fear' being resurrected in white myths of black violence, criminality, 'witchcraft', laziness and sexuality (Helg 1995: 17–18), and with de facto segregation operating in entertainment, hotels and catering establishments, and employment. While whites dominated commerce, white-collar employment, printing and prestigious cigar trades, blacks were limited to the sugar harvest (*zafra*), domestic service, laundry, dressmaking and female employment (Helg 1995: 26).

This was the context for a rapid politicisation of *criollo* attitudes, towards both a greater radicalism (especially among the working class) and a new separatism. The former arose especially from immigrants bringing radical ideas and practices into an unequal and oppressive context, and from the tobacco industry, although emigration to Florida removed some of this. The latter, reacting to broken Spanish promises and to a newly desperate situation, was guided especially by José Martí, who, in exile, propagandised as a journalist, raised funds tirelessly, and, above all, united the elite and middle-class émigrés of the eastern US seaboard and the radical Florida-based Cuban workers into the Cuban Revolutionary Party (Partido Revolucionario Cubano, PRC) in 1892. Finally, in 1895, stimulated by the prohibitive 1894 US sugar tariffs, the PRC launched its rebellion, Martí leading the invasion but being killed in battle in May. The resulting war was in some respects like the first, fought by some 40,000 *mambises* in the *Ejército Libertador* (Liberation Army), but was shorter and more successful, ending with a military stalemate. Then, after three months of populist sabre-rattling, Washington took the decision to intervene unilaterally, its April 1898 declaration of war on Spain converting the Cuban War of Independence into the Spanish-American War, which ended in August with a comprehensive Spanish defeat.

The immediate result of the war was a four-year American military occupation, ostensibly designed to stabilise Cuba economically and socially and prepare it for self-government, but whose unwritten intention was to de-radicalise Cuban politics (disbanding the PRC), weaken the black 'threat' (with the demobilisation of the *Ejército Libertador*), extend US economic interests and 'Americanise' Cuba sufficiently to persuade Cubans to gravitate towards US 'protection'. Although US laws forbade further penetration by US economic interests, the occupation saw those interests double. The process of stabilisation was, however, effective, with the modernisation (and partial 'Americanisation') of the education system (including a reform of the University of Havana), the creation of a racially hierarchical Rural Guard to maintain order (but, significantly, no Cuban army, since that role would be taken by US forces), and the reliance of the US administration on Spanish bureaucrats and Spanish commercial interests, to the anger of Cuban separatists. Finally, the seal was put on US intentions when, in 1901, the Cuban Constitutional Convention was cajoled and threatened into accepting the wording of the notorious 'Platt Amendment' (an amendment to a US Army Appropriations Bill) as part of the new Constitution; since independence was clearly conditional on acceptance, even the most radical nationalist had to accept the inevitable, although the vote in favour was not unanimous. This Constitution cemented Cuba's new status, of neocolonial dependence on the United States as a protectorate, allowing unilateral US military intervention to restore order as necessary, leasing Cuban territory in perpetuity for military bases, and effectively giving the United States economic control.

Hence, after emerging late, Cuban nationalism had seen itself radicalise rapidly, incorporate the black population successfully and to radical effect, unify Cubans more effectively than ever, and finally achieve independence after three rebellions and fourteen years of brutal and bitter fighting, only to see the fruits of struggle taken away. Instead of a weak and corrupt Spanish control, Cuba now faced control by the United States' growing military and economic power and with old debilitating divisions being replaced by new ones, between those prepared to accept the new order and those still harbouring dreams of the elusive *Cuba Libre*, the embodiment of the once vague aspiration of *cubanidad*. Cuba thus began its independent existence with a sense of national identity still in doubt, but at least with the vague notion of *cubanidad* having evolved into a more consensual and challenging ideology, as an emerging *cubanía* (belief in *cubanidad*).

Part 1: The City in the Shadows – Pre-sugar Havana (1550s–1750s)

Birth of the City

With the boom of Mexican silver and the fleet system, Havana especially reflected Cuba's two functions: to service and to protect the trans-Atlantic trade, particularly after Drake's 1586 sack of Santo Domingo. In the 1550s, the Santo Domingo *audiencia* moved the Governor's office from Santiago de Cuba to Havana, now authorised as the sole Cuban trading port (Segre et al. 1997: 13). After that Havana's rhythm depended on the fleets, the Mexico-bound *flota* leaving Spain in the spring and the Panama-bound *galeones* in August, both then joining in Havana in March for the return journey, taking on supplies, making repairs and waiting for clement weather. Although wealth still flowed through rather than into Havana (Segre et al. 1997: 18), the city had a central imperial role, a royal decree in 1634 endowing it with the epithets *Clave del Mundo Nuevo* (Key to the New World) and *Antemural de las Indias Occidentales* (Bulwark of the West Indies).

The impact was immediate. By 1608, Havana was Cuba's largest city (with 46 per cent of the population) and by 1620 the Empire's fastest growing city (Sorhegui and Fuente 1994a: 110). Moreover, sharing only with Vera Cruz and Porto Bello the right to receive goods, ships and people directly from Spain, Havana was Cuba's most Spanish and most privileged city.

Servicing the trade meant, firstly, providing supplies. In 1550, the *cabildo* raised a harbour tax to build an aqueduct (the *zanja real*) from the Chorrera river, which, when completed in 1592, was the Americas' first European water-supply system. Servicing also meant ship-repairs, which, while leading to the hinterland's deforestation (compounded by cattle-ranching and agriculture), encouraged artisan labour and established a small dockyard, subsequently replaced, in 1725, by the Astillero Real (Royal Dockyard) where, by 1796, 114 ships were built (Lightfoot 2002: 18), employing some 3,000 (Portuondo Zúñiga 1994: 189). Of course, servicing also meant 'rest and recreation' for those awaiting the fleet, especially lodging, gambling, alcohol and prostitution (setting a long-term Havana stereotype); by 1570, Havana had fifty taverns for a permanent population of only 330 (Sorhegui and Fuente 1994a: 134).

Around Havana, land was another source of wealth; in 1552–1601, the *cabildo* granted 148 *mercedes* (land grants), uniquely in Cuba (Segre et al. 1997: 18), producing supplies for both fleet and garrison, and, increasingly, more commercial crops. Havana's first *ingenio* (sugar mill) appeared in 1595 (Torrents 1989: 38), but most were small (Sorhegui and Fuente 1994b: 140), and tobacco, starting at Jesús del Monte and the Chorrera, spread southwards to Santiago de las Vegas,

Bejucal and Wajay and eastwards to Guanabo, but was also small-scale and limited.

Besides supply, defence was Havana's other role, garrisoning and protecting city and fleet. The construction of the Real Fuerza fortress was the first task, under governor De Soto; after completion (1544) and destruction by piracy (1555), it was finally completed in 1577, the first military stone building in the Americas (Segre et al. 1997: 13). In the 1630s, its cylindrical tower was completed, crowned by the Giraldilla. Governor Diego de Mazariegos then commissioned a wall, the Castillo del Morro (de los Tres Santos Reyes Magos), and the Castillo de San Salvador de la Punta, and, in 1597, a long defensive chain was suspended nightly across the Bay's entrance (Sorhegui and Fuente 1994a: 129). In recognition, in 1592, Philip II raised Havana from a *villa* to a *ciudad* (city) and awarded a coat of arms.

The next construction priority was ecclesiastical, and especially convents (most notably the Colegio de San Francisco de Sales, Santa Clara and Santo Angel del Custodio), churches (such as the Iglesia del Espíritu Santo, the oldest surviving church) and the Hospital de San Lázaro. Priority was evident in materials, seventeenth-century churches being begun in adobe and *guano* but finished in stone, while dwellings (apart from the wealthy stone and tiled houses) were more impermanent, fire destroying ninety-six adobe or wood thatched houses in 1622 (Eguren 1986: 123).

Havana's design followed imperial imperatives, with a grid pattern radiating from a central plaza, Spanish residence being central and the indigenous population peripheral. However, the Bay's shape made Havana's evolution more haphazard, and, from 1647, the emerging wall defined the city's shape, dividing it between *intramuros* and *extramuros*, although, by the time it was completed in 1767, it was already redundant, Havana by then bursting its bounds. By the 1760s, Havana consisted of two districts (*cuarteles*), Campeche (south of the Bay) and the northern Punta (or Cangrejos), and four parishes, the largely military Santo Angel, the south-western Santo Cristo del Buen Viaje (by the gate and commercial centre), the wealthy Parroquia Mayor (by the Cathedral), and the poorest, southern Espírito Santo.[1]

Social Development

Settlement in Havana was slow; by 1570 there were still only sixty Europeans (Sorhegui and Fuente 1994a: 109). Initially, immigration came mostly from Seville, the Canaries and Castilla (Sorhegui and Fuente 1994a: 110), but later was more Galician, Asturian, Basque and *canario* (Segre et al. 1997: 43), although all Spaniards were termed *gallegos* (Galicians). The major immigration was, however, forced African labour. By 1600, Havana alone had imported 800, a further 144 arriving from Cartagena in 1603 and 300 in 1692 (Sorhegui and Fuente 1994a: 140), mostly for construction, brush-clearing and domestic service, but for some artisan work (allowing an opportunity to buy freedom and land: Sorhegui and Fuente 1994a: 111–12). Hence, while in 1600, *intramuros* (with 12,000 inhabitants) was 70 per cent white and *extramuros* more mixed (Sorhegui and Fuente 1994b: 145), by 1700 Havana contained some 50,000 inhabitants (Portuondo Zúñiga 1994: 193).

Predictably, white–black divisions were legally and socially rigid, white *habaneros* thinking themselves European, and, with no indigenous population and thus no *mestizaje*, as superior to *criollos* elsewhere (Johnson 2001: 8). Initially, the Havana elite consisted of descendants of the early settlers, but, by 1600, an elite of merchants, administrators and landowners existed (Sorhegui and Fuente 1994a: 133), reinforced by intermarriage and mobility between land and commerce (Sorhegui and Fuente 1994b: 152). Meanwhile, by 1620, free blacks (often seeing themselves above slaves) dominated several artisan trades, often formalised in the guilds (*cofradías*), suggesting stability and the emergence of an incipient 'middle layer', many also joining the militia companies for blacks and *mulatos* (Sorhegui and Fuentes 1994b: 169).

However, the easy wealth, the transient population, the city's economic function, the relative Spanish neglect and the lack of settler women all meant a curious social development, Havana being a very male city, with women either as chattels (for sex or labour) or, if 'respectable', expected to remain indoors at night or protected in convents. It was a city of cock-fighting, bullfights and gambling (Torrents 1989: 40), and dangerous enough for a nightly curfew inside the walls (signalled by cannon round) and for the *cabildo* to order a stronger prison in 1577 (Eguren 1986: 65); it was also characterised by 'la abundancia de prostitutas' (the abundance of prostitutes': Torrents 1989: 24). It was also a dirty city, making disease inevitable, epidemics striking every few years, killing one third in 1649 (Torrents 1989: 41).

Religion might have offered some stability, the Bishopric transferring in 1561 to end 'sinfulness' (Torrents 1989: 29), but, lacking an indigenous population, the Church remained institutionally weak, although religion did determine white–black relations; in 1680, blacks or *mulatos* were banned from the priesthood and restricted to the lay brotherhoods (Sorhegui and Fuente 1994b: 162).

In this context of violence, filth and the supposed black 'threat', the elite inhabited a social cocoon, using the extra-mural space to display their wealth in the nightly carriage ride (*paseo de carruaje*), the Alameda de Paula theatre, and at dances and public band concerts (Segre et al. 1997: 26), always seeing Spain as their cultural yardstick.

Education was one badge of elite status. In 1597, the *cabildo* employed two teachers (Sorhegui and Fuente 1994a: 133), and, in 1689, the Colegio de San Ambrosio was founded by Bishop Diego, being endowed (in 1707) with chairs in philosophy, ethics and canon law (Le Riverend 1984: 848); finally, in 1728, the Real y Pontificia Universidad de San Jerónimo de la Habana was founded by the

Dominicans, in the Convento de San Juan de Letrán. However, public education remained rudimentary, with poorly educated and underpaid teachers (*maestros*), monks and private tutors taking up the slack (Portuondo Zúñiga 1994: 214).

The Emergence of a Culture

Havana's cultural development was therefore also rudimentary and belated. For two centuries, there was no learned stratum, most cultural activities being either associated with the Church (notably painting and sculpture) or popular and often raucous. With an elite slow to form, and with a profusion of cultural traditions and few white women, popular dance developed slowly, being initially limited to imported Spanish traditions such as the Andalusian *zapateo*. However, after the 1590s, public balls did appear, often being opportunities for riotous revelry (Eguren 1986: 113–14).

Interestingly, musical practitioners were, from early on, overwhelmingly black or *mulato*, since, with few European instruments or performers (Havana having no registered musicians in 1582), church orchestras needed black performers and African instruments (Torrents 1989: 40). When the first musical group (a quartet) formed in the 1590s, it used European and African instruments and consisted of a white *sevillano* violinist, a Hispaniolan free black, a *malagueño* violinist and a Portuguese clarinettist. In 1573, the Havana *cabildo* commissioned a *danza* for Corpus Christi, with pipes and drums, beginning the tradition of musical and theatrical Corpus Christi celebrations. Choral practice also emerged, for, although Havana had no tradition of indigenous choristers, by 1605 Gonzalo de Silva was teaching both organ and singing (Carpentier 1988: 49), and, by 1689, a choir school existed. Indeed, by 1700, Havana was associated with sacred music while Santiago had more lay musical associations (Carpentier 1988: 64–5).

Meantime, black music was evolving in many ways, helped by the religious segregation of Spanish rule (allowing slaves to continue their own cultural practices beneath or within Christian forms), by the forced fusion of different African cultures in a horizontal syncretism and by the protection of the black *sociedades*. Music was central to all forms, seen as a collective, participatory and celebratory activity (Roy 2002: 16).

In the space between the liturgical and the profane, a cultural tradition then evolved in Havana, especially in the popular festivals, rooted in Spanish traditions and celebrating patron saints, amounting to some forty-five different festivals in central and western Cuba. Beyond this, there were less religious carnivals everywhere and, in Bejucal, Santiago de las Vegas and Rincón, black *charangas* (Feliú Herrera 1999: 157–9). However, although carnivals were recorded in Havana in 1585, scarce resources were diverted to Corpus Cristi, leaving the carnival to 'elementos profanos' (Feliú Herrera 1998: 52), with African-origin processional dances (*comparsas*) and Spanish papier-maché giants.

It was also in theatre where a Havana culture began to emerge, uniting two traditions: the Spanish liturgical and the African ceremonial and religious, although there is evidence of masqued representations from the 1570s (Le Riverend 1984: 999). The first recorded play, *Los buenos en el cielo, los malos en el suelo* ('The good people in Heaven, the bad on earth'), supposedly the first recorded cultural 'event', came on 24 June 1598, the governor's saint's day, by the castle (Lightfoot 2002: 149; Le Riverend 1984: 999), a performance which was popular but rowdy (Torrents 1989: 40). Gradually, classical Spanish plays began to be performed in rich houses, and 1730 saw the baroque comedy *El príncipe jardinero y fingido Cloridiano* staged by a Havana militia captain, Santiago Pita (Lightfoot 2002: 75).

Written literature was, of course, held back by poor education, low literacy and the lack of a printing press, although other colonies possessed them (Fornet 2002: 11). Gradually, even the few writers to emerge – including the elusive José Augusto Escoto (writing as Miguel Velázquez) (Lightfoot 2002: 73) – tended not to be *habaneros*, such as the friar José Rodríguez Ucres (or Ucares), with his satirical *décimas jocosas* (Le Riverend 1984: 916) and the *canario* Silvestre de Balboa, whose epic poem on Havana's battles with piracy, 'Espejo de la paciencia', was published in 1608 (Lightfoot 2002: 73), and included the first known written use of the word *criollo* (Benítez Rojo 1996: 52). Finally, when in 1723, Havana's first press arrived via the Belgian Charles Habré, with a second in 1735, the stage was set and was the basis of Havana's cultural hegemony (Mata 1966: 104–5), with some seven presses by the time Santiago got its first in 1792 (Fornet 2002: 13). Thus, with infrastructure in place, and the population growing, Havana now only needed wealth to develop; sugar would soon provide that.

Part II: The Boom City – Sugar and the Evolution of a Capital (1750s–1901)

Havana's Political and Economic Evolution
Once the new sugar economy began to boom and, after the British departure, Spain conceded access to freer trade and slaves, Havana began to flourish. The shipyard was rebuilt under governor Ricla and the increased shipping exported sugar and imported manufactures, enhancing Havana's role as the Empire's focal point and the colony's core, the point where Cuba related to the outside world.

Other sectors also thrived, not least tobacco and coffee, the first coffee *fincas* being in Wajay (Torrents 1989: 49), but, as they collapsed (coffee) or shifted (tobacco), Havana's main non-sugar activity became cigar and cigarette manufacturing; even after the emigration to Florida, Havana still boasted thirty-six cigarette factories and 120 cigar factories, and, by 1898, small-scale manufacturing and a thriving level of petty-trading (Poumier 1975: 107–8).

However debatable the economic significance of 1762, its political effect was substantial, demonstrating Spanish weakness and boosting *criollo* self-confidence; as the 2,330 Spanish surrendered, the 4,753 *criollo* militia were left to resist a force of over 200 ships and 14,000 troops and marines (Keuthe 1986: 16–18). Moreover, once the occupation ended, it stimulated renewed military reform, which, recognising *criollo* importance, awarded military privileges and space for social advancement. While merchants and artisans enlisted alongside planters and shipbuilders, the militias included *pardo* (*mulato*) and *moreno* (black) battalions (Keuthe 1986: 38), helping Havana to resist another British invasion in 1782.

The occupation also, through external contact, stimulated intellectual development, especially in the Real Sociedad Económica de Amigos del País, which, echoing other colonies, was established by royal decree in 1792, seeking through Enlightenment principles of rational enquiry to improve the colony's economy, society and administration. In particular it created Havana's 'generation of 92' under people like Saco and Francisco de Arango y Parreño. The occupation also stimulated freemasonry, a Havana Temple des Vertues Theologales appearing in 1804 (Torres-Cuevas 1994b: 330), and the York Rite, with twenty-five lodges and 4,000 members in Cuba in 1821, spread progressive, and occasionally separatist, thought. However, the Spanish reaction to colonial independence also affected Havana, as one of the progressives' bases, the Academia de Literatura Cubana, was closed, Saco was expelled, and by 1837 a *peninsular*-dominated Junta de Notables ruled.

The new thinking had also affected Havana's slaves, where much unrest was evident from 1810 (Deschamps Chapeaux 1970: 17 *passim*), some slaves engaging in conspiracies, notably those led by Román de la Luz (1811), José Antonio Aponte (1812) and the Rayos y Soles de Bolívar group. When, in 1843–4, Havana province and Matanzas were beset by slave unrest, culminating in the 'Escalera conspiracy', the repression particularly targeted 'free blacks', many innocents being expelled or deprived of privileges (Barcia Zequeira and Toíres-Cuevas 1994: 435–6).

For the next two decades, heavily Spanish and militarised, Havana remained politically quiet, the more liberal *criollos* being either exiled, fearful or pragmatic. Even the *Guerra Grande* hardly affected Havana, confirming that separatism was often irrelevant to the capital, the *voluntarios*' base, and Havana irrelevant to the rebellion. The exception came on 27 November 1871 with the execution of eight medical students among the forty-three arrested following *voluntario* accusations of anti-Spanish remarks; the students were subsequently exonerated and the arrested freed.

After 1878, with Spanish retribution, rigid censorship and desperate shortages, Havana remained calm, although a new politics was emerging in the small working class and most particularly in the tobacco proletariat, through the custom of the *lectura*. Begun in 1865, this involved paying someone to read to the workforce from selected books (such as Verne, Russian and Spanish authors, Zola, and Marx: Poumier 1975: 182) or political newspapers (Fornet 2002: 187). It was a seminal method of democratic education, radicalising in a collective workplace. This radicalisation was also enhanced by immigration to Havana of two kinds: the increasingly political immigration from Spain, often using the new immigrant cultural centres as the bases for their new trade unions, and the displaced ex-slaves who now migrated to Havana's slums and shanties. Indeed, a black awareness was the newest political development, enhanced by the war and the effects of the peace (Ferrer 1999).

When that dissidence erupted in 1895, Havana was quite different from 1868. Although once again the base of Spanish resistance, with most of the 63,000 *voluntarios* (Helg 1995: 84), political affiliations were more variegated, and the 1895 rebels did not share their predecessors' reluctance to carry the war to the west. Hence, although little fighting occurred in Havana, its Spanish-ness was less marked.

Spatial and Social Evolution

Havana's visible character had also changed. The first boost to development was Ricla's fortification programme, including the new Príncipe and Atarés castles and the Arsenal. Governor de la Torre then prohibited guano construction, effectively expelling the poor to the outer *barrios* of Jesús María and Salud (Torrents 1989: 62–3), although Havana remained filthy and the Bay polluted (Eguren 1986: 209). Only under Tacón in the 1830s did modernisation seek to reduce crime, vagabondage and gambling (Segre et al. 1997: 33).

Initially, the commercial centre was the Spanish area around Obispo and O'Reilly (Eguren 1986: 299), the traditional centres seeing palaces built around the Plaza de Armas and the Plaza de la Catedral (the Cathedral itself being built in 1748), as well as Plaza Vieja, Obra Pía and the 1840 Palacio del Aldama.

Architectural styles were initially conservative, both the Baroque and the neo-Classical arriving late, the former because of the inappropriate local stone and lack of expertise, the latter because of its association with 'dangerous' French rationality (Segre et al. 1997: 28). However, Tacón encouraged the neo-Classical, inspired by L'Enfant's Washington work, encouraging 'ostentatious and symbolic' styles (Segre et al. 1997: 34), and designing the Prado (formerly the Alameda and now renamed Paseo de Isabel II) to enable women to ride unchaperoned in their *volantes* (Segre et al. 1997: 31).

The city also grew. Even in 1757, Havana and its hinterland had half of Cuba's population, most of its ninety-five sugar-mills, and almost all of the west's 2,763 tobacco *vegas* (Torres-Cuevas 1994a: 276). By 1810, the city and suburbs had grown sixfold, to 47,102, (Johnson 2001: 52–3), out of Cuba's 273,000 (Segre et

Figure 3 The Palacio de los Capitanes-Generales, the governor's palace in the central Plaza de Armas

al. 1997: 35), and, by 1832, 150,000 (Torrents 1989: 57), the adjacent San Antonio de los Baños, Guanajay, Guanabacoa and Campo Florido being also densely populated.

Despite five new gates in 1773, Havana burst its walled bounds, by the 1840s some 70 per cent living outside the old walls (Segre et al. 1997: 43). Tacón encouraged this, extending Reina and building the Paseo de Tacón (later Carlos III and now Salvador Allende) for his summer residence, Quinta de los Molinos. Cerro began to develop, with elegant *quintas* (country houses), as the elite fled disease and the mosquitoes. Already, in the 1770s, Governor La Torre had established the city police, and the 1780s had seen the first streetlight and bath-houses (Eguren 1986: 194); now, in 1832, the Bay was dredged, streets were paved, and 1837 saw the Havana–Bejucal railway (Latin America's first). This programme was followed by a slaughterhouse, public lighting, a fire brigade and fire alarm system (Segre et al. 1997: 35), and, in 1853, the first telegraph. In 1861, new building codes stipulated construction norms, and Vedado, to the west, was opened up, its two farms being subdivided in 1859 for development and 1868 seeing the new Cementerio de Colón. As Vedado grew, it followed a set grid pattern, with wide boulevards and new rules guaranteeing space around each house and introducing numbers and letters rather than street names.

As a result, Havana also boomed socially. As an indication, ice arrived in 1806 (Torrents 1989: 170), and the first steamship in 1821, connecting regularly with New Orleans (Torrents 1989: 63). Another indication was hotel construction, demonstrating outside interest: after the Santa Isabel (Plaza de Armas) and the Telégrafo, came the Perla de Cuba, Inglaterra, Europa, Progreso and Trotcha (Villalba Garrido 1993: 12). By the 1880s, Havana had eighteen consulates, a busy nightlife, cafés such as the Paloma and Comercio (Eguren 1986: 213), and a growing transport system with (successively) horse-drawn trams (1860), steam trams (1877) and the electric tram (1894) (Torrents 1989: 64). It also had book-shops such as the Minerva (selling the latest European novels), the Propaganda Literaria, Fernández's, and Spencer's (Eguren 1986: 376), and eighteen printing presses and lithographs (Barcia Zequeira and Torres-Cuevas 1994: 422–5).

However, the city still bore its old traits. The former violence had subsided, although 1820s visitors still reported weekly murders (Eguren 1986: 224), but Havana was still overwhelmingly unhealthy, the poor crowding into ten square kilometres (Segre et al. 1997: 51); in the 1800s, yellow fever, smallpox and cholera epidemics were still frequent, the 1833 outbreak killing 10 per cent of the popula-tion (Torrents 1989: 42; Torres-Cuevas, 1994a: 271). By 1894, visitors still complained of poor sewerage and disease (Poumier 1975: 102), all increasing dra-matically during the two wars, the 1868–78 *reconcentraciones* herding nearly 100,000 into *yaguas* (makeshift settlements) on the margins, ravaged by disease (Segre et al. 1997: 51; Poumier 1975: 132), and the 1895–8 war crowding some 120,000 women, children and old people into the city (Torrents 1989: 68). Havana's penchant for gambling and prostitution also continued, the former becoming rife (especially cock-fighting), the latter increasing with prohibitions on female labour (beyond laundry, tobacco and domestic service and certain profes-sions such as teaching and acting), leading to the founding of the dedicated hos-pital Quinta de Higiene San Antonio on Calzada del Cerro in 1898 (Barcia Zequeira 2000: 112). Meanwhile, the Church remained Spanish in loyalties, per-sonnel and control, with no Cuban bishops and with a visible public indifference to organised white religion (Torres-Cuevas 1994a: 298).

However, gradually, more stable patterns and hierarchies began to emerge. At the top sat the new *sacarocracia* (Moreno Fraginals 1977: 21) and its related oli-garchy, now more clearly divided between dominant *peninsulares* and *criollos* whose indebtedness created space for merchants (especially Catalans), acting as bankers (Torrents 1989: 59). This elite still engaged in conspicuous consumption in European-influenced housing, dress and leisure. In the 1820s, boosted by refugees, French influence was the strongest, through institutions such as the 1816 Academia de Música de Santa Cecilia and the 1818 Academia San Alejandro for painting; even house interiors were in the French style (Segre et al. 1997: 29). However, by 1898, ostentation was manifested more in the social club: the Havana Yacht Club (Marianao) and the Vedado Tennis Club (both opening in 1885), the latter moving to Tulipán in 1899 (Llanes 1993: 161–2). Elite social life focused on the *paseo*, the public dance or the theatre, the first (usually in horse-drawn *calesas* or *carruajes*) beginning each evening, in the Alameda de Paula, the Plaza de Armas or (later) the Paseo Extramuros and Paseo Tacón.

Dance was the least refined but most genuinely popular entertainment. In 1800, the public dances at the Teatro Tacón and the Liceo were the playgrounds of the elite's young, the Escanriza, Circo and Sebastopol being more popular (Santos Gracia and Armas Rigal 2002: 27–8). Fifty years on, the Liceo was still the only 'decent' one, the Escanriza being mostly for 'dependientes, tabaqueros, o criollitos de mala vida' ('shop-workers, tobacco workers or low-life *criollos*') and the Circo and Sebastopol being distinctly 'indecent' (Eguren 1986: 301–2). By the 1890s, dances were being organised on Sundays by hotels and, after performances, by theatres, with private dance schools proliferating (Poumier 1975: 114). What was being danced also changed: while in the 1820s European dances were the fashion, with the *minuet* still being popular and with the closest to a 'national dance' being the Spanish *fandango* (although the *contradanza* 'Cubanised' imported French, Spanish and possibly English forms, becoming known outside Cuba as the *contradanza habanera*: Roy 2002: 83), by the 1890s, the Cuban *danzón* reigned supreme, adapted and moderated by the new middle class (Santos Gracia and Armas Rigal 2002: 29; Poumier 1975: 114).

Theatre was increasingly a social event, especially as women could attend (although not in the plebeian and raucous *patio*), its status arising partly from the governor's patronage and partly because it was another opportunity for ostentation, richer families having their own boxes (*palcos*). Concerts offered similar opportunities and hierarchies: in the 1840s, the Filarmónica served the elite, the Santa Cecilia being more popular (Eguren 1986: 27), and, gradually, Sunday afternoon military band concerts in the Parque Central became popular.

This development was allied to the growth of education. In 1803, the Sociedad's Bishop Espada – one of the Cuban Enlightenment's seminal patrons (Leal 1986: 79) – unsuccessfully introduced the Pestalozzi method and, in 1816, the Sociedad's Ciencias y Artes section became the Educación section, which, until 1844, took responsibility for free public primary education, especially under José Agustín Caballero. This consisted in Havana of twenty-four boys' schools and eighteen girls' schools (Barcia Zequeira and Torres-Cuevas 1994: 420) and, from 1820, the Escuela Normal. Private education also developed, especially the Colegio San Cristóbal (Colegio de Carraguao), the Colegio Salvador and the Colegio San Anacleto. However, in 1844, Havana still had only one secondary public school, the University's Colegio, although, in 1857–68, another Escuela

Normal was opened for teacher-training in Guanabacoa, when secondary education was separated from the university, leading to the Instituto de Segunda Enseñanza.

Higher education was more impressive, especially the Colegio de San Carlos, which became a seminary and then, in 1773, after the Jesuits' expulsion, the Real Seminario de San Carlos y San Ambrosio, becoming the main forum for debate and research and shaping most of Cuba's leading thinkers and separatists. In 1842 the university was secularised as the Real y Literaria Universidad de La Habana, at the Convento de Santo Domingo.

As the century moved on, a new Havana middle class also grew, based in administration, education, commerce, the professions, petty trading and Spanish immigration. Tending to imitate aspects of elite society, especially its passion for dances – their preferred locale being, in the 1830s, the Tívoli garden (Eguren 1986: 244) – this class gradually developed its own patterns, viewing 'culture' as recreation and, by 1898, an instrument for advancement, 'para adquirir notoriedad y consideración social' ('to acquire fame and social status': Le Riverend Brusone, 1960: 404).

Equally, Havana's small and developing working class developed its own cultural patterns, although frequenting some of the elite's and middle class's dances. Immigration partly obscured the cultural differences between 'middle' and 'working' classes but also meant that no clear-cut cultural identity emerged at the bottom of the pyramid until the immigrants began to form communities. Hence, the most identifiable cultural forms among Havana's poor were those in the black community, especially as they outnumbered the white immigrant working class; in 1828 some 60 per cent of Havana's population was black (Deschamps Chapeaux 1970: 17) and as late as 1869, the west had 600,840 whites, but still 300,989 slaves and 141,677 free blacks (Pichardo 1977: 367).

However, being urban, Havana's black culture saw more adaptations. Drums, for example, were replaced by piano, flute and trumpet, and traditional religious dances by the waltz, mazurka and polonaise (Helg 1995: 31), a process strengthened by the 1887 law obliging *cabildos* to be open and inclusive educational or recreational societies, identified with a Catholic saint (Roy 2002: 14; Santos Gracia and Armas Rigal 2002: 32). The Afro-Cuban tradition that survived best was probably the Abakuá, the hierarchical brotherhood of male *ñáñigos*, with initiation rites, internal discipline, hermetic language and sacred signs (Helg 1995: 29), evident in Marianao, Regla and Guanabacoa and in the tobacco factories; in the 1870s, the Abakuá increased, eighty-three associations (*juegos*) with over 1,000 members being identified in 1882 (Helg 1995: 30), linked to dockers' unions, but increasingly being regarded as criminal, barbaric and engaging in witchcraft (*brujería*) (Helg 1995: 30), and with the emerging *santería* religion becoming associated in many whites' and official eyes as synonymous with *brujería*.

The *sociedades de color* soon became identified with specific trades (such as cooks or coachmen) or with specific baseball clubs, and some advocated black and *mulato* trade unions. This development, helped by decrees on education and social reform, led to greater black awareness and the evolution of Havana's black communities, which, by the 1880s, had regained some status in literature, journalism, philosophy, music and religion (Helg 1995: 29). From 1886, black activists created an integrationist movement, establishing the Directorio Central de las Sociedades de la Raza de Color, and launching an education drive, especially as the decrees allowing blacks into education were often ignored in reality, whites escaping to the increasing number of discriminating private secondary schools (740 by 1895: Helg 1995: 37). Black frustration was also expressed in the argument for a black private sector and a double existence of outward integration alongside inward cultural preservation (Helg 1995: 33).

Meanwhile, immigration from outside was changing Havana. The cohesion and adaptability of Spanish immigrants was achieved by the social centres, especially the Centro Asturiano (with over 10,000 members, a school and a hospital), the Casino Español (from 1869), the Basque, Galician and Catalan centres, the Centro de Dependientes and Círculo Habanero (Poumier 1975: 115). Besides the Europeans, the Chinese were most evident, 97 per cent of Cuba's 34,420 Chinese living in Havana in 1869 (Pichardo 1977: 367), making Havana's Chinese community Latin America's largest and most economically active.

Emergence of a Havana Culture

On the basis of these social developments, there were potentially at least two sorts of 'cultural community': an elite-based community, seeing itself as an extension and imitation of external patterns, and an evolving number of Afro-Cuban communities, with smaller, immigrant-based nuclei evident, if not yet evolving into anything more cohesive. Of these, the elite community was the best documented and the most self-confident; it possessed the necessary network of institutions (for legitimacy, guidance and the determination of boundaries), sites (defined spaces and opportunities for publication, performance or dissemination) and groups, gathered around and stimulated by leading interpreters and fostered and protected by the necessary patrons, either as entrepreneur (making things happen with finance, space and dynamism) or as 'mentor' (leading by example and prestige).[2]

1750s–1860s

The most important institution for the formation of an elite *criollo* cultural identity was the Sociedad Económica, the seed-bed for most enlightened and eventually separatist thinking in Havana, which, with royal patronage and the prestige of elite membership, left few areas of intellectual life untouched, establishing the canon and providing space for dissident thinking. The Sociedad created several institutions,

Figure 4 The original building of the Sociedad Económica de Amigos del País

notably the 1793 library; the first such non-clerical Cuban institution, based in the Convento de San Francisco and then, in 1844, the Convento de San Felipe. The Sociedad also had other offshoots, such as the Sociedad Patriótica de La Habana, which, in 1793, began the Cuban tradition of literary prizes, and, in 1830, the Comisión Permanente de Literatura (under Nicolás de Cárdenas and Domingo del Monte), from which, in 1831, emerged the seminal *Revista Bimestre Cubana* and, in 1833, the Academia Cubana de Literatura, the first institution to define and confer elite prestige on cultural forms. With twenty-seven leading academicians, it rapidly became the favoured site for Havana's progressives, until the increasingly conservative Sociedad closed it soon afterwards (Torres-Cuevas 1994b: 344; García 1980: 18).

Beyond the Sociedad, those years also saw institutions designed to spread the effects of progressive thinking, such as the 1861 Liceo Artístico de Guanabacoa and the 1844 Liceo Artístico y Literario de La Habana, which, under Ramón Pintó (Chió 1981: 65), the captain-general's patronage and the direction of Rafael Mendive and José María Hererra y Herrera, actively promoted culture through education, grants to poorer students and publications, and through its various dedicated sections (García 1980: 497).

Within these still nascent institutions, the role of the intellectual leaders, the leading interpreters, was often fundamental, especially (in defining *cubanidad*) Félix Varela, who, in 1816 (Torres-Cuevas 1994b: 333), began teaching at San Carlos, developing new thinking from his chair of philosophy and seeking Cuban solutions to Cuban problems, and who, elected in 1823 to the Spanish Cortes, proposed educational reform, abolition of slavery and Cuban autonomy (Torres-Cuevas 1994b: 338), before exile in the United States, where he published *El Habanero*.

The elite's sites were also the physical spaces of cafés, salons and *tertulias*, and the opportunity offered by the printing industry. The former began with the introduction of the coffee house, the Café de Tavern (later de la Taverna) appearing in 1772 in Plaza Vieja, followed after 1804 by the Café de los Franceses, Café de las Copas, Café de la Dominica (1812) and the 1825 Café de la Paloma (Segre et al. 1997: 30), while La Lonja and El Comercio offered less intellectual space. Later on, the Hotel Inglaterra's terrace, Acera del Louvre, became important, offering risqué young conversation (Goodman 1986: 241).

The *tertulia* (cultural gathering) was a staple of elite society and *criollo* identity, driven by patron-entrepreneurs, of whom the undoubted leader was the Venezuelan-born Domingo del Monte. After studying at San Carlos and the University and visiting Europe and the United States, he hosted regular *tertulias* (in 1836–43) in the Palacio de Aldama, where the latest European and Latin American ideas were discussed, where writers brought their work for criticism and where a free-thinking environment existed for Havana's intellectuals, notably Cirilo Villaverde, José Victoriano Betancourt and Felipe Poey (Le Riverend 1984: 1012). Del Monte also founded magazines (such as the 1829 *La Moda o Recreo Semanal del Bello Sexo*), contributed to the Academia Cubana and the *Revista Bimestre Cubana*, and was instrumental in encouraging the self-taught black Matanzas poet, Juan Francisco Manzano, to join the Havana literary community. Finally, in 1842, he left Cuba because of suspicions arising from his friendship with the abolitionist British consul, Turnbull, and the Escalera conspiracy.

Two other patron-entrepreneurs were the Sociedad's Poey (who organised *tertulias*) and Mendive. The latter in particular was the Liceo's literary secretary (1848), founded the Colegio San Pablo (1867) and the *Revista de la Habana* (1853–7), which sought to be a forum for activity, discussion, criticism and publication (Le Riverend 1984: 877), and directed the Escuela Municipal de Varones (from 1864); his *tertulias* became a seminal site for Havana's future cultural leaders (especially Martí), until in 1869 he too was obliged to leave for New York. Other *tertulia* hosts included José Antonio Cortina and José M. Céspedes (who also awarded prizes: Le Riverend Brusone 1960: 429), and Nicolás de Azcárate, whose Thursday Guanabacoa *noches literarias* (1865–7) became a cultural fixture, enhanced by the 1866–7 publication of the two-volume anthology *Noches literarias en casa de Don Nicolás Azcárate* (Le Riverend 1984: 1012).

Beyond these opportunities, doors were also opened by Havana's developing printing industry, the presses growing steadily, mostly associated with the Sociedad; Havana's ten printers in 1838 rose to twenty-eight in 1852 (Fornet 2002: 46–54). The presses' principal focus was the newspaper, starting in 1764 with the news-sheets *La Gaceta* and then (1782) *La Gaceta de La Habana*. In 1790, at Governor Las Casas's instigation, the first proper newspaper appeared, the *Papel Periódico de La Habana*, becoming, until 1848, the main forum for cultural expression and enlightened debate, adopting an almost evangelical desire to civilise and awaken 'la inquietud cubana' ('Cuban restlessness': Vitier, García Marruz and Friol 1990: 40). A flood of papers ensued, most notably *Diario de La Habana* (from 1810), all adhering to a view of culture as civilisation and education, engaging in intellectual and scientific debate, or informing through *costumbrismo*.

Only *Revista Bimestre Cubana* (1831–3) and a crop of ephemeral cultural magazines (usually by and for small intellectual groups) paid attention to culture as art, notably the 1822 *El Amante de Sí Mismo* (García 1980: 45), Mendive's monthly *Flores del Siglo* (1846–7 and 1852) and the most influential monthly *Album*, whose twelve issues (1838–9) disseminated cultural opinions and Cuban and foreign works, including Villaverde, Del Monte, Milanés, Manzano and the Condesa de Merlín (García 1980: 31). The small-circulation *El Plantel* (1838–9) also strove to increase Cuban awareness of outside culture (Le Riverend 1984: 797), and, throughout, the pro-Spanish *La Prensa* (1841–70) and *Diairo de la Marina* (after 1844) offered regular space for culture.

However, whatever the organ, 'culture' was always defined in terms of Cuba opening up to European 'leaders'. Only José Fornaris's *Cuba Literaria* (1861–3) consciously attempted to represent a 'Cuban' literature. This was partly because the cohesive network of cultural groupings or circuits did not yet exist to provide a 'Cuban' identity, although the raw material did, in the longest-lasting Havana movement of *costumbrismo*. Following the model of the Spanish movement and rooted in idyllic Romantic notions of nature, this depicted in detail the customs of daily rural life (such as Juan Francisco Valerio's 1865 *Cuadros Sociales*) or located realist narratives in a rural environment. Appealing to the more sophisticated tastes of a Havana cultural community, which either followed European fashions or were nostalgic for an imagined rural past, *costumbrismo* was the first manifestation of a Cuban cultural nationalism, even though few then either meant it or realised it, for the movement was simply a part of an older *criollismo*, which, referring to the various attempts by Cuban writers to reflect Cuban tastes, realities, sentiments and desires, had been the eighteenth-century cultural manifestation of a limited local pride in something called 'Cuba', which soon became the search for *cubanidad*;

hence, there never was a *criollista* movement as such, although Ramón de la Palma's 1854 studies of popular song (*Cantares de Cuba*) and Miguel Teurbe Tolón's *Leyendas Cubanas* (1856) are seen as *criollista* for seeking to rescue vestiges of a rural popular culture.

Instead, the most explicitly nationalist cultural movement was *siboneyismo*, the attempt to introduce into literature elements and themes from an imagined pre-Columbian past, represented especially by the poetry of Fornaris and Joaquín Lorenzo Luaces, and the prose-writer Pedro José Morillos. Fornaris alternated between Bayamo and Havana from 1840, producing his most famous collection *Cantos del Siboney* in 1855, while Lorenzo Luaces was an *habanero*, participating in Poey's *tertulias* from 1848, and, with Fornaris, producing the *siboneyista* magazine *La Piragua* (1856–7) and the 1861 anthology *Cuba Poética*, as well as unperformed *siboneyista* plays (García 1980: 512). Morillos's *El Rancheador* (1839) helped take the genre beyond the Romantic poetry of its main exponents, and, although not *siboneyista*, the *costumbrista* Julio Rosas (really Francisco Puig y de la Puente) also wrote an 'Indianist' novel, *Flor del corazón* (1857).

Within this overall picture, the cultural hegemony of the Havana elite was growing, especially given the Sociedad's enlightened criteria-setting and gate-keeping role and particularly in white Havana. However, outside the capital, another vibrant cultural pole was also flourishing in Matanzas, the centre of the booming sugar industry and the site both of the most progressive commercial and productive entrepreneurs and of a black and *mulato*-based cultural community. Indeed, the emerging Havana elite effectively attempted to appropriate this alternative community by attracting and including potentially dissident non-white writers such as Manzano or the *mulato* poet Plácido (Gabriel de la Concepción Valdés), who, having acquired fame in Matanzas, was welcomed into the Havana cultural community in 1832 with the award of the Aureola Poética prize for his poem, 'La Siempreviva'. Furthermore, Antonio Medina, whose 1842 *El Faro* (the first Cuban paper written by and for blacks) was an essentially dissident attempt at a counter-elite, was invited to belong to the Ateneo and hosted *tertulias* (Le Riverend 1984: 588).

Throughout, the small size of the Havana elite cultural community was problematic, particularly affected by the limited opportunities for publication, the favoured method being subvention through collective sponsorship achieved by the author (Fornet 2002: 114). This made poetry and prose minority activities, the first book of verse (Ignacio Valdés Machuca's *Ocios Poéticos*) appearing only in 1819 (Fornet 2002: 108) and the first novel (Cirilo Villaverde's *El Espetón Diario*) appearing as a book in 1838, after serialisation in *El Album* (Fornet 2002: 112). However, some attributed the lack of interest to wealth (Fornet 2002: 122), which had generated the infrastructure for an elite culture but produced newspapers rather than creative publications, the most popular printed form being for some time *proyectismo*, rationalist treatises on governance, which, when written by Spaniards stressed Cuba's importance within the Empire, but, when written by Cubans, focused on Cuba's distinctiveness, notably Martín Félix de Arrate's 1830 verse work, *Llave del Nuevo Mundo*.

A final obstacle was the persistent problem of 'exile', whether imposed or chosen in pursuit of opportunities or recognition. One outstanding case was the poet José María de Heredia, who, living in Santiago until fourteen and then moving to Mexico in 1823 (because of a marginal involvement in the Rayos y Soles conspiracy), returned in 1836, renouncing his views, but, after only two months of ostracism for that reason, returned to Mexico to die. Moreover, Heredia wrote in French as much as in Spanish (becoming part of the French Romantic canon), although his prestige and external recognition make him significant in the evolution of Cuba's culture. Another was María de la Mercedes Santa-Cruz y Montalvo, the Condesa de Merlín, who, after escaping from the Convento de Santa Clara in 1799, married a French general in Spain, returning to Cuba only for one brief 1840 visit. A third outstanding exile was Villaverde, who, after publishing serialised novels in newspapers and magazines, was arrested in 1848, for alleged involvement in conspiracies, escaping to New York in 1849; returning to Havana in 1858, following an amnesty, he ran the La Antilla press and edited *La Habana* (1858–60), but again left for New York in 1860, where he died soon after.

Absence was also, of course, internal, as with Manzano (whose years in Havana were limited to the 1830s, until he returned to Matanzas and, implicated in the Escalera conspiracy, was arrested) and Plácido, who, returning from Havana, was also arrested after Escalera and executed.

Within this context, the most evident and predictable manifestation of an elite culture was poetry, with almost 100 titles published in Havana in the 1840s, although dismissed as versifying (Fornet 2002: 126) and usually either tradition-ally neo-Classical or derivative, the traditional *décima* becoming a Cuban prefer-ence. Even Romanticism was slow to arrive, apart from the émigré Heredia, although Plácido and Manzano might have taken the movement further had they stayed in Havana. Nonetheless, Havana attracted aspiring poets from the interior, notably the Bayamo-born Juan Clemente Zenea (in Havana from 1845, apart from exile in 1852 and 1865–70, until his 1871 arrest and execution), José Jacinto Milanés (invited by Del Monte from Matanzas and enjoying great success in 1836–1843: Le Riverend 1984: 616), and the Oriente-born sisters Luisa Pérez de Zambrana (married to the Havana poet Ramón Zambrana Valdés from 1858) and Julia Pérez y Montes de Oca, both becoming stalwarts of Havana poetry circles, publishing and participating in the Guanabacoa Liceo and Azcárate's *tertulias*.

Prose was slower to develop, limited initially to poetic narratives or journalistic *crónicas*, most notably by Spanish-born Virginia Felicia Auber de Noya, who, in Havana from 1833 to 1872, contributed to the 1852 collection *Los cubanos pintados por sí mismos* (García 1980: 86). Embryonic novels emerged (for example Palma's 1837 *Matanzas y Yumurí*), usually in manuscript form or serialised in newspapers, most notably Villaverde's *Cecilia Valdés*, which, first published in 1839 as a short story and then serialised, only appeared as a novel in 1882.

Painting, at that time a minority activity given the lack of space, was really pioneered in Havana by the Frenchman Jean Baptiste Vermay, who, before being named Pintor de la Real Cámara in 1826 and Socio de Mérito of the Sociedad Patriótica in 1828 (Sánchez Martínez 1989: 405), founded the Escuela de Arte de San Alejandro in the Convento de San Agustín in 1819, under the Real Sociedad. This academy followed European models under successive directors (Vermay, Francisco Cuyás and Jean Baptiste Leclerc), and, from the late 1820s, two strands: aesthetic education and more applied art (Merino 1989a: 320). The latter meant lithographic illustration (Merino 1989b: 393), theatre scenery, especially at the Principal, and church painting (Sánchez Martínez 1989: 403).

In fact, it was theatre that really offered the best opportunities to the Havana cultural elite, especially with new sites; in 1776, the quayside Coliseo, on Paseo de Paula, was built (Carpentier 1988: 83; Sánchez Martínez 1989: 398), which, closed in 1788, was replaced by the 1803 Teatrico de la Alameda (known immediately as the Teatro Principal or Teatro de la Opera), copying Madrid's Teatro Príncipe (Sánchez Martínez 1989: 399), although that too, partly destroyed in the 1846 hurricane, was demolished, as was the 1830 Teatro Diorama (Sánchez Martínez 1989: 401). With both theatres destroyed, plays were staged in the Jesús María district (Rivero 1981: 34), but, in 1838, Tacón had the Gran Teatro built on Paseo de Isabel II, because the Principal was too small and distant; its opening performance, of *Don Jean d'Autriche* in translation (Eguren 1986: 385), saw 8,000 attending and 15,000 outside spectators (Rivero 1981: 35).

Tastes varied according to the period and the building. There were some Cuban plays, such as Milanés's 1840 *El mirón cubano* (Le Riverend 1984: 616), Francisco Póveda's *El peón de Bayamo*, at the Guanabacoa Liceo in 1879 (Le Riverend 1984: 827), and Alfredo Torroella's *Careta sobre careta* at the Tacón in 1866 (Le Riverend 1984: 1024). Most theatre, however, was foreign and musical. The Coliseo opened with Metastasio's opera, *Didone abbandonata*, but thereafter preferred Spanish theatre, with a permanent Spanish theatre company from 1790 and musical recitals and *zarzuelas*. The Principal preferred Italian operas (Rivero 1981: 34), by then generally popular (Eguren 1986: 250, 256), while the Diorama was more a concert hall than a theatre, under the Academia Filarmónica de Cristina from 1839. In 1802 the Fleury company started performing French dramas, and, in 1810–12, a Spanish company staged French and Spanish operas, also including the dancer Manuela Gambarino, whose repertoire began a taste for dance schools and the waltz (Carpentier 1988: 148–51); the Austrian Fanny

Essler's 1840 visit was indeed a moment of cultural recognition for Havana (Leal 1986: 93–4). However, the frequently poor quality of Havana operas brought criticism of one 1850 French work (Eguren 1986: 291) and an 1863 riot at the Tacón (Leal 1982: 16).

However, opera really ceded pride of place to light musicals. 1791 saw the first Spanish-style *zarzuela*, Joseph Fallotico's *El alcalde de Mairera* (Río Prado 2002: 2), but the *tonadilla escénica* remained the mainstay; essentially a Cuban version of the Spanish *sainete* (a one-act musical comedy), over 200 were performed in 1790–1824, becoming the basis for the popular and uniquely Havana genre of *teatro bufo* (Carpentier 1988: 87–8). The *sainetes'* popularity created so many opportunities for musicians that, in 1802, the cathedral authorities banned church musicians from the theatre. Between 1794 and 1800, theatrical performances were briefly replaced by spectacles and circuses (Vitier, Marruz and Friol 1990: 285), the Circo-Teatro opening in 1800 in the Campo de Marte.

Indeed, by 1815, both the *tonadilla* and the *zarzuela* had declined, replaced by the new *teatro bufo*. A two-act play aiming to entertain, display musical extravagance and pass ironic comment on the contemporary scene, this form was seen as more quintessentially Cuban, in popularity, social relevance and irreverent challenge to the 'ambiente operático y romántico de los grandes salones' ('operatic and Romantic atmosphere in the great salons': Leal 1982: 31). The first *bufo* came in 1868 and there were soon sub-genres (the witty *sainete,* the topical *apropósito*, the theme-less *revista*, the *zarzuela* with its clear story and varied characters, and the *parodia*) and the *bufo* followed the *zarzuela* pattern of stock characters: the sharp *negro curro*, the more African *bozal*, the learned *catedrático*, the *mulata de rumbo*, the drunk, the *chino*, the undertaker and so on (Río Prado 2002: 10).

New *bufo* theatres soon opened: the 1847 Circo Habanero (the Villanueva from 1848), the 1870 Albisú (briefly renamed the Lersundi), the 1874 Cervantes (ending each performance with a risqué dance: Rivero 1981: 36), and the 1877 Payret. *Bufo* plays were soon written, especially by Circo actor Francisco Covarrubias, who, in 1800–47, adapted Spanish *sainetes* and *entremeses* for Havana tastes with Cuban characters (Carpentier 1988: 208), pioneering a 'género único cubano' ('uniquely Cuban genre': García 1980: 241). Equally important, however, was the Spanish-born Bartolomé José Crespo y Borbón (known as Creto Gangá), whose contribution was to introduce African words and portray black characters (Lightfoot 2002: 150).

The 1868–78 war interrupted *bufo*'s evolution. On 22 January 1869, at a Villanueva performance of Francisco Valerio's *El perro huevero aunque le quemen el hocico*, Spanish *voluntarios* interpreted as treasonable the audience reaction to a seemingly patriotic phrase (possibly 'Viva la tierra que produce la caña': 'long live the land which produces sugar cane'), and opened fire, killing and wounding several. The Spanish authorities immediately banned the *bufo*, as seditious and excessively *criollo*, thereby guaranteeing its patriotic status thereafter in Cuban minds. One immediate effect was Martí's explicitly patriotic *Abdala*, which, published within days in *La Patria Libre*, rejected *bufo*'s perceived triviality and established a new committed *teatro mambí*. In the absence of *bufo*, Havana theatre briefly became a diet of European drama or opera, or patriotic Spanish plays, although a Chinese theatre opened briefly in 1873 on Lealtad (Leal 1982: 90).

Bufo's popularity introduces the other accessible art form, music, which mirrored other cultural forms in its steady 'Cubanisation'. In 1801, the *Papel Periódico* published the press's first concert programme of Pleyel, Hoffmeister and Haydn (Carpentier 1988: 91–2), alongside advertisements for instruments indicating a level of amateur interest. Certainly, music societies reflected this interest, with local groups, the Horcón-based Sociedad del Pilar (1848) and the 1851 Sociedad Casino Habanero; and the more prestigious 1824 Sociedad Filarmónica, the 1834 Sociedad Santa Cecilia (which fused with the Liceo) and the 1841 Sociedad Habanera. In 1866 the Sociedad de Música Clásica was founded by musicians and composers (including Cecilia Arizti, Carlos Anckerman and Nicolás Ruiz Espadero) to escape the 'tiranía operática' (Carpentier 1988: 193). Space was also offered by magazines (*El Filarmónico Musical*, 1812), the musical supplement of Del Monte's *La Moda* and educational institutions, such as the Academia de Música (1814) at Antonio Coelho's house (Carpentier 1988: 140–7), or the cathedral, where Juan París staged concerts, classes and a library (Carpentier 1988: 160).

However, the prime site for music remained the theatre, even attracting the Sociedad Santa Cecilia to Italian opera, and resisted only by small groups such as the San Carlos student orchestra and Santiago, which, between 1830 and 1860, became Cuba's centre for 'serious' music.

The community's musical life also, of course, depended on individual patron-entrepreneurs, such as the musician Antonio Raffelin, who founded the Academia Filarmónica de Cristina, organised concerts, taught music and toured the island, until a religious crisis halted him. Another was the Frenchman Jean Frédéric Edelman, who, after 1832, directed the Sociedad Santa Cecilia and whose music shop became a gathering site; it was under Edelman that the musical nationalist Manuel Saumell Robredo developed. His unfinished and unperformed opera *Dolores* was seen as a key moment in the trajectory of a Cuban 'national' culture, incorporating popular African and indigenous elements, and he pioneered recognition of popular dance, writing *comparsas* and being considered the father of the *habanera*, the *danzón*, the *guajira*, the *clave* and the *criolla* (Carpentier 1988: 171–6). Also influential was Espadero, who largely remained in his Havana house but in 1854 befriended the visiting American pianist Louis Moreau Gottschalk, who persuaded him to compose stylised 'primitive' and brooding music, including the 'Cuban' *Canto del Esclavo* and *Canto del Guajiro*. However, Gottschalk was, unquestionably, the leading patron-entrepreneur, who, visiting Havana repeatedly and befriending Espadero and other prominent Havana musicians, introduced European styles, and, in 1861, organised a spectacular event at the Tacón, *Una noche en el trópico*, with forty pianos played by Espadero, Saumell, Edelman and others, and with Afro-Cuban drummers, including a huge *tumba* played by a *rey de cabildo* (Carpentier 1988: 185).

Gottschalk's role highlights two issues in Havana's musical development: the attraction of the United States (Raffelin, Desvernine and Ignacio Cervantes Kawanagh staying there for long periods and Bousquet, Valdés Costa and Gáspar Villate touring: Acosta 2001: 57–8), and the role of black performers. In 1827, only forty-four white musicians were recorded in Havana, while the black community provided forty-nine from a much smaller total (Carpentier 1988: 123), blacks becoming the majority of musicians by 1840 (Carpentier 1988: 133; Deschamps Chapeaux 1970: 105–18). However, despite this, they faced discrimination and the post-Escalera repression affected musicians too, Pimienta being executed and Buelta y Flores and Claudio Brindis de Salas being tortured, despite the latter's prowess and status in teaching white Havana society to dance.[3]

1870s–1898

Thus, by the 1860s, a recognisable elite cultural community had begun to emerge in Havana, gaining in self-confidence and self-belief (as a community within a community) and with its boundary-defining institutions and patrons who provided the space and opportunity necessary for development and recognition. This community clearly looked in two directions: towards a European cultural community to which it felt it belonged and whose values it sought to imitate and spread, and towards the rest of Cuba with a mission of enlightenment. It was therefore simultaneously 'leader' (of something called 'Cuba') and 'led'. By the 1850s, *criollos* within that community had begun to propagate a tentative and derivative sense of their Cuban identity (in *siboneyismo* and *criollismo*) especially in music and the unlikely form of *teatro bufo*, the latter demonstrating the new reality that this community had been leavened by new elements, the infusion of black performers and the rise of a middle class that cared less about cultural fashion but more about what made them different from *peninsulares*.

The 1868–78 war, however, blew apart that emerging sense of community, exacerbating cleavages (between whites and blacks, Cubans and Spaniards, intellectuals and authorities) and leading some elite Cubans to doubt their separate identity, either retreating again to the protective custody of Spanish colonialism or resigned to the apparent fact of Cubans' inability to unite and cohere as an 'imagined community'. Defeat also scattered the community, into exile (exaggerating the old problem of absence) and to other parts of the island. This was also largely because, with the decline of the *criollo* sugar elite and the force of

Spanish retribution, there was nothing to which the Havana cultural elite could attach itself, for, after 1880, the Havana elite was more Spanish, more ensconced in positions of commercial, financial and political power, and bolstered by a middle class which was also considerably more Spanish than in the provinces.

Hence, for the aspiring community, space and access to power and prestige were more difficult than before; they either had to retreat into small groupings or into their private work, attach themselves to an ever more colonialist Spanish elite, or leave Cuba and seek space, recognition and opportunity in Spain, France or the United States. Two prominent examples of this new exile were the novelist Gertrudis Gómez de Avellaneda and Martí, the former living either in Puerto Príncipe or in Europe, and Martí spending only some eighteen of his forty-two years in Havana, from his birth in 1853 till his exile in 1871 and for two brief visits in 1877, and 1878–9.

With old institutions, formal and informal, having also either collapsed or decayed, the community's infrastructure was less auspicious, the Spanish elite now preferring not to encourage specifically Cuban cultural manifestations. The only exceptions were the new elite social clubs, which did sponsor events, such as the Círculo Habanero, one of the few sites of cultural activity, introducing *modernismo* and giving space to poets such as Julián del Casal (García 1980: 424). Patronage and recognition were also conferred by cultural (mostly literary) prizes, as yet not given 'official' status (by a colonial state uninterested in manifestations of a possibly subversive Cuban art), but linked to other institutions with limited social prestige, such as the Sociedad Provincial de la Catalana Colla de Sant Mus, which awarded an annual literary prize, Juegos Florales.

With exile taking its toll, the community lacked the mentors or entrepreneurs of the pre-1868 Havana, this role being left to critics or journalists; these were surprisingly influential in defining cultural directions, most notably Justo de Lara (José de Armas y Cárdenas), whose *Las Avispas* (1892–5) sought to spread knowledge of foreign literature through translation, and Ramón Meza, who started various magazines from 1884, taught at the University, hosted *tertulias* and sponsored poets such as Casal.

Therefore, not only was there no cohesive and self-confident Havana cultural elite but, equally, with no strong counter-elite, a vacuum existed and, with authority difficult to establish, respect was the best hope. This role was left to places like the Liceo de Guanabacoa, which, having been closed in 1868 (and replaced by the pro-Spanish Recreo Español until 1878), was resurrected by Azcárate, with Martí briefly as literature secretary (Enrique José Varona occupying the same post from 1882); this institution, helped by its geographical marginality, saw itself as somewhat self-consciously dissident, hosting Torroella's 1879 funeral where Martí spoke. A similar role was played by the more political Liceo Artístico y Literario in Regla (established in 1878, following a lecture by Martí), which, until it closed in 1896, founded various newspapers from 1887 (García 1980: 498).

Equally, *tertulias* (revived by Azcárate in 1879) never regained importance, rising from about three a year to seven in 1887–94 (Fornet 2002: 152), although the later sessions (until 1882) attracted Havana's cultural leaders, such as Manuel Sanguily, Diego Tejera, Fornaris and the union leader Saturnino Martínez. From 1880, the dramatist Luis Alejandro Baralt hosted regular *tertulias*, culminating in the Teatro Jané (1881) and the Nuevo Liceo de la Habana, which, between 1882 and 1895 under Azcárate, offered a cultural space for performance and publicity. In 1880–1 smaller *tertulias* were organised in social centres, *El Fígaro* sponsored the 'La Habana Elegante' series and the Teatro Alhambra ran a regular *tertulia* (Le Riverend 1984: 1012).

In this less auspicious context, cultural production declined. Poetry still enjoyed prestige, through association with Heredia and Martí and through its continued status as a cultured pastime for women, creating an exaggerated impression of a vibrant scene, although Antonio López Prieto's revealingly named 1881 anthology *Parnasio Cubano* did bring recognition to otherwise forgotten and diffuse Cuban poets. The exception was of course Casal, who most eloquently absorbed and expressed the new *modernismo* and French symbolism, and who, after studying and briefly visiting Spain (in 1888), worked as a proofreader and contributor for *La Discusión*, becoming a protagonist of Havana's few cultural gatherings, befriending Azcárate and Ramón Meza and editing (in 1891–2) the weekly *La Familia Cristiana*. Less obviously, Havana then boasted several prominent novelists, notably the naturalist Martín Morúa Delgado and Meza; the latter's *Carmela* won the 1887 Juegos Florales and his 1878 *Mi tío el empleado*, with its gritty realism, signalled a moment of collective self-discovery (Lezama Lima 1989: 225).

In the hitherto vibrant musical circles, a degree of retreat was also evident, the Havana scene returning fully to its traditional love of opera and musical theatre, and following the European fashion for band music, especially under Guillermo Tomás, director of the Banda Musical de La Habana, who aspired to educate Cubans musically. One problem was, however, the lack of patron-entrepreneurs, the exception being the Dutchman Hubert De Blanck, who opened a classical conservatoire in 1885.

However, two outstanding exponents of a distinctly Cuban non-operatic music were evident in Cervantes and Villarte, both benefiting from travel abroad. Cervantes (often considered the century's leading Cuban musician) studied in France after being dispatched by the captain-general in 1875 to prevent his arrest; besides his overtly experimental work, it was his dances and similar compositions that most expressed his beliefs. Villarte shared his nationalist or *criollista* consciousness; on returning from the United States and Paris in 1871, he developed *contradanzas* influenced by *siboneyismo* and composed with explicitly Cuban themes but with a clear French stamp.

Music however was exceptional, being somewhat enclosed within Havana but exposed to the outside world through travel. Instead, during the Havana community's three fallow decades, 'culture' in Havana meant two different things. At both elite and middle-class levels, it meant entertainment, whether the boom in 'light reading' (popular novels and newspapers), the continuation of popular musical theatre, or the popularisation of sport. Reading was clearly influenced by the development of bookshop-based publishing in the 1870s, Manuel de Villa's Obispo bookshop publishing magazines and José Gutiérrez's Plaza del Vapor shop stressing popular songs (Fornet 2002: 146). Meanwhile, non-literary publications increased, especially popular histories of Cuba, which indicated some new post-bellum desire among the middle class to 'imagine' their Cuban identity, and, in 1890, the Imprenta El Pilar began its Biblioteca Selecta Habanera series of 'serious' novels, publishing sixteen by 1896 (Fornet 2002: 156–7).

The newspaper boom copied American and European habits, especially with small-scale specialist organs, responding to rising literacy, a discernible middle class and imported fashions. These included sports magazines (most notably *La Joven Cuba* (1894–5), the 'órgano oficial del Base Ball Club "Cerro"': García 1980: 472) and magazines (such as the 1881–3 *El Almendares*) for the cultural edification of Havana's women, but most targeted the new commercial and fashion-interested Havana readership, such as the sports-focused *El Fígaro* and *La Ilustración Cubana* (Fornet 2002: 155). By the 1890s, Havana boasted a wealth of papers, reflecting the city's disproportionately high literacy levels, compared to Cuba's 70 per cent literacy in 1887.

In this context, elite culture was addressed by a few specifically cultural organs, notably *La Bibliografía* (1885–7), patronised by Havana's leading writers and introducing the latest Latin American developments, and, above all, *La Habana Elegante* (1883–91 and 1893–6), briefly the organ of the Círculo Habanero and the Havana Yacht Club (García 1980: 422) until replaced by *La Habana Literaria* (García 1980: 424).

Havana theatre also returned to something of its former popularity and vitality, old *bufo* theatres reopening (such as the Payret, though abandoned in 1883–90 through hurricane damage), and new ones appearing, such as the Yrijoa (often spelt Irijoa) in 1884 (after 1898, the Edén Garden and now the Teatro Martí). One factor was the arrival of troupes of American minstrels (Acosta 2001: 34; Leal 1982: 23) and American vaudeville at the Alhambra (Pérez 1999: 126). It was, however, the new Alhambra (initially, in 1879, on the old Cervantes site until moving, in 1890, to a former skating rink on Consulado and Virtudes) that best reflected this popularity. After the first plays by the Narciso López company in 1891 and José Ríos in 1894 (Río Prado 2002: 19), it became, for three decades, Havana's principal *bufo* establishment, particularly staging the work of the *autonomista* Raimundo Cabrera, Ignacio Sarachaga and, above all, Federico Villoch, who wrote some 400 *sainetes* and *zarzuelas* and whose plays were performed regularly at the Lara and Alhambra (Le Riverend 1984: 1102).

For all its trivialisation, therefore, *bufo* clearly laid the basis for a demonstrably Cuban theatre during this period, more than the derivative, melodramatic, declamatory and moralistic work of Torroella, Aniceto Valdivia and Justo de Lara (Le Riverend 1984: 1003). It often incorporated black elements into public white culture (ending performances with a *rumba* and being occasionally set in a black Havana community), and the Alhambra's plays revelled in familiar Cuban 'types', gently poking fun at the authorities. The two theatrical worlds, however, did not mix, the new generation of respected actors (such as Adela Robreño or Napoleón Arregui) looking down on the seemingly 'immoral' theatre where comic actors such as Elvira Meireles or Florinda Camps plied their trade (Le Riverend 1984: 1003). When war broke out in 1895, this somewhat killed off Havana's residual theatrical activity, although a few theatres did reopen in 1897, one with a visiting Italian company (Barcia Zequeira 2000: 133).

One middle-class cultural development was, however, sport, especially baseball. Although Cuban mythology records Cuba's first baseball game on 27 December 1874, at Palmar del Junco in Matanzas (between a Matanzas team and the Habana Base Ball Club) or, in another version, sees its roots in the *taíno* game of *batos*, baseball was in evidence some time earlier (González Echevarría 1999: 76–7). Certainly, in the 1860s, it was being played informally by the young of all classes, probably arising less from American sailors (one version) than from young Cubans' studies in the United States. In 1868, the Habana Base Ball Club was formed, although, in 1869, the sport was banned by the Spanish, given its supposed link with Cuban nationalism (by being American) and its potential for riotous behaviour. In 1878, the Club was re-formed, together with the impeccably bourgeois Almendares Base Ball Club (González Echevarría 1999: 91), and between 1879 and 1890 over 200 clubs were created in Cuba (Brock and Cunningham 2001: 207).

Despite its elite origins, baseball's popularity already went further; in 1879, the Jesús del Monte-based Alerta and Progreso clubs merged in the Fe Base Ball Club, creating the first national league (González Echevarría 1999: 92). In the 1880s, baseball became both amateur (among the elite and the middle class) and semi-professional, as enterprises paid (increasingly black or *mulato*) players to represent them (González Echevarría 1999: 104). By the 1890s, there was a boom in clubs and magazines, the leading clubs building bigger stadia in Cerro (especially the Parque Almendares in Tulipán). Already, as with football in Europe and Latin America, urbanisation was creating a mass 'market' for an exciting spectator sport, but also, uniquely to Cuba, another opportunity for popular gambling. Baseball was also clearly becoming enshrined as a culturally nationalist expression, through its popularity and the Spanish authorities' reaction and because, as with American habits and citizenship, being pro-American was a statement of Cuban distinctiveness against Spain.

Like baseball, musical cultural forms also now went beyond the urban middle class in post-1878 Havana, namely those recreational and signifying cultural manifestations evolving among Havana's black working class, where dance had developed steadily from its *peninsular* roots into the *guajira*, the *guaracha* and the *décima*. By the 1890s, the *danzón* was, unquestionably, the most popular dance; supposedly created by Miguel de Faílde (*Las Alturas de Simpson* being first played at the Liceo de Matanzas on 1 January 1879), it in fact already existed, several being published in sheet music and Faílde merely codifying it. By 1878, it had conquered Havana, a competition being held in the Teatro Albisú (organised by the black Centro de Cocheros, Cocineros y Reposteros de la Raza de Color), and with Raimundo Valenzuela's leading dance orchestra including it in their repertoire of *rumbas*, *guarachas*, *boleros* and *claves* (Carpentier 1988: 216–17).

The fact was that Havana's increased black population had always practised its own popular cultural dance forms, building on Catholic celebrations, especially the Epiphany (*Día de los Reyes*), Shrove Tuesday (*martes de carnaval*) – the latter celebrated by blacks as the date of abolition, until banned in 1884 – Corpus Christi and San Francisco (3 October), the church of San Francisco being the starting point for the Vía Crucis procession on Lenten Fridays. Indeed, so successful had been the black population's appropriation of the Catholic calendar that only Christmas and New Year's Eve were considered white feasts, and, by 1900, these festivities had become flamboyant displays with more stock characters and instruments.

The political implications of such manifestations led the Spanish to ban them after 1895, the *Día de los Reyes* processions being replaced by *comparsas*, ritual processional dances based on different *barrios* (Roy 2002: 36), incorporating African-origin dances and other immigrant forms, such as Chinese drums (*cajita china*) and trumpets (Esquenazi Pérez 1999: 170), into the white tradition of carnival, which, in the 1840s, would follow masked dances at the theatres with a procession passing along Alameda, Reina and the Campo de Marte (Feliú Herrera 1998: 54).

Clearly, by the 1890s, several processes were evident in Havana's different cultural communities. At the elite level, any sense of a cohesive community had been dissipated if not broken, increasing the cultural elite's self-perception as a minority within a minority. Equally, apart from *criollista* music and the occasional painting (Antonio Rodrígeuz Morey's *Bosque y riachuelo* or Domingo Ramos's *Atardecer*, where the Cuban landscape, hitherto a stylised backdrop to an essentially European form, now became more of a protagonist), any sense of Cuban-ness in the different elite cultural expressions had either disappeared, moved abroad or remained frozen in a picturesque *costumbrismo*, depicting Cuba's black population in formulaic and unthreatening ways. Below the elite, however, different cultural forms were emerging organically, with their own internal authority but, as yet, without the acquired prestige of the supposed cultural leaders. There was, in short, almost no overlap between the cultural authority of each community, but at the edges, fusion was taking place.

By the 1880s, Havana found itself poised uncomfortably and disoriented between two Empires and three cultures, between the residual pressure of Spain (reinforced by weight of numbers and the war's effects), the impact of North American culture (reinforced by exile and the new legitimacy) and a cautious emerging Cuban culture, which lacked any consensus on its definition, differences of perspective focusing on where and how Afro-Cuba might fit in organically. Until any consensus emerged on that issue, within any of the cultural communities, there could be no hope of a sense of national culture either to challenge the two metropolitan cultures or to provide the basis for a consensual identity for a new Cuba.

Epilogue: 1898–1902

In almost every sense, therefore, 1878–98 was a hiatus, a period of uncertainty, conflict and transition towards an unknown future, the American occupation really only confirming preceding economic trends.

That occupation, however, did change Havana's infrastructure, the US authorities and their subaltern Cuban elite following a coherent programme of infrastructural construction and development of services such as sewers, electric lighting, telephones, gas and street paving (Segre et al. 1997: 52). Furthermore, under Varona, the university was rebuilt on a new Vedado site (la Colina) and reformed along American lines, and, in 1901, the Biblioteca Nacional was created as an autonomous institution in the Castillo de la Fuerza, with an initial 3,000 volumes (García 1980: 128).

Although no public buildings were constructed, the occupation did improve building materials, and the biggest construction project, the Malecón esplanade, was begun for two reasons: to establish elite sea-front summer homes and to facilitate traffic access, especially for the military, to Habana Vieja. The Malecón thus helped take Havana westward into Vedado and Miramar, reversing the previous 'introversion' (Segre et al. 1997: 52).

Cultural spaces were slow to emerge after 1898, through exhaustion, poverty, uncertainty and continuing exile, and because the war's divisions had dispelled the remnants of a potential coexistence with colonialism, which had given the Havana cultural community its cohesion, allowing both cultural nationalism and foreign cultures (including Spanish) to be received. The Liceo de Guanabacoa did reopen in 1900 under José Lacret Marlot, but never regained its status and the fragile 1878–95 *tertulia* scene remained limited to irregular sessions at the Casino Café and the Parque Central, involving José Manuel Carbonell, Arturo R. Carricarte, Max Henríquez Ureña and Jesús Castellanos.

As in 1878–98, the only new spaces were those offered by newspapers and magazines, boosted by returning young Cubans enthusiastic to translate the new and burgeoning US magazine culture into Cuban conditions. The occupation thus saw optimistic organs such as *La Nueva Era*, *El Progreso*, *La Joven Cuba*, *la Juventud Liberal* and *La Juventud Cubana* (Pérez 1999: 35), but, more characteristically, saw the increased popularity of sports magazines sharing their pages with culture, especially Andrés Segura y Cabrera's 1899 *El Biciclista* (devoted to sport and poetry) and the 1899 *Correo de la Juventud*, also mixing literature and sport. There were still a few cultural journals, such as *Cuba Libre* (1899), which, under Rosario Sigarroa (with support from Varona, Alfredo Zayas and Diego Vicente Tejera), strengthened the hold of *modernismo* (García 1980: 255).

Yet, productively, the occupation was barren, Cuban plays being noted more for patriotic content than quality, such as Félix R. Zahonet's 1899 *Los Fosos de Weyler o La Reconcentración* and 1900 *Patria o Tumba* (Poumier 1975: 214). 1898 did see the first performance of Eduardo Sánchez de Fuente's *Yumurí*, the first Cuban opera, at the Albisú, significant for its explicit cultural nationalism though still heavily influenced by Romantic notions of the 'noble savage' and a mythifying *siboneyismo*, and still seeing Cuba through European eyes, musically ignoring Cuba's African heritage in its preference for European-style dance forms and Italian opera.

Avowed nationalism did not yet herald a renaissance. Indeed, the occupation saw an impact of American popular theatre, especially in the American Café (with vaudeville, minstrels and burlesque), the Jardín Americano (where the Cuban Extravaganza Company was based) and the Casino Americano, which only booked visiting American acts (Pérez 1999: 126). Moreover, in 1897, the first American film was shown in a theatre, delivering a powerful message about changing cultural tastes (Poumier 1975: 120).

Even in sport, Cuban tastes were being changed. In 1894, the Havana bullring had competed on Sundays with baseball, but that competition ended in 1899 when Governor Wood banned bullfighting, as part of the 'Americanisation' drive and in order to civilise Cuba away from barbaric practices (González Echevarría 1999: 87), also removing an element of Spanish influence in favour of a sport that, though associated with Cuban nationalism, was also quintessentially American.

As the former colony, demoralised, struggled painfully towards a conditional independence, the critical question culturally, therefore, was: would the coming Republic be able to develop a Cuban culture? Moreover, with Havana still so Spanish, and now the port of entry for Amcrican cultural influences, would the capital's cultural communities be able to rescue something of their previous role in spearheading the national search for cultural identity? Or would the patterns of

1878–98 continue, Havana being a battleground for cultural expression at best and possibly a 'Trojan horse' for pressures against the national imagining of a Cuban community?

Notes

1. In 1783, these became eight: La Punta now included Estrella, Montserrate, Dragones and Angel, while Campeche included Santa Teresa, San Francisco, Paula and San Isidro (Segre et al. 1997: 23).
2. I am grateful to Alison Sinclair, of Cambridge University, for her insights on this distinction.
3. In fact, Brindis's son, Claudio José Domingo Brindis de Salas, became one of Havana's leading musical figures, even though travelling and studying mostly in Europe and only briefly in the city.

–2–

The Republic (1902–1958)

Historical Overview

Because of the effects of the US occupation, the new Republic that emerged finally in 1902 (some eighty years after the rest of Latin America) was beset by inherent difficulties: the nationalist forces were divided, the Platt Amendment undermined formal independence, American economic interests had expanded, and there was a sense of disillusion among those who had fought or supported the war.

Yet the economic future seemed positive. The Republic's first treaty, the 1903 Reciprocity Treaty with the United States, guaranteed Cuban sugar privileged access to the vital US market, and Cuba's strength as a sugar producer at a time of high prices promised to continue expansion. Yet that same strength also spelled danger, as, firstly, sugar wealth fuelled a rampant corruption and, secondly, US capital flooded in, further challenging economic independence. Moreover, dramatic social change resulted, with even more Spanish migrating to Cuba in the first twenty years of independence than in the last years of the colony, with a working class beginning to form in the increasingly modernised sugar sector, but with the old inequalities remaining, and even worsening – between east and west, black and white, sugar and non-sugar, and even Cuban and Spanish (the latter still entrenched in business and finance).

Politically, however, the new Republic seemed ill-starred. A patronage system based on sugar wealth, wartime loyalties and US tolerance (especially after US troops occupied Cuba again in 1906–9) all ensured that political life became endemically corrupt. Meanwhile, over it all hung the reality of the Platt Amendment, producing an endemic instability that, ironically, made intervention more likely. Indeed, not only was the US ambassador always a key political actor, but on three occasions (1906–9, 1912, 1917–23) US troops intervened to end unrest; on two of these occasions (1906, 1917), that unrest arose from a rebellion by dissenting elite elements in order to activate the Amendment and effect the government's removal through US intervention.

The 1912 intervention, however, arose from more deep-rooted discontent among Cuba's blacks, whose economic, social and political marginalisation after 1902 generated a deep anger at being cheated of the fruits of their substantial participation in the three independence wars. As a result, the Partido Independiente de Color (PIC) was created, which immediately led the government to ban racially based parties. In May 1912, PIC plans to launch an 'armed protest' petered out into localised unrest, especially in Oriente, but that was enough to generate a fierce reaction from whites and the government, and also from American economic interests, which requested US intervention to protect them. The outcome was a Cuban Army massacre of an estimated 6,000 'rebels', most simply peasants and workers victimised in a racist rampage.

However, the wider discontent that this reflected was generated by the frustrations of nationalists and radicals in the face of a shameful corruption and growing dependence. Apart from the creation of a veterans organisation in 1911, however, it remained mostly inert until the 1920s, when the system began to unravel with economic collapse. In 1920–1, following a frenzy of speculation (the *Danza de los Millones*), a precipitate decline of sugar prices (by over 90 per cent in a few months) brought immediate problems for the sugar-dependent state, for employment, for sugar production and for finance. One effect was that many Cuban-owned sugar enterprises and banking interests were immediately replaced by US interests. Another was to revive the old radicalism, led this time by Havana students (from 1923) and the always radical trade unions, focusing on corruption, inequality and a perceived neocolonialism.

One result was the creation of the new Cuban Communist Party in 1925. Another was the 1925 election of the supposedly nationalist reformer, Gerardo Machado, who, in office, proved to be close to the United States and an increasingly brutal authoritarian figure, generating even greater opposition and, eventually, a widespread revolutionary violence, which, by 1930, even included elements of the new middle class (in the clandestine terrorist organisation, ABC) and the elite (in a 1931 rebellion). As the effects of the 1929 Crash weakened his regime and radicalised further, a nationwide labour insurrection began from 1930, until the Army finally removed him in August 1933, replacing him by Carlos Manuel de Céspedes.

By that stage, however, the Republic was in terminal crisis. Céspedes was himself overthrown on 4 September 1933 by an alliance of mutinous NCOs and radical students, a rebellion that, after a brief interlude of rule by a five-man junta (the Pentarquía), brought Ramón Grau San Martín to power. For four months, Cuba was paralysed as the revolutionary government struggled simultaneously to institute popular nationalist reforms and control the country; it was, however, squeezed between, on the one hand, a suspicious Washington (which withheld the necessary recognition and whose ambassador, Welles, meddled dangerously) and conspiracies by displaced army officers and civilian sympathisers (mostly in ABC), and, on the other, a spiralling violence, perpetrated by armed student groups, and a continuing labour radicalism that, mostly in the sugar industry, was now led by a largely reluctant Communist Party. Finally, backed by Washington, the NCOs' leader, Fulgencio Batista, seized power in January 1934, ending the chaos (to many Cubans' relief) and, with it, the 'First Republic'.

The eighteen years that followed were characterised by three things: populism, degeneration and radicalisation. From 1934 to 1940, Batista's control of Cuba (through a series of mostly puppet presidents) was a curious affair. On the one hand, he crushed the Left (especially in 1935),[1] encouraged American organised crime to invest and operate, and allowed an emerging 'new' Cuban elite to recover. However, he also enacted many of the 1933 reform proposals in a populist campaign that, although partly modelled on Roosevelt's New Deal, was mostly opportunistic, as when he struck an astonishing deal with the Communist Party in 1937, allowing them a free hand in labour organisation if they supported him politically. The results were, in 1940, a progressive new constitution (codifying what was already the 'Second Republic') and Batista's popular election (till 1944). Another result was that the Communist Party (renamed after 1944 the Partido Socialista Popular, PSP) became more integral to progressive Cuban politics.

Meantime, the force overthrown in 1934 – Grau and the students – had largely consolidated in the Partido Revolucionario Cubano-Auténtico (Authentic Cuban Revolutionary Party), the Auténticos; in 1944 they were elected, under Grau, on a remarkably similar platform of nationalism, social reform and opposition to corruption. However, the Auténticos (Carlos Prío following Grau in 1944–52) proved a huge disappointment to many, not least as corruption worsened – especially with the rise of a gangster violence that, arising from the 1930–4 student groups, was tolerated and even used by the government. That disappointment gave rise to a new populist and nationalist party, born out of Auténtico frustration, the Partido del Pueblo Cubano (Cuban People's Party), the Ortodoxos, led by the flamboyant ex-student Eddy Chibás.

The Second Republic was politically stronger than the First (especially as Roosevelt abrogated the Platt Amendment in 1934), but it lacked its predecessor's sugar strength, since the long post-1762 period of growth was now largely ended, especially by the new US-Cuban arrangement. On the one hand, the 1934 Reciprocity Treaty, replacing the 1903 version, responded to Cuban fears and demands during the Depression and guaranteed much-needed security of market in exchange for advantageous access for US manufactures, thereby eliminating any hope of an industrial-based economic independence. On the other hand the new US sugar quota system brought Cuba security but, with quotas determined annually by Washington, little incentive for development. As a result, Cuba remained as divided as ever – a booming Havana (based on American tourism, illegal wealth and patronage) was contrasted with the appalling backwardness and poverty of the *campo*, Oriente and even parts of the capital, where the conspicuous consumption of the *nouveaux riches* coexisted with the poor, forced into economic informality and prostitution.

This was the context for the revolution that developed from 1953, stimulated by and reacting to Batista's coup on 10 March 1952, which brought the fragile house of cards down with hardly a protest, except for some Havana students led increasingly by the young lawyer and ex-Ortodoxo Fidel Castro. After an abortive attempt to galvanise opposition (by attacking the Moncada barracks in Santiago on 26 July 1953), a period of imprisonment (till 1955) and then exile in Mexico, Castro organised an invasion of Oriente in December 1956 on the yacht *Granma*, which, though it failed, began the process of widespread insurrection, as the rebels ensconced themselves in the remote Sierra Maestra and waged a guerrilla struggle, while their urban wing engaged in destabilising urban guerrilla activity. Finally, as Cuba polarised, as more and more dissident forces rallied to Castro (including the PSP, which joined the rebel alliance in 1958) and as the guerrilla Ejército Rebelde (Rebel Army) began a relentless and victorious westward march, Batista fled the country on 31 December 1958, with the rebels' Che Guevara entering Havana the next day.

Throughout this period, inevitably, the question of national identity became a constant theme of political life, intellectual concerns and debates, and even cultural developments. Until the 1920s, the overriding concern among nationalistically minded Cubans was the implications of the apparent betrayal of the ideals of Independence by both Cuba's politicians and the formal and effective US hegemony. This was especially provoked by the 1906–9 US intervention, which, highlighting the reality of 'Plattism' and confirming the largely nationalist Liberal Party in government and as part of the consolidated elite, made nationalism part of elite politics and led the new elite to begin constructing a nation-state consciously, through institutions and patronage. Some argued that the fault lay with Cubans themselves, even advocating, as in the past, some sort of quasi-annexationist accommodation with the United States, while others blamed US imperialism and developed increasingly radical interpretations of Cuba's history and present dilemma. The latter tendency came to a head in the radicalism of the 1920s, when Marxist perceptions and nationalist explanations from elsewhere in Latin America (especially from APRA in Peru) began to penetrate and shape such interpretations, culminating in the 1933 revolution. After 1934, the old questions returned, as the power of the nationalism and radicalism of 1923–33 now seemed to be manipulated, frustrated and dissipated. Once again, debates about why this had happened led some Cubans, perhaps concluding that the mission of a truly independent *Cuba Libre* of which they could be proud was an unrealisable chimera, to seek 'escape' either in art, in hedonism or in exile; on the other hand, however, others increasingly began to read Cuban history in different ways, not least stimulated in this by the coincidence of three anniversaries in 1952–3 – fifty years of a questionable independence, the centenary of the birth of Martí, and twenty years of frustration of the hopes of 1933. As these debates again catalysed nationalist sentiment, encouraged by a plethora of historical publications and by more radical perspectives among some of Cuba's younger generation, the 'reservoir' of radical nationalism, the old *cubanía*, now began to be a source of strength for oppositionist struggle, resurrecting the sense of the 1920s dissidence, which had effectively seen the emergence of a *cubanía rebelde*. As it was precisely from that well where Castro and the rebels took their political water, this meant that, by 1958, the old questions of national identity, *Cuba Libre*, the heritage of Martí and independence in all its forms had again begun to assume a new significance.

Part I: A Nation without a Capital and a Capital without a Nation (1902–33)

Havana's Political and Economic Evolution

Although the 1895–8 rebellion was based outside Havana, the US occupation and the installation of a neocolonial apparatus restored the city's political primacy, for, despite Cuba's dependence on agriculture, the post-1903 US-Cuban arrangement relied on Havana to channel wealth out and goods in (70 per cent by the 1920s: Segre et al. 1997: 62) and to be the base of the government and the US embassy. Therefore, although Havana got richer (with a steady growth of small-scale activity), American economic interests were pre-eminent and the Spanish community retained much financial and administrative control, a dependence that meant that the 1920–1 crisis had a greater impact on Havana than elsewhere.

Before 1920, the new neocolonial patterns made Havana the focal point of the new patronage networks, affecting public life and the bureaucracy and making opposition reformist or personalist rather than radical; indeed, the disappearance of radicalism in Havana indicated either a resigned pragmatism or a general disillusion. Only Havana's black population dissented radically, exemplified in the two newspapers, *La Estrella* and *Refulgente*, and especially in the shift from the 1908 Agrupación Independiente de Color to the PIC, which had thirty-two regional committees in Havana and up to 20,000 supporters (Helg 1995: 156). The post-1912 repression therefore especially affected Havana, with 320 arrests in the city and eighty in Guanabacoa, and two deaths after racist mob attacks in Regla and Havana (Helg 1995: 215). There followed a campaign to marginalise black culture: in 1913, *comparsas* were banned (until 1937) and a 1922 decree banned displays that might be seen as 'símbolos de barbarie y perturbadoras del orden social' ('symbols of barbarism and disturbing social peace': West Durán 2000: 129).

After 1920, Havana became the principal site of radical opposition, especially from the university's students and the emerging unions, the former's cohesion arising from a group identity within the new campus and reflecting a wider unease among the middle class, threatened by the crisis and angered by elite and American domination, a dissidence resulting in the largely Havana-based ABC. Union radicalism was less evident than in the sugar industry, although both the anarcho-syndicalists and the Communists had a strong base in the capital. Hence, when opposition to Machado grew, Havana saw increased dissent in both groups, erupting finally in the 1930–3 insurrection and the 1933 revolution, the latter a substantially Havana phenomenon as the base of both the DEU and the NCOs and the site of the main struggles and bloodshed, especially the military challenges.

Spatial and Social Evolution of the City

In 1899, Cuba was already one-third urban, with almost a quarter of a million in Havana (Poumier 1975: 10), economic expansion and rural immigration doubling that by the 1920s (Segre et al. 1997: 520; Torrents 1989: 115), and trebling it by 1930 (Lightfoot 2002: 40). In Habana Vieja, some 86,000 lived in narrow streets in *solares*, tenements around a central courtyard (Segre et al. 1997: 56), while

Figure 5 The Gran Teatro (built in 1915 as the Centro Gallego)

thousands more lived in low-lying areas susceptible to flooding near the polluted Bay, often in wooden houses until the 1926 hurricane (Segre et al. 1997: 62), or near the emerging industry, although Havana's tobacco factories were mostly located just by the old city.

By the 1920s, the city displayed haphazard architecture. From 1909, a new 'Republican' neoclassical monumentalism emerged (Torrents 1989: 105) spear-headed by government and American commerce (Segre et al. 1997: 57), and typi-fied by the university, the 1910 Lonja de Comercio, the 1912 Central Station, the 1919 Palacio Presidencial, and even the decorative 1915 Centro Gallego. By 1910, there were apartment blocks in Centro Habana (Segre et al. 1997: 56), while new hotels added more styles, notably the pseudo-Arabic Sevilla, while attempts were also made to 'tropicalise' the core, by colonnades and flamboyant designs (Segre et al. 1997: 65).

The new suburban spread after 1902 followed two axes: southward from Cuatro Caminos and westward towards Miramar, eastward expansion being only briefly considered, with a planned Bay bridge in 1904 (Llanes 1993: 96–7). These devel-opments, with their American-style grid pattern and wider streets, stimulated res-idential construction, Cerro attracting all classes, but Vedado's population suddenly expanded between 1899 and 1907 from 9,980 to 26,046 (Pavez Ojeda 2003: 65), becoming the bourgeoisie's leisure and residential area, its remaining lots being filled by 1930, often with luxuriously built residences (Segre et al. 1997: 55). Indeed, the scale and speed of the property boom defied government regula-tions, which, in Marianao and Miramar, gave way to land speculation (Segre et al. 1997: 56).

The two axes had different architectures, the southern axis reinforcing the Spanish tradition and the western reflecting an admiration for American styles, although also becoming eclectic with the vogue for Catalan *modernismo* in 1902–9 (Torrents 1989: 104), reflecting the influence of the new School of Architecture and the 1920s Beaux Arts movement (Segre et al. 1997: 46). Influenced by Law Omsted's 'garden city' ideas, plans emerged to decentralise government and 'green' the city until the 1920 crisis. Machado's only monumental construction was the US-influenced 1929 Capitolio Nacional.

It was tourism that most impelled construction thereafter. By 1927–8, 62,547 tourists visited Havana annually, especially on twelve weekly cruise ships and on ferries from Florida (Lightfoot 2002: 41), fleeing Prohibition and seeking drink, gambling and sex. This stimulated more hotel construction (especially the 1927 Presidente and the prestigious 1930 Nacional), and, with the peak season between December (the start of horse-racing) and March (the closure of the casinos), devel-oped Havana's main racecourse, Oriental Park (Villalba Garrido 1993: 47) and the 1,000–seat Marianao Gran Casino Nacional, in 1928 (Pérez 1999: 179). Much of Havana's new building was, anyway, recreational, with cinemas especially reflecting new styles, notably the 1912 Miramar, the 1915 Fausto and Vedado's 1920 Olimpic and Trianón (Llanes 1993: 140), as well as the Marianao funfairs of Coney Island Park and Playa de Miramar. Meanwhile, the combination of tourist hedonism and poverty also produced a boom in prostitution, with Havana's red light districts flourishing, especially around Virtudes (Torrents 1989: 105), the Barrio Chino and the docks, Havana's prostitutes numbering some 7,400 by 1931 and 11,500 by the late 1950s, in some 270 brothels (Pérez 1999: 193).

This boom, of course, neglected Havana's poor (especially the increasingly marginalised black population), crowded into deteriorating formerly bourgeois properties in Habana Vieja and into squatter settlements (worsened by the 1926 hurricane). Only one publicly funded working-class project, Lutgardita, was built in 1929 on Rancho Boyeros for 100 residences (Segre et al. 1997: 69). This overcrowding was worsened by immigration: of Cuba's 660,958 arrivals in 1902–30, almost 30 per cent went to Havana (Segre et al. 1997: 52). Since 1902 legislation limited black immigration (apart from sugar labour in the east), this immigration was mostly Spanish or eastern Mediterranean. By 1902–7, 128,000 Spanish

Figure 6 A synagogue in Vedado, one of the few remaining signs of a once significant Jewish (*polaco*) immigrant community

arrived (60,000 permanently) (Helg 1995: 99), as part of a drive to 'whiten' Cuba; these incomers accentuated the Spanish dominance in employment and commerce (47,297 were merchants or salesmen; Helg 1995: 101). Meantime, after the collapse of the Ottoman Empire, thousands of Jews (all known as *polacos*), Greeks and Arabs (all known as *turcos*) came, increasing Cuba's non-Spanish Europeans from under a thousand to 5,619 (in 1917); a Jewish community in particular formed, based around its 1906 synagogue and shops around Sol and Muralla.

This complex of migration patterns had two curious effects on Havana's black population; on the one hand, it marginalised them even more, driving them into the protection of their somewhat isolated communities and away from the emerging mainstream of prestige, but, on the other, the continuing evolution of *santería* (by now referring both to the majority Afro-Cuban religion and to all black religious practices in general) began to attract white adherents too, bringing it a new, if not always recognised, prestige at the grass roots.

Immigration, together with the new Republic's steady bureaucratisation, visibly strengthened the Havana middle class and elite. At the top, the new elite's self-confidence came from wealth and access to power, manifested in the social clubs, especially the Havana Yacht Club, the new Club Almendares (mostly for social gatherings), the foreigners' clubs such as the American Club (or Club de Extranjeros) on Prado, which included the President (Llanes 1993: 157), or sports clubs, notably the Cuban Jockey Club, at Buenavista, and the golf Country Club, developed by British and American residents. There was also a new skating rink on Virtudes and the most prestigious Vedado Tennis Club, which, from 1902 organised polo, tennis, baseball and yachting competitions, an amateur baseball team (the Marqueses), and the 1905 Asociación Atlética (with the University).

However, though self-confident, the new elite lacked a distinctive style. For, while residual loyalists and the Spanish adhered to Spanish norms of architecture, lifestyle and culture, Cubans gravitated naturally towards new American paradigms, leading one 1899 visitor to observe that 'Havana is losing its charm to an excess of Americanization' (Robinson 1970: 85), an Americanisation that extended to the currency, with the peso and the dollar freely exchangeable (Segre et al. 1997: 89). Nonetheless, this elite proceeded to shape its own social life: within Habana Vieja, around the old Campo de Marte, the theatres, the Parque Central hotels and the 1894 Manzana de Gómez shopping centre, and, elsewhere, in Vedado and Miramar.

Evolution of a Havana Culture

As the Republic established its institutions and the new elite consolidated, a subsidiary cultural establishment emerged, albeit slowly as culture was not a priority for the governing elite in 1902. However, the 1906–9 US intervention changed that. For the new formal nationalism which followed created an awareness that a genuinely independent republic might need a 'national' culture, especially if political independence was questionable. Therefore, given the nature of post-1902 politics, the way to establish the norms, boundaries and forms of such a culture was by establishing a recognised cultural elite, through a parallel process of institutionalisation and patronage.

Of course membership of this cultural elite was complicated by the fact that the new Republic's governing class was formed from the pre-1898 Cuban 'counterelite', the rebellion's surviving leaders, the Spanish who remained in the bureaucracy or commerce, and those rising to prominence under the Americans. 'Elite-ness' thus depended less on lineage (although this did count) than on wealth, war experience and power. Moreover, just as elite-formation meant that erstwhile dissidents were now the political establishment, obliged to forget habits of dissent, this also applied to the emerging cultural elite, which encompassed pre-1898 establishment figures and those who were less recognisable as defenders of a status quo, expected to champion progressive aesthetic ideas while defending the increasingly conservative state.

Two factors also now militated against its formation. One was that much cultural activity flourished outside Havana, although never on the scale of 1840s Matanzas; for example, Cuba's four best-known poets of the period (Agustín Acosta, Regino E. Boti, Juan Manuel Poveda and Emilio Ballagas) all lived in the provinces, as did the leading story-writer Luis Felipe Rodríguez (in Manzanillo) and the novelist Carlos Loveira (in Camagüey in 1908–13, then leaving Cuba till 1920 because of his labour activism). The other weakening factor was the curse of emigration. While before 1898, this had responded to the repressive Spanish colonialism, emigration now occurred for economic reasons (apart from during the *Machadato*), a motivation that allowed them periodically to revisit Havana and rejoin the elite, bringing news of external cultural developments, but militated against any inclusiveness, which really only returned in the late 1940s and 1950s. This emigration was not permanent but professional or the self-discovering wanderings of a moneyed elite. Besides Luis Rodríguez Embil, José María Chacón y Calvo, Manuel Márquez Sterling and Mariano Brull, the most outstanding example of the former was Alfonso Hernández Catá, who became a diplomat (including a spell in Birmingham in 1911), eventually settling in Madrid, joining the vibrant *tertulia* scene and publishing his stories. His influence in Cuba, partly enhanced by this external recognition, was attributable to his long-distance patronage, especially through the story prize associated with him. The *intimista* poet Dulce María Loynaz who, after publishing in 1920, travelled and published abroad, exemplified the latter emigration.

Membership of or access to Havana's social elite was a sine qua non for this cultural elite. For some this was easily formalised through employment, since many worked as diplomats while others held political posts, such as the popular novelist and Partido Popular candidate Miguel de Carrión (who served in education), Jesús Castellanos (Director of the Academia Nacional de Artes y Letras from 1910) and Fernando Ortiz, an active Liberal who represented Havana province in the Cuban Lower House (Cámara de Representantes) for ten years from 1917 to 1927, and also, in 1915–26, occupied key political posts.

Institutionalisation also of course depended on the gate-keeping and boundary-defining spaces for determining the forms and principles for the new community to imagine itself, both formally (by institutions, leaders and organs) and informally (by groupings and some measure of cohesion). Through the Secretaría de Educación's Departamento de Cultura, the most basic Republican institutions were its public libraries, which helped spread active literacy, the foundations already being laid by the Biblioteca Nacional, which, although national, really served Havana from its post-1909 site in the Antigua Maestranza de Artillería and through its *Revista de la Biblioteca Nacional*. However, the Biblioteca Municipal de La Habana was not established (on Neptuno) until 1920. A further critical institutional step was the 1913 Museo Nacional, fundamental to the creation of a national heritage (a *patrimonio nacional*), which, as observed by García Canclini, needs to establish its repertoire of fixed traditions in an 'escenario-depósito que lo contenga y proteja, un scenario-vitrina para exhibirlo' ('a showcase to house and protect it and to exhibit it': García Canclini 2001: 165). In 1910, the Secretaría de Instrucción Pública y Bellas Artes created the Academia Nacional de Artes y Letras, which sought to promote the arts through its different sections, publishing opportunities, education, grants, and its own patronage system of prizes and favoured artists. Its Havana base and orientation were demonstrated by the fact that sixty-five of the eighty-nine founding members were *habaneros* (García 1980: 20). Also important in indicating and establishing a cultural self-determination were the 1910 Academia de Historia and, much later in 1932, the Academia Cubana de la Lengua, under Varona, Mariano Aramburo and Chacón y Calvo successively. Institutionalisation also depended on private bodies, such as the 1902 Ateneo Círculo de la Habana, with its different sections, an exhibition space and its aim of spreading cultural awareness (Merino 2002: 28).

Essential to any effective system of patronage of course was still the patron, responsible for leading, determining norms, conferring recognition and defining the community's boundaries. The outstanding example of the patron-mentor was Varona, the 'grand old man' of Cuban letters, fundamental to educational modernisation and, from his university post, bestowing criticism and advice and, sharing his contemporaries' pessimism, arguing for an abiding public morality. Many such mentors were literary critics or anthologists, who enjoyed special prestige, one such being Félix Lizaso, who produced no creative work but who was fundamental to the Havana cultural community, especially with his editing of *Surco* and *Cervantes*. Another was Juan Marinello Vidaurreta, who, in Havana from 1916, joined the seminal radical intellectual moments and wrote for *Social* and *Revista de Avance*, until, after imprisonment in 1932, left for Mexico in 1933 (Le Riverend 1984: 550).

It was, however, the patron-entrepreneurs who abounded. The most significant was the Dominican Max Henríquez Ureña, who mobilised the emerging Havana community, writing criticism, producing anthologies, directing *La Discusión*, *El Fígaro* and *La Lucha*, supporting cultural ventures, promotions and groupings, and creating the necessary spaces. From 1918, he directed the Ateneo and, most influentially, launched the Sociedad de Conferencias in 1910 with José Castellanos, which, offering lectures to *habaneros*, echoed the Sociedad Económica's didactic mission and demonstrated the impact of both Positivism and *arielismo* (Cairo 1978: 27);[2] until he returned to Santiago in 1914 (Chacón y Calvo succeeding him), the thirty-five who lectured at the Sociedad constituted the core of the Havana community. Also significant was Renée Méndez Capote, who used her wealth and quasi-aristocratic status to direct *Artes y Letras* with her sister Sara and, in 1928, co-found the Havana Lyceum Club. An elite institution designed to promote a collective cultural awareness among Cuban women, it offered night classes in such skills as sewing, typing and carpentry, but also taught art, literature, music, song and dance, and ran cultural competitions, yet, influenced by contemporary intellectual movements, it was actually a dissident pole, fundamental in shaping the Havana community and progressive thinking among the female Havana elite (García 1980: 534).

The polymath Fernando Ortiz combined both patron roles. Rarely in Cuba for his first twenty-six years (although he studied at the university in 1895–99), he studied in Spain till 1902, worked as a diplomat till 1905, and finally studied criminology in Italy. From 1905 his interest in the emerging anthropology led him to study black Cuban 'types' in a series completed in 1934, by when he had developed a more nuanced appreciation of black culture. After 1907, he joined (and, after 1923, led) the Sociedad Económica, refounding its *Revista Bimestre Cubana* in 1910. While a parliamentary deputy, he joined the emerging protest with his short-lived 1923 Junta Cubana de Renovación Cívica, and, in 1924, co-founded the Sociedad del Folklore Cubano and *Archivos de Folklore*; in 1931, he again left for the United States until 1933.

Patronage relied also on cultural prizes, now vital to the Republic's cultural infrastructure and to the elite's gate-keeping role. Most newspapers and magazines ran prizes (especially *El Fígaro* from 1910), and all cultural institutions, especially the Ateneo, the Academia Nacional and the Liceo de la Habana. With parallel provincial prizes, a culture of prize-giving evolved, which bestowed brief publicity and the possibility of partial or complete publication; in a real sense, therefore, the prizes were a powerful form for ensuring that cultural production conformed to the elite's preferred norms.

Indeed, newspapers, magazines and journals also offered a cultural space which, given the continuing lack of publishing, was invaluable. As well as the state institutions' organs, private publications were still mostly small-circulation and short-lived (notably the youth-oriented 1912–14 *Alma Cubana*), but offered space and a focal point for groups, especially *Letras* (1905–14), under Néstor Carbonell and Carlos Garrida, Ortiz's *Revista Bimestre Cubana* (edited by the historians Portell Vilá and then Elías Entralgo). However, it was the emerging general-interest magazines which offered most, such as *Bohemia* and *Azul y Rojo* (1902–5), and Havana's growing daily newspapers included much cultural coverage, notably *El Mundo*, the 1885–1909 high-circulation weekly *El Fígaro* and the *Heraldo de Cuba*, both under Bernardo Barros's literary editorships.

Within this network of spaces, cultural groupings gathered, either based loosely around *tertulias* (as ever, the lifeblood of the Havana community) or organised around a journal or magazine (Smorkaloff 1987: 37). From 1902, the Marianao *casa de las poetas* of Juana and Dulce María Borrero attracted luminaries such as Varona, Federico Uhrbach, Manuel Sanguily and Juan Gualberto Gómez (Le Riverend 1984: 1013), and, a decade later, Castellanos and Henríquez Ureña organised their peripatetic *veladas* and the Sociedad de Conferencias, really a formalisation of the *tertulia* but based on the idea of public lectures. By 1931, as the *tertulia* was dying out, Ortiz organised his regular sessions at the Hotel Ambos Mundos, attracting radical intellectuals such as Emilio Roig de Leuchsenring, José Antonio Ramos, Fernández de Castro, Carlos Rafael Rodríguez and Angel Augier (Le Riverend 1984: 1013).

In part, the *tertulia* lost out to magazines. The most notable of these was *Cuba Contemporánea*, a monthly founded in 1913 for 'writers who saw themselves and were seen ... as the progressive opinion of the day' (Wright 1988: 110), including Henríquez Ureña, Hernández Catá, Rodríguez Embil, Barros, Ramos, Chacón y Calvo, Loveira, Roig, Carlos de Velasco (editor 1913–20), Mario Guiral Moreno (editor 1920–6), Dulce María Borrero, Fransisco González del Valle, Enrique Gay-Calbó and Ernesto Dihigo (Wright 1988: 120). The magazine was explicitly preoccupied with 'la problemática de Cuba', taking up the banner of a Cuban national identity and aiming to spearhead a nationwide movement through satellite provincial magazines, disseminating as a 'revista de alta cultura' ('high-culture magazinc': Wright 1988: 113) and rejecting popular culture and politics. However, unlike later radicals, they made no connections between Cuba's cultural problems and the wider context, seeking to 'nationalise' culture in a vacuum (Wright 1988: 111); indeed, many, inspired by their elitist Positivism, saw Cuba's American connections as bringing stability. Hence, while Ramos's 1916 play, *Tembladera*, criticised American land purchases, he saw cultural improvement through contact with Anglo-Saxon culture (Wright 1988: 112).

Hence, the group really belonged to its time, as a 'tribuna de una intelectualidad comprometida con la reorientación *nacionalista* de un proyecto de nación' ('platform for intellectuals committed to a nationalist reorientation of a national project': Ubieta Gómez 1993: 56); after 1920, its increasing social awareness, driven by Roig, Chacón y Calvo and Gay-Calbó (Wright 1988: 117), led finally in 1927, after the more conservative-minded had tried to return to the original focus, to its closure. However, the group was seminal in generating debates on the failings of Cuban culture and on modern thinking, setting in motion future processes, and its 1917 publishing arm, Siglo XX Sociedad Editorial de Cuba Contemporánea, published novels on Cuban themes by writers like Loveira and Carrión, and works on and by the Independence leaders (Wright 1988: 110).

Those debates were especially driven by the notion of *decadencia*. A largely moralistic and pessimistic concern with corruption, influenced by psychology and Positivism, this notion explained Cuban problems either by habits inherited from colonialism, by racial stereotypes or by the new 'annexationism'. One clear manifestation of this concern with 'character' was the popular figure of Liborio, developed in fiction and cartoons: a thin, short, moustachioed white peasant (*guajiro*), Liborio represented a collective self-image of unsophisticated and self-deprecating common sense, a cunning ability to survive, and it was never clear when seeing Liborio as the embodiment of their character whether Cubans did so with stubborn pride or embarrassment. Liborio was clearly white, leading Julián Sierra to counterpose 'José Rosario', a black representative of common sense and nationalism (Helg 1995: 151).

Decadencia was boosted by Jorge Mañach's 1925 essay, 'La crisis de la alta cultura en Cuba' but especially, in February 1924, by the Ortiz lecture 'La Decadencia Cubana' at the Sociedad Económica, which declared 'Cuba se está precipitando rápidamente en la barbarie' ('Cuba is rushing headlong towards barbarism': Ortiz 1924: 9). Lambasting the parlous state of Cuba's education system, its corruption and a rampant criminality (making it, shamefully, the 'Montecarlo de América'), he identified causes deep in the colonial history of 'contrabandistas' (Ortiz 1924: 29) and in the dangerous fusion of 'unabsorbable' elements, but also blamed the Americans for giving power to non-patriotic elements. Generally, he mixed a view of an immoral colonialism, a cautious critique of neocolonialism and frankly racist notions of blood, and saw the solution in uncorrupted youth and women (Ortiz 1924: 31), explanations which struck a chord with many who shared his shame and despair.

Linked to *decadencia* was a parallel belief in 'pan-Hispanism' which, rejecting a slavish adherence to the United States, advocated a cultural return to Spain. Because it arose initially from a residual conservative loyalism, some nationalists rejected it as 'La reconquista de América' ('the reconquest of America', the title of an Ortiz 1910 essay); however, after the watershed of 1920, attitudes changed, conservatism fusing with a growing critique of imperialism to rediscover Cuba's Iberian cultural heritage. Indeed, unlike contemporary Argentine debates about the 'threat to national cultural unity' posed by immigration (Sarló 2000: 115), such concerns were largely not echoed in Havana, despite increased immigration. This was because, after 1909, the threat to Cuban identity was increasingly perceived as coming from the north, while the close Havana links between the new elites and Spain meant a more benevolent attitude to the latter.

Therefore, Ortiz, admiring the Madrid Instituto Libre de Enseñanza (Puig and Naranjo Orovio 2001: 199), argued that political rejection of Spain should not mean cultural rejection and that a new Cuban culture should appreciate and include Spanish elements, recognising common cultural roots and solving Cuba's ills by the 'rescate del Quijote' ('rescue of the Quijote': Quiza Moreno 2000: 47). Indeed, the Sociedad del Folklore Cubano aimed initially to examine Spanish, rather than African, traditions (Zaldívar 2002: 16). Ortiz therefore persuaded the Sociedad Económica to establish an Institución Hispano-Cubana de Cultura in Havana in 1926,[3] based in the Asociación de Dependientes (with activities also in the Teatro Principal and the University's Aula Magna), to improve Cuban-Spanish intellectual relations through a programme of lectures, through research and especially through exchanges, bringing to Havana a string of prominent Spanish intellectuals (including Fernando de los Ríos, Luis Arequistain, Américo Castro, Mario de Maeztu and Gregorio Marañón) and funding students (*becarios*) to study medicine and economics in Spain (Puig and Naranjo Orovio 2001: 203). The initial membership reflected the breadth of the contemporary Havana elite, including prominent Spaniards (such as the owner of the El Encanto store and the editor of *Diario de la Marina*), as well as the radical historians and writers Ramiro Guerra y Sánchez, Marinello, Loveira, Portell Vilá, Mañach and Lydia Cabrera, the expert on black culture (Puig and Naranjo Orovio 2001: 202–3).

One might therefore observe that the lack of cultural self-confidence evident in Havana intellectual debates about Cuba's cultural identity affected subsequent historiography of those years, a period often relegated to a lesser importance. Yet those years were by no means insignificant and certainly no cultural wilderness, for, while the new elite successfully incorporated the leading protagonists of Havana culture into a hegemonic cultural community, to direct the Republic's cultural development, they also produced many who challenged cultural orthodoxy. Indeed, in the 1920s, as the Cuban state's economic stability crumbled and dissidence emerged, the hegemony of the new cultural establishment was undermined by a number of alternative 'poles', one example of which was a new focus on Cuban history, encouraged by the Academia and exemplified by Guerra's 1921 and 1925 volumes of *Historia de Cuba*.

In fact, a counter-elite was emerging, a *vanguardista* dissidence from within the elite rather than an outright rebellion, since its exponents mostly still believed that Havana's intellectuals had a role in defining a Cuban culture, their dissidence lying in their focus on resisting imperialism and on defining the national rather than

'Cubanising' imported models. This dissidence also reflected its elite character by adopting the old mechanisms to bestow authority and patronage and create spaces, although, after 1928, many were forced into more radical postures or caught up in the repression; thus the police ended a Hernández Catá lecture and, in February 1931, arrested eighty-nine Havana university lecturers (Aragón 2002: 12), leading Mañach, Ortiz, Le Riverend and Alejo Carpentier into exile.

The new patrons were now mostly patron-entrepreneurs, especially Ortiz (who moved from his Positivist-influenced anthropology to a reassessment of Cuba's African roots) and Carpentier. Using his elite credentials (he was educated in the United States and France, speaking French fluently) to bring contemporary art, literature, music and architecture to Havana's younger generation, Carpentier flirted with *negrismo* (his novel, *Ecué-Yamba-O* was written in a Havana prison after being arrested for communist links), edited *Hispania* and *Carteles*, participated in cultural events and groupings, and then, after visiting Mexico in 1926 (and befriending Diego Rivera), co-founded *Revista de Avance* and co-organised concerts of avant-garde European music, writing scripts for Amadeo Roldán's ballets. The more genuinely radical patrons included José Zacarías Tallet, who, moving from Matanzas to Havana, became integral to the 1923–4 ferment, writing *vanguardista* and committed poetry and editing *Revista de Avance* and *El Mundo*. However, the radicals' main leader was Rubén Martínez Villena, the *vanguardista* poet who organised the Protesta and Grupo Minorista (see below), edited *Azul*, founded the Universidad Popular, the Liga Anticlerical and the Liga Antimperialista, was a leading activist in the Movimiento de Veteranos and, after 1928, led the Communist Party.

Other nodes of patronage now developed, although few formal counter-institutions, except the Academia Universitaria de Literatura, which, founded in 1925 by graduates of Havana's Schools of Letras and Pedagogía, aimed to encourage the study of world and Cuban literature, the latter through annual prizes (García 1980: 20). Meantime, in the visual and plastic arts, awareness of new developments was furthered through José Manuel de Poveda's Grupo Nacional de Acción de Arte and, from 1923, the Club Cubano de Bellas Artes, under Sergio Cuevas Zequeira and Marinello.

Understandably, *vanguardia* spaces were found in less formal places, specifically in emerging groupings. Of these, one really mattered: the Grupo Minorista. This group was rooted in different related manifestations of dissent, especially the the Grupo *Clarté* and one specific regular but peripatetic *tertulia* (initially led by Martínez Villena, Andrés Núñez Olano and Enrique Serpa), successively in the Café Martí (1920–2), the *Fígaro* offices, Martínez Villena's house on Amargura, Emilio Roig's office, and then, after the Protesta, the Hotel Lafayette, but occasionally the Hotel México or the Lirio del Prado restaurant (Núñez Machín 1974: 74).[4] Initially an accidental grouping of like-minded young intellectuals, characterised by their unpublished status and spirit of challenge, the *tertuliantes* reflected both contemporary *vanguardismo* and subsequent radicalisation, and were progressively joined by other radicals.[5]

This movement of dissent was political from the start, linked to the various radical manifestations of 1923–4, notably the Protesta, the Veteranos (to which Mella, Marinello, Tallet and Martínez Villena belonged briefly), and the Universidad Popular, which, modelled on the APRA institution in Peru and aiming to educate and radicalise Havana's workers, was inaugurated in the university's Aula Magna in November 1923, then becoming peripatetic, but especially based in the Centro Obrero on Zulueta (Núñez Machín 1974: 169). The most seminal moment came on 18 May 1923 with the Protesta de los Trece (Protest by the Thirteen), the collective walk-out from an Academia de Ciencias event whose platform included a minister implicated in the corrupt sale of the Santa Clara convent, the thirteen who staged the protest then explaining their motives and broader targets.[6]

The group was characterised by its impulse for radicalism and desire to reject formal structures, even refusing to follow norms by establishing a lecture programme or publishing outlet, although they were increasingly associated with *Social* (García 1980: 393). This distinction led to their epithet *minorista*, since, although they claimed to be the 'mouthpiece, platform and index of the majority' (Wright 1988: 122), they constituted a self-conscious *vanguardia*. Their publications included denunciations of American imperialism, corruption and the police occupation of the university, and the eight demands of Martínez Villena's 1927 Declaración de Principios included educational reform, Cuban economic independence, opposition to dictatorship, popular political participation, improved social conditions and Latin American unity. When the Grupo began, neither the Communist Party nor APRA existed and, in that vacuum, their political position was somewhere between 'proto-communist' and indeterminately radical, meaning an intellectual rejection of Positivism, a cultural embrace of the European avant-garde, and the popularisation of all art, seeing itself as the 'crisol del vanguardismo en Cuba' ('crucible of the Cuban *avantgarde*': Martínez Carmenate 2002: 61). By 1925, the gatherings attracted bigger names such as Ortiz, Hernández Catá and Miguel Mariano Gómez, and included painters (Arturo Gattorno, Jaime Valls, Eduardo Abela and Juan Sicre), the musician Diego Bonilla, the architect José Bens Amarte, Carpentier (Cairo 1978: 58), and other avant-garde activists, such as Mariblanca Sabas Alomá, Conrado Massaguer, Juan Antiga, Mariano Brull, Henríquez Ureña, Armando Maribona and Graciela Garbalosa (García 1980: 395).

Given the divisions and radicalisation of the time and the Grupo's eclectic nature, their loose cohesion could not last, especially with the *Machadato*'s repression and after Lamar Schweyer supported Machado and rejected the concept of *minorismo*.

Therefore, in 1928, the Grupo disbanded, fragmenting in three directions. The political radicals (Marinello, Martínez Villena, Tallet) gravitated towards the Communist Party, espousing revolution and maintaining *vanguardismo* through *Atuei* magazine. The more conservative moved to the right; Mañach joined the corporatist ABC (directing their *Acción*: Le Riverend 1984: 545),[7] although he continued *vanguardismo* in his prize-winning play *Tiempo Muerto* (1928) and his radio cultural programme, 'Universidad del Aire' (1932), and Ichaso entered parliamentary politics and edited *Diario de la Marina* (García 1980: 451), while Fernández de Castro edited the *Diario*'s cultural pages. Those still committed to a strictly cultural *vanguardismo* sought to perpetuate the Grupo's principles in new magazines such as *El Estudiante* and the hitherto radical *Alma Mater*, but they tended at that stage to lack of focal point, a patron or a clear-cut space.

Indeed, the Grupo's rejection of the traditional association between groupings and magazines broke down, and, the post-1927 years saw a return to that earlier pattern of ephemeral and limited magazines, notably *Ariel*, Martínez Villena's *Azul*, the poetry magazine *Castalia* (1920–1), the *vanguardista Hélice* (two editions only in 1932), *Surco* (1930–1) and *Alma Cubana* (García 1980: 37). Only *Cervantes* (1925–46) survived, revealingly as a forum for Spanish literature. Besides these, general-circulation magazines now paid more attention to culture, such as the new weekly, *América*, and the popular weeklies *Bohemia* and *Carteles*, now publishing short stories rather than, as before, poetry.

Two magazines above all now proved fundamental to cultural developments, *Revista de Avance* and *Social*. *Revista de Avance* (1927–30) especially reshaped Havana's *vanguardia*. Edited successively by Carpentier, Tallet, Ichaso and Martín Casanovas (and, after 1928, Ichaso, Lizaso, Mañach and Marinello), it was a fortnightly, avowedly *vanguardista*, magazine, with sections for different genres and for criticism, and sections on non-Hispanic letters, Spain and Latin America. Partly informative (with news of cultural events), it was campaigning in purpose, bringing into Cuba the latest avant-garde culture, especially from Spain (indicating its roots in the Institución Hispanocubana) and the new *Generación del 27*, Rubiera describing it as 'antología periódica de literatura española' (Zaldívar 2002: 16). Hence, in debates on cultural identity, it leaned towards 'Hispanism', seeing itself as belonging to and legitimised by a Hispanic cultural community. However, it also published Marinello, Boti, Mañach, Chacón y Calvo, Luis Cardoza y Aragón, and Eugenio Florit, as well as Carlos Montenegro's stories, Raúl Maestri's study of Cuban *latifundismo*, and a Lizaso and Suárez Solís poetry anthology (Smorkaloff 1987: 51), and clearly played a decisive role in the struggle between 'el academicismo y el vanguardismo' (Barquet 1992: 16), not least encouraging Havana intellectuals to look at Cuba differently.

Social had been founded in 1916, by Conrado Massaguer, as a general-interest monthly, modelled on *Vogue* and *Vanity Fair* (Merino Acosta 2001: 78). In 1918,

Emilio Roig edited its cultural-historical section, welcoming the emerging Grupo Minorista and other Havana *vanguardista* manifestations (Wright 1988: 122), until it closed in 1933, reappearing in 1935–8. Indeed, *Social* was the Grupo's principal vehicle (Cairo 1978: 126), although it shared *Revista*'s fascination with contemporary Spain, publishing Lorca, Alberti and Alejandro Rodríguez Alvarez (Martínez Carmenate 2002: 20).

This universal interest in Spain created a fertile soil for cultural links with the former metropolis. Thus, when Lorca visited Cuba in March–June 1930, he was received with adulation and general acclaim, feted by *vanguardistas*, nationalists and Spanish alike, welcomed, on his disembarkation, by a large crowd including leading progressives and the director of the Institución Hispanocubana, Santiago Guardiola (Martínez Carmenate 2002: 20). Lorca responded appropriately, with a suitably broad programme, which included five lectures at the Teatro Principal, a Sociedad Pro-Arte Musical Prokofiev concert, a Loynaz *tertulia*, the University (Martínez Carmenate 2002: 41–50), and even the haunts of the elite, such as the Havana Yacht Club. Yet, on reflection, the visit seems to have affected Lorca much more than it affected Havana, leaving few immediate traces (apart from legitimising the *negrista* search for the Cuban *duende* ('spirit' or 'soul') and inspiring Guillén); being part of Lorca's search for the *duende* of Afro-Cuban or Afro-American culture, it seems to have been, for *habaneros*, an opportunity more to display culture than learn, to bathe in the reflected glory of implicit recognition by a visiting cultural celebrity. It was, indeed, Lorca's death in 1936 that engendered a greater response in Havana (Martínez Carmenate 2002: 195–214). As with *Revista*, therefore, the Lorca visit seemed to indicate that, for some of the cultural establishment and even the *vanguardia*, the cultural community to which they all aspired was 'Hispanic' rather than 'Cuban'. In one sense, this attitude was surprising, since the visit coincided with a new artistic interest in social questions that shared an affinity with Lorca, namely the Cuban peasant (with a less *costumbrista* approach) and, above all, black culture, yet it was also unsurprising, given the collective lack of cultural self-confidence and the weight of cultural colonialism. It was also of course, logical in a context where the 1912 black 'rebellion' frightened white Cubans sufficiently to want to gravitate towards a definition of *cubanidad* which was white (and thus Hispanic) rather than racially mixed.

Within this changing environment, cultural production also changed, the more 'minority' genres reflecting the radicalising divide of 1920. Initially, after 1902, poetry, (though enhanced by the prestige of the now dead Casal and Martí, and also by the press's tendency to use its limited cultural space for poems) stagnated in its development, with few innovators to point new directions and with *modernismo* surviving well into the century (Sainz 2000: 113). This tendency was increased by the fact that poetry continued to enjoy the greatest prestige, among both the cultural and the social elite (although this did, of course, also mean that most Cuban poets only managed to publish their work in books some years after they had become known). The 1904 collection *Arpas Cubanas* reflected the new Republican poetry, publishing the work of twenty-nine established, lesser-known and new poets, mostly from Havana.

In 1926, with *modernismo* in decline, a seminal moment was the 1926 Lizaso and Fernández de Castro anthology (revealingly, published in Madrid), *La Poesía Moderna en Cuba, 1882–1925*, bringing attention and prestige to a Cuban poetry seen as part of a Spanish-language avant-garde, signalled by poets such as Tallet and Félix Pita Rodríguez, the latter leaving Cuba for Europe and Morocco in 1929. The work of Brull and the Spaniard Florit was now noticed, both part of the Havana community (despite Brull's absences from 1917 as a diplomat) and both advocates of Juan Ramón Jiménez and Lorca. Generally, however, 'versifying' traditions continued, not least with Gustavo Sánchez Galarraga's thirty collections of anachronistically Romantic verse (Henríquez Ureña 1967b: 361), and even the better poets published only individual poems, the Grupo and *Revista avantgarde* not penetrating deep into the community. Instead, until *negrismo*, Havana poetry was characterised by either residual French symbolism (Rubiera, Serpa and Esténger) or an 'ironía sentimental' (Henríquez Ureña 1967b: 368), as in Tallet, Federico de Ibarzábal and, most successfully, Martínez Villena.

That changed after 1928, with the genuinely new formal and conceptual note of *negrismo*. The roots of the movement came in 1923, with Montori's *El tormento de vivir* (on a black theme), followed by Manuel Villaverde's 1924 novel *La rumba*; even the highly conservative *Diario de la Marina* published a regular column 'Ideales de una raza' (in which Marinello and Mañach were prominent) and (in April 1928) Ramón Gurirao's poem 'Bailadora de la rumba', while Tallet's 'La Rumba' appeared in August in *Atuei*. However, initially this interest arose more from a vanguard search for aesthetic 'popularisation', being largely limited to white writers stylistically adopting supposedly black themes and language, with the later doyen of *negrismo*, Nicolás Guillén, largely unnoticed, marginalised by being *mulato*. Hence, these writers were almost 'exoticising' Cuba through European eyes, finding a 'primitive' subject in their own backyard, without absorbing the truths of Cuba's racism, social structures or black culture. Only later did the Havana community, led by black or *mulato* writers, incorporate the Afro-Cuban into their conception of a Cuban culture; in the 1920s, they were largely following traditions of seeking legitimacy through external paradigms, although the moment was significant in fusing the traditional outwardly oriented search for novelty with the inwardly focused search for identity.

Narrative genres now grew in popularity, with increased readership, magazine serialisations and stories, and with novelists influenced by naturalism, albeit that Havana novelists tended to be rural in focus, such as Castellanos (whose story, 'Ciénaga', won the Ateneo's 1908 Juegos Florales); one exception was Loveira, whose acerbic urban political novel *Generales y Doctores* (1920) was enormously popular. Only Serpa (winner of the 1925 *Diario de la Marina* poetry prize and the 1928 Premio Nacional de la Novela) and Ofelia Rodríguez Acosta (Havana's leading feminist) showed any impact of *vanguardismo*.

The visual and plastic arts showed the same pattern of derivative styles until the 1920s and the cautious movement into *vanguardismo*. The former was evident in the Republic's institutions and spaces: the 1916 Asociación de Pintores y Escultores, the Ateneo's 1907 and 1908 French art exhibitions, and the magazines *Salones* and *Revista de Bellas Artes* all espoused symbolism, pre-Raphaelism and impressionism (Merino 2002: 29–30). *Vanguardismo* then became evident in the Cuban art of Alfred Barry Jr's Galería el Prado (Merino Acosta 2001: 80) or in the 1927 *Revista de Avance* Exposición de Arte Nuevo, the magazine also offering opportunities for illustration to Víctor Manuel García, Eduardo Abela, Carlos Enríquez, Antonio Gattorno and Marcelo Pogolotti, with their 'búsquedas formales y conceptuales, nuevos temas, nuevos lenguajes' ('formal and conceptual searches, new subjects and new languages': Merino 1989b: 397), while other magazine illustrations copied *art nouveau* (Merino 1989b: 394).

However, although many of these still saw Cuba through European eyes, albeit in more avant-garde ways, the visual arts most successfully incorporated popular culture into their emerging definition of 'una afirmación nacional' (Merino 1989b: 398), often introducing Cuba to Paris as much as Paris to Cuba. Indeed, the visual arts, more than other forms, depended on continuing contact with developments in these established cultural centres, since art reproductions were less readily available in Havana than copies of the latest European poetry or novel. However, that same need to travel to the source seems to have led Havana artists to see Cuba more with Cuban eyes in Paris than their literary counterparts did in Havana. Indeed, there is a case to be made that, during the Republic, the vibrancy, self-confidence and novelty of painting influenced Havana writing.

In this enclosed community, classical music seemed, initially, to be boosted by Independence: Guillermo Tomás continued his Banda Municipal concerts from 1900 with a wide European repertoire, in 1908 organising the Orquesta Sinfónica, which irregularly performed concerts of modern music (Carpentier 1988: 245). In 1922, Havana's first regular symphony orchestra, the Orquesta Sinfónica de La Habana, specialising in Cuban music, was founded by Gonzalo Roig, Alejandro García Caturla and the *bufo* composer Ernesto Lecuona. In 1923, the Spaniard Pedro Sanjuán Nortes founded the more *vanguardista* Orquesta Filarmónica, and in 1922, a series of Conciertos de Música Típica Cubana began in Havana, under Sánchez de Fuente (then president of the Academia Nacional) and then Lecuona, who always sought to incorporate Cuban elements. In 1919, the Sociedad Pro-Arte Músical (often also called the Sociedad Pro-Arte Música) was founded, subsequently publishing *Pro-Arte* magazine; in 1928, it built the Teatro Auditorium

Figure 7 The Teatro Roldán (formerly the Teatro Auditorium), in Vedado, now the principal concert venue for classical music

(now the Teatro Roldán) in Vedado, also housing a ballet school, a Sociedad Guitarrística de Cuba and an Escuela Cubana de Guitarra (Linares 2001: 134).

As with other forms, Havana music was initially Europeanised; however, from the 1920s, composers strove consciously to create a genuinely Cuban music, and, by incorporating African elements, continuing the theme of the closing colonial decades. For example, Sánchez de Fuente, composer of *Yumurí*, continued to recreate an imagined indigenous past, with 'Indianist' operas such as *Doreyra* (1918) and the cantata *Anacona*, performed in Barcelona in 1929 (Carpentier 1988: 257–8). Yet this echo of *siboneyismo* was paralleled in music by an awareness of Cuba's African roots, José Mauri Estévez writing an opera *La Esclava*, performed in 1921 and incorporating African themes in choral and symphonic language, affecting Lecuona, Roig, García Caturla, Roldán, Eliseo Grenet and Moisés Simons (González 1989: 426).

Meanwhile, Havana's musical community had moved into the avant-garde earlier than its counterparts; in 1919, María Múñoz de Quevedo and Roldán created the Sociedad de Música Contemporánea, the former also founding the

Sociedad Coral de La Habana and the influential *Musicalia*, which, in 1928–32, became a forum for Havana's musical *vanguardia*. Roldán certainly did most to innovate; having studied in Spain and worked as a Havana cabaret and restaurant musician, in 1923 he began to compose and joined the modernist Orquesta Filarmónica, which, in 1925, performed his *Obertura sobre temas cubanos*, considered Cuba's most important twentieth-century musical event (Carpentier 1988: 280–1). He continued prolifically, composing especially the ballets *La Rebambaracha* (1928) and the jazz-influenced *El Milagro de Anaquillé* (1929), with lyrics by Carpentier. In 1930, he incorporated Afro-Cuban drums in his work, notably in *Tres Toques* (1931), with the drums as musical protagonist (Carpentier 1988: 282–6). By then, he had institutionalised the avant-garde, especially through his chair of composition at the Conservatorio Municipal de Música de La Habana (Linares 2001: 134). He was supported by García Caturla, who, after studying ballet in Paris under Boulanger, returned to synthesise Cuba's musical traditions, composing prolifically, especially with Afro-Cuban themes and rhythms; his *Danza del Tambor* (sung by the new Conjunto Folklórico de Remedios) used folk interpreters and set a pattern of fusing 'high' and 'popular' musical forms (González 1989: 427).

Beyond these somewhat minority interests, theatre in Republican Havana continued straddling an increasingly blurred line between art and entertainment. For two decades, Havana remained on the American circuit for European companies (Matas 1971: 429), with an even clearer shift towards the light musical rather than the serious dramatic. The 1920s saw new Cuban companies forming, such as Arquímedes Pons's 1923–5 Teatro Cubano (later Molino Rojo) and Teófilo Hernández and José Orozco's 1926 company at Teatro Actualidades.

The Alhambra was, however, still the mainstay of the popular Havana theatre and of the *bufo*, especially after Jorge Anckermann (composer and orchestral director) took over with Villoch as principal librettist. The plays staged there conformed to a pattern, being largely satirical and topical (when *comparsas* were banned, many of their political songs were incorporated into the Alhambra's repertoire), and tending towards the sexually suggestive, making it a 'teatro para hombres solos' ('theatre for single men': Henríquez Ureña 1967b: 344). Besides the Alhambra, *bufo* continued until the 1920s in the Regino, the Molino Rojo, the Cuba, the 1909–10 Polyteama (really two separate theatres on the roof of the six-storey Manzana de Gómez), the constantly mutating theatre on Animas (successively the Armenonnue, Olimpia, Chantecler and finally Teatro Heredia: Rivero 1981: 38), the old Albisú (reopened in 1905 as the Campoamor, until demolished in 1914 for the Centro Asturiano), and even the more prestigious and serious Nacional, Payret and Yrijoa theatres (Le Riverend 1984: 1004). Throughout, *bufo* gave ample opportunity to theatrically skilful playwrights like Villoch and Gustavo Robreño (Henríquez Ureña 1967b: 345) and offered a valuable tool to 'Cubanist' playwrights which written literature lacked. For its capacity for improvisation, with each performance being unique and allowing audience response, gave it an unusual organicity, making it often more in tune with popular sentiments and nationalist impulses, and, in the process, making the Havana middle class a very much more significant ideological battleground than one might have expected.

Meantime, Lecuona, director of the Spanish company at the Martí from 1919, sought to return to Spanish-style *zarzuela*. In 1927, the Molino Rojo was rebuilt as the Teatro Regina, under Lecuona, where the future doyenne of the Havana musical stage, Rita Montaner, appeared (Río Prado 2002: 45), and, in 1931, Lecuona set up again at the Martí, engaging, with Gonzalo Roig, in an indigenous 'cynical' theatre (Matas 1971: 444).

Inevitably, countervailing pressure was exercised to shift Havana theatre in more aesthetically demanding and culturally progressive directions, absorbing European dramatic ideas: in 1910, Henríquez Ureña, Ramos, Barros and Castellanos founded the Sociedad de Fomento del Teatro, under Luis Alejandro Baralt, whose bold first season at the Nacional, in May, with plays by Martí and Gómez de Avellaneda, closed after poor attendances (Henríquez Ureña 1967b: 346). Ramos in particular led this campaign with an Ibsenian theatre of ideas and with openly political theatre, especially with his 1914 *Calibán Rex*, published in *Cuba Contemporánea* (Le Riverend 1984: 844), his *Tembladera* winning the 1917 Academia Nacional prize. Others with him included Hilarión Cabrisas, whose opera *Doreyra* (performed at the Nacional in 1918) won the Concurso Bracale, and Salvador Salazar, who sponsored various activities and groups. However, demands for 'serious' theatre were usually met by visiting companies or by Cuban performances of traditional Spanish plays, although, in 1915, the Sociedad Teatro Pro-Cubano was created (with its 1919–20 magazine *Teatro*) to persuade visiting companies to stage Cuban plays (Matas 1971: 429). This was because resistance to the *bufo* largely came from small groups of enthusiasts whose emphasis on non-Cuban drama meant the 'serious' commercial theatre's reliance on the conventional, with the avant-garde arriving via Salazar's University theatre group, the Institución Cubana Pro-Arte Dramático (also supporting a seminal journal, *Alma Cubana*), which staged Synge, Evreinoff, Sacha Guitry and Valle Inclán (Matas 1971: 429), echoing the Sociedad Pro-Arte Músical's efforts in music.

By the 1930s, therefore, both the elite and *vanguardista* Havana cultural communities were at a crossroads. The old canon was staid, stagnant or light, either stressing entertainment over art or mimicking established foreign forms. Hence, the establishment's desire to identify with a community centred in Paris or Madrid made for an unsatisfactory definition of the new Republic's cultural identity. Yet the *vanguardia*'s challenge from 1923 had not delivered much, divided between the political or socially committed and a new search for external legitimacy and models. Indeed, the new *vanguardia* had rejected their predecessors' identification with an external cultural community only to do the same, albeit with one based in Paris or Madrid.

Meantime, both traditional and new cultural forms were acquiring authority within emerging popular communities, seeking to develop culturally and educationally. In 1917, for example, Club Atenas began, a recreational and social club for blacks and *mulatos*, which, under Pantaleón Julián Valdés, sought to raise cultural and educational levels, publishing *Atenas* (García 1980: 217). Also, social boundaries were, to some extent, breaking down culturally, and, as traditional folk culture declined with urbanisation, the middle class adopted some popular dances, usually black in origin.

It was, in fact, in music and dance where this fusion and greater awareness were most notable, popular music being linked increasingly to dance and song. This was especially seen in the *décima*, which followed a strict musical pattern, with words rather than sounds as the personal element (Carpentier 1988: 274–5); the first two decades saw an enormous popularity in Havana of its exponents, the *trovadores*, notably Sindo (Gumersindo) Garay, Alberto Villalón, Manuel Corona and Rosendo Ruiz (West Durán 2000: 127), mostly playing in restaurants or at cinemas (Roy 2002: 106). Radio especially revived its popularity.

Mostly this period saw dance emerge as a new urban expression and as a possible form of cultural nationalism, as what was later observed (in the 1990s) was already beginning to be true: 'la única manifestación donde este pueblo participa con un espíritu creador es la música popular cubana bailable' ('the only manifestation in which the people take part creatively is popular Cuban dance music': Fornet 2002: 166). Although lacking prestige outside its own community, popular dance in Havana was beginning to show the creativity that distinguished it from folklore traditions and elite cultural production.

An outstanding example was the processional *comparsa*. From 1902, this had become part of both white carnivals (sponsored by breweries) and Havana election campaigns, making a black dance form (still with African-influenced names, La Culebra or El Alacrán) into a site where black and white working classes merged. Indeed, although their boisterous nature officially brought their 1913 prohibition, it was this embryonic fusion that most alarmed the elites.

Yet the tide could not be so easily turned. As we have seen, by 1898 the *danzón* was becoming dominant in public balls; now, after 1902, it was enshrined as the national dance, popular at all levels (Poumier 1975: 172; Acosta 2001: 38). By the 1920s, however, the *son* had replaced it, driven by the garrisoning policies of the new Ejército Permanente (Permanent Army) of 1909, which brought *orientales* to Havana, where it was standardised and popularised (Roy 2002: 127). Long established, its rhythmic quality, enhanced protagonism of drums and opportunities for individualism gave it a special prestige outside black communities. By 1916 Havana had its first professional *son* group, the Cuarteto Oriental, then spawning the Sexteto Habanero with its distinctive *habanero* form: an introduction by the (guitar-like) *tres*, multivoiced songs and long instrumental passages (Roy 2002: 129). In 1918 RCA Victor recorded it in the Hotel Inglaterra, opening a Havana studio in 1920, after which it developed, adding the double-bass (1920s) and trumpet (1927). In 1925, the *son* was legitimised when the Sonora Matancera played at Machado's birthday party, Machado approving it for clubs, cabarets and restaurants (West Durán 2000: 129), and, in 1929, international recognition (the first for a Cuban musical form) came when the Sexteto Nacional won a Seville prize (Linares 2001: 133), after which Beny Moré and Trío Matamoros were successfully marketed in Latin America (Chanan 1985: 48).

However, the *rumba* which it had spawned now challenged it successfully (although the *rumba* later known in Europe and North America was actually the *son*), its novelty coming from being a new urban form rather than an urbanisation of a traditional dance, created in Matanzas and Havana's black communities and associated with the *solar*'s central courtyard. Relying more on atmosphere rather than specific forms, rhythms or words, and also allowing for variation and improvisation, with a wide range, from the faster Havana male performance *columbia*, through the slower couple-based *yambú* to the most common and erotic *guagancó* (Roy 2002: 55–9), the *rumba* also represented for most Cubans the music of the *mulato* rather than either white or black communities.

The Republic, of course, coincided with two genuinely new popular cultural forms: film and radio. The moving picture had arrived in 1897, Gabriel Veyre (the Lumière brothers' agent) arriving in January, the Edison version in February and the Biograph version in April. The first Cuban film was made by José E. Casasús, *El brujo desaparecido* (Chanan 1985: 29). In 1906 Havana's first purpose-built cinema was opened, the Teatro Actualidades, showing Enrique Díaz Quesada's short scenic films (Chanan 1985: 34), and setting a pattern of sponsored advertising films. In 1913 Díaz Quesada made Cuba's first full-length feature film, tapping into popular culture and the drive for national identity, with *Manuel García o el Rey de los Campos de Cuba*, based on the legends of an 1890s bandit and folk hero.

By then, cinema was becoming less a spectacle than both a business and an ideological tool (Chanan 1985: 47), the theme of nationalist legitimation ensuring government provision of equipment, manpower and finance for *El Capitán Mambí o Libertadores y Guerrilleros* (1914) and *La Manigua o la Mujer Cubana* (1914) (Chanan 1985: 45). Indeed, with novelty, lower costs and the possibility of repeated performances, cinema now threatened Havana theatre, contributing to the *bufo*'s decline. By 1914, the Campoamor was renting space for film screenings (Rivero 1981: 37) and by 1915 there were forty cinemas in Havana alone (Llanes 1993: 139), rising to fifty by 1920, Cuba having some 23,000 cinema-goers in a population of half a million (Chanan 1985: 48). It also challenged the spectacular appeal of *bufo*; in 1928, Abel Gauce's silent film, *Napoleón*, at the Payret, was accompanied by a fifty-strong orchestra and a thirty-strong choir, under Gonzalo Roig (Río Prado 2002: 41).

Initially, Cuba was a battleground for cinematic influence, between the French and the Americans, the former initially dominating with the Actualidades buying Pathé films regularly and with the first distributors, Santos y Artiga, being agents for Gaumont and then, buying the Actualidades in 1909, for Pathé (Chanan 1985: 49). However, the First World War ended French competition and, in 1917, Paramount entered Cuba; by 1926, Cuba represented a greater proportion of overseas American film distribution than many European countries (Chanan 1985: 52) and 'nowhere in Latin America did US motion pictures so thoroughly saturate a natural market as in Cuba' (Pérez 1999: 287). However, as US film's ideological power began, studios needed Latin Americans for translation or dubbing, creating opportunities for Cubans like Ramón Peón who, Cuba's first professional film-maker, dominated Cuban production until 1939 (Chanan 1985: 59).

Radio presented a different panorama and different opportunities. October 1922 saw the first transmissions from the Cuban Telephone Company's Radio PWX, inaugurated by President Zayas, and, by 1923, fourteen of Cuba's twenty-four transmitters were in Havana, rising to forty-three by 1930, more even than in New York or Britain (López 2002: 80). Popularity grew rapidly, the Teatro Campoamor and the Reguladora restaurant playing broadcasts to their clients (López 2002: 22), with the first advertisement (for a government bond issue) in 1926, and with two fan groups created, the Sociedad Cubana de Radiofusión (1923) and the Radio Club de Cuba (1928). Radio now gave itself a special place in Havana hearts and culture by broadcasting popular music.

Another area where social change had affected boundaries was sport. In 1907, the increasingly middle-class Centro de Dependientes (with 25,000 members) boasted a gymnasium, shooting-range, swimming-bath and billiards, alongside the usual library, reading room and vast *sala de fiestas* (Llanes 1993: 167), but it was baseball that now enjoyed its 'Golden Age' (González Echevarría 1999: 113 passim), coinciding with sugar money, the influx of Americans and an incipient cultural nationalism that rejected football as Spanish (González Echevarría 1999: 187). The Club Almendares now built its Parque Almendares in 1916, in Pozos Dulces, and the tradition began of US Major, Minor and Black League players wintering commercially in Cuba. Gambling now also became integral to the sport.

Machado's awareness of sport's potential led him, in 1930 (in the depths of the Depression), to bring the Central American Games to Havana, through Porfirio Franca (an ex-amateur baseball player for the Vedado Tennis Club and later member of the 1933 Pentarchy). The Games, held in the Estadio Cerveza Tropical in Marianao (now the Estadio Pedro Marrero), were a success, Cuba winning gold in the baseball, setting a long-term pattern.

Figure 8 The status of baseball revealed by this tomb to a Havana baseball association's members

It is appropriate to end this section in 1933, with an economic crisis that would change Cuba irrevocably, with a pro-American dictator manipulating an increasingly popular cultural manifestation with some resonance for the question of national identity, and with one genuinely popular genre (film) beginning to cement a cultural neocolonialism, another (radio) beginning to offer space for popular musical manifestations of identity. Yet, among Havana's elite cultural community, the battle-lines for cultural identity were still being drawn tentatively.

Part II: Havana as 'the cultural problem' (1934–58)

Havana's Economic and Political Evolution

With the post-1934 double-process of sugar stagnation (affecting areas like Oriente) and partial boom, Havana now saw small-scale industrialisation, especially in American subsidiaries, tertiary sector growth (almost 60 per cent of the working population by 1953: Segre et al. 1997: 77), a boom in tourism and gambling, and, with the new state apparatus, greater employment in public works and the state. This unusual juxtaposition created problems within Havana, however, with a growing informal sector driven by rural emigration. Tourism, after declining in the early 1930s, provided the greatest boost, a record 188,519 arriving in 1951 (Villalba Garrido 1993: 25) and 347,508 in 1957 (Villalba Garrido 1993: 116), of whom almost 90 per cent were American (Villalba Garrido 1993: 119).

In this context, just as the 1933 revolution unravelled almost entirely in Havana, the new politics after 1934 also had particular effects in the city. Populism in Havana, for example, meant especially a tendency towards large spending projects and a public nationalism that sought to foment manifestations of a Cuban national culture, not least through a new wave of institutions. Degeneration had very specific manifestations in Havana: in the various student gangs whose activities plagued street and university life between 1938 and 1950, affecting even the intellectual and cultural world and perhaps contributing to the apparent 'escapism' of the *Orígenes* group, and in the entry of American organised crime which had already been evident during Prohibition, in rum smuggling and race-fixing (Cirules 1999: 42), but which was now given full rein by Batista who, in 1938, invited Meyer Lansky to streamline two Havana casinos and the Hipodromo, and again in 1953 to lead gambling reforms (Lightfoot 2002: 46). Again, the effect on Havana's social and cultural fabric was considerable, not least providing a space for the evolution of the new popular culture. Meantime, radicalism had changed and evolved, Havana seeing much continuing unrest, especially in the 1935 general strike, in the rising Communist Party (increasingly institutionalised in national and local politics), in the leftists among the Auténticos and Ortodoxos, and eventually in the student-based dissidence that responded to Batista's 1952 coup.

Spatial and Social Evolution of the City
As Havana grew economically, so did the population, reaching 1,216,762 by 1953, especially in the newer areas. Meanwhile, a post-1940 construction boom in the suburbs and in infrastructural development, saw the Carretera Central boost ribbon development of housing and industry to the south-east and west (Segre et al. 1997: 70), and saw the new airport develop the areas around Rancho Boyeros and Santiago de las Vegas, while the commercial hub began to move to the Rampa in Vedado (Segre ct al. 1997: 123–4).

The city centre now also saw the first high-rise offices and apartment blocks in Centro Habana, with prestigious department stores (notably Fin de Siglo), and, in Vedado and Miramar, new supermarkets and shopping malls, all changing the familiar pattern of street vending and small-scale shop-front selling, except for the *bodegas* in working-class areas.

Housing development was mostly unplanned, apart from the 1947 Barrio Residencial Obrero de Luyanó in Reparto Aranguren, which only built 177 of the projected 1,500 houses and services (Segre et al. 1997: 73). Instead, poor housing proliferated, ranging across the different types: twelve-roomed *casas de vecindad*, the *solares* (twenty to thirty rooms), *ciudadelas* (over 100 rooms), *cuarterías* (rooming houses), *pasajes* (blocks between two streets, linked by a 'passage'), and *accesorias* (one-bedroom ground-floor flats). Meanwhile marginal squatter settlements mushroomed at Las Yaguas, La Timba, Cueva del Humo and La Tambora, housing some 300,000 inhabitants (Segre et al. 1997: 73).

Conscious and sustained planning tended to concentrate on public construction. Both Batista's first period and the Auténticos stressed labour-intensive public works and infrastructural modernisation, but the 1950s saw the tourist boom affect building patterns, with hotels and leisure complexes, especially in Vedado and Miramar, public works being limited to projects such as the 1953 Almendares tunnel and the 1958 Bay tunnel. Even these had ulterior motives: to ease military movement, open up the east to development, and (after a 1957 attempt on Batista's life) develop a safer government centre in Habana del Este. There were ambitious plans (by José Luis Sert) to transform Havana by building high-rises along the Malecón, demolishing low-income housing in Habana Vieja for car-parking and creating an artificial island off the Malecón (with hotels, casinos and shopping malls) (Segre et al. 1997: 118). Central to these plans was the idea of the independent, Corbusier-influenced Plaza Cívica Forum, under Pedro Martínez Inclán at the university, which aimed to shift the centre of gravity to Vedado, south east of the Príncipe. However, little was actually completed, apart from the Tribunal de Cuentas (1953), Ministerio de Comunicaciones (1954) and Teatro Nacional (1958); everything else was completed after 1959, including the contentious Martí monument, built by Enrique Luis Varela who came second in the competition but was awarded the contract by Batista (Segre et al. 1997: 78).

Architectural styles changed substantially, the Modern movement not really taking hold until the 1950s, influenced by Wright, the 'Arts and Architecture' ideas, a 'Californian Mission' style and Latin American vanguards (Segre et al. 1997: 121), compounding the existing eclecticism.

By 1958, the future Havana seemed to be moving towards American models, but with Third World patterns; its population density was especially great in the area around Belascoaín, Galiano and Malecón and half of its housing was in a poor condition (Segre et al. 1997: 77). However, this was precisely the Havana social elite's heyday, boosted by American money and tourism, as the city became the playground of rich Americans. This Americanisation confirmed the shift westward, indicated by the development of some twenty elite clubs in Vedado and Miramar, notably the Vedado Tennis Club, the Lyceum Lawn Tennis Club, the more middle-class and Jewish Casino Deportivo, the Casino Español, and the new Country Club de la Habana. The acme was the Habana Yacht Club (el Yacht), which, by the 1930s, had replaced the Tennis in prestige, with a membership so exclusive that it rejected Batista, the rival Havana Biltmore Yacht and Country Club accepting him, in exchange for marina investment (Segre et al. 1997: 106–8). This was a self-confident and ostentatious elite; in 1949, Cuba had the world's highest per capita ownership of Cadillacs (Lightfoot 2002: 47), and, by the 1950s, many had second homes east of Havana, in Santa María del Mar and Tarará (Segre et al. 1997: 109). However, Havana also had a large, self-confident middle class, boosted by state employment, education and retailing, and evident in increased car ownership, the growth of Vedado and other residential areas, the popularity of television (from 1949), the growth of private schools and the fashion for American lifestyles.

Below them was Havana's small but growing working class and the burgeoning urban poor, seeking employment at the margins of the booming urban economy, which meant a reliance on tourism and related activities: this was the heyday of the nightclubs (the Tropicana, with dancing, bingo, restaurants and gambling, the Montmartre and the Sant Souci), of Sloppy Joe's, the Bodeguita del Medio and Floridita bars, of numerous casinos (especially the Riviera's Salón Rojo, complete with exotic dancing: Cirules 1999: 21), and of gambling at the Miramar greyhound track (Pérez 1999: 196). Indeed, one of Havana's booming activities was the sex industry, offering a gradation of supply from the cheapest brothels on Pila (in Atarés) and by the port, to the most notorious around Colón, Paseo, Neptuno, San Lázaro and Galiano, with other red-light districts existing on Zanja, near the Plaza del Vapor and on the Rampa (Segre et al. 1997: 110). In all, Havana had become a byword for corruption, seediness and crime: 'No había un sitio vital en la ciudad que no contara con un expendio de drogas, una mesa de juego, un apuntador y cientos de prostitutas' ('there was no residential area in the city without a drug supply, a gaming table, a pimp and hundreds of prostitutes': Cirules 1999: 24).

Hence, Havana's social fabric had changed dramatically and partly broken down, traditional patterns of social control and hierarchy disappearing to leave no clear sense of cohesion, order or deference. Those who had wealth displayed it, those who lacked it either scrabbled to survive or became marginal, while those in between imitated American manners and aspired to American standards. Even the Catholic Church had retreated to an urban, white, elite or middle-class constituency, leaving the poor (black and white) to seek religious expression and comfort in an evolving *santería*. What social cohesion existed operated within rather than between classes, the rich mixing in their social clubs, the poor seeking their belonging in religious groupings, trade unions, self-help or recreation and sport.

Evolution of a Havana Culture
The 'Second Republic' obviously sought to repeat the post-1902 process of institutionalising its avowed nationalism; this was especially the case under Batista after 1940, when he explicitly sought to emulate the Mexican nation-building exercise under Vasconcelos by creating a range of new cultural bodies and encouraging the

study of history, even chairing the inaugural session of the 1943 Segundo Congreso Nacional de Historia (Miller 1999: 239). However, certain differences emerged, notably the cultural elite's relative marginalisation from a social elite that, more managerial and commercial, based less on lineage, historical ties and family connections, and with different aims, attitudes and models and a more fragile economy behind it, was less respectful of culture, seeing it more as another commodity, fashions being more North American than European.

Therefore, the contours and boundaries of any new cultural elite would inevitably be different, enjoying even less prestige than before, although its elements were already in place, occasionally occupying socially prestigious positions. For example, José Antonio Ramos returned to a diplomatic career after 1934, and many 1930s radicals now had close links to the ex-radical political elite, and could thus aspire to be cultural leaders. Carpentier, for example, worked for the Ministry of Education after 1939 (and also taught history of music, after 1941, at the Conservatorio Nacional), the communist Marinello returned from exile in Mexico and Spain (1936–7) to be elected to the Constituent Assembly and, in 1944, become a Minister in Batista's cabinet, Renée Méndez Capote became Director of Bellas Artes in the Secretaría de Instrucción Pública (1933–4) and then, from 1940, worked in the Ministry of Education, Raúl Roa (one of the intellectual activists of 1927–33) led the Dirección de Cultura under Prío (where Lizaso also worked) and Serpa worked throughout the Batista regime as a press attaché in Paris.

These apart, however, the relative separation of social and cultural elites meant that, unlike 1902–34, instead of a clear-cut distinction between a cultural establishment and a counter-elite or vanguard, there were three layers, which complicated and fragmented the formerly cohesive gate-keeping role of the cultural elite. At the top were the formal, public cultural institutions, which, run by the more established intellectuals associated with the new order, defined standards and boundaries (through literary prizes, publishing opportunities, and so on) and determined and legitimised cultural production; at the bottom were the groupings, which, seeking vanguard status, either experimented with new European or North American ideas or strove to make Cuban culture socially and politically relevant. Between these two, the main manifestations of a Cuban culture could be found: partly establishment-oriented (led by university-based intellectuals, in private clubs, centres or institutes) but more politically critical and willing to experiment or go outside accepted artistic norms, a 'middle' where prizes, newspapers and other private means of recognition kept writers and artists afloat financially and kept popular and tentatively avant-garde forms in uneasy coexistence.

Therefore, the establishment and the counter-elite were now more difficult to identify, partly because, given that the cultural elite never controlled or exercised hegemony in defining prestige, it consisted of different groupings or even 'sub-elites', occasionally enjoying access to power and decision-making but mostly feeling more marginalised, seeking reinsertion either as established exponents of a declining cultural definition or by vanguard status. In this grey area *Lyceum* survived (1936–9 and 1949–61), as a partly elite and partly marginal organ, while, by 1935, *Social* was in decline, having returned to elite entertainment.

In this period, however, absence and emigration became suddenly more significant than before, the old political exile being replaced by self-exile until the second *Batistato*; the exceptions were many Communist/PSP activists who were obliged to flee after 1934 and then again after 1948, such as Guillén (1937–8 and 1953–9) and the critic José Antonio Portuondo (1944–53). Instead exile now meant a personal decision to flee the stultifying effects of a perceived philistinism, a dearth of publishing, performing or exhibiting opportunities, and an undiscerning and limited public. Those leaving in this way included Carpentier (who largely spent 1924–39 in Spain and Paris and 1945–59 in Venezuela), Virgilio Piñera (in Buenos Aires from 1942), Pita Rodríguez (in Buenos Aires and Venezuela, 1949–58), and José Rodríguez Feo (studying in the United States in 1939–49), while Paris in 1953–6 saw a whole colony of young Cuban writers, including Jaime Sarusky, Fayad Jamís, José Baragaño, Rolando Escardó, Roberto Fernández Retamar and Walterio Carbonell, whose experience of deracination and contact with new European or American culture shaped their artistic development and attitudes.

Moreover, outside Havana, there was still much cultural activity, some writers preferring not to be lured by the capital; a node of poetic activity existed in Las Villas, while the communist poet Manuel Navarro Luna, apart from periodic visits to Havana, spent most of his productive life in Manzanillo, and Portuondo, returning to Cuba in 1953, remained in Santiago.

Nonetheless, even without support, a new cultural hierarchy inevitably evolved, to define and create spaces within the city's elite cultural community, largely following the 1902–34 models, although with a notable lack of cultural patrons; this was mostly because the surviving 'leaders' now either preferred to work abroad or had become part of the establishment, cutting themselves off from legitimacy within the cultural community. It was therefore left to institutions and the activities of individuals within small groupings to determine either the new canon or the new vanguard.

The old institutions continued, now more as defenders of the faith and of the 'academy', including the Ateneo and the Lyceum, which, in 1942 (as the Lyceum y Lawn Tennis Club) established Vedado's first public library with the Henríquez Ureña collection bequeathed to it. Another survivor was the Institución Hispanocubana de Cultura, which, in 1936–47, published *Ultra*, offering mostly translations of, and articles by, foreign authors; however it now lacked its former impact and mostly focused on Spain, especially after 1936, when it helped exiles such as Juan Ramón Jiménez, Ramón Menéndez Pidal, Luis Amado Blanco, Adolfo Salazar and Américo Castro (Puig and Naranjo Orovio 2001: 207).

Cultural prizes, now more than ever, were thus a vital element in sustaining and renewing the cultural elite. The bourgeois El Encanto department store ran the Justo de Lara journalism prize (1934–57), the businessmen's Club de Leones de la Habana offered the Eduardo Varela Zequeira prize for *reportaje* (1941–7), the Dirección de Cultura offered, from 1935, seven prizes in its Concurso Nacional, the Municipio de La Habana offered the Ruy de Lugo-Viña journalism award. One effect of this focus on non-fiction was to make essay writing, criticism and histo-riography into the most dynamic elements of the new culture, especially as a gen-eration of former political activists confronted the new reality, including Marinello, Mañach, Ichaso, Lizaso, Chacón y Calvo, Roa and Raimundo Lazo, plus the historians who had emerged from the 1920s: in 1942, the Sociedad Cubana de Estudios Históricos e Internacionales, conceived as a radical and inde-pendent alternative to the institutional Academia de Historia (Miller 1999: 239), organised the Primer Congreso Nacional de Historia, under Ortiz. To some extent, these were the leading intellectuals of the Havana community, who challenged society by addressing the issues which others avoided. Meantime, more creative writing was patronised largely by private prizes, notably the Lyceum, the Asociación Cubana de Bibliotecarios, the Club Atenas and especially the Hernández Catá short-story prize which (established by *Mundo Contemporáneo*'s Antonio Barreras from 1942) stimulated the genre (García 1980: 226).

The Municipio de La Habana also now began to disseminate its Biblioteca Municipal provision through branches in Santos Suárez (the first Havana building specifically constructed as a library) and Cerro (García 1980: 128), and its Departamento de Bellas Artes created the Academia Municipal de Artes Dramáticas in 1947 (until 1949 in the Conservatorio Municipal de Música under Martínez Aparicio). In 1938, the Oficina del Historiador de la Ciudad de La Habana was established under Emilio Roig, a defining moment formalising the political importance of history as a discipline and signalling a drive to make *habaneros* aware and proud of their own roots; indeed, Roig used his position to sponsor groups such as the Sociedad de Folklore, the Sociedad de Estudios Afrocubanos and the Sociedad de Estudios Históricos. Alongside this, private sponsors included the 1940–52 Archivo José Martí, founded by Lizaso, Suárez Solís, Roselló and others to increase knowledge of Martí, and the Círculo de Bellas Artes, under Salazar, to further awareness of contemporary artistic devel-opments.

It was, however, the greater lack of publishing opportunities which most adversely affected Havana's elite cultural community; Antonio Sánchez Bustamante and Emeterio Santovenia created an Instituto del Libro in 1935, but the venture failed without a single publication. One underlying weakness, moreover, was now the impact of imported material, notably *Readers Digest* condensed books and USAID-funded matter (Smorkaloff 1987: 67).

Even culturally oriented or general-interest magazines were in shorter supply, not helped by the influx of syndicated American material. Chacón y Calvo's prestigious 1935–57 *Revista Cubana* (under the Dirección de Cultura) sought to define the parameters of prestige; *América* (1939–58), the organ of the Asociación de Escritores y Artistas Americanos, spread the word about contemporary Latin American culture; Cosme de la Torriente's short-lived and largely conservative *Revista de La Habana* tried to echo its eponymous predecessor's role without success; and the *Revista Bimestre*, under a succession of editors, never regained the leading role to which it aspired. General-interest magazines did occasionally publish literature, especially *Carteles* which, from 1937, published contemporary Cuban story-writers and, from 1954, devoted an entire section to Latin American stories.

Whereas, before 1934, the evolution of the elite cultural community could be traced through the effects of the 1920 dividing line, no such dividing line existed now, blurring the differences between the elements of the existing and the aspiring cultural elites. Instead, the only real division was not between canon and avant-garde but between a cultural ethos grounded in political or social commitment and another based on artistic excellence and aestheticism.

The former was followed by *Línea* (the 1933–7 journal of the leftist Ala Izquierda Estudiantil, Student Left Wing), the Liga Antimperialista's *Masas* (1934–5), Portuondo's unaffiliated *Baraguá* (1937–8) and *Germinal* (1949–57). However, the prime exponents of this current were the two journals associated directly with the Communist Party/PSP, *Mediodía* and *Gaceta del Caribe*. *Mediodía*, a 1936–39 monthly edited by Guillén, Portuondo, Marinello, Angel Augier, Edith García Buchaca and Carlos Rafael Rodríguez, played a seminal role in Havana culture, helping to forge a small grouping which survived long after it was replaced by *Magazine de Hoy*, the cultural supplement of the Party's daily, *Noticias de Hoy*. *Gaceta del Caribe* only ran for ten issues in 1944, but it too provided space for Havana's cultural radicals and, under Guillén, Portuondo, Augier, Mirta Aguirre and Pita Rodríguez, defended committed literature, advocated public art and publicised Cuban writers.

This pole was best manifested in *negrismo*, now boosted by Roig's Sociedad de Estudios Afrocubanos and the weekly *Estudios Afrocubanos* (1943–6). While the movement's earliest manifestations had been largely artistic fashion by white writers and artists, 'el fruto del maridaje de lo pintoresco y lo folklórico' ('the product of the marriage of the picturesque and the folkloric': Henríquez Ureña 1967b: 378), Guirao, the real pioneer, went deeper into the underlying social and historical context in his *Órbita de la poesía afrocubana* (1939), and Lydia Cabrera's study of Afro-Cuban mythology and culture resulted in *Cuentos negros de Cuba* in 1940. It was, however, Guillén who really took the movement to new levels, seeking to speak from inside the black experience by incorporating vibrant rhythms into his verse and writing about exploitation. After alternating between Camagüey and Havana, he settled in Havana in 1926, working as a government stenographer and, after becoming involved in Havana's radical politics, joined the Communist Party in exile in 1937, returning in 1938 and enjoying recognition as a cultural leader.

Meanwhile, the alternative pole saw small-scale magazine activity, some already existing and some new, such as *Poeta* (1942–3), under Piñera. As before, many were ephemeral, such as *Presencia*, which appeared irregularly from 1957 under Ramón Azarloza Blanco, José Jorge Gómez (known as Baltasar Enero) and Francisco Chofre. However, the outstanding exponent of this pole was, unquestionably, *Orígenes*, which grew out of a grouping stimulated by the November 1936–January 1939 visit of the Spanish poet, Juan Ramón Jiménez, to whom several already acknowledged a debt (Sánchez Eppler 1986: 30).

That visit was long but intense, with Jiménez taking over the vacant patron-entrepreneur role, lecturing, presiding over poetry readings in the Institución Hispanocubana, and sponsoring the preparation and publication of the Institución's anthology, *La Poesía Cubana en 1936*, in collaboration with Ortiz, Chacón y Calvo and Camila Henríquez Ureña, which constituted a seminal moment for Cuban culture, gathering together a poetic 'generation' which, through Jiménez, was associated with contemporary Spanish poetry. The established writers, such as Brull and Ballagas, welcomed him, and he in turn brought Cuban literature international recognition through his portraits of Enrique and Dulce María Loynaz, Serafín Núñez and Eugenio Florit in his *Españoles de Tres Mundos*. It was, however, among the younger poets (such as twenty-six year old José Lezama Lima and fifteen-year old Cintio Vitier, who had moved from Matanzas in 1935) that he had the most lasting impact, as 'the principal cultural landmark of their early years of artistic endeavour' (Sánchez Eppler 1986: 14).

They welcomed his arrival for several reasons. Firstly, as with Lorca's 1930 visit, it placed Havana on the international cultural circuit, but now not just for passing opera singers but for cultural leaders, thereby bringing these writers into a cultural community wider than Havana. Secondly, it refreshed a community dominated by the cultural academy. Thirdly, it helped legitimise their own emerging ideas and postures, Jiménez's work coinciding with them (Sánchez Eppler 1986: 16). This was immediately evident in the 1937 publication of Lezama Lima's 'Muerte de Narciso' and in the short-lived *Verbum* (1937), the organ of the Asociación de Estudiantes de Derecho, which, under Lezama Lima, published stories, cultural news and criticism, but, above all, new Cuban poetry and Jiménez. Thus, unlike Lorca's visit, Jiménez left an indelible mark in Havana. Although there were several differences between the visits and the context, to explain the different impact, the principal reason was these writers were effectively the 'third' current of the fragmented post-1928 *vanguardia*, in search of a patron until Jiménez's visit.

Inspired, the emergent group produced a string of equally ephemeral journals, all devoted to their emerging ideas and poetry. The first was *Espuela de Plata* (1939–41), dedicated mostly to earlier and new Cuban and Spanish poetry and run by Lezama Lima, Guy Pérez de Cisneros and Mariano Rodríguez. This was followed by the simultaneous *Clavileño* (run by Baquero, Vitier, Ballagas, Rodríguez Santos, Fina García Marruz and Eliseo Diego) and *Nadie Parecía* (1942–3). Then in 1944, *Orígenes* was born, produced from Lezama Lima's house on Trocadero (thus briefly reviving the *tertulia* tradition) and backed by Rodríguez Feo's sugar money. For, by now, the group had two clear patrons: Lezama was mentor, for his drive for literary quality, his fostering of younger writers and his personality and prestige, while Rodríguez Feo was unquestionably its entrepreneur.

During its twelve years, *Orígenes* created a movement of like-minded artists, also bringing in the poets Octavio Smith and Lorenzo García Vega, the artists Mario Carreño, Víctor Manuel, Raúl Milián, René Portocarrero, Mariano Rodríguez and Wilfredo Lam, and the musicians José Ardevol and Julián Orbón. Moreover, Ediciones Orígenes produced twenty-three books, dramatically increasing publishing space in Havana.

The group's aim was clear: the pursuit of artistic quality as a priority, and, linked to Jiménez's *intimismo*, embracing metaphysics, mysticism and hermeticism (García 1980: 395), while, like *Revista de Avance*, shaking the Havana community out of cultural provincialism by publishing foreign writers (Barquet 1992: 46). Hence, given the divisions in that community, the group was inevitably accused of escapism, of seeking the solace of the ivory tower, of being exclusive to Havana and ignoring the rest of the island. These accusations were not without foundation, since there was something elitist and even disdainful about their implicit rejection of a path that addressed black culture, poverty and exploitation, and in their search for inspiration in Europe rather than Cuba. Moreover, their isolation was furthered by the fact that so many were patently homosexual. However, this misjudges the 'heroism' (Barquet 1992: 68) of their intention of seeking nothing but excellence for a genuinely Cuban poetry and their stance against the degeneration of contemporary Havana by reaffirming the 'purity' of art and by their defence of 'una actitud ética' ('an ethical stance': Vitier 1975: 154). Indeed, their posture was ultimately as committed as the *negrista* poets, since they sought Cuba's 'soul' not in writing about topical issues or addressing Cuba's history but in a commitment to artistic principles that might ultimately produce an art to equal those they admired, whom the Havana community had long copied with a sense of inferiority. They were also equally in search of *lo cubano* ('Cuban-ness'), as they saw no value in a Cuban culture that was artistically poor, arguing that Cuba deserved better; their mission was 'a través de la empresa cultural independiente y consecuentemente ejecutada, el rescate y dignificación de lo cubano y de lo nacional' ('through an independent and consistent cultural strategy, to rescue and dignify both the Cuban and the national': Barquet 1992: 59).

The group's immediate impact was limited but its legacy was enduring. Until 1944, poetic *intimismo* among Havana's older poets had owed more to Romanticism (Henríquez Ureña 1967b: 385), although newer female poets, such as Mirta Aguirre, Graciela Garbalosa, Teté Casuso and Rafaela Chacón Nardi did show an awareness of *vanguardismo*; now this had been given a new impetus, affecting subsequent poetry and stressing, among younger poets, a complete dedication to the artistic vocation, with 'seriedad, profesionalismo y constancia' ('seriousness, professionalism and constancy': Barquet 1992: 25). However, its legacy was also negative, dominating Havana poetry so much that the next generation of poets felt obliged to reject it, with the only link between generations being Vitier, who effectively closed the movement with his 1957 Lyceum cycle of lectures on 'Lo cubano en la poesía'.

The group's demise was stimulated by a bitter personal dispute between Lezama and Rodríguez Feo over the unauthorised publication of a Jiménez article on Vicente Aleixandre (García 1980: 214), leading Rodríguez Feo to found a rival fortnightly publication from 1955, *Ciclón*. Produced with Piñera as secretary, it sought to publish new works by the more avant-garde Cuban and foreign writers, but, not distinguishing itself from *Orígenes* by any rejection of hermeticism, remained studiously apolitical until the editorial board closed it in 1957 as inappropriate under repression. The dynamism undoubtedly came from Piñera, who, although attached to *Orígenes* after moving to Havana in 1938 to study at the University, had always been a maverick, engaged in different groups, magazines, genres and activities. However, since *Ciclón* succeeded in attracting many of the next generation, such as Luis Marré, Ambrosio Fornet, Escardó, Luis Suardíaz, Rine Leal, Antón Arrufat, César López, Víctor Agostini, Roberto Branly, Jamís, and the Oráa brothers, it was more of a sequel, than a rival, to *Orígenes*.

Instead, rivalry came from the Sociedad Cultural Nuestro Tiempo, which explicitly represented the alternative 'pole'. Rooted in meetings at the Conservatorio Musical in 1950 (Otero 1999: 43) and founded in 1951 by composers Harold Gramatges, Juan Blanco and Ñico Rodríguez, it adopted, from 1952, a more frankly radical posture, hoping to 'traer el pueblo al arte' ('bring the people to art': Hernández Otero 2002: 19), and, from 1954, produced *Nuestro Tiempo*, publishing emerging writers, looking to Latin America rather than Europe and attracting the radicals among the young cultural community, such as Chacón Nardi and Fernández Retamar, novelist Surama Ferrer, *cuentista* Guillermo Cabrera Infante, essayist Fornet, and film-makers Alfredo Guevara, Saba Cabrera Infante, Néstor Almendros and Tomás Gutiérrez Alea. In addition, the publishing house Editorial

Páginas, linked to the Communist Party PSP and run by Rodríguez, offered space for committed art, as well as a bookshop (which also became a *tertulia* space) and a regular review of new books, *Nuevas Letras*.

To some extent, the apparent escapism–commitment dichotomy was simply a divergence between poetry and prose, for narrative tended to continue the old patterns of social concern, although now mostly in the short story, with novels tending to remain unpublished or being published abroad. The story's popularity was attributable to four factors: the space provided by magazines, Federico de Ibarzábal's 1937 *Cuentos Contemporáneos* (the first anthology of Cuban stories, which enhanced the genre's prestige and identified a group of Cuban writers), the Hernández Catá prize, which, unusually, encouraged provincial writers, and, in the 1950s, developments such as the workshop of the Buró del Cuento group under Agostini and Rosa Hilda Zell.

Stylistically, the story seemed heavily influenced by French and American forms, especially Hemingway, but the themes and treatment still followed naturalism, exposing exploitation with gritty realism and a *costumbrista* tinge of the picturesque. This was certainly true of Enrique Labrador Ruiz (who began publishing in 1933), Lino Novás Calvo (who mostly published abroad), and Galician-born Carlos Montenegro, who, after a colourful and violent past (including imprisonment for killing someone in a street brawl), developed as a journalist and writer after 1934, especially with his popular *Cuentos de la manigua* series. Dora Alonso was another such writer: having belonged to Guiteras's Joven Cuba and then the Communist Party (García 1980: 42), she wrote one successful novel, *Tierra Adentro*, winning the 1944 Secretaría prize, but was principally a story-writer.

The novel, meantime, seemed stuck in 'social realism', often an updated *costumbrismo*, almost as though novelists were still 'writing the 1930s' well into the 1950s.[8] Thus writers such as Alcides Iznaga, Esténger and Alonso belonged politically to their time (associated with progressive politics), but aesthetically to an earlier period. Writers such as Carpentier tended to avoid this as, being outside Cuba, they engaged in artistic fashions that had more to do with Latin America; while his early novels were part of *negrismo*, his 1956 novel, *Los Pasos Perdidos*, leaned more to emerging continental ideas of 'magical realism' with his notion of *lo real maravilloso*.

However, if the avant-garde was missing from narrative, it was fully present in Havana's visual and plastic arts, where the activity of Salazar's Círculo de Bellas Artes began to bear fruit, with exhibitions, lectures and discussions on the latest developments, creating the Escuela Libre de Artes Plásticas (García 1980: 215), while the San Alejandro school, now in Marianao, continued its activity. Here, the divisions evident in literature did not seem to apply; instead, *vanguardismo*, political commitment and the search for *lo cubano* fused easily, continuing patterns evident from the 1920s. Thus the seminal 1937 Exposición del Salón de Dependientes displayed the latest in the Cuban avant-garde (largely associated with the *Revista de Avance* but with greater self-confidence), while painters such as Marcelo Pogolotti, especially with his 1933 *Paisaje Cubano*, fused a critical vision with openly futuristic forms, and sculptors such as Ernesto Navarro and Rita Longa Anótegui bore the imprint of the latest European movements with clear Cuban referents. Meanwhile, the awareness of black themes became more common.

However, it was undoubtedly in Wilfredo Lam and René Portocarrero that the fusion was most successful, the former with his distinctive adaptations of Cubism and surrealism to Afro-Cuban myths and culture (*Huracán*, 1945, and the *Jungla* paintings of 1942–3), the latter with his expressionist use of colour for Cuban themes, in forms that owed much to Afro-Cuban cultural artefacts. Once again, the visual arts had proved most capable of fusing the outward gaze and endogenous expression.

Yet while, before 1933, that had also been true of the Havana music scene, this seemed less true now. The innovation characterising pre-1934 expression did continue, through the post-1942 Grupo de Renovación Musical, under the Catalan José Ardévol, cultivating young talents like Gramatges and Francisco Formell. However, Havana's musical activity in the 1940s and 1950s tended to focus on perfecting the musical academy, especially the Orquesta Sinfónica de La Habana which, reorganised under Erich Kleiber in the early 1940s, gave weekly performances in the summer in the Plaza de la Catedral, sponsored by the Ministry of Education (Matas 1971: 444). Meanwhile, the trend towards fusing classical music with Cuban popular music continued, especially in the University's summer schools from 1942 (Linares 2001: 135).

One new development was ballet; introduced into Cuba in the early Republic, backed by the Sociedad Pro-Arte Música, it had faded by the 1940s, but was boosted in the 1950s by the enthusiastic commitment of Alicia Alonso, who as Alicia Martínez Hoyo, had worked at the New York Ballet Theater from 1943. Returning, married, to Havana in 1950, she founded a company and a school, which, though still a minority activity, allowed ballet to survive.

In theatre, where *bufo* had blurred distinctions between art and entertainment, the old cohesion tended to fragment into light commercial theatre, experimental theatre, political theatre and radio. For a while, the tradition of light theatre and *costumbrismo* found a new outlet in politically satirical *sainetes costumbristas* at the Cueva theatre after 1936 (Le Riverend 1984: 1004), creating a generation of playwrights such as Carlos Robreño, Víctor Reyes or José Barreiro. Meantime, *zarzuela* survived at the Teatro Martí, especially 1931–6 (interrupted by the 1933 revolution), while *bufo* continued in a more stylised form, with a reduced range of characters and now preferring historical themes and melodrama over political satire (Río Prado 2002: 150).

However, a general decline set in once radio became popular. Initially, radio's dramatic repertoire was left to theatre experts, selecting according to artistic rather than entertainment criteria, with some inappropriate choices. Gradually, radio playwrights emerged, such as Franco D'Oliva, F.B. Caignet, Eduardo Zamacois, José Angel Buesa and Antonio Felip (López 2002: 101), who took account of the new medium where plays were broadcast live after one rehearsal, and radio began to bring theatre to a public which even *bufo* had never reached, changing the boundaries between art and entertainment, and between an enclosed theatrical community and a new audience for popular culture. In particular, the *radionovela* now took off, the first serial being broadcast in 1937 (*La Serpiente Roja*, with the Chinese detective Chan Li Po), a series that lasted ten years (Sellera 2001: 139). This provided opportunities for writers such as José Manuel Carballido Rey (the PSP activist and short-story writer, Hernández Catá winner in 1943, who worked throughout the 1950s as a scriptwriter for radio and television: García 1980: 177), Jesús J. López (*zarzuela* and musical librettist), Renée Méndez Capote, Enrique Núñez Rodríguez (writing, from 1948, especially for Rita Montaner) and Pita Rodríguez, named best radio author by the Asociación de la Crónica Radial in 1943.

Outside radio, *bufo*'s decline left the field open for more experimental or political theatre, but this could never hope to challenge light theatre or radio drama, and rarely enjoyed the internal prestige of painting, poetry or the story. Nonetheless, there were developments, boosted after 1942 by Luis Alejandro Baralt's Patronato del Teatro, which, supported by Suárez Solís, Ichaso and José Manuel Valdés Rodríguez, introduced its members monthly to the latest outside developments (Henríquez Ureña 1967b: 394). Based in the Teatro América, Teatro Auditorium and Sala Talía, it also offered the annual Premio Talía for Cuban authors from 1946. The small but prestigious monthly *Prometeo* (1947–53) was also significant, as was the post-1936 La Cueva company, which, formed under Baralt, adopted Pirandello's ideas (Matas 1971: 429), and, after 1948, the Las Carretas group, which staged Lorca (Martínez Carmenate 2002: 215). Modern theatre was also boosted by the influx of Spanish Republican exiles, especially director and writer Cipriano Rivas Cheriff and actor Margarita Xirgu, who founded the Academia Municipal de Artes Dramáticas in 1941, initially as a school, but, from 1953 (under Mario Rodríguez Alemán), as an experimental theatre (García 1980: 20). Another Spanish exile was Luis Amado Blanco, who became drama critic for *Información* and won the 1946 Premio Talía for his representation of Casona's *La Dama del Alba* (García 1980: 45), while Rafael Marquina founded, in 1940, the government-backed Teatro-Biblioteca del Pueblo, inspired by Lorca's La Barraca group (Martínez Carmenate 2002: 214). During this activity, the most seminal development was the 1941 Teatro Universitario and Seminario Universitario de Artes Dramáticas under Shajhowicz (Matas 1971: 430), which rapidly became Havana theatre's main experimental workshop.

Therefore, although this ferment was limited to a small circle within an increasingly isolated cultural community, it did, nonetheless and despite little money, succeed in planting new ideas in a fertile soil for later development. It also provided a supportive environment for the more avant-garde work of the largely absurdist Piñera (notably *Electra Garrigó*, 1945) and Carlos Felipe (*El travieso Jimmy*, 1943). Indeed, 1951–4 saw another 'new wave', consisting of Andrés Castro's Las Máscaras group (based at the Teatro Universitario), Julio Matas's Arena and Erik Santamaría's 1954 Salón TEDA (beginning in 1952 as the Teatro Experimental de Arte), mostly backed by Nuestro Tiempo, whose Sección de Teatro (under Vicente Revuelta and Mora Badía) organised a Ciclo de Estudios, launched *Cuadernos de Cultura Teatral*, staged writers such as Tennessee Williams and advocated the Stanislavsky method (Matas 1971: 444; Hernández Otero 2002: 155–58). This movement especially launched writers such as Fermín Borges (who, in 1958, founded Los Comediantes Cubanos), Matías Montes Huidobro, José A. Montoro Agüero, and Dysis Guira (Hernández Otero 2002: 160–2), while the young David Camps set up his Teatro Estudio in 1957 and Adolfo de Luis set up his Stanislavsky-influenced Atelier group (Pogolotti 2001: 146).

By 1958, the outcome was an unprecedented range of small experimental theatres (notably the Talía, Hubert de Blanck, Atelier, Sótano, Arlequín, Idal and Arcoiris) and drama workshops, which meant that, having long laboured under the weight of tradition, theatre now became Havana's most innovative and avant-garde artistic form. For, if an avant-garde needs an oppressive academy against which to rebel, then, while the lack of such an academy in poetry, prose, art and music meant that former innovators had become established, theatre had such a target for rebellion in musical theatre.

Rebellion brings us to Havana's fourth theatrical form, the politically committed drama, especially by writers like José Montes López, José Cid, and Pita Rodríguez (whose *El relevo*, about Chinese resistance to Japan, was performed in the Teatro Principal in 1944). The Communist ex-*zarzuela* singer Paco Alfonso was the doyen of this form. Having founded the small Teatro Cubano de Selección and the 1930 Teatro Juvenil, and won the 1936 *4 de Septiembre* prize for *Reivindicaciones*, he now developed the Brigadas Teatrales de la Calle (which, operating during 1930–40, prefigured post-1959 experiments) and the Teatro Popular from 1943. This theatre, founded by Raquel Revuelta in 1941 and supported by the Federación de Trabajadores de La Habana, played in factories and the *barrios*, often using workers as actors. In 1950 Alfonso's *Cañaveral* won the Premio Nacional de Teatro, and, in 1956, he founded the Teatro El Sótano (García 1980: 36).

Apart from a new Chinese theatre around Zanja (especially the Teatro Chino de Zanja, which became the Shanghai before evolving into a pornography theatre and sex club), Havana also had the puppet-theatre Teatro Guiñol Nacional from 1949, which, contracted by the Ministry of Education in 1950 for a national tour and by television in 1953, opened its own premises in 1955.

Given this wide range, theatre attendances rose, with performances going from fifty-four in 1936 to 145 in 1945, including plays by Strindberg, Hoffmansthal, Anouilh, Williams, Sartre and Saroyan, as well as Spanish classics (González 2003: 167–86), peaking in 1956 at 218 separate performances (González 2003: 291).

This was even more surprising given the rapidly increasing popularity of radio and film. In 1939, thirty-four of Cuba's fifty-eight medium-wave broadcasters were in Havana (López 2002: 91), and by 1956 radio reached some six million people, with two thirds of Havana's 77,271 vehicles having radios (López 2002: 332–3). After *La Voz del Aire* broadcast news in 1933, others followed suit, such as CMQ's *La Palabra* and *El Noticiero*, CMCY's *Radiario Nacional* and CMCO's *El Periódico del Aire*, and 1947 saw the birth of the idiosyncratic Radio Reloj (whose main purpose was constant timekeeping).

The cultural implications were considerable: radio (through advertising revenue) was increasingly where artists could earn and create. Rosa Hilda Zell, for example, after studying art, became a scriptwriter in the Instituto Cubano de Radiofusión, even writing on cookery, while in 1932 Mañach began his Universidad del Aire educational programmes, followed, in 1937, by the popular series, *La Corte Suprema del Arte*, on CMQ. The most popular aspect of radio was, unquestionably, the *radionovela*, which counted four of the listeners' top ten favourites in a 1951 poll (*Bohemia* 43, 11: 40).

Once again, popular music benefited most from radio, with music programmes spreading the popularity of *trovadores* and *décima* singers, jazz bands and *son* interpreters (such as Clavelito, the Duo Perfecto or the Trío Oriental), while the 1936 CMCY programme, *La Hora Cubana de Cultura Popular* (organised by the Hermandad de los Jóvenes del Pueblo, linked to the PSP's Liga Juvenil Comunista), raised the national prestige of these forms, leading to the Instituto Popular del Aire (López 2002: 150–1). Indeed, the Communists were quick to recognise radio's power, creating their own popular station, Radio Mil Diez (*La Emisora del Pueblo*) in 1943, which led the drive to fuse art and people in the 1950s and gave opportunities to more radical writers.

Radio was so powerful, indeed, that it dwarfed both television and film. Television was less successful partly because of its cost, but also because *telenovelas* were scripted according to themes determined by advertisers (Cid 1986: 361).

Film in Havana had become genuinely popular by the late 1940s, magazines paying attention to celebrity gossip and photographs; by then, Cuba had fifty-seven million annual admissions (Chanan 1985: 16), and, unlike in Britain and the United States, television did not affect this.

Havana film-making was, however, now dominated by the demands and fashions of Hollywood and Mexico. At the end of the 1930s, Ramón Peón, building on that experience, created a Havana production base, Pecusa, which made six films in 1938–9, mostly musical comedies (Chanan 1985: 61). However, Mexican hegemony led to a crop of Cuban melodramas, especially after 1951, when Peón teamed up with Rita Montaner in films such as *La renegada* (1951) and *La única* (1952) (Sellera 2001: 140).

Moreover, by the 1950s, cinema was accepted by the cultural *vanguardia* as an art form, evident in the University's 1940s film studies course, and Nuestro Tiempo gathered a group of young radical, *cineastas*, such as PSP activist Alfredo Guevara and Roberto Branly, who looked towards the European new wave rather than Hollywood, Gutiérrez Alea and Julio García Espinosa studying in Rome's Centro Sperimentale in the early 1950s and learning from Italian neo-realism. Manuel Barbachano Ponce's weekly 10–minute television 'magazine', *Cine Revista*, also became a training-ground (Chanan 1985: 73). Thus a generation existed whose politics and artistic aspirations made them a potential *vanguardia*, waiting only for resources and space to rebel against the weight of Hollywood, seen as the 'punto de lanza' ('spearhead') for US imperialism (Fornet 1982: 8). Some did produce shorts, notably Gutiérrez Alea's *La Caperucita Roja* (1946), and García Espinosa's 10–minute neo-realist documentary on the Ciénaga de Zapata charcoal-burners, *El Mégano* (1955), which, after a showing at the university was seized by Batista's police, and is now considered the 'único antecedente legítimo del cine cubano contemporáneo' ('the only legitimate predecessor of the contemporary Cuban cinema': Fornet 1982: 15).

Film's political power was appreciated everywhere. While the Prío government, in 1952, established a finance bank and the Patronato para el Fomento de la Industria Cinematográfica (Chanan 1985: 62), the PSP's *Noticias de Hoy* organised a programme of newsreels, leading to Cuba-Sono-Films under José Tabío, reflecting a growing 'oppositional film culture' in Havana (Chanan 1985: 78). This was also expressed in an emphasis on appreciation, for the period saw a flourishing movement of *aficionados*, Cine Clubs showing foreign films and arranging discussions, imitating the Photographic Club of Cuba which, after 1943, organised a competition for amateur film-makers. One of the most active was the Cine Club de La Habana, founded in 1948 by Fornet, Almendros, Gutiérrez Alea and Guillermo Cabrera Infante, which, from 1951, screened borrowed French avant-garde films (Otero 1999: 44), but one of the most successful was the Cine Club Visión, which sponsored the musician Leo Brouwer, as well as Norma Torrado, Nelson Rodríguez and Gloria Argüelles (Chanan 1985: 81). Indeed, the Catholic Church also created its own network, which, by 1957 numbered forty-two clubs (Chanan 1985: 81).

Clearly, traditional patterns within the elite Havana cultural community were breaking down, the old cohesion being replaced by a more fragmented and less confident vision, enhanced by the lack of a clearly canonical elite. Not only was there mostly no fruitful divide between academy and *vanguardia*, but the search for a Cuban culture that might combine artistic quality with both national and popular senses of belonging had fragmented too. The paths indicated by *negrismo* had either petered out into fashion or exile or had proved unrewarding, while the 1920s attempts to fuse *vanguardismo* and identity seemed unachievable. Yet there were signs of possible new developments in all genres.

Ultimately, it was left not to the elite community to point the way, but rather, as suggested before 1933, by various exponents of popular forms outside that enclosed environment, as Mil Diez had sensed. Here, music and dance offered the most, especially for the *trovadores*, as late-night live broadcasts brought provincial performers to Havana, such as Guyán, Codina, Duo Carbó, Quevedo, Berto González and Terral (López 2002: 82). It was the traditional *décima*-based *punto* (solo improvisation) or *controversia* (two-handed improvisation) that radio developed most in 1940–4. Audiences filled the theatre-studios where *decimistas* performed or gathered in bars to listen on the radio, and cinema owners employed *decimistas* to perform *punto* between films, some performances attracting coach-loads of fans (Bode Hernández 1997: xxv); the peak came with the *controversia* between Bando Azul and Bando Tricolor on COCO's *Bohío Cubano*, between December 1940 and January 1942 (Bode Hernández 1997: 2).

Radio also continued to develop groups such as the Sexteto Habanero or Sexteto Nacional. By the early 1950s, Havana witnessed a boom of quartets, duos and trios, led above all by Beny Moré; after arriving from Las Villas in 1940 as Bartolo Moré and performing in bars and on radio, he joined Miguel Matamoros in 1944 and then the Pérez Prado Big Band in Mexico in 1944–52. By 1953, he had his own Big Band, whose distinctive music he took to Latin America and the United States.

However, the implicit need to gain American recognition had a significant impact on popular forms in Havana bars, radio and television. For, while before 1933 popular music had touched a chord of national identity sometimes better than the elite's efforts, popular music now seemed vibrant and famous outside Cuba, but perhaps offered less that was 'authentic'. While there were technical developments, such as the introduction of the piano in the 1930s, or through Lecuona and Ignacio Jacinto Villa Fernández (better known as 'Bola de Nieve', 'Snowball'), few genuinely new Cuban forms emerged.

Certainly, the weight of American music was considerable. From the 1930s, jazz's popularity in Havana indicated the potential to challenge Cuban music, and, by the 1950s, the proliferation of Cuban jazz bands (such as Tito Gómez's Orquesta Riverside) led to the popularity of *descargas* (jam sessions) and the Orquesta Hermanos Castro, based in Radio CMBZ and a music shop on San Rafael (López 2002: 84); in 1957–8, the Club Cubano de Jazz invited over twenty American bands (Acosta 2001: 46). However, it was in less adventurous forms (through radio) that the American influence was most clearly felt, as in the emergence of the *movimiento de filin*. Based on the *bolero* and the *trova*, but heavily influenced by Nat King Cole, *filin* (a corruption of 'feeling') began with Angel Díaz in Callejón de Hamel, and, publicised by Mil Diez, evolved a style of melody, singing and lyrics that 'Cubanised' it (Roy 2002: 115).

However, it was the fate of the *mambo* that really showed the weight of American taste, almost as though Cubans in Havana were being asked to recognise an Americanised form of their own music as a cultural product of which they could be proud and with which they could identify organically. A similarly revealing development came from radio. CMG's 1930s weekly news programme *El Suceso del Día* ('Events of the Day') used a theme tune based on traditional Spanish *romance*, Oriente melodies and the *guajira*, to which a singer, Joseíto Fernández, following the tradition of *punto*, would improvise a 'narration' or comment on the day's events or political issues of import. This became so familiar that the melody and rhythm were adopted by others; then, in the 1950s, at a gathering in his home, the classical musician Julián Orbón set some lines from Martí's *Versos sencillos* to the tune. An ex-pupil present at the performance, Héctor Angulo, then took it and, eventually, it found its way to the American folk-singer, Pete Seeger, after which it became the internationally recognised 'Guantanamera' (Roy 2002: 136). Indeed, after 1963, it was the Seeger version that was adopted in Cuba, played repeatedly to visitors, confirming that external recognition still seemed to determine Cuban preferences.

The American role inevitably leads us again to sport; here, the popular form was still baseball, football only briefly challenging its hegemony in the 1930s, responding to its growth elsewhere, Cuba's relative success in the new World Cup and the Central American Games, and to Spanish immigration. Batista especially backed baseball; in 1936, the new commissioner of baseball, fellow 1933 conspirator General Galíndez, reformed its national structure, including a youth league (the Juveniles), and, in the 1940s, created the Dirección Nacional General de Deportes y Educación Física under Colonel Jaime Mariné. He also emulated Machado by bringing the World Amateur Series annually to Havana between 1939 and 1943. The *Auténticos* followed suit, Grau appointing Luis Orlando Rodríguez head of the Federación Nacional.

Clearly, baseball meant both money and popularity, with businesses (especially brewing) now investing considerably and with the Liga de la Federación and Liga Cubana increasingly becoming feeder leagues and wintering facilities for both US-based baseball and the predatory Mexican League, then challenging US baseball for continental hegemony (González Echevarría 1999: 20). In 1947, American money financed the new Gran Stadium on the edge of Cerro and by the late 1940s radio broadcast baseball regularly (González Echevarría 1999: 58). The epitome of this commercialisation were the 1950s Cuban Sugar Kings, seeking to sell Cuban baseball to the United States and become the 'farm team' for the Cincinnati Reds and win a major-league franchise (González Echevarría 1999: 336); it was the epitome because it sold itself in English, invested vastly and sought American recognition.

Clearly, therefore, the cultural confidence manifested within the clearly defined elite cultural community and popular forms in the late 1920s and early 1930s had, by the 1950s, begun to dissipate. While *Orígenes* may have indicated directions in quality and experimentation, echoed by theatre groups, and while artists around the PSP and Nuestro Tiempo may have sought an explicitly committed art, taking art to the people rather than the people to art (as the *negristas* had done), the pre-1933 promise had not generally borne fruit. Neither the elite cultural community in Havana nor exponents of popular forms seemed any closer to discovering or creating forms which they, and most Cubans, could identify as genuinely expressive of a national identity. Instead, it seemed, they either struggled under the weight of North American influence, norms and demands, or developed forms whose 'Cuban-ness' was determined by American consumers or Parisian artistic groups rather than by Cubans for Cubans in Cuba, reflecting the dilemmas facing all Cubans in the 1950s. What the *mambo* represented was the fact that Cubans were being encouraged to doubt their own identity and reshape it as a poor imitation of their powerful neighbour, especially in Havana, where Americans flocked in pursuit of the delights which Cubans could give them to suit their needs and tastes; if a Cuban cultural identity did exist in Cuba in 1958, there were few clues in Havana as to where that might be and how it might emerge.

Part III: *Bohemia* case study

When seeking to discover the post-1902 patterns of cultural awareness and changes in cultural attitudes in Cuba generally, and specifically in Havana, a magazine such as *Bohemia* becomes a valuable source of evidence. This is because, being the Republic's longest lasting, most prestigious and most popular weekly magazine, it often reflected the shifts in social, cultural and political attitudes during a volatile period. Moreover, from its foundation in 1910 (after a few trial editions in 1908) until 1928, under Miguel Angel Quevedo, the magazine consciously tried to mirror Cuban society and to promote the arts, reflected in its subtitle, *Ilustración mundial* ('world enlightenment'). In the 1930s, under Quevedo's son, Miguel Angel Quevedo y de la Lastra, it became more openly political, recording firstly Havana's radicalisation and then, from the 1940s, its daily political violence, until, after Batista's coup, it opposed the dictatorship and recorded the growing rebellion. For the duration of the Republic, therefore, it was a window onto social attitudes and changes, and, with its historical feet in both the elite and the emerging middle class, onto the ways in which culture was presented, seen and appreciated, and, more specifically, which aspects of culture were privileged by both the elite and the changing readership, which cultural models were proposed for guidance or imitation, and which popular cultural forms were acknowledged. This is because, although a magazine's cultural focus can reflect editorial prefer- ence, its development necessarily leads to a reliance on a market; hence, as Havana changed, the magazine changed, enabling us to gauge how cultural attitudes also evolved.

The changes in readership were of course identifiable by examining certain key indicators: these include advertising (to see which groups were being targeted), sports coverage (given that different social groups practised different sports) and revealing issues such as religion, education and society pages.

Equally, one can tell the magazine's evolution through its changing politics. After 1930–3, it opposed Machado (being closed in 1931) and, having welcomed the September 1933 revolution, then became more critical of its disintegration into chaos and violence, adopting positions close to some of the more elitist student groups. After 1936, it supported the Spanish Republic, its anti-Fascism leading it to a curious admiration for Stalin's Soviet Union, while, in Cuba, it tended to be sympathetic to Batista's nationalism, economic interventionism and stability. By 1944, however, its politics seemed to reflect 'New Deal' postures.

Of course, given forty-eight years of *Bohemia*'s existence, practical considera- tions of space determine a necessarily selective examination of its pages; hence a particular pattern has been adopted here (and continued in the chapter 3 case study), namely to examine in detail all the March editions every ten years from 1911. March has been selected for two reasons: firstly, in Cuba's essentially com- memorative political culture, March was until 1959 a relatively uneventful month, making the magazine's content more likely to be typical, and, secondly, March was either the month of *Carnaval* (allowing us to judge *Bohemia*'s treatment of popular cultural celebrations) or of Easter (allowing us to gauge its treatment of religion). Finally, the choice of 1911, 1921, 1931, 1941 and 1951 arises from the knowledge that 1921 might be expected to reflect something of the elite's self-doubt immedi- ately after the *Danza de los Millones*, 1931 might reflect both Depression-induced crisis and the process of radicalisation, while, after 1959, 1961 was a critical year for culture (with the *Lunes* affair, UNEAC and Castro's *Palabras*) and 1971 included the *caso Padilla* and the Cultural Congress.

March 1911

After only nine months, *Bohemia*'s readership was clearly the largely commercial, substantially Spanish, white Havana upper-middle class, especially demonstrable from the weekly 'society' column 'Crónica', recording ladies' buffets in Marianao residences, a list of 'lindísimas señoritas' ('loveliest young ladies') at a Reina party (II, 11: 538), events at the Ateneo, and the births, deaths, marriages, betrothals and holidays of an elite whose Vedado Tennis Club *fiesta* was 'una tarde agradabilísima … en tan aristocrática sociedad' ('a most pleasant evening … in such aristocratic company': II, 12: 551). Certainly the existence of a small elite was borne out by the familiarity of references to cultural leaders, such as 'nuestro distinguido amigo, el reputado profesor de música, señor Hubert de Blanck' ('our distinguished friend, the famed professor of music, Hubert de Blanck': II, 12: 551). Moreover, the magazine's minimal advertising indicated a substantial financial base; the few advertisements were for French or *afrancesado* fashions (at Maison de Blanc, for example), for English tailoring, and for health and beauty preparations. The readership was also evident from the religious themes, either in the poetry (mostly for the coming Lent or Easter – Chrisanthème's 'Magdalena y Jesús' (II, 11: 530) and Miguel E. Oliva's '¡Oh, el vía crucis de las almas …!' (II, 12: 544)) or in the 'Crónica Religiosa', announcing the coming week's religious calendar.

Poetry stood out immediately; traditionally the most socially acceptable genre, associated with female readers, this unsurprisingly took pride of place, with twelve poems in three editions, twice on the first page. These were often by Cubans, such as Esteban Foncueva (II, 10: 519) and Agustín Acosta (II, 10: 517), perhaps reflecting familiarity within the small enclosed Havana elite, and were usually in *modernista* sonnet form. March 1911 also included Amado Nervo poems (II, 11: 530) and a homage to the Puerto Rican José Mercado (II, 12: 542). Music, however, challenged poetry; this month saw various musical news items, such as the inaugural concert of the Agrupación Artística Musical (II, 11: 533), a Wagner concert (II, 11: 538), *Tosca* at the Teatro Payret, with Italian singers (II, 10: 523), a forthcoming Juan González baritone recital at the Academia de Canto (II, 12: 551) and news of the dance bands at society events, such as the Orquestra de Escarpentier (II, 12: 550). It also published sheet music. Painting had surprisingly little coverage in the month's issues, considering that *Bohemia*'s artistic director was the painter Antonio Rodríguez Morey; mostly, Cuban artists were given space for illustrations. In the visual arts, there were photographs of Julian Lorieux sculptures (II, 10: 522) and of the gold medal winner of the Exposición Nacional (II, 12: 551).

The cultural models evident were almost universally European, in fashion, content and focus, as in La Hija del Caribe's 'La Reina Primavera' (II, 10: 518), depicting a frankly European spring, complete with skylarks and nightingales, although there was one curiosity – a Fernando de Salgado story, 'Miseria Impía' (II, 10: 519), about a *guajiro*, an almost mythical figure with whom readers might be expected to sympathise romantically.

Of popular culture there was predictably almost no trace and no hint of a black Cuban population. Even the coverage of *Carnaval* was with society references, to *bailes infantiles* (children's dances) at the (Spanish) Palacio de la Asociación de

Dependientes del Comercio (II, 12: 545) and fancy-dress balls with young ladies dressed as *princesas orientales* (II, 10: 524). Even sporting references were few (despite the media's new interest in sport), aimed at a social class that practised fencing and tennis; baseball was beyond the magazine's interests.

March 1921

By 1921, *Bohemia* still clearly targeted a readership that was self-confident and even more moneyed, demonstrated by the advertisements for sea cruises, New York hotels and new customised houses in the exclusive Country Club Floral Park (XII, 11: 15). The closely knit nature of the elite readership was demonstrated by the 13 March list of the Josés and Josefinas of established Havana society who would be celebrating San José on 19 March (XII, 11: 17), and the bourgeois and possibly Spanish focus was evident in religious themes, notably the paintings 'El Nazareno' (XII, 12: 1) and 'Cristo y el joven Rico' (XII, 12: 7), Roger de Lauria's Good Friday poem (XII, 12: 10), the accounts of the Cuban film, *Cristus*, and the diatribe against the 'blasphemous' play, *Los Siete Dolores de María Santísima*, a 'mamarachada literaria' ('literary tastlessness': XII, 13: 14). However, much of the increased advertising was for women's health and beauty products in remarkably explicit ways.

However, *Bohemia* was now a little more aware of a Cuba beyond Havana, with the regular 'Crónica Social de Provincia' recording the comings, goings and activities of the provincial bourgeoisie, alongside the Havana society columns, 'Sociales' and 'Actualidades'. Moreover, the inclusion of a regular 'Directorio Profesional' indicated a shift in readership towards the professional classes, and the advertisements for window-cleaning fluid indicated that *Bohemia*'s readers included those without servants.

Bohemia still clearly saw itself in the Cuban cultural vanguard. Poetry remained prominent, though somewhat conventional, as in the sonnets by Modesto Campos Julián, 'En el mundo no existe mi quimera', and Primitivo Herrera, 'Musgo' (XII, 10: 8), and fewer of the poets were Cuban. Music tended to consist of reports of small recitals and news: the Sociedad Pro-Arte Musical's success in bringing Kubelin, Rubinstein and Augières to Havana (XII, 10: 16), the American soprano Myrtle Leonard's visit, an Academia de Canto Filarmonia de Italia concert at the Asociación de Propietarios del Vedado (XII, 11: 17), a recital by Ursulina Páez Medina at the Conservatorio Nacional's Sala Espadero (XII, 12: 17) and a coming Saint-Saëns recital by Alberto Falcón (XII, 12: 18). Visual arts received less attention than before, although with more colour reproductions (of somewhat kitsch European paintings); the only news was of the London sale of a Breughel painting (reproduced in black-and-white) (XII, 12: 3) and of an exhibition by the Cuban Enrique Crucet (XII, 13: 15).

Theatre took the lion's share of cultural coverage, with detailed reporting of the New York theatre scene (XII, 10: 9) and with a regular column, Gerardo de Noyal's

'Teatros', which recorded a Cuban season by the touring Spanish Guerrero-Mendoza company (XII, 10: 11), operettas at the Payret (especially a Mexican operetta, *El Doctor Argesola* (XII, 12: 13), and the Bracale company's Nacional performance of Breton's opera, *Dolores* (XII, 13: 14).

Two new developments indicated changing fashions. One was the short story, mostly non-Cuban (usually French), with the few Cuban ones (by Mario Sorando and Rosario Sansores) being much shorter. The other was the cinema, above all in Gypsy's weekly 'Arte Silente' column (keeping Cuban film-fans updated with gossip and news from the US film scene), in the attention paid to possible Cuban stars (with a weekly competition – 'Galería de Nuestro Concurso' ('Competition Gallery') – for a Cuban beauty to challenge the US film industry's best) and Cuban films (for example, *La Maldita*, starring María Luisa Santos (XII, 11: 12)), and in news of the documentary *Víbora Social y Progresista* at the Tosca cinema (XII, 11: 14).

Hence, the conclusions for 1921 are, firstly, that the audience was growing (reflecting greater literacy, a more urban society and a larger middle class), but with the tone still determined by the traditional readership, now richer and more cosmopolitan, and, secondly, that an awareness of a Cuba beyond Havana was greater. However, *Bohemia* was looking even more to foreign 'models', especially beginning to shift from Europe (though still looking to Paris for fashion, beauty and literature and Britain for a genteel aristocratic tone) to a greater interest in North American products and news. Curiously, when the 'exotic' appeared, it followed European notions, although European cultural fashions were then seeing countries like Cuba as exotic; clearly, the *Bohemia* readership did not wish to be considered primitively exotic, so it replicated traditional European views, in part reflecting the Havana elite's Spanish origins, manners, orientation and interests (witnessed in the attention to Spanish companies, actors, writers and news). Once again, beyond cinema, there was no hint of popular culture, neither traditional dance (seemingly abandoned as a possible interest) nor sport, where coverage still reflected elite tastes, in fencing, *frontón*, shooting and hunting.

March 1931

March 1931 had only three editions, *Bohemia* being closed down between 12 January and 15 March. By then the magazine had almost doubled its size and had changed visibly, reflecting changes both in Cuban society and politics and also in editorial direction, with a greater focus on political events.

By now, the old confident elite had gone, reflected by the lack of 'society news' (replaced by photographs of businessmen's lunches or dinners or of 'celebrities' and politicians) and the absence of any religious themes; in March 1931 'religion' meant just one photograph of the Pope, while the editions carried an article on civil marriage (XXIII, 5: 23) and Ofelia Rodríguez Acosta's series in favour of women's rights (XXIII, 3: 9; XXIII, 4: 28; XXIII, 5: 19). The greater length now accommodated two things: world news and a vastly increased number of advertisements, all aimed at the middle class and increasingly for American goods. Indeed, it was now clear that *Bohemia*'s readership was middle-class, evident from the sports coverage of football and baseball and the greater attention to the United States, despite a residual fascination with European royalty. The class's aspirations, usually following American criteria, were now evident in articles on motoring and advertisements for American military academies. However, unlike the old elite readership, this one now sought information about Cuba: instead of stories of European landscapes, there were travel articles on Gibara (XXIII, 3: 54–5), pictures of Santiago, and football reports from outside Havana (XXIII, 5: 49).

Cultural patterns had also therefore changed, evident in the growth of more popular forms. The traditional interest in poetry had disappeared completely, apart from one picture of poet Graziella Gierbalosa (XXIII, 4: 30), and theatre and opera received much less attention, with only one article on Paris street theatre (XXIII, 3: 50) and a serialised biography of Strindberg, but nothing on Cuba. Visual arts included only a short item on the painter Maripepa Lamarque (XXIII, 3), and dance had an article on the Mexican ballerina Adelita Trujillo (XXIII, 4), while Pita Rodríguez (described as an avant-garde poet) wrote one ironic piece from Paris (XXIII, 4: 74–5).

One of the signs emerging in 1921 became clearer with the prominence of the short story. There were now several in each edition, some being serialised; these were, however, mostly foreign (especially French or American) with only three Cuban stories (out of twenty-one) – by Sansores (XXIII, 3: 94; XXIII, 5: 78) and Antonio Roselló Bonilla (XXIII, 4: 46) – once again usually shorter and coming towards the end of each edition, although several Cuban story writers by then existed. Interestingly, apart from Chekhov, most of the foreign stories were sensationalist, romantic or crime tales by fashionable but second-rank practitioners (such as J.H. Rosny, Jacques Constant, G.G. Toudouse, Jack Carter or Brayton Eddy). Indeed, this crime theme was echoed in news stories on the United States, such as Juan Giró Rodés, 'Como son descubiertos los asesinos' ('How murderers are found': XXIII, 3: 23) and José Juan Tablada, 'Nueva York de día y de noche' ('New York by Day and Night': XXIII, 5: 11).

Cinema now had pride of place, especially G. Barral's weekly film review, 'La Emoción del Momento', always including a still and a plot *resumé*; such films were always American and the focus of attention always Hollywood (with no evidence of a Cuban film industry), usually with photographs of stars or interviews with visiting actors, pandering to the appetite for glamour.

One new development was the appearance of radio, and especially radio drama or the *radionovela*, confirming the gradual replacement of live theatre by

American cinema or radio, indicated by an article on the new Teatro Sintético del Aire (XXIII, 5: 65).

This more popular tone was reflected in music; the previous focus on classical recitals and news had largely gone (apart from news of Alberto Falcón's appointment to the Escuela Municipal de Música: XXIII, 4: 30), replaced by sheet music for popular Cuban waltzes and tangos, but also including one *son*, and by information about popular orchestras (XXIII, 4: 30). It was also reflected in sport, which was now clearly a priority (with four or five pages each week); now, instead of the old elite activities, sports were firmly middle-class or American. Horseracing, for example, got weekly photographs, and football had Pablo Ferré Elías's weekly column '¡Goal!', clearly aimed at the Spanish community – demonstrated by the Havana team names reported (Deportivo Centro Gallego, Real Iberia, Juventud Asturiana and Catalunya Sport: XXIII, 5: 50) and the Spanish league tables. Boxing also now appeared in the magazine, but largely as photographs of American boxers, which, together with baseball (the curious coverage privileging the American game, with Cuban baseball as a more marginal activity), seemed to imply that popular sporting culture was acceptable only if it was foreign.

Therefore, in 1931, cultural models were obvious. Europe clearly remained the pole for some things (France for the short story, beauty, fashion (as in Mme Andrée Bizet's weekly 'Correspondencia de la Moda'), Britain for aristocratic pastimes and 'society', Spain for some sport) but the United States was overwhelmingly the yardstick for more popular pursuits. It seemed that, since 1921, the Cuban cultural elite, having lost self-confidence, increasingly sought guidance and celebrity abroad. Even an article 'Los Hombres de Mañana' ('Tomorrow's Men': XXIII, 3: 51) displayed photographs of American rather than Cuban children.

March 1941

1941 presents a slight flaw in the selective March methodology, for *Bohemia* dedicated an expanded edition on 23 March to Britain at war, distorting the usual pattern, although the other four weeks still provided useful evidence.

By March 1941, the 'new Cuba' since 1933 was reflected in *Bohemia*'s target readership, more firmly and more comfortably middle-class, evident in the greatly increased advertising (covering several pages), and by advertisements for goods such as horse-feed, indicating a class now more likely to be horse-owners. This class was, however, now even more Americanised, buying American goods (such as Rosenkranz's various teach-yourself courses), following American politics and military activity and sending their sons to US military academies; on 30 March there was a page of photographs of returning pupils from Riverside Academy (33, 13: 39). *Bohemia* too now imported translated American articles and regularly carried 'La Marcha del Tiempo' ('The March of Time'), a column of extracts from *Time* magazine, but also copied American magazine models, with 'agony pages' –

'Lo que nos trae el Correo' ('What the Postbag Brings Us') and 'Confesionario del Amor' – sewing and crochet patterns, and a taste for sensationalism and titillation, with articles on a five-year old Peruvian mother, on the asteroid threat and on trepanning. Although football coverage had disappeared, remnants of the old pro-Spanish preferences remained in articles on Alfonso XIII (33, 10: 42–3) and Spanish flamenco in New York (33, 10: 66–7).

Curiously, however, the 1941 focus partly echoed 1921, with social events reported from places such as the Casino Español and the Club Náutico de Marianao, and the *Carnaval* photographs being taken in the Liceo de Jovellanos and the Liceo del Perico, indicating a wealthier middle class. This class also seemed to be targeted in sport, with René Molina's weekly column on basketball (then largely played in private schools), while baseball still only appeared once, in a short article on the New York Yankees, and with no other hint that Cubans were playing and following baseball passionately.

In culture, the magazine had curiously changed its focus to a more 'up-market' direction; instead of 1921's 'establishment' culture or 1931's 'downmarket' focus, *Bohemia* was now seemingly more aware of cultural fashion, with signs of modernist and *vanguardista* tastes. Poetry, for example, reappeared, in the form of a full Lorca poem (33, 9: 19), a Ramón Rubiera poem to a British soldier (33, 12: 41), and 'celebrity' photographs of two Cuban poets, Esther Costales and Mary Mirandeyra. The visual arts, too, received more attention, with reproduced Catalan paintings from a current exhibition (33, 9: 44), with 'Arte Fotográfica' recognising photography as an art form (33, 9: 45), and with news of the Salón de Bellas Artes Gold Medal for Pintura Decorativa for the Cuban Carlos Fernández, three of whose paintings were reproduced (33, 10: 35).

There was also a curious reference to the European fashion for primitivism, in Antonio Ortega's 'Las Comparsas' (33, 10: 38–9), which, mimicking European stereotypes of Cuba, with its caricatured graphics of black dancers and drummers and its steamy and mysterious account of an Afro-Cuban club, showed some awareness of a Cuba outside the moneyed white circles of *Bohemia*'s readership. This demand for the sensational and exotic was also conveyed in the serialisation of a Sax Rohmer Fu Manchu story.

If the magazine was shifting towards *vanguardismo* in some respects, however, its continuing fascination with the still dominant short story did not reflect that, for once again (despite many Cuban writers being available) there were no Cuban stories at all, although Lino Novás Calvo had an article in the edition on Britain. Instead, the stories published were French (four), American (two) and English (two), and again (apart from the English 'classics' in the special edition) still following the fashion for sensation, crime and romance.

As for popular culture, this now clearly meant cinema and radio. The treatment of cinema again focused on Hollywood, with glamorous pictures of stars (one

Cuban) and gossip (33, 13: 14–15), but radio now received more attention than cinema and had evidently replaced theatre in the magazine. Coverage of radio now included an interview with the Cuban radio singer Hortensia Coalla, just returned from a Latin American tour (33, 10: 36–7), and interviews with well-known Cuban radio actors (33, 9: 36–7; 33, 13: 27) and with a Cuban radio guitarist (33, 11: 32–3), and news of a new radio theatre company (33, 10: 36–7).

March 1951

Ten years later *Bohemia*'s target was still evidently the Havana middle class, although with signs that it was beginning to look further down the social scale, notably in a vastly increased advertising (in a regular 150–page edition) now directed at a market for small household goods, cosmetics, clothing and food (often American), and, with regular features on cookery – Adriana Loredo's 'El Menú de la Semana' ('The Week's Menu'), at a new breed of American-style housewife. However, the full-page property advertisements indicated a greater disposable income among a readership with ambitions for personal improvement and social advancement.

Only in sport did the 1951 *Bohemia* go beyond this middle class. With coverage still of middle-class sports, such as athletics, *frontón* and *jai alai* (43, 12: 98–104), baseball now figured more prominently in three of the four weeks, and boxing had two references. This was also borne out by the absence of religion: only the Easter issue dealt with it, in a strangely sentimental, and even prurient, manner, with sickly representations of Christ's passion and crucifixion on the cover and one inside page (43, 12: 3), and with 'Figuras de la Pasión', photographs of posed scenes from the Passion, including one sensual-looking Mary Magdalen, with the caption: 'Belleza, tentación, poder diabólico' ('Beauty, temptation, devilish power': 43, 12: 52).

Although *Bohemia* now included a significantly more political focus, on only two occasions did it refer to Cuba's relationship with the United States: on the Cuban Telephone Company monopoly (43, 11: 38–9), and an article by Herminio Portell Vilá on US oil concessions in Cuba (43, 9: 23–4), although an article he also penned on political corruption dealt not with Cuba (the obvious target) but the United States (43, 11: 20–1). Yet the weight of the United States was palpable in familiar ways. Firstly, it was evident in the advertising of American products and companies. Secondly, it was evident in the syndicated articles: apart from the continuing 'Marcha del Tiempo' section, March 1951 included a Herman Volk article on American ghosts (43, 9: 26–7) and sensationalist stories that were either imported or copied the American model – 'Los grandes criminales del siglo' (43, 10: 10–12), 'La vida íntima de Jesse James' (43, 12: 21–2) – a piece on Empress Maria Teresa (43, 11: 10–11), and 'believe-it-or-not' stories. It was also evident in the format, for the magazine now copied American models explicitly, with the weekly columns 'Así va la ciencia' ('This is Science'), Miguel Angel Martín's 'Gotas de saber' ('Drops of Knowledge'), 'Siguiendo al mundo' ('Following the World'), 'Agilidad Mental', 'En Cuba', 'Lo gráfico' and Guido García Inclán's 'En la Feria de la Actualidad' ('The Market of Current Affairs'), all full of news snippets, while 'En pocas palabras' gave largely US news and Jorge L. Martín's 'Comentario Internacional' reported on Latin America.

What then of culture? While members of the cultural elite wrote some of the leading articles (for example, Félix Pichardo Moya, Portell Vilá, Ichaso and Mañach), March 1951 included little other than short stories in the way of cultural products. Moreover, as before, these were mostly foreign crime stories, as with those by Rohmer (43, 9: 6–8; 43, 12: 30), Jack London (43, 10: 24–5), André Paul Duchateau (43, 11: 30), J.S. Fletcher (43, 11: 36–7) and Maurice Level (43, 12: 48–9). There was only one Cuban story, by Gerardo del Valle (43, 10: 30–1), again relegated to the later pages. Beyond this, 'culture' usually meant cultural news or articles about foreign artists, as in the regular sections 'La Farándula Pasa' and 'Teleradiolandia'; the former dealt mostly with film news and gossip, mixing items on American Hollywood stars with photographs of Cuban stars (such as the actor Estelita Rodríguez or the baritone Enrique Vila), although one issue included graphic representation of Cuban ballet (43, 11: 82), and the latter was devoted to radio and television news, copying the 'Farándula' approach, with short articles on the popular singer Joseíto Fernández, photographs of an exotic Tahitian dancer or the cast of the 'Gran Teatro Radial' (43, 9: 52–6). Beyond this, there were references to cultural activities and cultural 'stars', as in the pictures of Lecuona (43, 9: 60–2), or, in the regular history section 'Poblaciones Cubanas', pictures of the Roldán Quartet of the 1930s or the nineteenth-century Cuban poet Sofia Estévez (43, 9: 141–2). Any longer or more serious articles were reserved for non-Cuban artists and writers, such as Indalecio Prieto's piece on Vicente Blasco Ibáñez (43, 12: 40–1), a syndicated American article on Sibelius (43, 10: 3), and an Ambrosio Fornet article on, and interview with, the visiting Stravinsky (43, 11: 46–7). The message seemed to be that *Bohemia*'s readers preferred to treat Cuban culture in terms of celebrity at best, but foreign culture somewhat more seriously.

Conclusions

The most obvious conclusion from this analysis is that *Bohemia*, throughout, reflected the attitudes, aspirations and tastes of the social elite of each period. While, in 1911, this elite was somewhat equated with the cultural elite, ten years later there seemed to be two separate cultural entities, a cultural elite and an emerging *vanguardia*; the latter seemed more visible by 1931, as the elite's power and influence declined – commensurate with the political and social elite's declining concern with culture. By 1941, there was even less evidence of either, as

Bohemia's readership and tone were more materialist, 'Americanised' and middle-class, defining culture in ways unimaginable in 1911.

Culture clearly meant different things at the five different stages. In 1911, it was narrowly and traditionally defined, according to established European criteria and the tastes of the Europeanising elite. Only theatre (and perhaps music) seemed to aspire to popularity in the taste for light musical entertainment rather than drama, continuing a long Cuban tradition. By 1921, culture had become something broader, beyond elite tastes; there were hints of an avant-garde and of a desire to be au fait with European aesthetic fashions. Theatre had clearly begun to decline both in popularity and as an art form, while the first hints of popular culture gaining prestige were evident in cinema, although this was then considered as both art and popular entertainment. By 1931, the separation of the cultural and social elites meant a more materialistic definition of culture, defined by a middle class that aspired to elite status and sought to consume culture as a commodity, especially the short story and the cinema, whose attraction was now mostly in its glamour. By 1941 and certainly by 1951, that pattern had become firmly established, with little substantial change from the 1930s, but with the weight of American influence ever more evident.

This therefore raises the question of cultural identity, in seeing culture as expressive of a Cuban identity and as identifiable with 'the people'. From this selective examination, the evidence seem to indicate that, while culture was initially defined by the elite in narrow, traditional and European terms, the 'popular' never entering their vision, by 1941 the new elite had dropped its mimicking of European fashion and had begun to aspire to increasingly commercialised American cultural tastes, 'popularising' culture by removing any concern for aesthetics. At no stage did this elite consider genuinely popular Cuban culture (dance, song or sport) as something to be taken seriously, as desirable or as identifiable with 'Cuba'; certainly, only briefly was there any sense that 'a Cuban culture' might take new directions.

A further recurrent piece of evidence is the clear preference for Havana, for, however vibrant the cultural activity in Matanzas, Las Villas, Manzanillo or Santiago, this was not evident in *Bohemia*, confirming the pattern of Havana as the locus for an externally oriented search for cultural identity, with efforts to define and produce a more 'Cuban' culture being forced into the periphery or abroad. In fact, the evidence seems to be that, after the 1920s, a Cuban cultural identity was neither the preoccupation of, nor associated with, the hegemonic Havana policy-formers who, instead, followed others' fashions, becoming consciously a conduit for non-Cuban cultural definitions to enter Cuba. Hence, if the Havana cultural elite sought protagonism in anything, it was not in defining and defending a Cuban identity but in being recognised outside as cultured and in bringing external criteria to the attention of Cubans. Whatever moves towards cultural identity were being made within the *vanguardia*, they were not yet taken up by the elite, and whatever popular forms were preferred by most Cubans had not yet acquired sufficient prestige to become the basis of any coherent 'Cuban cultural identity'.

Hence, *Bohemia* seems to have been reflecting the cultural elite's gate-keeping intentions, since, with an ever-increased readership and with considerable prestige, it can be assumed to have shaped tastes and attitudes as much as it responded to them. If certain forms seemed privileged in its pages and other forms neglected, that corresponds to what the cultural gate-keepers wished at any given time; that this was less clear-cut by the 1950s simply reflects the fact that by then the elite's hegemony within the Havana community was less clear-cut.

Notes

1. This repression especially resulted in the death of Antonio Guiteras, the popular and radical nationalist Interior Minister in Grau's government, who had formed an action group Joven Cuba in 1934 to challenge Batista from the left.
2. In 1900, the Uruguayan Enrique Rodó published his essay *Ariel*; with its message of rejection of Northern materialism and exaltation of the region's 'Latin-ness', this had a deep influence on Latin America's educated youth.
3. The Institución was variously Hispano-Cubana and Hispanocubana.
4. The Grupo *Clarté* had been founded in 1919 by Lauro Rayas Bazán and Enrique Lluria, modelled on Barbusse's Parisian group and meeting mostly clandestinely (because of their pro-Soviet views), dissolving itself in 1921 to fuse with the Martí *tertuliantes* (Cairo 1978: 36), in particular bringing Luis Gómez Wangüemert and Luis A. Baralt into the emerging grouping.
5. These especially included Rafael Esténger, Guillermo Martínez Márquez, Alberto Lamar Schweyer, Miguel Angel Limia, Arturo Alfonso Roselló, Regino Pedroso, Ramón Rubiera and Juan Marinello (Núñez Machín 1974: 72, 74). After the merger with *Clarté*, the group was joined by Roig, Lizaso, Francisco Ichaso, José Manuel Acosta, Tallet, Calixto Masó, Primitivo Cordero Leira and Mañach.
6. Those involved were Martínez Villena, Mañach, Marinello, Ichaso, Lizaso, Acosta, Tallet, Fernández de Castro, Primitivo Cordeiro Leiva, Lamar Schweyer, Gómez Wangüemert, Masó and García Pedrosa.
7. After the 1933 revolution, Mañach served as Education Minister under Batista's protégé Mendieta and then Batista himself (1944).
8. I am grateful here to the ongoing work of University of Wolverhampton doctoral student Jill Ingham.

–3–

The Revolution from 1959 to 1990

Historical Overview

The first three decades of the Revolution saw a complex and often contradictory process of change that was, overall, characterised by four things: a rapid and continual (if somewhat chequered and occasionally interrupted) revolutionary transformation; a search for paths to, and definitions of, a new form of appropriate and independent development; recurrent cycles of crisis, debate and certainty; and the gradual discovery of a new form of revolutionary national identity, *cubanía revolucionaria* (Kapcia 2000: 125 *passim*).

The first burst of radicalisation lasted approximately nine years, once the initial uncertainties were clarified by mid-1961. Until then, the Revolution was characterised by political confusion, ideological discovery and economic disruption, all underpinned by an ever-deepening process of radical social change, partly directed from above but mostly generating its own empirical momentum on the ground. The confusion owed as much to the initial revolutionary alliance as to the uncertainties of the leading political actors and the external context; from early on, the broad anti-Batista unity began to fragment in the face of increasing US opposition (to what it saw as an incomprehensible and possibly Communist-influenced challenge) and of a radicalisation of perspectives among elements of the new leadership and a radicalisation of demands in a population increasingly enrolled in, and empowered through, the various tasks of defence and socio-economic revolution. Defence especially consisted of the seminal Committees for the Defence of the Revolution (CDR), set up after September 1960 to prepare for the coming US-backed exile invasion, and also the civilian militias which armed and enlisted thousands of mostly young Cubans in a politically transforming experience. Socio-economic revolution especially consisted of a string of radicalising mobilisation campaigns, such as the regular mobilisations for *trabajo voluntario* (voluntary labour) especially for each year's sugar harvest (*zafra*), but especially in the defining 1961 Literacy Campaign. This episode transformed Cuba's political and cultural landscape and also all those who participated, by enrolling thousands of mostly young urban Cubans as educators (*brigadistas alfabetizadores*) and bringing life-changing and empowering benefits to many thousands more, especially in the *campo*.

As social benefits (especially in housing, education and racial equality) increasingly accrued to a hitherto unequal and disunited population, the daily experience of improvement and revolution rallied popular support behind the ever more radical vanguard of the 26 July Movement. Their political resolve was in turn by now backed by the PSP, which, in a move that cemented many aspects of the Revolution, gave unconditional support to the rebel leaders. However, inevitably, that same process increasingly alarmed those in the elite and the middle class who had expected little or no deep change, but at best a cleaner version of the old politics. As a pro-US, liberal or social democratic alternative to the Movimiento's definition of revolution began to lose authority, the internal and external battle lines began to be drawn.

The principal factor in this cleavage was, increasingly, the divergence between an uncompromising political vanguard – radicalised by its guerrilla experience – and an uncomprehending, suspicious and more hostile Washington. In April 1959, during Castro's goodwill visit to New York, US Vice President Nixon met him, and immediately authorised the CIA secretly to train an invasion force of former *batistianos* and disenchanted elements – henceforth a source of concern and anger to Havana, fully aware of the plans. Ultimately, it was the Cubans' search for economic independence – specifically, the search for new markets, resulting in a small, but significant, sugar-for-oil swap with the USSR in February 1960 – that triggered the final unravelling of US-Cuban relations, as a series of reciprocal measures (starting with the US oil companies' refusal to refine Soviet oil) saw Havana expropriate US property and Washington progressively cut the sugar quota. The culmination was the first, partial, trade embargo of autumn 1960 and the breaking of formal relations in January 1961, the moment which really began the 'siege' of the Revolution.

By this stage, however, the revolution had radicalised itself irrevocably, not least as the initial economic strategy (largely a mixed-economy development model of industrialisation, diversification, land reform and social welfare) failed in the absence of capital, leading Havana to turn to Moscow for aid, advice and trade. In April 1961, after the US-backed invasion had been soundly repelled at the Bay of Pigs (Playa Girón), not least by the efforts of the CDRs and militias, the whole process proceeded to radicalise even further. The three main forces in the rebel alliance – the Movimiento, the PSP and a small guerrilla group, the DRE (Directorio Revolucionario Estudiantil) – were first fused into one single organisation, Organizaciones Revolucionarias Integradas (ORI). Meantime, the economic move towards Moscow produced its own effects, shifting the original strategy in a more collectivist, centralising and state-owning direction, especially witnessed in the politically vital sector of agriculture. The May 1959 land reform (which had provoked much liberal and US criticism) had actually been relatively moderate and reformist, attacking only the excesses of ownership, but the subsequent momentum of expanding participation, increasing demands and radicalising perspectives saw the land reform agency, INRA, become the principal arm of social as well as economic revolution in the *campo*, culminating in the 1963 reform, which drastically reduced the maximum landholding (to sixty-seven hectares) and effectively put some 60 per cent of Cuban land in state hands, mostly in state farms (*granjas del pueblo*). However, economic difficulties deepened, especially given the vain drive for over-rapid industrialisation to escape the 'curse' of sugar dependency, the costs of rapid social revolution and the effects of the full US embargo, formalised in 1963.

By 1963, however, Cuban-Soviet relations had begun to deteriorate, exacerbated by the Soviet climb-down in the October 1962 Missile Crisis (the Crisis del Caribe), which left the Cubans feeling abandoned and marginalised. This coincided with internal tensions, between the Movimiento (now disbanded but still forming the bulk of the Ejército Rebelde/Fuerzas Armadas Revolucionarias, the FAR) and the PSP; based on old antagonisms and on generational, as well as ideological, differences, these sharpened in 1962 when Aníbal Escalante, the PSP activist charged with organising the ORI, was criticised and punished for abusing his position to give the PSP an excessive influence in the body. The PSP were then relegated within the political hierarchy, and a new, guerrilla-dominated organisation, the Unified Party of the Socialist Revolution (PURS), was established.

These crises now led to a fascinating period of open, encouraged debate, as the political vanguard took stock, reacting to disappointments and also using the space provided by US assurances (not to invade) resulting from the Soviet-US settlement in October 1962. This debate was above all formalised in the public 'Great Debate' over a revolutionary development strategy (1963–5), but was also reflected elsewhere in the cautious moves to adjust and reconsider, after the hectic rush of 1959–63. By 1965, the new direction was confirmed (not least towards the *campo*, the peasant and 'ruralism') and a renewed period of intense radicalisation began.

In the economy, this meant two things. Firstly, it meant a drive towards what was called the 'moral economy', a Guevara-influenced attempt to achieve communism as rapidly as possible, rejecting Soviet models, moving away from material and capitalist mechanisms towards an increasingly 'voluntarist', mobilising organisation of labour, and driven by revolutionary consciousness, embodied by the symbol and model of the 'New Cuban Man'. Secondly, the immediate goal of this strategy was the drive to produce ten million tons of sugar in 1970, to be the launching pad for a truly independent development and definition.

In politics, this meant, domestically, replacing the PURS by the still guerrilla-led Cuban Communist Party (the PCC), but its definition of 'communism' was clearly Cuban rather than Soviet, and real grass roots power actually resided not in the Party but, rather, in entities like the CDRs, INRA and the FAR, and accompanied, as any tendencies towards institutionalisation were resisted in an ever more mobilising political style, by a 'guerrilla mentality'. Abroad, this new radicalism was seen in the strategy of encouraging (through training, finance, personnel and logistical support) armed insurrection in Latin America – a means of breaking the isolation but also of challenging both US 'imperialism' and Soviet complicity in 'peaceful coexistence'. It was this strategy that saw Che Guevara leave Cuba in 1965, to lead guerrilla struggles in Africa and then, fatally, in Bolivia in 1966–7. As a result, by 1968, Cuba seemed to epitomise a concept of 'total revolution' – with an unorthodox economy (taken even further in March 1968 by the Revolutionary Offensive, which nationalised the remaining 55,000 non-agricultural enterprises), an anti-institutional and constantly mobilising political system, and a collective sense of being an embattled enclave, besieged by the USA and challenging Moscow (although still trading with the Socialist countries). This was when the post-1960 'siege mentality' was at its clearest, epitomised when Escalante was again disgraced, in 1968, for apparently trying to shift the Revolution back towards orthodoxy and the USSR.

Meantime, the social changes had continued apace, helped especially by the exodus by 1969 of some 400,000 Cubans, mostly white and middle class (Olson and Olson 1995: 63), an exodus that helped fortify the sense of siege and unity, but also helped equalise socially (as their former property was redistributed to solve housing and educational shortages), but which had a cost. Economically, it drained valuable expertise which had to replaced expensively (especially in health, education and technology), while politically it formed a powerful bloc in the United States, especially in Florida, with access to policy-making circles and wielding an electoral influence capable of ossifying US policies towards Cuba for decades to come.

The whole period of radical change, however, ground to an embarrassing halt in 1970 when the much-vaunted *zafra* fell short of its target, in the process disrupting the whole economy and threatening to undermine the legitimacy of the system and leadership among a population whose morale had already been damaged by the shortages, pressures and demands of the preceding years and by the loss of Che. This potential alienation was generally evident in growing absenteeism and falling productivity, but could also be seen in the tensions within the cultural world and the vanguard.

Once again, as in 1962–5, these crises generated a debate and another stock-taking at the top, but this time with Moscow entering the discussions as it agreed to bail out the failed economy. Inevitably, the result was that the radical experimentation of the preceding seven years was abandoned and a series of reforms between 1972 and 1976 set the process on a course of necessary consolidation along more orthodox lines. Economically, strategies were coordinated with the other socialist countries (Cuba joining the CMEA, the Council for Mutual Economic Assistance, in 1972), and greater emphasis was placed on efficiency (rather than need), on decentralisation and on material (rather than 'moral') incentives, resulting in something of a consumer boom, soaking up higher wages by acquiring Comecon-imported goods. Politically, mobilisation was not abandoned but was certainly slowed down, and political institutions took over from the old participation mechanisms as the preferred and characteristic forms of representation.

In particular, a new Soviet-style pyramidal structure, People's Power (Poder Popular), was set up in 1976, bolstered by the Revolution's first Constitution in the same year. Also, the Party – somewhat dormant since its creation – had its first Congress (1975), was greatly expanded, and became increasingly influenced by the former PSP leaders and activists, supported now by a new generation of Soviet-trained 'technocrats'.

The only 1960s element that seemed to resist this 'institutionalisation' was Cuba's foreign policy. Although the new orthodoxy saw a rapprochement with Moscow (Cuba ceasing its public criticisms and no longer challenging Soviet ideas) and also, surprisingly, a degree of détente with Washington (especially under President Carter, who set up limited mutual recognition via Interest Sections in Havana and Washington), in the Third World Havana seemed to continue its commitment to *conciencia revolucionaria*. Shifting attention from a less promising theatre of revolution in Latin America (where leftist challenges had given way to reformism and then, gradually, to military dictatorship), Havana now began a coherent and sustained strategy of 'internationalism', seeking to lead the Third World politically (with alliances with new radical governments in the Caribbean, Central America and Africa) and even militarily, as Cuban troops successfully defended Angola against South African invasion (1975–89) and Ethiopia against the Somalis (1977–80). Thus, Cuba seemed still to be flying the revolutionary flag abroad if not at home, while the engagement with Africa helped reawaken a long dormant interest in Cuba's African roots, now expressed as both a cultural movement towards Afro-Cuban forms and traditions and a political opening to *santería*.

However much the Revolution might have seemed to abandon revolution at home, however, institutionalisation was popular, as the 1960s pressures disappeared, living standards rose, life became more materially comfortable, and the social revolution began to bite deeply and permanently. Health reforms, in particular, now began to take concrete shape, as the 1960s investments began to pay off, and new developments were seen in a much expanded education system (more geared to technocracy than participation) and in something of a cultural boom. Certainly, by 1989, Cuba (which, in 1958, had counted only a hundred libraries, six museums, and fewer than one million books published annually) could boast some 2,000 libraries, 250 museums, and 50 million books annually (Levinson 1989: 488).

However, institutionalisation had a political cost, for the combination of an expanded and inevitably more bureaucratised Party with a greater focus on materialism meant fundamental changes within a political structure that, for all its faults, had never been characterised by problems of privilege and corruption. Indeed, in the 1960s, the problem had been one of a mediocrity of equality rather than a case of austerity for the many and privileges for the few. Now, however, a new problem began to appear, as Party membership for the first time conferred economic status and access to privilege, within a system that was more inert and self-satisfying than before. This generated its own frustrations and complaints, although Cubans were generally materially better off than at any time since 1959; these tensions emerged especially in 1980, when a mass occupation of the Peruvian embassy by visa-seekers led to turbulent counter-protests and, finally, to the government's permission for the disaffected to leave via the port of Mariel. The result was the largest exodus since the early 1960s, as 124,779 Cubans, their numbers swelled by released prisoners (up to 26,000 had criminal records of some sort), made their way from Mariel to the United States in five months (Olson and Olson 1995: 81). As on earlier occasions, the 'safety valve' of emigration had been brought into play to relieve tensions, but the underlying grievances remained. Hence, when, after 1985, the impact of Gorbachev's reform process in the USSR began to felt in Cuba – through Soviet proselytising in the imported press, through pro-Gorbachev elements in the Party hoping to unseat Castro or, above all, through the decision to put Cuban-Soviet economic relations on a commercial footing after 1989 – the threat to the system began to seem considerable.

Once again, therefore, crisis generated debate; in 1986, the Party Congress was preceded and characterised by a long and fierce debate that finally enshrined 'Rectification' ('of Past Errors and Negative Tendencies') as the new strategy, although in fact its characteristics – political 'cleansing' of the problem elements within the Party and economic streamlining through management reforms, to prepare for the coming shock of new, less beneficial, relations with the USSR and in recognition of a deepening crisis in Comecon – were already evident in 1984. What the new process now also meant, however, was something of a rescue of the 1960s: blaming the USSR and pro-Soviet elements for many of the political failings of the 'grey' years, the leadership – still under Castro and many of the former guerrillas – now encouraged Cubans to look back to the first decade for models, inspirations, and even ideas (as Che Guevara's works were revived, for example), and also began to talk more of 'nation' and Cuba's pre-1959 past than of more orthodox definitions of 'communism'.

This now confirmed some trends of the preceding decades of revolutionary change. For, while one should of course look at the 1959–89 experience as one of dramatic social and political revolution, oriented towards varying definitions of 'socialism' and 'communism' and governed by an explicitly Marxist ideology of change, the fact is that that same process was also a search for the elusive 'national identity'. After all, the same revolution that had sprung, in 1958, from the frustrations of many decades of the search for a genuinely independent *Cuba Libre* and from a growing, if disoriented, tradition of *cubanía rebelde*, was never likely to abandon that goal and subsume the national preoccupation into a supposedly internationalist project. The different tensions with Washington and the Soviet Union, the erratic strategies for economic development, many of the internal tensions in the leadership and even between the cultural world and the political vanguard were signs of something other than personal ambition, political challenge or circumstantial crisis and pressure.

In fact, over those three decades, despite (or perhaps because of) the seeming oscillations of policy, strategy and alliance, one thing had become clear: that the old search for national identity had become increasingly identified with something called 'the Revolution'. The idea had evolved, empirically rather than through a process of conscious debate, that Cuba's historical destiny of *Cuba Libre* was in fact essentially a revolutionary one, and that *Patria* now meant *Revolución*. What this therefore also meant was that the long-standing and evolving dichotomy between 'outwardly oriented' perspectives of *Cuba Libre* and the 'inwardly oriented' perspectives had now been given a new impetus and direction. While at certain moments and in certain periods it seemed that the former perspective was in the ascendancy (for example, 1961–3, 1975–85, when imported Soviet models were preferred), the latter – more inherently nationalist in its origins and emotional identification – seemed to dominate at other critical moments, such as 1959–60, 1965–70, and from 1986 onwards. Indeed, as the Revolution approached its fourth decade, it seemed to have reached a point of ideological confidence and certainty in this respect, recognising that survival had demonstrated the truth of the latter, 'inward', paradigm; indeed, if the 1960s strategy had effectively been based on the belief that, with Cuba under siege and alone, its only reliable resources were its land and its people (both of which should therefore be the objects of investment and attention), that same realisation was again beginning to dawn in the late 1980s, only this time attributing success and development, rather than embattled survival, to that focus.

Part I: Dark Days and Revolutionary Enlightenment (1959–71)

Transformation of the City
From 1959, Havana's economic life changed irrevocably. One of the most dramatic changes was the collapse of tourism (as a major currency-earner and job-creator), visitors falling from 179,752 in 1959 to 4,180 in 1961 (Villalba Garrido 1993:

164), rising again to 8,400 in 1974 (Segre et al. 1997: 266). Industrialisation was also dramatic, new factories appearing, often without regard to the environmental effects on nearby housing, especially in Habana del Este and La Lisa, a problem exacerbated with the shift of focus to the *campo*. Equally, the disappearance of the private sector changed retailing, as American-owned enterprises were closed or nationalised, followed by Cuban-owned businesses (including the Encanto) and culminating in the 1968 Revolutionary Offensive, which, taking over the traditional corner shops (the *tencéns*) and the few remaining private bars and restaurants, left *habaneros* with only the ration-book *bodegas* for food supplies and boosted a black economy that kept Havana's economic heart beating. Even new construction affected the *campo* more, apart from the large Havana projects (for schools, hospitals and civic buildings) or specialist-built rehousing projects. Certainly, by 1970, Havana seemed an empty shell, compared to its 1958 character, the ravages of time and salt air being increasingly unchecked and older housing beginning a process of decay. Consequently, Havana stopped growing exponentially, reversing its old characteristic primacy.

Political life also changed fundamentally. While peasants enjoyed a new political involvement, increasing centralisation meant the growth of a Havana-based state apparatus and a boom in state employment, converting the old Plaza Cívica area into the Plaza de la Revolución, the Revolution's political centre of gravity and prime public political space. Hence, all the 1960s crises occurred in Havana: the split with the 'liberals', the 26 July Movement–PSP tensions, and the ideological and political battles at the university: Armas, Cairo and Torres-Cuevas 1984: 643–9). Indeed, apart from the Sierra Escambray peasants, most opposition to the Revolution was initially based in Havana, where the middle class and the Catholic Church were strongest; indeed Havana's other image was as the last refuge of the *ancien régime*, either plotting or attempting to leave, making the city again 'the problem' in radicals' eyes, all confirmed by the fact that Havana was where the CDRs, in April 1961, detained most potential collaborators with the invasion.

In fact, the rise of the CDRs reflected political change: as the middle class left, political activism shifted to Havana's *barrios*, the areas most affected by militia mobilisations or the Literacy Campaign (although most *alfabetizadores* came from the more comfortable areas). The October 1962 crisis also focused on Havana more than anywhere, creating a sense of siege and doom, but also of unity and defiance, while, even after the Revolution's 'agrarianism' from 1963, Havana was still where volunteers were recruited for *zafras* or other campaigns. However, the new post-1966 Poder Local system of representation mattered less in Havana than in the *campo*.[1]

Yet, initially, Havana saw enormous benefits, especially with the 1959–60 Urban Reform Laws, which redistributed income by halving rents (March 1959), regulated land use, fixed low prices and ended speculation (December 1959) and then transferred all housing titles to tenants (October 1960), making Havana one of Latin America's greatest concentrations of owner-occupation. Simultaneously, Havana's shanties (especially Hega y Pon, Las Yaguas and La Cueva del Humo) and worst slums were eliminated, and many of the poor were rehoused in new complexes (Perla, Martí and Zamora) and in new prefabricated developments in Habana del Este (Bahía, Guiteras, Alamar), Boyeros, Cotorro and La Lisa (Segre et al. 1997: 131). Indeed, unlike before 1958, Havana now developed eastwards (Torrents 1989: 113). Meantime, the poor (often black or *mulato*) also moved into vacated bourgeois properties in Vedado and similar areas, transforming them socially and further alarming the already threatened middle-class residents.

However, urban planning was affected by skill shortages, as Havana's architects left (Torrents 1989: 129), leading to ad hoc developments that answered urgent problems but often paid little attention to the quality of life, such developments often becoming a rather soul-less 'Alphaville socialista' (Torrents 1989: 131). The Revolutionary Offensive then exacerbated this by converting inappropriate commercial premises into housing. Hence, what was hitherto architecturally eclectic now became chaotic and characterless, larger projects often being functional but ugly, arising from 'el conflicto entre estética, ideología y tecnología' ('the conflict between aesthetics, ideology and technology': Torrents 1989: 133), although the 1970s Instituto Superior de Arte (at the old elite Country Club), designed by the Italians Roberto Gottardi and Vittorio Garatti and the Cuban Ricardo Porro until construction was halted in 1965, was truly imaginative.

Havana's social fabric also therefore changed fundamentally, especially with the changes in residential patterns. Indeed, besides the white middle class leaving, Havana's Chinese community also largely emigrated, thereby dismantling one of Latin America's most vibrant Chinese communities, while the 1960s also saw an increased provincial immigration (until official restrictions after 1964), usually into the new *barrios* of El Romerillo and La Corbata or to the already overcrowded Atarés and La Güinera districts (Segre et al. 1997: 132).

The other notable social changes were the break with pre-1958 patterns of racial discrimination – Havana's beaches being opened to all in April 1959 – and the campaign to eliminate the characteristic prostitution, especially by retraining former prostitutes for respectable and socially useful roles. Havana's public spaces were also transformed politically and socially as new areas opened up, most notably the Coppelia ice-cream parlour by the Rampa, largely appropriated by the young after 11 p.m.

Less visibly, the Catholic Church also changed. In particular, the clergy's implication in the Bay of Pigs invasion (followed by a September 1961 incident) led to hundreds of (mostly Spanish) clergy being deported (Azicri 2000: 252).[2] The remaining Church retrenched, its spiritual space among Havana's poor being occupied by *santería* and its buildings falling into disrepair, and, in 1969 (ostensibly because of the demands of the *zafra*), Christmas celebrations were suspended (ultimately restored in 1996).

The Evolution of a Havana Culture

The Revolution changed Havana so much that, for culture, nothing in the past served as a guide for the future; 1959 was not simply to be 1902 rewritten, with the patronage system broken, wealth no longer determining power, patterns of social distinction being disrupted, and the relationship with the United States (the traditional model) breaking down irretrievably, while the experience of reform and empowerment gave *habaneros* new behaviours and expectations, with little deference.

Yet it was inevitable that the Revolution would mean a new culture, since, if the post-1902 period had heralded cultural nation-building, then the Revolution would inevitably mean cultural rebuilding. However, with the old institutions, patrons and spaces irrelevant, any 'new' culture would respond to different expectations: of a government with ever clearer views on the role of culture, of a society being transformed daily, and of a cultural community lacking clear parameters for operation and definition of its role. Indeed, that community was itself problematic, especially in its heterogeneity. For it combined the remnants of the old establishment who chose to remain and adapt (often with difficulty) or to wait until emigration became possible, the pre-1958 political activists with definite ideas about their role and the nature of a new culture, and the many who had returned from self-imposed exile in Europe, Latin America or the United States, enthusiastic but with different experiences, models and patterns of thinking.

For the government, the importance of culture was clear, having figured large in the rebels' manifestos since 1953 and being evident in its early moves, including Che Guevara's foundation of a cultural school in the Cabaña fortress (under Armando Acosta and three radical film-makers, Alvarez, García Espinosa and Massip) and Camilo Cienfuegos's leadership of the Rebel Army's Dirección Cultural (Chanan 1985: 89). However, given the early Revolution's other priorities, precise plans were unclear, partly because the political leadership included no figures with cultural authority; it was thus always likely that any cultural policy would either follow the priorities and perspectives of the political vanguard or emerge organically. Cultural policy as such would thus for some time be somewhat empirical, subordinated to political needs, perspectives and dictates, determined by people who, although sympathetic to the need for a parallel cultural revolution, would make political rather than strictly cultural decisions.

There were, however, some parallels with 1902, most clearly in the conscious creation of a 'new Cuba' by a political vanguard committed to a role for education and a notion of culture as serving the process of nation-building. Furthermore, as before, the existing Havana cultural community was at a low ebb of respect and self-esteem, and many were still abroad. Two important differences, however, were that while, in 1902, cultural influence came from Spain, North American mass culture had now become the model, and, secondly, that the Revolution was characterised by a relative, and even deliberate, lack of institutions, reflecting the constantly changing context.

Hence, the only institutions to guide the cultural community for the first two years were either educational or politically oriented. The major official entity to promote culture until 1961 was the Ministry of Education's Dirección de Cultura, which, although lacking resources, had responsibility for two areas: the Biblioteca Nacional (which, under María Teresa Freyre de Andrade and then Aurelio Alonso, became instrumental in all the Revolution's educational initiatives) and the new publishing industry. The latter was reorganised in March 1959 as the Imprenta Nacional (from 1962, the Editorial Nacional, under Carpentier) and, combining the presses of the Ministry, the new Consejo Nacional de Cultura (CNC), the Consejo Superior de Universidades and the Editora Juvenil, became a key instrument for both the educational revolution and the drive for national identity, one of its first undertakings being Martí's *Obras Completas*.

Figure 9 The 1950s modernist façade of the Casa de las Américas building

This vacuum created a special place and importance for two particular cultural institutions, Casa de las Américas and ICAIC. Casa de las Américas was established in an imposing modernist Vedado building by the 26 July Movement leader Haydée Santamaría in April 1959, conceived of then as a 'dinámico centro de alto nivel intelectual que promoviera la cultura viva joven y pugnaz de la América Latina' ('a dynamic centre of high intellectual quality, designed to promote Latin America's living, young and combative cultures': Campuzano 2001: 33), to inform Latin America and Cuba about each other's cultures. However, with no models from which to learn, Casa's empirical development thereafter reflected three processes in the Revolution: its increasing radicalism, its regional purpose and its growing discovery of Cuba's Latin American identity.

As Casa evolved, it became a leading determinant of evolving cultural policies in Cuba and one of Havana's major cultural spaces, establishing new actors and bringing prestige and protection to hitherto marginalised genres and activities, partly filling the role of the disappeared *tertulia*. It also therefore defined directions, boundaries and criteria, not least through its seminal Centro de Investigaciones Literarias, its library and its annual prizes from October 1959 (which, although privileging Latin American rather than Cuban artists, established both Casa and Havana as one of Latin America's prime cultural spaces, bringing a new prestige to the cultural community). Its magazines were also seminal, such as *Conjunto* (for theatre, from 1964), *Boletín de Música* (from 1970), and especially *Casa de las Américas* which, founded in July 1960 and edited till 1965 by Santamaría and prominent Latin American writers (and thereafter by Fernández Retamar), became the Revolution's leading cultural forum.

This highlighted a fact of revolutionary life: that the spaces traditionally offered by magazines and newspapers were also being constantly redefined. Initially, most pre-1959 organs remained, but increasingly problematically as they adopted a more oppositional line, especially *El País*, *El Mundo* and *Diario de la Marina*; the latter's increasingly reactionary stance led to the workforce's regular insertion of dissident pro-Revolutionary *coletillas* (disclaimers) and, in May 1960, to its closure. For radicals, the new demands were less problematic, as with the Directorio's *Combate* and the PSP's *Noticias de Hoy*, although less coherently progressive organs such as *Bohemia* found it more difficult to adapt from anti-Batista opposition to supporting an increasingly radical Revolution which expected the media to serve and which was creating its own organs, most notably the 26 July Movement's *Revolución*, under former PSP activist Carlos Franqui. Hence, *Bohemia*'s pre-1958 editor Quevedo remained in post until his departure from Cuba in 1960, succeeded by the more radical Enrique de la Osa and then Angel Guerra.

Simultaneously, the new environment also removed another pre-1959 feature: the importance of cultural patrons. For, as the Revolution did not replicate the old patrimonial structures, a similar system of cultural patronage could not emerge, especially as the new cultural community's leaders changed continually, with individuals being either left behind, discarded (into self-imposed exile or a marginal existence) or moved to other duties. Moreover, there was no consensus, within either the community or the revolutionary vanguard, about who the cultural 'leaders' should be, the established 'giants' who were returning to Cuba (such as Carpentier, immediately appointed vice-president of the CNC, or Marinello, after 1962 rector of the university) or members of the new generation.

This all created a vacuum and tensions, in which two groups above all represented alternative 'poles' of 'cultural revolution'. One was *Revolución*'s Monday cultural supplement, *Lunes de Revolución*, where Franqui gathered a disparate group of young, rebellious writers, artists and musicians (some having before 1959 been associated with either Nuestro Tiempo or *Ciclón*); having mostly lived abroad before 1959, these responded with unbridled but occasionally unfocused enthusiasm to the new freedom. However, their criteria were by no means clear, other than a desire to rebel against their elders (especially against a perceived suffocation by the *Orígenes* generation, against whom they unleashed fierce and often personal criticism) and a didactic commitment to bringing Cuba up to date with the latest cultural ideas and movements, an explicit aim to be a 'formidable instrumento de actualización de la cultura cubana' ('formidable means of bringing Cuban culture up to date': Otero 1999: 76), modelled on the 1920s Spanish *Revista de Occidente*.

Lunes was important for two reasons. Firstly, it grouped together this dynamic younger generation of individuals who saw themselves as the Revolution's cultural arbiters and 'first generation'. Secondly, since *Revolución* was (by its association with the rebels and the changes) the popular newspaper, *Lunes* gave an unprecedented opportunity to spread the cultural word to a captive and eager audience, and thus became the early Revolution's leading cultural organ, doing more than most to set a new cultural tone; indeed, it was the first Latin American literary magazine with a circulation of some 200,000 (Cabrera Infante 1994: 64). It also became a leading space, its offices operating like a *tertulia* for like-minded individuals. Under Guillermo Cabrera Infante and Pablo Armando Fernández from September 1959, it developed a particular focus, devoting whole issues to the cultures of less familiar Third World and Socialist Bloc countries and also publishing new Cuban writers. *Lunes* also sponsored regular peak-time television programmes on culture – 'Lunes en Televisión' – and a publishing house, Ediciones R, whose first book was José Baragaño's *Poesía, Revolución del Ser* (Cabrera Infante 1994: 66).

There were, however, inevitable problems. Firstly, the group's heterogeneity soon began to conflict with the radicalising tenor of the political environment. Secondly, the individuals' alienated experience before 1959 had led to a collective tendency to see the writer as critical conscience rather than the servant which the

Revolution was beginning to demand; some found it increasingly difficult to adjust and then proceeded to leave Cuba (most publicly, Guillermo Cabrera Infante in 1965). Thirdly, their focus was less on Cuban culture (as Cuba's leaders and many Cubans increasingly expected) but more on educating Cubans in world culture; this was evident from the contents of the magazine's many issues, which saw relatively few Cuban authors published, until March 1961 when, perhaps aware of the impending crisis and celebrating the magazine's hundredth issue, all the authors were new Cuban writers of the *Lunes* generation and group. Finally, their assumption of the role of cultural arbiters was increasingly challenged by the political leaders, by the evolving process of cultural democratisation, which was fundamentally altering Cuba's cultural landscape, and by at least two other alternative poles: the cultural activists gathering in the new CNC and the Instituto Cubano de Artes e Industrias Cinematográficas (ICAIC).

The CNC was established in January 1961, under Armando Hart's Ministry of Education.[3] Although its hierarchy included Carpentier and Lezama Lima, many of its most influential leaders were former PSP activists (notably Joaquín Ordoqui and Edith García Buchaca) who tended to bring cultural perspectives closer to 'socialist realism' (Otero 1999: 77) and who broadly believed in educating Cubans *up* to a level of cultural appreciation (although, simultaneously, the CNC's Centro Cubano de Investigaciones Literarias, under Mario Parajón, sought to publicise Cuban authors). Inevitably, there were tensions between the CNC and *Lunes* positions, especially as other processes of change were determining the new cultural environment.

If Casa established the norms and boundaries for the evolving external cultural policy, then the institution that most seminally shaped the domestic cultural environment was ICAIC. Founded as early as March 1959, under Alfredo Guevara (a former PSP activist and colleague of Castro), ICAIC rapidly became a relatively autonomous and prestigious forum, gathering film-makers and others who gravitated naturally towards ICAIC's more directed radicalism. While *Lunes* and ICAIC were never openly antagonistic to each other, there were personal and political tensions that reflected the competing perspectives of the early Revolution and also the different pre-1959 experiences, since, unlike the exile background of the *Lunes* group, most of those around ICAIC had spent the 1950s in Cuba, many of them politically active.

It was, indeed, partly because of these tensions that the first major, but seminal, cultural crisis emerged. The specific cause was the May 1961 production, by Saba Cabrera Infante (Guillermo's brother) and cinematographer Orlando Jiménez, of the fifteen-minute film, *PM*, which (without comment but with a free camera style) portrayed Havana's 'lower depths', depicting an array of drunks and prostitutes in a bacchanalian cabaret culture of drugs and alcohol. It was offered first to Havana's only private cinema, whose request for a licence was refused; ICAIC then delayed distribution, but, after protests, organised a screening and discussion of the film at Casa de las Américas to an invited audience. Those favouring the film were led by Néstor Almendros (especially through his weekly *Bohemia* film column) but those against argued that, coming only weeks after the Bay of Pigs, it was irresponsible, creating a misleading impression of a 'segmented reality' and pretended an erroneous neutrality (Chanan 1985: 101–3). Moreover, some felt that the film's portrayal of Havana's blacks was offensively and anachronistically stereotypical (Pérez Sarduy 1983: 26).

This was, of course, the tip of the iceberg of tensions between alternative cultural poles and perspectives, rather than, as often argued, between artistic freedom and Stalinism (Cabrera Infante 1994: 69). For the PSP did not then have a monolithically restrictive approach to art, as its pre-1959 record showed, and the apparent 'hardening' of attitudes was as evident among the 26 July leaders as within the PSP and CNC. The fact was that all of them increasingly felt that Cuba's new situation and the process of radicalisation demanded greater responsibility and commitment from everyone, including the cultural community.

However, the *PM* affair was a watershed, indicating to all concerned that the situation demanded changed structures and criteria. One immediate result was a series of Saturday meetings (in the Biblioteca Nacional, on 16, 23 and 30 June) between political leaders (including Castro, the president Osvaldo Dorticós, Hart, Santamaría, Alfredo Guevara, García Buchaca) and Havana's worried artists and intellectuals. Supposedly to prepare for the Primer Congreso Nacional de Escritores y Artistas, but also designed to clear the air, the meetings were remarkable affairs, addressing the artists' fears of state control, the question of the role of culture and allegations of cultural elitism, and displaying the disagreements within Havana culture. Indeed, whatever the outcome, the meetings did set a pattern which would thereafter characterise the Revolution's internal workings, namely the recurrence of moments and periods of open debate within certain parameters.

The debates were ended by Castro's closing *Palabras a los Intelectuales* ('Words to the Intellectuals'), which, although becoming the Revolution's definition of cultural policy thereafter, actually did more to reflect changing priorities, patterns and processes than to establish any new criteria. The speech was revealing, admitting the differences between the CNC and many artists (upbraided for failing to see the need for the CNC), and, while neutral on *PM*, defended the right to determine its publication (Castro Ruz 1980: 19). In particular, however, Castro criticised *Lunes* for becoming an exclusive cultural grouping (Castro Ruz 1980: 22) and identified the criteria for creating cultural debate and activity:

La Revolución ... debe actuar de manera que todo ese sector de artistas y de intelectuales que no sean genuinamente revolucionarios, encuentren dentro de la Revolución un campo donde trabajar y crear y que su espíritu creador, aun cuando no sean escritores o artistas revolucionarios, tenga la oportunidad y libertad para expresarse, dentro de la Revolución. Esto significa que dentro de la Revolución, todo; contra la Revolución, nada.' ('The Revolution … must behave in such a way that all those artists and intellectuals who are not genuinely revolutionary can find space to work and create, within the Revolution, and that their creative spirit, even if they are not revolutionary writers and artists, can have the opportunity and freedom to express itself, within the Revolution. That means within the Revolution, everything, and against the Revolution, nothing': Castro Ruz 1980: 14.)

Those final words have subsequently been taken by critical commentators to have established strictures determining control of artistic freedom, or at best to have left ambiguity. However, this understanding has arisen especially from misquoting *contra* ('against') as *fuera* ('outside') (Franco 2002: 89; Weiss 1985: 121; Camnitzer 2003: 129), thus changing the meaning of what Castro was actually saying. For his statement indicated not 'if you are not with us, you are against us' (which the use of *fuera* would have meant) but the more inclusive 'if you are not against us, you are with us'. This is not mere semantics, for one characteristic of the Revolution's processes subsequently has, indeed, been its 'argumentalism' (Kapcia 2000: 254–5), its willingness to allow and even encourage internal debate, within clear parameters and behind metaphorically closed doors, which has allowed writers, artists and intellectuals to know and even define the bounds of the acceptable; apart from moments of crisis or of exaggerated internal tensions, exclusion and a 'hard line' have tended to be applied only to those publicly going beyond those 'doors' and those parameters.

Whatever the long-term implications, however, the speech closed this particular debate and began the necessary process of institutionalisation, defining the new parameters and context, and, with that, the new spaces for the cultural community. The CNC's authority was enhanced; in 1963, it was given greater autonomy, under the Consejo de Ministros, with a brief to organise, coordinate and direct all cultural activity nationally and locally, and, most significantly, to rescue national cultural traditions (García 1980: 231).

Another immediate outcome was the creation of the Unión Nacional de Escritores y Artistas de Cuba (UNEAC), following the August Congreso; with a clear political purpose and with Guillén as president, Lezama Lima and Carpentier as vice-presidents and Fernández Retamar as secretary, it carried cultural weight, respectability and prestige to counter fears of it becoming a controlling rather than facilitating mechanism. In fact, UNEAC soon became a more protective body, separate from the CNC, with its own spaces and structures of legitimacy, especially in its journals from 1961. *Unión* (under Carpentier, Fernández Retamar and Guillén) was where cultural policies were outlined, defended and expressed, while the fortnightly *Gaceta de Cuba* (under Otero), though lacking *Unión*'s 'official' status, was perhaps more influential, publishing more widely and more frequently, and especially publicising newer artists and writers. In 1965, UNEAC also established its own prizes, thereby providing an officially sanctioned domestic parallel to Casa, while the UNEAC building also paralleled Casa, as a space for the cultural community to gather.

Meanwhile, even after 1961, ICAIC retained autonomy and purpose. Indeed, at the 1962 Primer Congreso Cultural Nacional, Che Guevara defended it against PSP criticism, while ICAIC criticised the CNC's 'populism' and defended artistic experimentation. This debate continued into 1963, when twenty-nine Cuban film-makers wrote a *Gaceta de Cuba* manifesto defending their right to challenge dog-matism, provoking a riposte by García Buchaca in *Cuba Socialista* and a vigorous debate at the university. In 1964 Alfredo Guevara, in *Revolución*, publicly defended the Cubans' right to see the Italian film *La Dolce Vita*, against criticisms in *Hoy* by the PSP's Blas Roca.

The new institutions, of course, in a context of isolation and of demands for internal unity, reflected several existing processes. The first was cultural democra-tisation, arising both from a Literacy Campaign, which empowered thousands of new readers and legitimised reading and writing as never before, and from the par-allel drive to create *instructores de arte*. This latter campaign was one of the most fundamental changes in Cuban culture, arising from Castro's *Palabras*, which, referring to the need to take culture to the people, talked of creating 'instructores de música, de baile, de teatro' ('teachers of music, dance and theatre': Castro Ruz 1980: 26), although the process was in fact already under way. The idea was a network of *escuelas de instructores de arte* (schools to train cultural teachers) all over Cuba, available to all, regardless of social class; from 1961, *instructores* were trained intensively, usually by leading artists and musicians and often in presti-gious commandeered buildings (such as the Copacabana, Sevilla and Habana Libre hotels or the Teatro Nacional). By 1963, the first graduates were working in local schools and factories, targeting the young, and, by 1969, there were some 20,000 *instructores*, with an inevitable momentum.

Although less publicised than the Literacy Campaign, the movement's cultural and social significance should not be underestimated, being both a long-term enterprise and affecting more of the population, but sharing the Campaign's trans-formational effect on thinking, behaviour and social divisions. For the movement popularised culture in more effective ways than decrees or reforms, culturally empowering those hitherto lacking any opportunity to develop an artistic talent, and becoming an explicitly participatory experience, bridging the potential divide between the personal and the collective. It took the ownership (if not yet the defi-nition) of 'culture' beyond the previously narrow confines of the established spaces of the cultural community, and thus challenged the latter's claim to be cultural arbiters. It was therefore no coincidence that, just as the *Lunes* crisis was arising from differences over definitions of role, the event that triggered the debate set in motion a collective experience which promised to democratise culture empirically through participation rather than the nostrums of a self-appointed vanguard. Hence, while *Lunes* focused on the cultural *products* of established cultural *producers*, in the *barrios* a real revolution was taking place involving consumers in the processes of cultural *production*. It was a change with fundamental implications, asking Havana's cultural activists to identify with a different cultural community, the Cuban world they had previously ignored, taken for granted, or perhaps theorised, instead of their natural tendency to identify with a wider global community of cultural producers.

The second process was the sharpening of the tensions underlying the 1961 debates, the *Palabras* (and other seminal events) forcing a *toma de conciencia* ('realization', or 'coming to terms') on intellectuals who, since 1959, had not questioned their politics. 1961–6 were, indeed, years of pressure, separation and cleavage in the cultural community, when some (notably Cabrera Infante, Calvert Casey, Lydia Cabrera, Gastón Baquero, Carlos Montenegro, Lino Novas Calvo, Eugenio Florit, Juan Arcocha and Severo Sarduy) chose to go into exile, while others encountered difficulties, reinforced by an increasingly defensive atmosphere in which 'deviation' was decreasingly tolerated. In culture, this was expressed as an intolerance of perceived inappropriate behaviour, for example by writers whose known homosexuality led to personal difficulties, notably Lezama Lima, whose writings briefly disappeared from bookshops (Black 1989: 128), and Piñera, who was briefly detained in 1965 and whose 1967 UNEAC prize-winning *Presiones y Diamantes* was criticised as an absurdist vision (Black 1989: 120–2). Intolerance also played its part in the creation in 1965 of the Unidades Militares de Ayuda a la Producción (UMAP, 'Military Units to Aid Production'), re-education camps for those 'deviating' from the norm (notably Jehovah's Witnesses, Seventh Day Adventists and also several of Havana's gay community), until UNEAC pressure and Castro's intervention closed them in 1967 or 1968 (Yglesias 1968: 14; Chanan 1985: 284; Lumsden 1996: 70). Indeed, gays in Havana's cultural community had experienced a chequered time since 1959; when a 1961 round-up took place, as part of the drive to clean up Havana's streets and image, some were swept up in that, notably Piñera (briefly detained in Guanabo) and Arrufat, who lost his *Casa* editorship over the publication of a homosexual poem (Lumsden 1996: 59). Moreover, when Arrufat arranged, in 1965, for Casa to invite the openly gay American poet, Allen Ginsberg, to visit, the resulting furore (caused not least by some of Ginsberg's statements) played a part in both justifying harassment and tarring all intellectuals with the same brush.

The same pressure also affected the El Puente publishing house, which, founded privately by José Mario in 1960, gathered a group of young writers (mostly poets) who, meeting after 1964 at the Gato Tuerto café in Vedado, argued for the experimental and for the ideas of *Orígenes*, thus challenging the new mainstream. In 1965, El Puente was closed and Mario dispatched to an UMAP camp, while some

Figure 10 The Gato Tuerto café, site of the Puente group's meetings

(Mercedes Cortázar and Isel Rivero) left Cuba and others (Miguel Barnet, Belkis Cuza Malé and Nancy Morejón) returned to the mainstream (Casal 1971: 450).

The third process was the ending of independent poles of influence. *Lunes* closed, being replaced by UNEAC's journals, and publishing was centralised further in the 1967 Instituto Cubano del Libro. In April 1967, copyright was abolished; partly a revolutionary challenge to capitalism's control of intellectual freedom and partly allowing Cuba to publish non-Cuban authors, this also eliminated any possibility of royalties to individual writers, making them even more dependent on the Revolution's benefices and employment.

The fourth process was the replacement of old external models by new ones, meaning a separation from New York, Paris and Madrid as the cultural poles of a community to which Havana's writers might belong, and the affirmation of new communities. One such had its centres east of Berlin, a result of decree but also organic development, reflecting the new isolation and reorientation, and also the awareness of the models that did indeed exist in Poland, Czechoslovakia or the early Soviet Union. The second was Cuba itself, seeking inspiration not in Paris but in Cuban history and Cuban writers. This was especially evident in two new magazines. *Cuba* was created by INRA in 1964, under Lisandro Otero, and became another space for new writers, artists and photographers (Otero 1999: 86). *Caimán Barbudo* was created in 1966 as the weekly cultural supplement of *Juventud Rebelde*, the newspaper of the UJC (Unión de Jóvenes Comunistas, or Young Communists); partly responding to El Puente's closure and, indeed, involving some of the same people (often meeting in the Coppelia), it sought to provide space 'within the Revolution' for otherwise problematic young writers, a tolerance denoting the end of the short period of harassment and intolerance. Rejecting both the 'hysterical-liberal' tendency of some (*Lunes* and El Puente), but also the 'terrorist-dogmatic' trends of others (Casal 1971: 451), the magazine, under the young Jesús Díaz, had difficulties positioning itself comfortably, its editorial committee changing with baffling rapidity, reflecting both uncertainty and tensions. By the fifth issue, for example, Guillermo Rodríguez Rivera had become editor, replaced three issues later by Luis Rogelio Nogueras, who was in turn replaced six issues later by the longer-lasting Víctor Casaús (García 1980: 169). However, the magazine clearly distinguished itself from *Lunes* in two respects: it focused almost completely on Cuban writers and culture, and it always had a more openly political concern.

This new mood (stimulated when Otero became CNC Vice-President) was, however, limited to 1966–8, 'the period of greatest tolerance' (Black 1989: 109); this was reflected especially in the 1967 Salon de Mai art exhibition brought by Lam to Havana, which hailed the latest European avant-garde and advocated experimentation, taking its cue from both Che Guevara, who had spoken repeatedly in favour of experimentation and against conformity (Guevara 1968), and the still experimental new cinema.

By 1968, however, the mood had again shifted. Often interpreted as further evidence of Stalinism, rooted in 'Communist dialectics' (Cabrera Infante 1994: 74), this shift in fact had other causes, especially the growth of a notion of cultural decolonisation, rooted in the Revolution's radicalised nationalism and new 'Third Worldist' militancy, challenging both US imperialism and Soviet revisionism. Both roots were amply evident in the 1968 Cultural Congress in Havana: part of Cuba's drive for recognition as a new revolutionary entity (many of the invited participants being 'New Left' intellectuals from Europe and Latin America), its militancy and demand for '[l]a descolonización cultural' (Fornet 1980: 317) also echoed the impulses which had created ICAIC, and also Casa's shift towards Latin America as a new cultural pole and even towards a still unknown African culture (Fernández Retamar 1982: 54). It also represented a new defiance, expressed by Desnoes: 'No nos satisface nuestra realidad subdesarrollada pero tampoco nos interesa someternos a una estética, a una concepción del mundo que nos niega; no queremos ser ni bárbaros atrasados, ni colonizados culturales' ('We are by no means happy with the reality of our underdevelopment, but, on the other hand, we are certainly not interested in following an aesthetic and a conception of the world which denies our existence; we want to be neither backward barbarians nor cultural colonials': Desnoes 1967: 49).

These were indeed the impulses which now determined the denouement of the old *Lunes* battles, in the start of the so-called *caso Padilla*. Once part of *Lunes* group and increasingly disenchanted with the new cultural directions, Heberto Padilla published in *Caimán*, in 1967, a scathing criticism of Otero's new (and much praised) novel, *Pasión de Urbino*, comparing it unfavourably with the émigré Cabrera Infante's recent *tour de force*, *Tres Tristes Tigres*, published abroad. In 1968, Padilla's provocatively titled poetry book, *Fuera del Juego* (Out of the Game), won the UNEAC prize (with a largely foreign jury), but UNEAC inserted a disclaimer in the published volume dissociating them from its content. Then, in November, two fiercely critical articles appeared in the FAR's *Verde Olivo*, under the pseudonym of Leopoldo Avila, after which UNEAC decided to limit its prize juries to Cubans (followed, in 1969, by the FAR's Dirección Política's decision to create its own *26 de Julio* prize).

Padilla himself survived this particular furore, but others were less fortunate; in 1969, José Lorenzo Fuentes was expelled from UNEAC and then arrested for passing missile secrets to Washington (Otero 1999: 46; Lorenzo Fuentes and Díaz Martínez 1994: 144). However, simultaneously, belying visions of Stalinism, 1968 saw two new journals (*Pensamiento Crítico* and *Revolución y Cultura*) whose positions emphasised the Third World and an almost Guevarist position regarding the intellectual's role. Indeed, anti-imperialism was now the basic criterion for much in Cuba, obliging the Havana cultural community to examine its possible subservience towards 'imperialist' culture and to seek a cultural decolonisation, bringing those still following the path of *Lunes* into inevitable conflict with the new mood.

Moreover, this was also a time when pressure increased again on Havana's gay writers and artists, as a CNC directive sought to reduce their supposed influence, leading to sackings from the ISA and UNEAC's rejection of Reinaldo Arenas's *El Mundo Alucinante,* culminating in the 1971 Congress's explicit criticism of the 'anti-social' behaviour of homosexuals (Lumsden 1996: 71–3).

One of the realities underlying these tensions was that literature now enjoyed a curious status in Cuba. Poetry in particular continued to be feted, partly because of its traditional prestige, partly because its immediacy allowed it to reflect the changing environment best and partly because of the political and cultural authority of the poets dominating the post-1959 cultural institutions, such as Retamar, Guillén and the *Lunes* poets. Hence, much of the Revolution's early cultural output of the Revolution was poetic.

Within this panorama, certain patterns stood out, not least something of a differentiation between generations, which was itself partly a product of different collective experiences. Thus, the older established poets within the community tended to respond to the new environment either by leaving, seizing the welcome opportunity to publish unpublished material (such as Eliseo Diego or Cintio Vitier) or by seeking to adjust, often uncomfortably, although those who had previously written more openly 'social' verse engaged immediately with the Revolution, not always with literary merit, notably Alcides Iznaga, Félix Pita Rodríguez and Justo Rodríguez Santos.

However, the first years of Revolution undoubtedly belonged to the poetry of the so-called 'Primera Promoción', the younger, previously exiled, writers who (born between 1925 and 1940) now gathered around *Lunes* or Casa: Retamar, Pablo Armando Fernández, Marré, Escardó, Jamís, Arrufat, Padilla, César López and Baragaño. Enjoying both the prestige of the genre and the immediacy which the form offered (not to mention the space which newspapers and magazines offered it), these poets tended to respond with a mixture of catharsis (publishing hitherto unseen work) or welcome, a response which shortly toned down to a more measured reaction, focusing on the mundane, the conversational and the understated (notably in the verse of Domingo Alfonso). This lead was then followed by the 'Segunda Promoción' (born after 1940), whose work either deliberately rejected open commitment or took it for granted, until the 1965–9 pressures forced something of a retreat; in the meantime, however, their work dominated the late 1960s, especially the verse of Georgina Herrera, Pedro Pérez Sarduy, Miguel Barnet, Joaquín Santana and Nancy Morejón.

Within this new environment, the short story also blossomed, sharing something of poetry's inherent advantages: a vestigial prestige (with established writers), an immediacy (enabling it to respond quickly and expressively) and publishing space (in the media). This was especially evident in the work of Humberto Arenal, Cabrera Infante (till 1965), Arrufat and the younger writers, Ana María Simo, Evora Tamayo, María Elena Llana, Esther Díaz Lanillo, Rogelio Llopis and Angel Arango (the latter two specialising in a growing penchant for science fiction).

However, while poetry and the story tended to enjoy prestige and pride of place, culturally and politically, the novel was less forthcoming. In great part, of course, this may have been a result of the novel form's necessarily longer gestation period and need for time to reflect, since reflection and time were commodities in short supply during the frenetic years of transformation of Cuba in the 1960s. Hence, the early novels were largely the publication of extant manuscripts now able to be published, such as the work of Jaime Sarusky, Juan Arcocha, Edmundo Desnoes and Lisandro Otero. The genuinely new works however, tended either to be rapid and immediate, and of variable quality (such as those dealing with the insurrection, by Humberto Arenal, Hilda Perera and José Soler Puig) or to emerge after 1964, often addressing the post-1959 trauma and changes, notably works by Desnoes, Víctor Agostini, Soler Puig, Otero, Reynaldo González and José Lorenzo Fuentes. Even then, the ones that did emerge were often problematic, in that they constituted something of a challenge to the new norms, especially when some chose to leave Cuba, such as Severo Sarduy or Calvert Casey. The outstanding examples of this were Cabrera Infante's *Tres Tristes Tigres* (published in Barcelona in 1965), Severo Sarduy's 1969 *De Donde son los Cantantes* and Lezama's Lima's challenging novel of homosexuality, *Paradiso* (1966), although the young Reinaldo Arenas's work was also challenging and often ignored.

Whatever the differences between the genres, most early works were written individually for individual consumption. Hence, although readership and publishing opportunities had increased, the new poetry and narrative were, essentially, still produced by a minority for a minority, adapting uncomfortably to the Revolution's emerging cultural preferences for public art, participation and popularisation. Therefore, the new revolutionary environment especially affected more public genres and cultural forms, such as theatre, cinema, visual arts and music, all more immediately accessible and, in some cases, more participatory, and all therefore with a potential to be seen by the political vanguard as either important instruments of social and political change or, alternatively, as potentially subversive forms.

Havana theatre, of course, had several advantages, with a traditional popularity, an active community of innovators, and an immediacy and capacity to deliver to the public. Certainly, the Revolution's impact was immediately evident in the quantity and range of Havana productions, with a record 215 performances in 1959, rising to 264 in 1960 (González 2003). Even *bufo* and melodrama flourished briefly at the Teatro Martí, with the new Teatro Cubano Libre in 1959–65 and then the Grupo Nacional (Río Prado 2002: 187), while the Teatro Guiñol Nacional enjoyed the patronage of the Dirección de Cultura in 1959 and the CNC from 1961, acquiring its own theatre in 1963 in the Focsa building.

An official preference for experimental theatre was demonstrated from the outset. In 1959, Fermín Borges became director of the new Teatro Nacional's Departamento de Artes Dramáticas and (from 1960) theatre school, while in 1962 the CNC nominated David Camps as advisor, the same year that Adolfo de Luis staged José Brene's *Santa Camila de la Habana Vieja* at the Mella, a seminal moment in Havana theatre in its path-breaking adoption of the Stanislavsky method (Muguercia 1995: 116).

Since the new theatre therefore trod where narrative would not, it reflected the ideological challenges more immediately, as in Berta Martínez's 1964 staging of Abelardo Estorino's *La casa vieja* (about surviving patterns of thinking), Vicente Revuelta's 1966 staging of José Triana's *La noche de los asesinos* (symbolically depicting the new social conditions), and Roberto Blanco's 1967 staging of Eugenio Hernández Espinosa's *María Antonia*, about the survival of old rituals and beliefs (Muguercia 1995: 117–18). However, as the political mood changed and the siege deepened, this willingness to challenge and question made theatre more vulnerable to criticism; while absurdism might be revolutionary in 1950s Cuba, it could be considered counter-revolutionary in 1967. Hence, the greater intolerance around 1966–8 affected Havana theatre, subduing the urge to experiment. Here, of course, theatre's inherent advantages – each performance's uniqueness, a capacity for improvisation, and a potential for stimulating audience reaction – gave each performance a potential for subversion in official eyes. Hence, Antón Arrufat's play on a siege theme, *Los siete contra Tebas* ('Seven against Thebes'), shared Padilla's fate in 1968, winning the UNEAC theatre prize but with an inserted disclaimer.

Of course, theatre was an obvious instrument for cultural democratisation. While the *instructores de arte* identified drama as a preferred form for developing cultural awareness and latent talent, stimulating a boom in local amateur performance, the late 1960s saw new theatrical developments outside Havana. In 1966, the Conjunto Dramático de Oriente began its activities, leading to the formation of the Cabildo Teatral in 1971, while 1969 saw the new Teatro Escambray (begun by ten Havana professionals under Sergio Corrieri), take revolutionary theatre outside Havana to the peasantry, copying early Soviet efforts in the use of culture as an instrument of revolutionary change, and leading to the creation in the Sierra of the Grupo La Yaya (Weiss 1985: 129). In Havana, the only hint of this was the development of the amateur-based Teatro de Participación Popular in Centro Habana (Weiss 1985: 129).

In this sense, cinema was less problematic, with identical 'performances' and less scope for grass-roots improvisation and response. Hence, from the outset, film offered an unparalleled opportunity for cultural revolution, as an 'arte revolucionario … como instrumento de cultura y arma de combate' in Alfredo Guevara's words ('revolutionary art … as a cultural instrument and weapon': Fornet 1982: 16). This, indeed, partly explains ICAIC's early creation and enduring autonomy, for film enjoyed a unique status: with an existing popularity with the capacity to spread ideas, images and messages rapidly and acceptably, and with the possibility of cheap mass dissemination (despite expensive production). Certainly, after January 1959 cinema remained Havana's leading form of regular entertainment (Clytus 1970: 48), 120 million cinema visits being recorded (seventeen per year for every Cuban), concentrated especially in Havana (Chanan 1985: 16).

In this context, ICAIC's mission was to organise, establish and develop a national film industry, the expropriation of Alonso's studios and cinemas giving it complete control of the industry (Chanan 1985: 20). ICAIC's first productions were mostly didactic documentaries and political features about the Revolution, the new reforms, mass mobilisations, Cuban history or social problems (as in Tomás Gutiérrez Alea's 1960 *La Tierra es Nuestra*). These productions generally followed a stark neo-realism arising from both the industry's pre-1959 Italian influences and the growing austerity, which demanded efficiency, sparseness and directness, as in García Espinosa's *Cuba baila* (1960) and Gutiérrez Alea's 1960 *Historias de la revolución* (Chanan 1985: 116).

The new cinema also looked elsewhere, to the French *nouvelle vague* (seen as a young and rebellious cinema: Chanan 1985: 129) and, increasingly, to Eastern Europe, confirming the Revolution's evolving politics and also the reality that, if Cuban cinema were to become Latin Americanised, it needed to adopt an ideologically anti-imperialist posture (Fornet 1982: 17). This eclecticism was also evident in the films which ICAIC imported and distributed; in 1959, of the 484 films shown in Cuba, 266 were American, 79 Mexican, 44 British, 25 Italian, 24 French and 19 Spanish (Chanan 1985: 104).

Evidently, ICAIC was as fundamental to the new culture as Casa, encouraging a genuinely revolutionary and innovative art that was seen as 'national', and ensuring that public tastes were both met and shaped. For ICAIC also sought to develop cinema appreciation through the 1961 creation of the Cinemateca de Cuba (becoming, under Héctor García Mesa, a forum for debate), the 1960 magazine *Cine Cubano*, and Cuban television, with regular educational programmes on film and screenings of Cuban and foreign films.

Inevitably, this boom could not be maintained, especially as the shortages and the 'siege' worsened. By the mid-1960s, film production declined and some prominent film-makers left, notably Fernando Villaverde and Néstor Almendros. However, the new mood also saw the tone shift from earnest documentaries to ironic feature films such as Gutiérrez Alea's *Muerte de un burócrata* (1966), Solás's *Manuela* (1966), Octavio Gómez's *Tulipa* (1967) and García Espinosa's *Las aventuras de Juan Quin Quin* (1967). These were then followed, in 1968–9, by some of the Revolution's acknowledged masterpieces, such as Gutiérrez Alea's *Memorias del Subdesarrollo*, Solás's *Lucía*, and Octavio Gómez's *La Primera Carga del Machete*.

ICAIC was also influential in two other, significantly public, art forms. On the one hand, it sponsored the rapid and innovative development of cinema poster art, boosted by the acquisition of a graphics studio, from which, in 1960, the first poster came – by Eduardo Muñoz Bachs for Gutiérrez Alea's *Historias de la Revolución* (Trujillo 1996: 41)[4]   and from which, under Saúl Yelín, a vibrant group of artists and graphic designers evolved, who developed this new form into a flourishing, adventurous and eventually recognisable genre.[5] These new posters had a deliberately political purpose, seen initially as an artistic challenge to the hegemony of the essentially commercial Hollywood poster, so prevalent before 1959 and still evident in Cuba (Trujillo 1996: 41); hence, while posters had previously sold 'noventa minutos de evasión' ('ninety minutes of evasion': Pogolotti 1996: 50), they now became an instrument of political education. However, the artists, supported by ICAIC, also sought to make posters innovative and attractive, challenging the banality of the ubiquitous political posters (Chanan 1985: 132). By the late-1960s, therefore, poster designers displayed an exciting virtuosity, using collage, montage, pop art, op art, psychedelic art and the more familiar styles of art nouveau, to create an art form in and of itself, with exhibitions in 1966 (in the Pabellón Cuba) and 1969 (at the Primer Salón Nacional de Carteles). Moreover, Havana's collectors now also bought posters for decoration, making the Cuban poster a 'testimonio decorativo de vida, de cultura, de acción revolucionaria y sentimiento internacionalista' ('decorative element, bearing witness to life, culture, revolution and internationalism': Trujillo 1996: 48), recognised in the massive 1979 exhibition at the Museo Nacional's Palacio de Bellas Artes. In 1967, ICAIC began the practice of decorating the facades and areas around cinemas, making Havana's streets into an unparalleled street gallery (Juan 1996: 33).

Poster art, however, was also part of a wider flourishing of the graphic arts in general. As book production accelerated and new newspapers and journals emerged, this created new opportunities for illustration (by artists such as Umberto Peña, Fayad Jamís and Raúl Martínez), echoing the early Republic before photographic illustration. However, this new space depended not on private enterprise and beneficence but on the revolutionary state's patronage after the 1962 nationalisation of the media and publishing, and after the coincidental creation of the Guanabacoa Escuela de Artes Gráficas Alfredo López, followed shortly by the Taller Experimental de Gráfica.

This institutional impulse was also part of the wider artistic patronage, evidenced in the Escuela Nacional de Arte, which, created in 1962 and producing graduates from 1967, shaped most of Havana's subsequent generations, creating opportunities but also establishing the parameters, criteria and principles to guide Havana's and Cuba's youngest and newest artists. Meanwhile, other spaces opened up, notably the influential 1963 exhibition of Expresión Abstracta at the Galería de La Habana, and the new and influential Club Cubano de Bellas Artes and its bi-monthly *Gaceta de Bellas Artes*. Meanwhile, the old Grupo de los Once continued, under Raúl Martínez, stressing the important of both public and socially useful art (Levinson 1989: 494).

The outcome was a refreshing vitality and sense of innovation, although, as with film, the growing shortages affected styles, notably the reliance on silk-screen painting and the tendency to use limited colours and tones, making a virtue out of necessity in the exaltation of simplicity and even blank spaces (Juan 1996: 26). Yet the positive sense of innovation also took the new art from the cautious eclecticism of established artists such as Agustín Fernández and Angel Acosta León (seemingly releasing pent-up energies and styles), through a Mexican – or Soviet-influenced monumentalism (as in Servando Cabrera Moreno's 1961 *Milicias Campesinas*), to a new confidence after 1964, intertextually blending materials into a new identifiable style, as in Raúl Martínez's abstract expressionism (*26 de Julio*) or pop-art (*15 repeticiones de Martí*, 1966).

In this new environment of opportunity and service, the spaces for and demands on Havana's musicians and composers were also inevitably enhanced. However, the pre-1959 evolution of Havana's music made it a more problematic field for the new cultural policies. On the one hand, the Revolution's commitment to cultural democratisation meant, in music, either giving prestige to popular forms (such as dance and song) considered by the musical vanguard as insufficiently serious, or educating the public into a new appreciation. This was clearly a new dilemma for definitions of culture: should the Revolution develop a music *for* the people or a music *of* the people, and, if the latter, what form should this take, folkloric (taking up the banner of the 1920s) or entertainment?

In the event, the answer was given by the political momentum, since the nation-alisation of Havana's hotels and cabarets and the disappearance of tourism closed many popular entertainment venues, leading some musicians to leave for overseas opportunities, a process reaching its peak with the Revolutionary Offensive's closure of the remaining clubs, although radio and television continued with a diet of popular music. However, the post-1960 embargo cut the links between Cuban musicians and both the external market and developments, creating something of a musical autarchy, freezing styles in their 1950s forms, as in the continuation of *filin* at the St John's Hotel.

Yet the new emphasis on invention did affect Havana jazz, before 1959 a largely minority taste. Now, despite some media and professional disapproval (for its sup-posedly decadent and American associations) and despite the departure of some leading exponents, jazz experienced a small boom (Acosta 2001: 47), culminating in the CNC's 1967 creation of the Orquesta Cubana de Música Moderna, a forum for 'Cubanisation' from which, in 1973, Irakere would emerge.

However, Cuba's cultural leaders, already cautious about the implications of popular American forms, faced a dilemma in the mid-1960s as the new youth music emerged in the West: did they welcome these forms as something to enhance Cuban music or reject them as commercialised, decadent (given their behavioural associations) and threatening? Ultimately, the die was cast, when, in 1967, Washington policy-makers decided to make political use of what they saw as subversive British and American rock music, by beaming it into the Cuban air-waves, leading the Cubans to jam the broadcasts, and then to operate a de facto ban of any such music on Cuban radio and television. This ban was limited to official channels (although zealous local activists often enforced it in the private sphere too) and limited in effect, since tapes of the new music, not least the Beatles, were easily smuggled in or recorded and passed around among the young. However, it was effective enough to drive this music underground and limit its influence until the late 1960s, when, in a different atmosphere, a few Cuban rock groups emerged, such as Los Vampiros, Almas Vertiginosas, Flores Plásticas, Los Kent, Sesiones Ocultas, los Dada, Sonido X and Los Magníficos (Rodríguez Quintana 2001: 90).

Figure 11 The statue to John Lennon in Vedado, a sign of shifting attitudes to a music disapproved in the 1960s but now enshrined as part of the canon

Simultaneously, however, one aspect of the new Western music was welcomed, namely protest song, as it fused with traditional and indigenous forms to become an instrument of Latin American resistance. Between 24 July and 8 August 1967, Casa de las Américas organised in Havana the Primer Encuentro Internacional de la Canción Protesta, including many well-known singers (three Cuban) from sixteen countries, and, in 1967–69, a Centro de la Canción Protesta existed, organising monthly *encuentros* (gatherings or concerts) for practitioners and public.

Meantime, in 1969 ICAIC, seeing the potential damage in prohibiting any popular youth music, established the Grupo Sonora Experimental, building on developments such as the 1962–4 compositions of Hilario González and Pablo Milanés (Díaz 1994: 15), the Canción Protesta movement, the July 1967 *Caimán Barbudo* anniversary concert in the Museo Nacional de Bellas Artes, a general aesthetic dissatisfaction with Havana musical broadcasting (as too staid and focused on entertainment), and the ideas of the young avant-garde composer Leo Brouwer. The group had clear aims: to research and create cinema music, to develop music as an art form through new technology and all available forms, including rock music (Padrón Nodarse 1997: 101), and to protect and promote traditional music.

The first aim was immediately successful, notably in Manuel Octavio Gómez's music for *La primera carga al machete* and the compositions of Carlos Fariñas,

Sergio Vitier and José M. Vitier. The second aim was equally successful in the emergence of the Nueva Trova, which, heavily influenced by both the traditional *trova* and the *canción protesta*, grouped together people like Silvio Rodríguez, Pablo Milanés, Noel Nicola, Eduardo Ramos, Leonardo Acosta, Sara González, Amaury Pérez, Martín Rojas, Belinda Romeu, Vicente Feliú, Agosto Costales, Gerardo Alfonso, Pedro Novo, Roberto Novo, Emiliano Salvador and Pablo Menéndez, and groups like Grupo Moncada (consisting of social scientists who researched and composed Latin American music: Weiss 1985: 126) and Grupo Manguaré (Levinson 1989: 495). The Havana musical establishment was initially cautious about the movement's form and content, but the powerful patronage of both ICAIC and Casa, which also provided space (Costales 1978: 81), made it one of Cuban culture's longest lasting products. The phenomenon also, surprisingly, led to the UJC's creation of the Brigada Hermanos Saíz, as the junior wing of UNEAC, to promote culture among the young, many of its leaders graduating from Havana's music schools and the ISA.

It was, therefore, music that seemed to be finding the elusive fusion between the popular (traditional or entertainment), the Cuban (produced by Cubans and responding to Cuban tastes and needs), and the innovative. This was partly attributable to the ideas and commitment of its leading exponents, but also by its unique ability for universal dissemination, its long-standing traditional associations and its participatory potential. Music also provided an outstanding example of the drive to educate the people *up* to a cultural appreciation in the surprising development of ballet, once the Ballet Alicia Alonso became the Ballet Nacional de Cuba in 1960 (based in the Gran Teatro). Thereafter ballet (under Alonso's firm direction) was for the first time established as a national art form, and, in the process, provided yet another space for innovation and for sheltering artists whose lifestyle otherwise made them vulnerable to discrimination (Lightfoot 2002: 155).

Once again, therefore, we return to the meaning of 'cultural revolution'. For, by 1969, it was becoming clear that, in addition to the evolving definitions (of preserving traditional forms, bringing prestigious forms to the people, or responding directly to the Revolution's concerns), it now had acquired another definition: a culture developed *by* the people. Indeed, this now took on a special and seminal form as the *movimiento de artistas aficionados* ('movement of amateur artists'), initially an informal and loose 'movement', without headquarters, definition or system, but with an evident and real existence and clear organic roots, whose heyday (with an estimated million *aficionados*) was yet to come.

Meantime, perhaps revealingly, the Revolution seemed unsure what to make of the very cultural forms which, before 1959, had begun to offer possible routes to a cultural identity, namely Afro-Cuban popular culture. On the one hand, some in the cultural hierarchy saw dance and musical forms as little more than entertainment, while others viewed the religious forms of *santería* as somewhere between

superstition and an authentic if folkloric manifestation of Cuba's past, but not necessarily its future. This was especially true as the revolutionary process (which
increasingly stressed unity and integration, and believed that all social changes
would de facto eliminate capitalist discrimination) tended to view any cultural
expressions that stressed the distinctiveness of any one group as suspicious at best
and dangerous at worst. Hence, the early Revolution restricted the activities of the
black *sociedades* and famously preferred the visiting American Black Power
activists to take their arguments away from Cuba, but also, from 1960 (after the
visit of Senegal's Sekou Touré), began to organise seminars on ethnology, folklore
and culture, leading to the creation of the Institución Nacional de Etnología y
Folklore in December 1961. This pattern – of an uncertain oscillation between
'folkorism' and an emphasis on political liberation of other countries' black citizens (in Africa, the Caribbean and the United States) – remained the characteristic
until the 1970s, with little or no evidence of a new *negrismo* appearing in literature, and the popular forms of black-originating dance enjoying a marginal existence as entertainment or folklore.

Meantime, other popular cultural forms were continuing to be practised and to
develop in a new revolutionary environment that encouraged a collective self-confidence and self-awareness. This, for example, was the case with sport, whose
political potential was now realised by the vanguard. In February 1961, the
Instituto Nacional de Deportes Educación Física y Recreación (INDER) was
established, responsible for all sports promotion, training and investment, and all
professional sport was abolished. This latter move especially affected baseball,
which had, initially, continued after 1959 apparently unaffected by the changes
(the Cuban League continuing even into 1961). However, the sport's past com-
mercialism and American business and professional links made it ripe for change.
The Cuban Sugar Kings folded in 1960 and the abolition of professionalism led to
an exodus to Mexico and the United States, leaving Cuban baseball as a solely
amateur sport, with a new structure and season, and with Cuba now dominating
the Amateur World Series, although many outside Cuba questioned precisely how
amateur sport was, with a sustained programme of identification, isolation and
preparation of leading athletes and players. Nonetheless, sport was directly relevant to the questions addressed here, since it too had now the capacity to be both
participatory and 'Cuban', and thus part of a new national cultural identity. Yet this
too was relevant, since one important aspect of a cultural identity, as we have seen,
is the notion of identification with a community to which a people feels it can and
should belong, in other words of which it is proud.

Overall, by 1970, despite the 'dark days' of austerity and 'siege' (or even
because of them), Havana's elite/vanguard cultural community had undergone
profound changes; it had broadened (beyond the would-be gatekeepers of *Lunes*,
Casa or ICAIC) and had deepened and popularised in ways that promised (or

threatened) to open up definitions of culture in revolutionary directions, threatening the stability and self-regard of elite groups and vanguards. In other words,
to take up the theme of 'sweetness and light', the new art and the new opportunities might be sweet and the light thrown by expanding education and cultural revolution might be the brightest it had ever been but a bitterness was all too evident
in many in the community, especially as it became increasingly clear that Havana
was no longer the centre of Cuba's cultural universe. The community's boundaries, once so clear and limiting, were now being redefined so fundamentally that
'belonging' was unclear; did Havana's artists and writers belong to a definable
Havana-based community, to a wider global community or to some sort of
emerging 'Cuban' community?

Part II: The Grey Years – Conformity and Stagnation (the 1970s and 1980s)

Evolution of the City

The crisis following the failed 1970 *zafra* affected Havana considerably, given the
vulnerability of its infrastructure, its housing shortage (which the early reforms
had addressed in the short term) and the overall neglect of the 1960s. Moreover,
the end of the 1965–71 emigration agreements also removed an important safety
valve. Thus, 1971–4 were especially hard years for *habaneros*, discontent being
manifested not in protest or rebellion (since few wished to challenge the system)
but in an absenteeism and *vagancia* ('loafing'), the tendency for younger
habaneros to loiter in the streets or on the Malecón rather than endure the drudgery
of a meaningless workplace. When the economy began to recover, from 1973, the
effects of a decade of austerity, overstaffing and declining commitment to work
made Havana a curious mix of greater consumerisation and poor productivity, but,
by the mid-1980s, it was more vibrant and again attracting Cubans from the interior, who previously had little reason to abandon the *campo*'s benefits for the
Havana 'pressure-cooker', where political demands were greater but economic and
social benefits less easily identifiable. By the end of the 1980s, Havana's authorities were again worried about increased immigration.

Hence, the decision to allow emigrant relatives to visit from 1979 and the 1981
liberalisation of the peasant markets were both aimed at easing *habanero* discontent, since the nature of post-1959 emigration made Havana most affected by the
influx of dollars and goods that relatives brought in, bringing welcome hard currency and material relief, and the markets were designed to satisfy the growing
demand for food beyond the demoralising *libreta* and stave off food protests.
Equally, housing pressures were addressed in 1984. Until then, home-owners,
unable to sell and buy, were locked into existing property, regardless of changing
family size, leading to overcrowding and under-use; the new law, however, allowed

limited renting, legalised self-help housing cooperatives and especially allowed property 'exchange' via the *permuta* system. Inevitably, the reality of more valued locations and properties, together with the inefficiencies of the Cuban administration, meant an illegal housing market (payments being made to address differences in 'values'), leading to some retraction, but a safety-valve had been inserted, allowing movement and releasing income into circulation. Equally, the 1970s 'Havana Green Belt' campaign, although of questionable efficacy, ensured that more food was produced closer to the consumers.

Meantime, the unused infrastructure of Havana's tourist industry, dormant since tourism dried up in the early 1960s, was reused as Havana saw a partial recovery of the industry once INTUR was created (1976), tourists initially arriving from the Socialist Bloc (leading to the new, functional, concrete hotels outside Havana) and then low-budget subsidised tourism from the West (notably Italy, France, Britain and Canada). By 1978, Cuba was receiving 69,500 tourists per year (Segre et al. 1997: 266), bringing Havana another source of hard currency, legal and illegal, and producing small-scale developments such as the *sábados en la Plaza* ('Plaza Saturdays'), which, until ended in the mid-1980s, sold artefacts and handicrafts to tourists in the Plaza de la Catedral. Hence, Havana's legal and black economies both flourished until the mid-1980s, when recession began to be felt and 'Rectification' began.

Social change in Havana was inevitably slower than the 1960s, until the effects of new construction were felt and provincial immigrants started to arrive. Gradually, Havana became younger, blacker and more mixed than in 1959, with average income levels low but with greater equality of access. Social benefits now began to affect Havana more immediately, given the 1960s neglect, especially in health and an education development that led young *habaneros*, less aware of old shortages, to demand opportunities commensurate with their skills. Therefore Havana *barrios* began to become focal points for youth activity and even some noticeable youth alienation, especially Habana del Este and Cerro, and the centre became a social space for youth, notably the Malecón and the Coppelia corner.

This had a curious political effect. Firstly, it created a pool of disaffected youth, which, while mostly apolitical ('dropping out' rather than challenging), did occasionally vent frustrations in rowdy rock concerts or in street protests (such as that preceding Mariel). Secondly, it affected young activists within the political system, who welcomed Gorbachev's Soviet reforms by forming groups to push for a Cuban *perestroika* and *glasnost*, buying hitherto unread Soviet magazines and worrying Cuba's leaders enough to reform the UJC in 1987. Havana was the epicentre of this activity, confirming older leaders' prejudices about Havana as the 'problem', a political site contaminated by external contact.

However, these political problems were rooted deeper in the post-1975 political changes. As the Poder Popular system was implemented, it more effectively represented than its predecessor, Poder Local, delivering goods and services more succesfully and easing political pressure in the city. However it also meant downgrading the CDRs and reducing the number and frequency of rallies and the demands of *trabajo voluntario*, thereby involving people less, especially as Poder Popular moved the level of representation from the *barrio* to the larger *municipio*, creating a distance between ordinary citizens and the decision-making processes. Efficiency and effectiveness thus meant reduced participation, which, for all its material benefits, risked greater alienation. Now participation tended either to be specific (responding to national emergencies, such as hurricanes or the 1981 dengue outbreak in Havana) or ritualised in May Day rallies and the CDRs' *guardia nocturna*. Hence, while life visibly improved in Havana, a sense of belonging and responsibility within the collective began to decline.

By the early 1980s, there was therefore a sense of disaffection, which helped create the atmosphere for Mariel, since most of the unrest around the Peruvian embassy was generated by *habaneros* and many of the emigrants were from the city, the reaction from angry citizens and the *brigadas de respuesta rápida* (Rapid Reaction Brigades) indicating new divisions in Havana.

However, simultaneously, Havana was beginning to grow as a community and become more self-confident, indicated in a new willingness to display signs of deviation from the norm, an example of which was the rise of an unprecedented definable youth culture. Hitherto, its absence was largely attributable to the absence of space or opportunity and the later tendency towards revolutionary zeal and conformity, which, in 1965, for example, saw long male hair incur official disapproval and lectures on revolutionary responsibilities. Before that, its absence had probably resulted from the phenomenon of a 'young' revolution empowering children and teenagers more than their elders, making a whole generation lose its adolescence overnight, without any opportunity to experience it as its counterparts were doing in the West, driven by a commercial world in search of a market. Thus, while Western youth were rebelling in hairstyles, music or drug experimentation, Cuban youth were standing armed guard to defend the Revolution in the militias, or being mobilised in the Literacy Campaign, the *zafra* or some other campaign which gave them a role in the process. Hence, the attractions of youth rebellion often made little sense to Havana teenagers, who, though seeking and playing the disapproved Beatles or American rock, rarely saw the need to express this as rebellion.[6]

By the 1980s, however, much had changed. Now, young *habaneros* had time, space and reason to rebel, frustrated at lack of opportunity, the perceived mediocrity of their futures and the niggling restraints on self-expression. Hence, they were more attracted by outside cultural models in music and behaviour, Havana manifesting its own variant of punk and the following for rock bands beginning to see such music as an opportunity for collective identity and, occasionally, to challenge authority through behaviour (as *roqueros* or *friquis*) that generated official denunciations of 'decadence'. One side-effect was the emergence of a generation of gays more prepared to challenge norms by open homosexuality.

Another deviation became evident in the rise of religious practice, in both formal structures (the weakened Catholic Church and the more acceptable Protestant churches) and informal Afro-Cuban religions (often by now collectively termed *santería*), which, as Havana grew, experienced a revival, attracting even more white Cubans. This had much to do with an ambivalent official attitude to *santería* (which created a unique space) and the association between black religion, the new prestige of Afro-Cuban culture and the need for 'belonging' among inhabitants whose lives, having been changed fundamentally twenty years before, had now set down roots that demanded recognition in religious practice.

Havana also changed spatially and physically, one factor being the ongoing housing shortage. By 1971, the possibilities of 'quick-fix' solutions had been exhausted with the end of middle-class emigration. Hence, longer-term planning was needed. Accordingly, in 1971, the Master Plan of the Instituto de Planificación Física prepared for a 2.3 million population by 2010 (Segre et al. 1997: 149), and decided to expand eastwards in Habana del Este. Here the construction *microbrigadas* came into their own; established in December 1970, they were characteristic of the 1960s ethos (in voluntarism and improvisation), but, throughout this period, became useful for meeting immediate needs, building residential units in new developments in Plaza, Alta Habana, Rancho Boyeros, Alamar, Reparto Bahía, San Agustín and La Coronela (Segre et al. 1997: 204). A typical *microbrigada* consisted of a thousand workers, who, recruited from 'surplus' labour in over-staffed enterprises and with professional guidance and rudimentary training, built housing for themselves and their fellow-workers with imported Yugoslav technology and prefabricated materials. By 1975, there were 1,150 brigades and 30,000 workers (Segre *et al*, 1997: 204), building 20,000 units annually and sixty per cent of all units constructed in 1971–5 (Segre et al. 1997: 137–8), Havana seeing most of the 100,000 built by 1983. However, simplicity meant monotony, and the combination of voluntarism and a faith in technology meant poor construction and a neglect of traditional local materials (Segre et al. 1997: 138).

Moreover, although addressing immediate problems, the *microbrigadas* could not keep pace with demand, especially as provincial immigration increased, and, by then, quality had become important, the 1960s short-term measures making repairs, refurbishment and demolition long overdue; by 1987, 357,000 *habaneros* still lived in sub-standard accommodation (Segre et al. 1997: 209). Therefore, 1976–86 saw a new drive on house-building, emphasising self-help projects by local *municipios* using professional builders and provided materials, culminating in the resurrection of the *microbrigadas* in 1986, to build on vacant city-centre spaces, social projects, and the complex for the 1991 Pan American games.

Monotony referred to life in the new developments often without adequate social facilities, transport connections or a sense of identity (especially in Alamar), and also architectural style, the period being characterised by an emphasis on the functional and social need rather than aesthetic quality. The result was a 'mediocridad apabullante' ('overwhelming mediocrity': Torrents 1989: 82), which clashed with the old dynamic jumble of styles, eventually producing a reaction in the 'founders' movement', designed to reverse the worst aspects of recent development since 1959 (Segre et al. 1997: 207). By the 1980s, a new generation of architects was seeking to decentralise and restore some aesthetic criteria into their work, leading to the Arquitectura/Cuba group and, within the Hermanos Saíz organisation, a architectural subsection within Artes Plásticas (Segre et al. 1991: 43). The outcome was an architectural revival as younger artists (such as Eduardo Rubén, Rafael Fornés, Emilio Castro and Rolando Baciel) focused on cultural expression and imagination, leading to the innovative 1986 Taller Le Parc (Segre et al. 1997: 44).

Evolution of Havana Culture

Havana's culture partly followed and partly deviated from these patterns. Overall, the emphasis on institutionalisation and greater economic space had an inevitable impact on the expression of the cultural community, which, by 1971, had felt marginalised, battered and uncertain. Now, with the apparent reversal of the 'Guevarist' approach, it seemed likely that those against whom he had argued in the early 1960s, associated with the perceived CNC 'hard-liners', would be in positions of power, although, equally, the end of the pressure-cooker atmosphere of 1968–70 signalled some promise of reprieve for the harassed community, although the definition of 'cultural revolution' was still unclear.

In April 1971, one clear definition was given by the Congreso de Educación y Cultura, which extolled cultural revolution as the massification or popularisation of culture. While that Congress seemed, outside Cuba, to signal a new 'hard line' on creative freedom, the ensuing policy seemed to follow the 1960s ethos, the new focus on deepening the social revolution being paralleled by a drive to develop Cuban attitudes to reading and to privilege the reader as well as, or even more than, the writer.

A second definition was of cultural revolution as the overt politicisation of culture. Here the starting point was less the Congress than the final denouement of the *caso Padilla*. On 20 March 1971, Padilla was arrested and then, released a month later, directed an *autocrítica* ('self-criticism') to an UNEAC gathering of intellectuals on 27 April, confessing to having unjustifiably played the part of dissident writer and inviting other writers (notably Manuel Díaz Martínez, Norberto Fuentes, Lezama Lima, Pablo Armando Fernández, César López and his own wife Belkis Cuza Malé) to follow (*Index* 1972: 83–122). The episode became a *cause célèbre* in relations between the Revolution and European intellectuals; an open protest letter, signed by fifty-four formerly sympathetic prominent Latin American and European intellectuals, generated a fierce Cuban riposte and condemnation at the Congress, while some original signatories retracted their participation in what they saw an inappropriate bourgeois criticism of a Revolution they supported. In short, the *caso Padilla* was when many foreign intellectuals (most notably Mario Vargas Llosa) broke with the Revolution permanently, some, already disenchanted, long seeking an opportunity to break. It was also a cathartic moment for the Revolution's attitude to outside culture.

Whether the *caso* was the end of the 1960s or the start of the 1970s, it indicated a shift which the Congress then confirmed, with the decision to monitor the selection of cultural prize juries. Yet the Congress simply confirmed the message of post-1961 Cuban cultural policy, its significance lying in its tone and its coincidence with the *caso*. Its resolutions certainly set a new tone, emphasising more firmly that art in Cuba should be judged on its political worth – as a 'weapon of the Revolution … against the penetration of the enemy' (*Paths of Culture* 1971: 12) – and not its aestheticism, that art 'against the Revolution' had no place, and rejecting 'the aspirations of the mafia of bourgeois pseudo-intellectuals to become the critical conscience of society' (*Index* 1972: 124). The Congress also defined culture in a collectivist society as 'a mass activity, not the monopoly of an elite' (*Paths* 1971: 12), arguing that 'true genius is to be found among the masses and not among a few isolated individuals' (*Paths* 1971: 13). It thus identified 'cultural revolution' as mass culture, by and for the masses, and, significantly, stepped away from cultural nationalism and cultural identity: 'While the art of the Revolution will be drawn from the roots of our nationality, it will also be internationalist' (*Paths* 1971: 13), going on to talk of the need to express the struggles of the Third World and to offer Cuban institutions as 'tools for the real artists of those continents' (*Paths* 1971: 13).

Indeed, the Congress condemned the 'social aberrations' of 'false' intellectuals, removed from the masses and the Revolution, targeting identifiable individuals and behaviours as counter-revolutionary, while Castro's closing speech was even more characteristically explicit, referring to 'a small group of sorcerers acquainted with the rituals of culture' (*Paths* 1971: 33).

Evidently, the 1965–7 experience looked to be repeated, 1971 ushering in the *quinquenio gris* (grey five years), a period when, as now admitted, a 'corriente de intolerancia' reigned ('current of intolerance': Campuzano 2001: 54). For some, the threats were real: Piñera's works were unpublishable, his movements limited, his manuscripts seized and he was briefly detained in 1978, a year before he died (Black 1989: 120–1), while Reinaldo Arenas spent eighteen months in prison in 1974–5, found his new works unpublished and was expelled from the *talleres literarios* ('literary workshops'), founding a group of young writers to rewrite confiscated manuscripts (Black 1989: 123). Meanwhile, Antonio Benítez Rojo remained unpublished and lost his job as director of Casa's research centre, his writings (as with Lezama Lima's) disappearing from bookshops (Black 1989: 134), René Ariza had constant battles with CNC officials over his plays and was eventually imprisoned for smuggling a manuscript abroad (Black 1989: 122), and Eduardo Heras León was dismissed from the *Caimán Barbudo* editorial board in 1971.

In these circumstances, a state of enforced quiescence descended on the Havana community, artists either keeping their counsel or conforming resignedly to the new ordinance, unsure of how far they could go in their work and preferring to lie low until the mood changed again. The effects on cultural production were noticeable, as all literary genres seemed to decline in vitality and ambition, the only new developments seemingly being the rise of the detective novel after 1971, stimulated by the prize offered by the Ministry of the Interior (MININT), Concurso Aniversario del Triunfo de la Revolución, and then flourishing after 1976 (Alvarez 1987: 160). However, in poetry and the story, the pattern seemed to be less dynamic and much more cautious. Nonetheless, in one of characteristic paradoxes of post-1959 Cuba, those very years saw a boom in general cultural activity, measured (not untypically) in quantitative terms: by 1975, the CNC employed 19,540 people in all activities and proudly boasted a 65 per cent increase in activities since 1962 and a 50 per cent increase in cultural participation (Weiss 1985: 121).

There is, of course, another possible explanation for the apparent, but partial, decline in creativity, more complex than the simple tendency to see restraints on creativity as identifiable with political obstacles, namely in the processes of change itself. For, in the 1960s, regardless of political pressures and supposed 'hard lines', the whole exciting and destabilising process of dynamic social change and political interaction generated a context for cultural creativity to flourish, while, after 1971, as institutionalisation slowed down that process, the resulting decline in the dynamism of Cuban life may well have contributed to a loss of creative tension. Certainly, as we have seen, the *quinquenio* did not apply equally to all in the cultural community.

In 1976, the climate did indeed change again for the better, perhaps somewhat surprisingly, since this coincided with supposedly the period of greatest political 'orthodoxy' with institutionalisation. However, that same institutionalisation also saw, in 1976, a new Ministerio de Cultura replace the unpopular PSP-led CNC. Since the new body was led by Armando Hart, always part of the governing 'inner circle' and instrumental in the early revolutionary processes as Minister of Education, it seemed to endow culture with a new power and offer the prospect of change.

Hart used that power to effect. Recognising the *quinquenio*'s damage to creativity and morale, he sought to end the institutionalised intolerance and bring a 'descongelamiento' ('thaw': Muguercia 1995: 118), creating 'new institutional forms to fulfil the demands of the grass roots artistic-literary movement' (Pérez 1991: 33). Firstly, he established organisations to reflect the needs of 1976 rather than 1968, reducing bureaucratisation to ease communication with artists; these included new research centres (to study key issues and provide protective space), especially, in 1976, the Centro de Estudios Martianos. The latter, under Fernández Retamar until 1986, represented a significant moment, providing space for expression in tasks fundamental to both education and revolution and recognising the Revolution's Cuban roots. In the embattled Havana cultural community that significance was welcomed.

Secondly, Hart opened communication with the cultural community, encouraging them to look outside for inspiration, in a real break with the patterns of 1968–76. One example was the welcome for the young Cuban-Americans of the Areíto group who visited in 1977, breaking the ice and opening up the enclosed cultural world to Cuban-American culture (Campa 2000: 91). Thirdly, many of the community who had suffered personally since 1971 were rehabilitated and either published or able to create and travel, a freedom enhanced by the abrogation of the old ban on copyright (which gave writers partial ownership and the opportunity to be professionals rather than cultural bureaucrats) and the 1975 abrogation of the CNC's strictures on homosexuality. In 1977 the de facto 'blacklist' was ended and, in 1979, imprisoned intellectuals were released and many allowed to leave, some (such as Arenas) seizing the opportunity of Mariel and others (such as Padilla or Leante) leaving more discreetly. Hence, Heras León was again published from 1977, and Benítez Rojo's isolation ended in 1979 when he became director of Casa's Centro de Estudios del Caribe. This rehabilitation even included older exiled writers whose work now appeared in bookshops, such as Lydia Cabrera and Lino Novás Calvo. As unpublished manuscripts appeared and new groups formed, debating issues unquestioned since the 1960s, the Havana elite cultural community came alive again.

Hart's fourth strategy was to build on the network of *escuelas* and *instructores de arte* and formalise the *movimiento de aficionados* by creating the Casas de Cultura. Beginning with a *sistema de instituciones de base* (to guarantee that each *municipio* would minimally have a library, a museum and a Casa de Cultura), the Casas were established until 1978 under the Ministerio's Dirección de Casas de Cultura y Aficionados, although many already existed; although one commentator argues that they responded to imported Soviet models (Weiss 1985: 124), they were clearly a formalisation of a more organic process. By the 1980s, their activities had expanded to include literature (usually in a separate Casa del Escritor), *instructores* again regularly going out into schools and workplaces, their quality being now enhanced by a new university-trained *asesor cultural* in each Casa, by the provision of resources, equipment and *instructores* from the Ministerio, and local support from mass organisations (who would organise competitions) and the municipal Poder Popular. Their quality and vibrancy, however, varied enormously, ranging from a 'forced decorum' (Weiss 1985: 125) to a responsive local forum for untapped talent.

This was all helped by the expansion of publishing. Until it was dismantled in 1977, the Instituto del Libro remained in control of all publishing (outside Casa de las Américas and UNEAC), with thirteen different presses subordinated to its centralised management decisions.[7] While Rolando Rodríguez was at the helm, decisions were enlightened, following the prevailing revolutionary ethos, but the new intolerance affected publishing too. Even the new Central Committee-linked Editora Política (1970) and a decentralisation through the 1972 Juan Marinello printing plant in Guantánamo (before 1970 only Editorial Oriente existed outside Havana) represented a move to take publishing away from potential contamination by the 'problematic' Havana community. Therefore, the Instituto's disaggregation was welcomed, as it split into several separate presses: Editoriales de Cultura y Ciencia (including Letras Cubanas, Arte y Literatura, Gente Nueva, Ciencias Sociales and Oriente), Pueblo y Educación (for textbooks), UNEAC's Ediciones Unión, Ediciones Casa de las Américas, Ediciones MINFAR, the Biblioteca Nacional and the University presses, along with Editorial José Martí (largely for overseas publicity) and Editorial Abril, printing youth magazines and, from 1986, books (Smorkaloff 1997: 128–9).

The Ministerio also encouraged an acceleration of publishing; while in 1967, Cuba had published 781 titles in 15.9 million copies, 1977 saw 1,1143 titles and 31 million copies (Smorkaloff 1997: 127). For literature publishing, in particular, this was a golden age, Letras Cubanas between 1977 and 1986 publishing 958 titles including 124 totally new writers (compared to 1,544 titles by Cuban authors published in the whole of Cuba in 1959–76 (Smorkaloff 1997: 165). Interestingly, of these 124 no fewer than 99 were from Havana, indicating both a revival of the capital's cultural life and the magnetic tendencies of the city as a place, once again, to seek fame and publishing space. One effect on cultural production was an evident increase in the ambition of new narrative, with the appearance of intimate themes, psychological novels and a 'neo-picaresque' vein inconceivable in 1971–6 (Alvarez 1987: 163).

Inevitably, perhaps, 1980–2 saw a brief retrenchment in the face of Mariel and threatening noises from the incoming Reagan Administration, although, in fact, fears arising from the 1968–76 experiences left many Havana artists and intellectuals still cautious, for, while Hart's reforms were welcomed, they were not fully trusted until they had passed the test of time; anyway, some in the political elite still mistrusted a community seen as a seedbed of potential dissent. Thus, when people like Arenas, Padilla and Leante left, that mistrust seemed confirmed, and the whole atmosphere of condemnation around Mariel made many intellectuals fearful. Moreover, this mood was not helped by the new ideological war with Washington, who (especially through the Miami-based Radio Martí from 1985) focused accusations of Cuba's repression of human rights on recent memoirs of exiled writers and the campaign to release Armando Valladares, whose decision to start writing poetry while imprisoned for counter-revolutionary sabotage made him into a new *cause célèbre* for a critical outside intelligentsia, seeing him as a new Padilla, leading to the 1986 publication of his *Against all Hope*.

By 1982, however, the fears were largely over, the reality of the new tolerance being confirmed for many by an encouraging article by Fernández Retamar in Issue 131 of *Casa de las Américas* (Campuzano 2001: 54); given his proximity to Hart and his general access to political authority, his words seemed to indicate that the new post-1976 freedoms were real.

Certainly this seemed to be proved further in 1984 when the first Bienal de La Habana took place (largely for Latin American art), followed by the Second (focused on the Third World) in 1986 and the Third in 1989. Seen then and since as a seminal moment in the plastic and visual arts, the 1984 event established a welcome space for new artists to exhibit and have dialogue, as well as bringing new art into Havana and, in the process, acting as a 'vaccine against provincialism' (Valdés Figueroa 2001: 21), a provincialism that many in the cultural community had feared with the 1960s 'siege'.

This opening was reinforced by 'Rectification', to the surprise of many outside observers who read that process as a return to an old militancy.[8] That, however, is to misread Rectification, a campaign as much about finding a new ideological impetus (inspired by the 1960s) as about returning to old patterns, its implicit rejection of Soviet orthodoxy (deemed the cause of Cuba's current problems) also meaning a desire to open up to new debates. Indeed, Rectification itself became such a debate, seeking solutions more than defined certainties, which meant, in culture, applying the principles of self-criticism under Hart's guiding hand, condemning 'past errors and negative tendencies' in culture too.

After two years of debates, the 1988 Congresses of UNEAC and Hermanos Saíz became the forum for a full-blown debate and a confirmation of a new tolerance, a new questioning and a new condemnation of past approaches. The UNEAC Congress in particular (only its Fourth) addressed three issues. The first was the need to criticise and question, delegates condemning the 1970s' lack of communication and demanding to be heard and involved in decision-making. In Castro's presence, participants in the Hermanos Saíz assembly criticised their working conditions and leadership, their comparatively poor premises and the quality of cultural education.

The second issue was the need to clarify whether Castro's 1961 *Palabras* had indeed allowed the space it seemed to offer, and whether those who were not explicitly *for* the Revolution but were not *against* it were included. Clarification came from Carlos Rafael Rodríguez, whose closing speech reiterated the exclusion of the 'incorrigibly counter-revolutionary' but the inclusion of honest creators who broadly supported the Revolution, and, rejecting art produced by apologists and acolytes, reminded delegates and authorities of the need to appreciate the quality of non-revolutionaries' work. On the third issue, the question of quality, Congresses and leaders were in harmony, especially the new UNEAC president (later Minister of Culture) Abel Prieto, reiterating that poor quality served no purpose and demeaned the Revolution.

Given this tortuous experience of change and the uncertainty about the parameters of tolerance, the Havana cultural community spent much of these two decades in a state of shock, flux and cautious re-formation. Their working conditions were indeed often deplorable, as the head of the Escuela Nacional de Ballet complained in 1988, indicative of their marginalisation. Yet, until 1986, few felt able to complain openly, this persuading some to leave in the 1980s. Confusion was especially acute among the supposed cultural vanguard of 1959–61, which had borne the brunt of criticism until 1976, domestically for being insufficiently revolutionary and internationally for being seen to serve the official cultural apparatus. By the time relief came, some of these, spent and disoriented, chose to leave Cuba. With their emigration, a degree of leadership and disaffection also left the community, and, with the provincial influx yet to have an impact, the Havana community of 1976–89 generally lacked direction, cohesion, purpose and self-confidence.

There were, of course, exceptions of protective space, notably ICAIC and Casa. With the Havana Festival of New Latin American Cinema from 1979 opening Cuba up to external scrutiny and talent, and with the prestigious Latin American Film School being founded in 1986 through the initiative of Fidel Castro and García Márquez, film was obviously still a hallowed space. Indeed, ICAIC continued to protect its own, enabling film-makers to address controversial issues, such as machismo (in Gutiérrez Alea's 1983 *Hasta Cierto Punto*), housing (in Juan Carlos Tabio's 1983 *Se Permuta*) and emigration (in Jesús Díaz's 1985 *Lejanía*). ICAIC also continued to be open to the outside: by the late 1980s, it was importing 120 films annually (Aufderheide 1989: 502). ICAIC's power evidently derived from film's political importance and enduring popularity; although other distractions (television and an expansion of public cultural performances) meant a decline, in the 1980s a leading Cuban film could still expect a one million audience in its first two months. Moreover, in 1985, there were still 500 cinemas nationally, at 1960s prices, and 741 cinema clubs (Chanan 1985: 16–17). In the late 1980s, ICAIC still produced weekly newsreels, and an average of up to forty documentaries and eight full-length feature films annually (Aufderheide 1989: 499; Soles 2000: 125), although in 1971–76 ICAIC too seemed to suffer from the *quinquenio*, producing twenty-three films in six years compared to the twenty,

twenty-four and twenty-seven in 1986, 1987 and 1989 alone (García Borrero 2001: 377).

Casa de las Américas was of course another such space. This was because it was protected by Haydée Santamaría's patronage until her death in 1986 and then because of the status and political skill of her successor Fernández Retamar, but also because of its contacts with Latin America and, after the 1979 Carifesta, the non-Hispanic Caribbean, the new Centro de Estudios del Caribe establishing its *Anales del Caribe* in 1981.

Throughout this period, the meaning of cultural democratisation was again central. While writing experienced a boom in the new atmosphere and opportunities, the relative obscurity of the Casas del Escritor indicated a perhaps more marginal function, seemingly limited to providing space and equipment rather than emulating the *talleres literarios* or boosting participation. The visual and plastic arts and theatre were, however, emphasised in the Casas de Cultura and *movimiento de aficionados*, although somewhat divorced from the professional world, where the former drive for popularisation and relevance seemed less evident, theatre and art both tending either to retreat into a shell or seek innovation rather than relevance.

The Havana art world, after its 1960s heyday of 'public art' through posters, spent much of the 1970s relatively silent, the principal development being a movement of 'photo-realism' in 1973–9 (Camnitzer 2003: 9), which, linked to the vogue for *testimonio*, offered at its worst echoes of Socialist Realism and at its best a degree of formal novelty. In the 1980s, however, it seemed to blossom again, especially with the promise of new space and opportunity. Besides the promise and encouragement of the 1984 Bienal, it was above all the January 1981 exhibition, 'Volumen I' at the Centro de Arte Internacional which stimulated this (Mosquera 2001: 13); with eleven artists exhibiting and some 8,000 visitors in two weeks (Camnitzer 2003: 3), and with its almost iconoclastic tone, it offered hope to the emerging generation which it seemed to represent.

This new art, however, only resembled the 1960s boom in its self-confidence, notably in the detailed monumentalism of Gilberto de la Nuez Iglesias's 1980 panorama of Havana, *Esta es la Historia*. This was partly generational, the 1970s being a hiatus between the pre-1959 artists who had dominated the 1960s and the emergence of the graduates of ISA, of the reformed San Alejandro and other art schools. There were also other factors. In the first place, the end of the material shortages (which had helped determine the 1960s' innovation) and the greater availability of paper boosted a resurgence of drawing (Eligio 2001: 31) and a willingness to experiment beyond the previous minimalism. Secondly, the effect of institutions such as ISA and the ENA was positive and negative; on the one hand they guaranteed employment after graduation, which changed the Havana art world drastically, but, on the other, they also determined the potentially rigid criteria and parameters for the new art, as the new art hierarchy (using its prizes, spaces and training opportunities) effectively laid down the rules for acceptability. This was enhanced by the fact that Cuba still only had four middle art schools, two in the east (Holguín and Santiago) and two in Havana, thereby ensuring greater conformity with official norms. Professionalisation was thus a double-edged gain.

The result was, however, something of a 'golden age', when 'cultural discourse became separate from "official discourse"' (Mosquera 2001: 13) and with young groups acted on their determination to question orthodoxy. This newness was especially exemplified by groups such as the Grupo Hexágono, with its desire to exploit collectively a range of materials in the field (Camnitzer 2003: 73), and especially the so-called 'Third Generation' which followed, characterised as it was by a number of groupings. These especially included the Grupo Provisional, the iconoclastic Arte Calle, the collectivist anti-celebrity Grupo Puré, 1, 2, 3 ... 12, and the Grupo Reunión/Grupo Imán (Camnitzer 2003: 79), plus various individualists such as Tomás Esson, whose iconoclastic *Mi homenaje al Che*, which, when exhibited in 1988, caused the brief closure of the gallery, because of its supposedly disrespectful eroticism.

However, this new art found little resonance among the public, exhibitions being largely enclosed within the small circles that revelled in their freedom but, unlike their predecessors, paid little overt heed to the demands of Revolution or public. Hence, not only did it risk isolation and condemnation for excess in a still cautious atmosphere but it seemed to break the link between the visual arts and the needs of cultural democratisation, the search for cultural identity seemingly being replaced by a concern for individual or group identity, and by a drive for artistic eclecticism, which at its best was a 'consciously assumed stance' (Camnitzer 2003: 314), reflecting confidence and Cuba's cultural reality, but at its worst was a chaotic melange of styles and individualism. Indeed, the fact that many of the 1980s generation subsequently left Cuba was no surprise.

A similar pattern was evident in Havana theatre, where the 1970s pressures had dampened innovation, experimentation being replaced by safety; given theatre's intrinsic capacity for immediate challenge, its exponents certainly felt more exposed to critical scrutiny and, by the late 1970s, the range of activity was reduced by several factors. Firstly, the general caution made performances necessarily more serious and didactic in intent, although, conversely, Havana audiences retained a taste for light comedy, either clinging to old traditions, responding to a relatively new cultural education or seeking relief from the greyness of Havana life and the earnestness of other cultural forms; the Teatro Bertold Brecht was specifically dedicated to such comedy. Curiously, this lack of vitality coincided with improved provision, as new theatres were opened (notably the Sala Alejo Carpentier within the Gran Teatro García Lorca) and a huge class of professional playwrights was created – including pre-1959 survivors such as Carlos Felipe and

Rolando Ferrer and newer artists such as Matías Montes Huidobro, José Triana, Manuel Reguera Saumell, José Brene, Arrufat, José Ignacio Gutiérrez, Nicolás Dorr and Héctor Quintera – although, while bringing a welcome stability, this generated a tendency to conformity and caution (Matas 1971: 435). Experiment, while less obvious now, was nonetheless evident in Piñera and the young Abelardo Estorino, in the Teatro Nacional's Noveno Piso theatre, and the García Lorca's Artaud theatre. Even in the 1970s, Vicente Revuelta's Los Doce troupe adopted Grotowski's ideas and Ramiro Guerra's experimental dance was beginning.

In the 1980s, however, theatre paralleled the visual arts' new mood, although its purpose was less innovation for its own sake and more engaged, addressing themes of daily life and questions of alienation, disillusion and identity, as in Estorino's *Morir del cuento*, Revuelta's *Historia de un caballo*, Flora Lauten's *Electra* and Abilio Estévez's *Lila la mariposa* (Muguercia 1995: 119). However, these efforts were often launched into a void, as Havana theatre lacked its former popularity and audiences tended to come from a smaller constituency, and it was again left to film to address social issues more publicly, albeit focusing on the question of cultural identity.

In the 1950s, of course, the cultural form most explicitly addressing that question had been music, although subsequently somewhat disoriented by the lack of consensus on what cultural revolution might mean in music, a pattern apparently continuing for the 1970s. For example, 'serious' music continued its link with cinema, through ICAIC, the 1980s seeing significant compositions by Mario Daly, Aneiro Taño, Gonzalo Rubalcava and Edesio Alejandro, culminating in the music for *La Bella del Alhambra* (1989), while Carlos Alfonso's Grupo Síntesis took classical music into rock-influenced forms from 1976, eventually becoming a rock group with its Afro-Cuban influenced 1987 album *Ancestros I*.

In this context, jazz experienced a revival, being stimulated after 1977 by the opening to its American roots, the improvement in US-Cuban relations being celebrated with a 'Jazz Cruise' to Havana by leading US performers (including Dizzy Gillespie, Earl Hines and Stan Getz), followed in 1978 by an *Encuentro Cuba-USA* in Havana's Teatro Karl Marx, including several American jazz and rock performers. However, American influence was only one cause, jazz having already begun to be incorporated into the music of Chucho Valdés's Irakere from 1973 and, from 1977, Afro-Cuba and Opus 13, all influenced by the awareness of Afro-Cuban rhythms and forms. Interestingly, this new development was often led by graduates of Havana's music schools; thus, while art graduates' self-confidence had pushed them towards individualism (and often emigration), music graduates were evidently seeking to 'belong' to traditions which they felt they were rescuing.

This rediscovery was paralleled by a rescue of other popular music forms, boosted considerably by ICAIC's search for cultural identity through its documentary series on Cuban music, notably Giral's *Qué bien canta Vd* (about Beny Moré) and Oscar Valdés's *La Rumba* (Chanan 1985: 264–5). Certainly, *rumba*'s recognition was now taken further; in 1975, the Conjunto Folklórico Nacional began regular Saturday events in Vedado, which, from 1982, became the *Sábados de la Rumba* (Rumba Saturdays). Partly encouraged by the Angola-inspired rediscovery of Cuba's African forms as more than entertainment and an expression of Cuba's cultural identity, this recognition now extended in other ways, especially by groups who either fused traditional dance and music forms with rock instruments and technology or sought to revitalise those forms. Thus, from 1976, the Sierra Maestra group took up the *son*, which, until then, only Juan Formell's Los Van Van had really used from 1969 (Roy 2002: 158). This was developed further in 1983 when a visiting Venezuelan *salsa* band played *son* at a Varadero festival, with such an impact on Havana's youth that Los Van Van developed its own *conga-son*. While this process seemed to echo previous patterns of recognition, legitimisation by external criteria came this time, significantly, from Latin America and not the United States, although, while the 1960s and 1970s development of *salsa* in New York was ignored, in the 1980s it was adopted with some pride in its Cuban *son* roots (Acosta 2001: 49).

Meantime, the Nueva Trova movement, which, in the 1960s, had tried to learn, and differentiate, from new Western youth music while using the *trova* tradition, became the 1970s' popular musical form. 1973 saw the UJC's Segundo Encuentro de Jóvenes Trovadores, in Manzanillo, found the Movimiento de la Nueva Trova; although much of the early impetus came from Oriente and Matanzas, Havana soon saw its greatest development, exponents taking the music with proselytising zeal into the city's factories and schools and boosting the *movimiento de artistas aficionados*. Certainly, the majority of performers eventually came from, or moved to, Havana, notably Los Cañas (founded in 1967 from FAR *aficionados*), Manguaré (1971) and Mayohuacán (1972), plus individuals such as Alfredo Carol, Vicente Feliú, Rubén Galindo, Alejandro García (Virulo), Sara González, Enrique Núñez, Amaury Pérez, Angel Qunitero, Eduardo Ramos and Miriam Ramos, and the best known Silvio Rodríguez and Pablo Milanés (Jorge Gómez 1981: 271–85).

Although the Movimiento's innovation and dynamism eventually faded, it had a lasting impact on youth music in Havana, for the *son* revival produced the more frenzied and anarchic *freneticia* and the sexually explicit *despelota*, both characterising Havana youth venues in the mid to late 1980s, while the 1988 emergence of NG La Banda, with its complex rhythms and challenging lyrics, appealed immediately, generating a Cuban rap and David Carzado's defiant Charanga Habanera.

Indeed, by now, it was possible to talk for the first time of a Havana youth culture emerging from the margins. For, while in the early 1980s, the deliberately self-marginalising *roqueros* and *friquis* had been harassed and denounced as decadents, in 1984 María Gattorno, head of the La Tumba Casa de Cultura Roberto

Branly (in Cerro) allowed young punk-influenced groups (often incorporating traditional rhythms) to rehearse and perform, despite official and local objections. Hence, the Casa de Cultura became known as the Patio de María, giving rise to later successful rock groups and hosting other youth cultural activities, poetry readings, exhibitions of art and youth theatre workshops (Lightfoot 2002: 211). Although the Casa was eventually closed for repair, it had already been seminal, legitimising and including a youth culture which would evolve in the 1990s and help shape Havana's cultural identity.

The significance of this musical explosion (so different from the atmosphere in literary, artistic and dramatic circles) was that music was again fundamental to the process of cultural identification, not only in finding a space where a Cuban national identity could be recognised, but also fusing elite production with public demands and finding a specifically *habanero* cultural identity. In fact, on the eve of the crisis that would challenge all cultural preconceptions in Cuba, it was possible to detect several different routes towards that goal.

The participatory definition had already been given by the Casas de Cultura. However, by 1989, many of their inherent problems surfaced, notably a bureaucratic rigidity that gradually overpowered the original democratising instinct. Most notably, there was a growing confusion between professionals and *aficionados*. Outside Havana, the local Casa had often become the local theatre or concert-hall, occasionally preventing the development of more professional local entities; hence local professionals increasingly resented the amateur Casas. Conversely, in Havana, the Casas could not compete with the available professional activities, making them seem distinctly second-best. This was compounded by an inherent tension in the original concept, whereby the *aficionado*, regardless of talent, could not become an artistic professional without specialist training, having only been coached by *instructores* trained to teach rather than develop their own art. Moreover, *aficionado* resentment of professional counterparts was mirrored by the latter's tendency to look down on the *aficionados*, because, by the late 1980s, the *instructores* (trained in earlier artistic mores and ideas) were seen to be peddling culturally outdated ideas, in comparison with professionals more geared to new ideas and foreign patterns. There was thus a growing perception within the Havana vanguard cultural community that the Casas were mediocre, lacking potential for a creative and politically acceptable fusion between popular and vanguard, the latter therefore retreating into their protective circles.

The Casas had been paralleled by the *talleres literarios*, which, in 1974, numbered about seventy with a thousand members (Smorkaloff 1997: 140). These were based in schools, factories and military units, structured to allow the best participants to progress from *barrio* to *municipio* level, culminating in an annual Encuentro Nacional, with public readings and professional judging of the work, the best being then published in a Letras Cubanas anthology series, *Talleres*

Literarios. By 1983, there were some 1,500 groups of *aficionados* or *talleres* (Smorkaloff 1997: 140), the latter in their heyday offering an imaginative space for aspiring writers, with established writers encouraged to be mentors. Their decline therefore said as much about changing attitudes in the cultural establishment as about popular interest.

Yet this participatory approach was also evident in the programme to develop reading habits. Following the 1961 Campaign, educational authorities had sought to address the limited educational impact of a rapidly acquired literacy, hoping to create a discerning literacy. One result was Salvador Bueno's Campaña Popular de Lectura, seeking to broaden new readers' literary tastes. However, in the 1970s, such campaigns were neglected, limited to short-term exercises such as the post-1977 *Sábados del Libro* (book Saturdays) in the Moderna Poesía bookshop, Havana's first book fair. In the 1980s, however, the new mood of self-examination led to two sequential campaigns: Raúl Ferrer's 1984 Campaña Nacional por la Lectura and the Biblioteca Nacional's 1988 Campaña Nacional (later the Programa Nacional de Lectura under Víctor Fowler Calzada: Fowler 2002: 243). In the 1990s these efforts became a national priority.

Meanwhile, some in the cultural authorities preferred to see democratisation as either mass culture (television and radio providing a diet of traditional popular Cuban music) or traditional popular culture. The latter was evident in carnival, which, in the 1960s, enjoyed a revival as a genuinely cultural expression, stimulated by state funds (channelled through trade unions) rather than *barrios* (Feliú Herrera 1998: 58), although the increasing shortage of materials made them less than flamboyant affairs. By the late 1970s, however, they were in decline, although the authorities still considered them an autochthonous form of entertainment and popular culture, preferable to the increasingly tumultuous youth concerts (Roy 2002: 152).

What this question raises, therefore, is the 'official' policy towards defining the 'popular', which, as we have seen, had oscillated between folklore (based on traditional forms), entertainment (based on 'mass' tastes) and democratisation (whether top-down, where artists raised cultural levels, or bottom-up, where participation was the driving impulse). The uncertainty and variation reflected differing opinions as much as policy changes. However, the judgement of Renato Ortiz (talking of 1930s–1950s Brazil) is relevant here, namely that 'samba, carnival and football' legitimised a notion of 'Brazilianness', and that '[F]aced with the still insubstantial development of modern life, the social imaginary was left to seize upon traditional popular culture, transforming it into the "national-popular" (Ortiz 2000: 142), into a cultural populism. The relevance in Cuba is that, whereas the political and cultural leadership occasionally attempted to formalise a Cuban cultural identity as based on Afro-Cuban roots (thus superficially corresponding to Ortiz's description of the Brazilian state's efforts), the Cuba of 1959–89 hardly resembled the evolving nature of 1930s-1950s Brazil, where social change and dislocation made 'modernisation' (and the resulting obsession with 'modernity') universally relevant. In revolutionary Cuba, however, the crucial concern was not modernisation but democratisation, participation and a destabilising pace of revolutionary transformation (the 1960s) or an occasionally stultifying process of consolidation (the 1970s). In this context, the 'traditional' had little organic meaning for most urban Cubans, and the official creation of a folkloric culture (echoing the 1920s) largely failed to take root; however, the pace of change obliged more and more Cubans to seek a cultural 'belonging' (to match their political 'belonging') in something meaningful – in modern 'traditional' music, dance or grass roots movements of cultural participation.

Sport was, of course, another meaningful area, where official efforts easily met popular tastes and where the drive for socialist improvement resulted in all sport (and especially where Cuba was strong, notably boxing, athletics or baseball) becoming a valid part of the construction of a political identity. Hence, in the 1970s, institutionalisation meant increased construction of facilities, high levels of state funding, new equipment, and national networks for identifying, encouraging and training sporting excellence (especially the primary-level Escuela de Iniciación Deportiva Escolar and the senior Escuela de Superación y Perfeccionamiento Atlético), which created a new generation of sportspeople and outside accusations of 'shamateurism'. Throughout, baseball continued to be the archetypal Cuban sport, the 1970s seeing an apogee, as Cuba repeatedly won the Amateur World series (the 1972 Games being in Havana) and the International Cup (also in Havana in 1979). Crisis, however, came in the 1980s, when complacency and inadequate competition led to International Cup defeats by Canada and the Dominican Republic and then a narrow victory in the 1984 Havana-based World Championship.

The year 1989 therefore found the relationships between culture, politics and national identity in a curious position. By then, the relationship between the elite cultural community and the political elite had reached a significant stage in its trajectory. In 1902, a new socio-political elite had created a subsidiary cultural elite, which was later challenged by a counter-elite; after 1959, however, those relationships became much less clear. Instead of a self-perpetuating political elite (seeking consolidation), Cuba was run by a political vanguard (seeking change), while the cultural 'leaders' saw themselves as an adjacent vanguard, yet behaved as a would-be cultural elite. After 1971, the political vanguard was, until Rectification, replaced by a political elite, but the cultural 'leaders' notably failed to constitute either an adjacent elite or a dissenting vanguard, and the cultural community lacked a strong sense of community.

What this signified above all was a profound change in the nature of cultural gate-keeping within Havana. Before 1959, as we have seen, this necessary function had been exercised by a self-conscious and recognised elite, using its network of institutions, prizes and spaces to bestow prestige and determine boundaries; the nature of this exercise was such as to allow room for dissidence from within the social elite, from an equally self-conscious vanguard, but to allow little or no recognition (or prestige) to popular cultural forms emanating from outside these circles. After 1959, however, as a similar cultural elite failed to form, the gate-keeping role was inevitably taken over by the state, but, with state structures and definitions fluid for many years, that meant in reality two things: the lack of insti-tutions, spaces and a perceived academy against which a dissident vanguard might form publicly, and little space or inclination for any real cultural opposition to operate, whether at elite or popular level. The result was an inevitable tendency towards cultural conformity, both out of resigned caution and out of commitment and adherence to shared principles, in which any gate-keeping was actually diffi-cult to enforce credibly, being realised somewhat clumsily at times when institu-tions were dominant (such as the CNC) and more subtly when key individuals were paramount (such as under Hart after 1976). Hence, in this context, the param-eters for artistic creation were actually far from clear at any one time, leading either to cautious self-control or to wilful or accidental breaching of any unseen bounds; equally, however, in the same context, the traditional boundaries between the elite/vanguard norms for cultural practice and popular cultural forms became increasingly blurred, especially as differentiating social layers became less clear-cut and cultural education (in all its forms) became more widespread.

Therefore the relationship between the Havana elite cultural community and others had evolved. As we have seen, the pre-1959 tendencies of elite culture to attach itself to a presumed global community whose poles lay abroad, seeing them-selves as the standard-bearers in Cuba of that broader community, had been replaced after 1959 by a new set of relationships. For two or three years, the old patterns continued, followed by a period of flux when new poles appeared (prima-rily in Latin America, but also, for the first time, in Cuba itself, and, to a lesser extent, in the Socialist Bloc), when the development of a national cultural com-munity began to be realised empirically but with few clear links with the elite/van-guard community. In the post-1971 disorientation, however, these relationships became even more problematic and unclear: largely isolated from the 1960s poles and broader communities, the elite community found itself also disconnected from the national community. Hence, by 1989, we could talk of the coexistence in Havana of two separate and remarkably disjointed (rather than overlapping) 'cir-cuits': the cultural 'leaders' being either abroad (reconnected to the pre-1959 global community) or isolated and internally disjointed, unclear about political-cultural directions and priorities and about their own role or parameters, while the 'lower circuit' was developing a series of separate routes.

This therefore leads to the third key relationship: between the Havana commu-nity and a national cultural identity. Certainly, by 1989, this community was less certain than ever about what constituted such an identity, with cultural attitudes and differing interpretations being underpinned by a constantly changing environment. However, at the grass roots, some significant developments were taking shape, in the Casas, an emerging youth culture and popular music, the latter two being particularly relevant by being especially focused on Havana, making it possible to talk of an emerging Havana identity, leading the 'national'. Given the vicissitudes of Havana's relationship with the rest of Cuba and its previously problematic role within a national identity, this was potentially significant, providing it did not again become marginalised.

Hence, another development was of fundamental importance: the rediscovery of Havana's identity in its process of restoration and reconstruction. For the post-1976 cultural changes also saw a long-term sustained effort (especially through the dynamism of the Eusebio Leal-led Oficina del Historiador de la Ciudad) to restore the crumbling Habana Vieja. After two years of research by the Departamento de Patrimonio Cultural of the Ministerio, Habana Vieja was declared in 1978 a Monumento Nacional, the key moment when Cuba discovered an important part of its cultural identity in Havana, and Havana discovered its identity in the act of restoration rather than neglect. Instead of seeing the city as a 'problem' and a focus of deviancy and anti-nationalism, the Revolution was now formally declaring its pride in Havana, an act of cultural nationalism which had an immediate impact.

One effect was felt among Havana's cultural community. A July 1981 issue of *Revolución y Cultura* (Issue 107) effectively became a cultural manifesto for a national battle to save Havana: 'Esta ciudad se salvará, si nosotros somos capaces de hacerlo. Esta es nuestra tarea, la tarea de todos, la parte que nos corresponde en el sostenimiento victorioso de la patria' ('This city will save itself if we can manage it. That is the task of all of us, our role in the whole victorious defence of the nation': Leal 1981: 9).[9] That same year, the state agreed a budget dedicated to reconstruction, and, in 1982, UNESCO declared the *municipio* a World Heritage Site, after which the campaign became one of the Revolution's most significant, imaginative and consensual acts of national cultural identification, of particular significance in the 1990s.

Part III: Case Study – *Bohemia* and *Granma*

The new Cuba after 1959 necessarily demands a slightly different case study approach from the 1902–58 period, especially as the print media changed substantially over the decade. For comparison with the pre-1959 pattern, *Bohemia* remains the focus for the first decade, but *Granma* thereafter replaces it, a change that recognises that *Bohemia* by 1971 had become less reflective of social shifts, while *Granma*, then Cuba's sole daily, provides an incomparable window both onto 'official' cultural attitudes and news (and thus onto the emerging patterns of official criteria and parameters) and onto readers' tastes. Moreover, while the previous chapter examined editions at ten-yearly intervals, this chapter's approach adopts a five-yearly pattern (but still using March as the criterion), recognising both the need to track changes during Cuba's astonishingly rapid transformation and also the fact that 1961, 1971 and 1976 were years of considerable cultural significance.

1961–71: Bohemia

March 1961   The 1961 *Bohemia* had most obviously grown (to some 130 pages) and had become more didactic in purpose, educating readers about the Revolution's achievements (especially rural), about culture and about science, in the regular informative columns, while still seeking to entertain. Advertisements no longer indicated social changes, but did reflect political shifts. Alongside the surprising survival of American products and correspondence courses (and even the Rosicrucians), the magazine included full-page advertisements for nation-alised (formerly American) enterprises and hotels, and for the CDRs; however, arguments with the United States and the movement towards the Socialist Bloc were not really reflected, the international focus tending to be Latin American, and the Socialist world appearing somewhat apolitically in the new 'Paz y Progreso' ('Peace and Progress') column. Furthermore, many of the pre-1959 features remained, including syndicated American material in two editions and the regular columns such as 'Agilidad Mental' (Mental Agility'), 'En Pocas Palabras' ('In Short') and Nitza Villapol's recipes, although new columns indicated change, notably the news digests 'En Cuba' and '7 Días en el Mundo' ('Seven Days in the World'), the miscellany of 'Cantaclaro' ('Out Loud') and '¿Qué Hay de Nuevo?' ('What's New?'), and the readers' letters column, 'Aquí, el Pueblo' ('The People Speak').

The magazine's greatest change, however, indicating the new priorities, came in its coverage of culture. This now occupied much more space than ever (some fifteen to twenty pages in each edition), both in the continuing columns 'Teleradiolandia' (still mostly news snippets and gossip, but now from Cuba) and 'Baraúnda' (on television's cultural offerings), and in the new column 'Cine' (including regular film reviews by Almendros); it was also in general articles and the inclusion of cultural features (such as book announcements) in the news columns. These articles were wide-ranging, every edition containing several pages of items: Issue 10 included the Casa contest's stimulation of talent (53, 10: 83) and an Almendros article on the American 'new wave' (53, 10: 90), Issue 11 a Salvador Bueno history of the Cuban novel (53, 11: 102–4), a piece on Byron (53, 11: 30) and news of the new Academia de Arte (*escuela de arte*) in the Copacabana hotel (53, 11: 40), Issue 12 carried news of a cultural workshop in the Santos Suárez dis-trict (53, 12: 8–10) and an article on Havana street booksellers (53, 12: 25–6), while Issue 13 included items on puppet theatre (53, 13: 43–5) and the Argentine novelist José Bianco (53, 13: 23). Overall, the most notable aspects of the new *Bohemia*'s cultural coverage for March were the omission of anything on theatre (other than an announcement of a Pirandello play at the Payret: 53, 13: 49), a decline in the number of stories (only five, one by a Cuban, the unknown 17–year old Guido López Gavilán: 53, 13: 26), and the pride of place for cinema, Almendros's reviews, ratings and educational articles dominating the coverage regularly.

Popular culture now figured, in the majority of items in the regular cultural news columns, in Orlando Quiroga's 'Rebambaramba' article on the *rumba* (53, 10: 48) and in sports, the focus now having shifted to boxing and baseball (the really popular sports), with celebrity coverage of motor racing. However, the overall cultural tone was focused more on education than entertainment or recreation, strangely echoing the magazine's avowed purpose in 1911, and it was clear that *Bohemia* in 1961, like the Revolution, stood at a crossroads between the continuity and radical change.

March 1966 Five years later *Bohemia* (now under de la Osa) had clearly changed. No longer were the advertisements commercial or foreign but Cuban and educational (on safety, health or diet) or political, with some publicity for Varadero and women's beauty treatment, while the news focus was on Latin American radicalism and repression and, domestically, on the Revolution's progress. The educational purpose was made most explicit by the regular 'Laminario Escolar', a small-print article on Cuban history or thought, designed to reinforce educational courses, and in the Dirección Nacional de Educación Obrera y Campesina cut-out section 'El Placer de Leer' ('The Pleasure of Reading'), a large-print reading exercise following up the 1961 Campaign. Of the old columns only 'En Cuba' survived, now much longer and subdivided into sections, and also 'Ría con Nosotros' ('Laugh with Us'). The majority of the magazine now consisted of regular news columns from Cuba and elsewhere, but also included the regular three-page 'Esta es la Historia' ('This is History') feature; in this, established historians educated readers on themes ranging from Cuban prehistory (58, 11: 101) to Cuban radio (58, 9, 104). There were also historical articles (on the anti-Batista struggle or Marx, for example) throughout the editions and the regular 'Aquí por primera vez' ('The First Appearance'), column, examining the first appearance in Cuba of things like the printing press (58, 11: 104) or the typewriter (58, 10: 106). This was clearly a Revolution that now sought as a priority to educate its citizens in a pride in their own past, but also in their own sport, as the new emphasis on athletics and chess indicated, alongside the now permanent focus on baseball and boxing.

Culture was now even more evident, in the fortnightly thirteen-page and twenty-six-page 'Arte y Literatura' section of 'En Cuba'. There were still few stories (and still only one of them Cuban, by Onelio Jorge Cardoso), there were regular interviews (with Sartre and with the 1966 Casa jurists), regular sections on theatre (including reviews by Calvert Casey and David Camps), regular film reviews (now by Loló de la Torriente, Almendros having left Cuba), and the new column 'Cámaras, Escenarios y Micrófonos' on film, theatre and television, which included stills and news but also educational articles. Yet, even outside this section, culture was evidently a priority, with no cultural form left unmentioned and with articles on Cuban cultural history or Rubiera poems on the *zafra* (58, 10: 14–16), and the weeks with no special section still included interviews (with Santiago Alvarez or the songwriter Tania Castellanos) and items on art exhibitions and film reviews.

It was now evident not only that culture was a priority but that it was more a matter of education than entertainment. Popular culture now figured with a firmly educational slant, *Carnaval*, for example, being now extolled as a collective political act, as *Carnaval de la Solidaridad* (58, 9: 46–9), and the traditional *trovador* now enjoying a new prestige. Yet the focus was mostly on educating Cubans *up* to cultural appreciation, evident in Félix Pita Rodríguez's article on 'Cursos de Apreciación del Arte para los Trabajadores' ('Workers' Art Appreciation Course': 58, 9: 36–7), focusing on one factory's inaugural session, and the overall focus of this section was on established culture.

March 1971 Bohemia showed a few changes in format five years on, but almost no change in its focus on rural Cuba and the Revolution's achievements, although there was now a greater emphasis on economics (in the regular 'Bohemia Económica' column). Yet the interest in history (still in 'Laminario Escolar' and 'Esta es la Historia') seemed now more focused on international labour and socialist history than exclusively on Cuba, reflecting Cuba's shift back to the Socialist Bloc (a shift also evident in the sports coverage, which now included football and cycling, then mostly un-Cuban sports).

Culture was still prominent, but now scattered more generally throughout the edition than solely in the 'Arte y Literatura' section, which only appeared in Issue 11 in this month, that dealing entirely with Isidoro Méndez, Martí's recent biographer. Cultural coverage was still broad, with Nicolás Cossío's film reviews and articles, with the results of a readers' poll on their favourite films (63, 10: 15), with Naty González Freire's writings on Cuban theatre, with Loló de la Torriente's book reviews in 'Lecturas para un viernes' ('Readings for a Friday': 63, 11: 101) and with news of Cuban cultural recognition abroad (63, 10: 26). By now the traditional preference for the short story had practically disappeared, with one story at best.

Curiously, however, the cultural tone was generally less earnest than in 1966 and more prepared to return to the old preference for news snippets, gossip and popular entertainment, as in Orlando Quiroga's 'Temas y noticias para un fin de semana'

('Topics and News for the Weekend': 63, 10: 38–41), with the weekly columns 'Recuerdos Musicales' ('Musical Memories'), combining musical history of both the popular (*trova* and popular song) and the classical, and 'Do-Re-Mi-Fa-Sol', of interviews and news on current popular musical entertainment.

Overall, the cultural changes in *Bohemia* reflected the changes in the Revolution, with culture evidently a priority for news and education, with the emphasis on improving the cultural and historical knowledge and appreciation of the ordinary Cuban, and with popular entertainment disappearing or at least relegated for a while, but returning without embarrassment by 1971. The notion of cultural identity was now, for *Bohemia*, clearly a mixture of cultural recognition abroad, pride in history and building a cultured and educated readership and citizenry. However, it was also clear that *Bohemia*, like the Revolution, was much less interested in Havana as a cultural site or in Havana's cultural community than before 1959, and thus was less useful as an indicator of cultural development in the capital.

1972–86: Granma

It is partly for that reason that we now turn to *Granma*, since the newspaper's coverage can offer us more information about Havana from March 1976, especially through the television schedules (since these were prepared in Havana and aimed mostly at a Havana audience), the cinema programmes (entirely focused on Havana) and the weekly 'Cartelera Cultural' notices of events.

March 1976 In 1976, culture was generally scattered throughout the paper's pages, except for the weekend, when one full page was dedicated to news, programmes and events; for example, on 13 March, there was extensive coverage of the Casa prize, an Eliseo Diego piece on Pushkin and an article on children's theatre (12, 61: 5). Outside these pages, culture tended to appear to record a Cuban success abroad, such as London's reception of Carpentier's *Recurso del Método* (12, 62: 7), or some politically important event, such as the Carifesta (12, 64: 3) or the Sancti Spiritus Festival Nacional de la Trova (12, 67: 2), or to herald the arrival of a prominent Cuban film, such as the extensive coverage of Solás's *Cantata de Chile*, premiered at ICAIC (12, 6: 3). In fact, ICAIC's continuing political importance was evident, highlighted in the report on 18 March (12, 65: 3) in the national news pages, which recorded with pride ICAIC's 1959–76 production of 71 full-length features, 541 documentaries, 739 news bulletins and 90 cartoons, talking of its importance for 'patrimonio nacional' ('national heritage'), and also Alfredo Guevara's references to the 1976 Party Congress's report on Cuban cinema as part of the process of 'decolonisation' (12, 68: 3).

The weekend schedules of television, cultural and film events were inevitably revealing. In 1976, theatre tended to be minimal, only about five programmes being advertised (and none at all in one week), usually the García Lorca, the Mella, the Teatro Musical and the Guiñol, with the Sótano occasionally appearing, although an article on 19 March covered the Grupo de Experimentación Sonora's adaptation of Sara Gómez's film *De Cierta Manera* (12, 66: 3). Music, however, appeared even less, usually limited to solo recitals (at places like the Museo Napoleónico, the Museo de la Ciudad, the Museo de Bellas Artes or the Biblioteca Nacional) or Teatro Roldán Sunday concerts; interestingly, however, music recitals seemed to be the one cultural activity advertised for locations on the edges of the city, at places like the Biblioteca José Machado in Guanabacoa (12, 59: 3), the Sala Teatro de Regla (12, 59: 3), the Casa de la Trova in Güines, or the Casas de Cultura in Bejucal, Artemisa and Santiago de las Vegas (12, 64: 4). Cuban traditional music was also the subject of lectures, notably at the Biblioteca Rubén Martínez Villena in Obispo and the Biblioteca Nacional (both on the *danzón*) (12, 64: 4). The visual arts were almost always limited to exhibitions of artisan crafts or *aficionado* art at the Galería de La Habana and the De Galiano, with only the Taller de Experimentación Gráfico indicating some specialist art.

There was little doubt that cinema was the prime cultural form, both for the editorial team (with regular reviews and articles) and for the public. Here, the regular weekly *cartelera* of film programmes is revealing: on 13 March, of 73 film showings in the 100 Havana cinemas, only one was of a Cuban film, apart from the ICAIC documentaries, with about one fifth being American and about one third from eastern Europe. However, film was by now evidently challenged by television's two channels, Canal 6 and Canal 2, especially from Canal 6's focus on musical entertainment (with programmes like 'Saludos amigos', 'Palmas y Cañas', 'Album de Cuba', 'Canción con Todos', 'Algo Especial' and 'La Revista de Domingo' providing a constant diet of variety-style and more traditional musical shows), from the television serial (during this month, adaptations of Gorky's *Mother* and *Les Miserables*), and from televised films, especially Canal 2's nightly 'Cine del Hogar' ('Cinema at Home'), which showed three on Sunday nights. Television was also evidently then a medium of cultural education, with the Cinemateca de Cuba's regular 'Historia del cine' programme, with programmes on Cuban and foreign composers and writers, with weekly discussion programmes such as 'Escriba y Lea' ('Write and Read'), and with the weekly bulletin 'El Mundo del Arte', but also with a Jorge Cardoso story being read.

What, therefore, was clear from this snapshot was that the activities of Havana's cultural community were either somewhat isolated from the public or marginalised in small circles, unless they were of political importance, but that cinema, television and music, the latter increasingly geared to entertainment, were at the forefront of popular cultural tastes and also of any notions of popular culture. Moreover, it was also clear that official attitudes tended to reflect a quantitative approach to success as much as any qualitative judgements.

March 1981   Five years later, *Granma*'s treatment of culture consisted of a daily half-page, which, though seeming to indicate an increased coverage, simply concentrated it more, with no cultural news on other pages. By now, treatment included attention to the serious prestigious cultural forms, the popular, folkloric or artisan forms and the usual billing of events, although the regular page did have the effect of allowing space for items and articles on unusual cultural issues, such as piano-roll music or carnival. Cuban successes were still, of course, celebrated, notably a French staging of a Carpentier play and a Leo Brouwer international tour (17, 51: 5). It also allowed for a fuller advertising of events, disseminating such information more effectively than before, with a smaller *cartelera* also appearing on some Tuesdays: besides the usual notices of plays (now including Beckett at the García Lorca), the cultural page for this month included notices of forthcoming radio programmes (which had never figured previously), lectures (such as Diego on the *décima*), poetry readings (such as Morejón) and almost weekly notices for book launches, always critical events for publicity, cultural identification and access. The usual billing of exhibitions continued, although these now included the *Sábados de las Plazas* artisan fairs and somewhat fewer music recitals, while the weekend *Cartelera* indicated either an increase in, or a raised profile for, theatrical activity, plays now also being advertised regularly for the Hubert de Blanck theatre (home of the experimental Gran Teatro Estudio) and the Teatro Alejandro García Caturla in Marianao, where the Teatro Joven de Marianao performed and from where it evidently toured other districts (17, 52: 4). Interestingly, the number of museums advertised had also increased to sixteen, perhaps indicating a greater material well-being and degree of collective self-confidence in nation-building.

The *Cartelera* now also regularly included a full notice of the activities in the Parque Lenin, which more than anything indicated the new emphasis on popularisation and participation, the activities always including popular music performances and recitals but also the weekly Peña Literaria, where readers were encouraged to bring their own books to read in a collective experience. Indeed, participation was a theme echoed frequently, with notices of *aficionado* events, such as the Gala de Trabajadores Aficionados al Arte at the CTC's Teatro Lázaro Peña (17, 50: 3), the news of Casa de Cultura inaugurations and programmes, such as the theatre groups at the Plaza Casa (17, 74: 4), the opening of the Marianao Casa (17, 60: 3) and the full programme for the Luyano Centro Cultural Recreativo (17, 75: 5). The latter's programme was, indeed, revealing, including *trovadores campesinos*, tango, sports, dance and excursions, with 500 members paying a peso each a month. However, at the other end of the scale, the offerings of the Orquesta Sinfónica Nacional were, for the first time, advertised in full (17, 67: 4), indicative of Brouwer's enthusiasm and the prestige which he brought to the form.

Popular culture still, of course, meant film, Havana now boasting 104 cinemas (with new buildings in Guanabacoa, Cotorro and Habana del Este), but the pattern of screenings had changed, with far fewer American films, more Latin American ones, still about one third from the Socialist Bloc and slightly more Cuban films, there being three different ones on show, although ICAIC organised a 19 March anniversary programme of Cuban films (17, 66: 4). It also meant television, where the range of programmes was largely unchanged since 1976, with as many variety-style music programmes (especially 'Buenas Tardes', 'Palmas y Cañas' and 'Para Bailar') and films still being a staple, in the regular weekend 'Telecine' and 'Cine en TV'. There were, however, more television dramas, including a full-length Emilio Carballido play (17, 64: 3), and serialisations of *Don Quijote* and Pérez Galdós's *Fortunata y Jacinta*, although the *telenovela* (here a Mexican serial, 'El carruaje') had finally appeared. While there were frankly 'down-market' comedies (such as the imported British 'Man about the House'), the 'Escriba y Lea' programme still remained, along with programmes on Hemingway and musical recitals. Most clearly, however, 'popular' now meant music, evident both in the television coverage, the Casa de Cultura programmes and the EGREM awards announced on 30 March (17, 70: 4), which indicated a huge popularity for the *son* and Nueva Trova performers.

Evidently, by 1981, Havana culture was booming in level of activity, self-confidence and participation, and the old image of marginalisation seemed distant. This was confirmed by the quantitative record given by the Deputy Minister of Culture on 18 March, indicating for 1980 an impressive array of activity in Cuba generally, including no fewer than six festivals organised for theatre, reading, ballet, cinema and the *son* (17, 65: 4).

March 1986   The most notable aspect of *Granma* in 1986 was its much reduced length, down to a mere six pages, although culture still enjoyed a half-page coverage, mostly consisting of short items (usually on Cuban successes), reviews and notices rather than sustained articles; indeed the information disseminated about activity was still considerable, certainly in comparison with the 1990s. These notices included book launches, but above all an indication of the rise of music in public state and esteem, with announcements of recitals at the new Casa de la Música, the Semana de la Cultura at the Plaza Casa de Cultura (22, 63: 3), and the IX Jornada de Música Contemporánea Cubana at the Nacional's Sala Covarrubias (22, 66: 4). Other evidence pointed to the continuation of participation as a priority, with notices of a Tarde Cultural at the Museo de la Ciudad (with performances by the Banda de Conciertos del Hospital Psiquiátrico and the Peña de la Trova) (22, 56: 3), of the *Sábados del Libro* at the Moderna Poesía bookshop, of the televised Programa Contacto (with the Movimiento de Aficionados de la FEU) 22, 60: 2), and with the weekend programme at the Museo de Bellas Artes, which included video screenings, fashion shows, puppet theatre, *aficionado* performances, poetry readings and recitals.

Film, despite coverage of ICAIC's twenty-seventh anniversary, seemed to have a somewhat lower profile, reflected in the decline in the number of cinemas to seventy-nine, but now showing no fewer than eight different Cuban films at fifteen of those, only Latin American cinema competing. That meant, of course, that television's profile had risen, still with its diet of popular Cuban music (with new programmes such as 'Discograma' and 'Joven, Joven' indicating an awareness of different youth tastes), confirmed by the Saturday late-night programme of American and British rock by satellite, by the 1986 EGREM prizes, which now, revealingly, included a category of 'Contribución, reafirmación y desarrollo de la identidad nacional' ('Contribution, reaffirmation and development of national identity': 22, 74: 3), and by the results of the *Opina* survey of tastes, in which the winners were all television performers or popular exponents of both traditional and new Cuban music, such as Los Van Van (22, 64: 4). Interestingly, television now showed fewer films, but the *telenovela* was clearly popular, with the Colombian 'Amalia' being shown twice a week and with the British serialisation of *War and Peace*.

However, for all the impressions that 'popularisation' meant going downmarket, television in 1986 seemed to include more programmes of cultural education, 'Escriba y Lea' (now covering more than literature) being joined by 'A través de la música' ('Through Music'), on Cuban composers, and the thirty-minute 'En primer plano' ('Front-stage') with its bulletin of cultural events and discussion, in addition to the other evidently educational programmes.

Clearly, therefore, Havana culture was still booming, but above all in participation, and the growing preference for popular music seemed to be relegating more traditional forms such as the visual arts, classical music and even theatre, to the sidelines as specialist activities. Therefore, on the eve of the crisis, some aspects were promising while others still held ammunition for fears of marginalisation or atomisation.

Notes

1. By this system, each *municipio* was run by a Party-selected president and ten elected delegates.
2. The incident came when the annual Caridad del Cobre procession became a 4,000–strong protest, provoking counter-protests, one death and 130 arrests (including Monseñor Boza Másvidal).
3. Hart had, before 1959, been the main coordinator of the 26 July Movement's urban wing and remained part of the Revolution's 'inner circle'.
4. Vega (1996: 6) gives 1961 as the date for this pioneering poster.
5. These were especially Rafael Morante, Holbein López Martínez, Ricardo Reymena, Antonio Fernández Reboiro, René Azcuy Cárdenas, Alfredo

Rostgaard, Julio Eloy Mesa (known as Julioeloy), Luis Vega, Pulido, Silvio, Servando Cabrera Moreno, Dima, Saura, Orlando Hernández Yanes, Raúl Oliva, Antonio Pérez (Ñiko), and Raúl Martínez González.

6. I am grateful for many of the insights contained in this perspective to the ongoing doctoral work of Anne Luke (University of Wolverhampton).

7. These were: Edición Revolución, Ciencia y Técnica, Pueblo y Educación, Ciencias Sociales, Arte y Literatura, Huracán, Gente Nueva, Cuadernos Populares, Ediciones Deportivas, Pluma de Ristre, Organismos, Ambito and Coordinación de Revistas.

8. For some of the perspectives that follow on Rectification, I am indebted to Kate Quinn's November 2003 paper on 'Cuban culture and intellectuals in the age of perestroika', given at the Institute of Historical Research, London.

9. The whole issue was dedicated to Havana, with contributions by Marta Arjona (the Director of the Patrimonio Cultural), Arrufat, Mosquera, Rivero and Victori Ramos.

–4–

The Revolution in a New Light?:
Havana as a New Cultural Space

Historical Overview

With 'Rectification' still under way, Cuba was suddenly hit by an unimaginable crisis; in 1989–91 the Socialist Bloc disintegrated and the Soviet Union imploded, demolishing in an instant Cuba's whole protective edifice. The outgoing Bush Administration in Washington then tightened the twenty-two-year old embargo, through the 1992 Torricelli Act. The economy was immediately plunged into its deepest crisis since 1933, declining in 1990–3 by over a third, bringing unprecedented unemployment, drastically reduced production, the collapse of infrastructure, plummeting oil supplies (reducing sugar production from an average seven million tons to under four) and producing demoralising power-cuts. It recalled the darkest days of the 1960s, but without that decade's hope, eating corrosively into social provision and morale.

To survive and keep loyalty in order to weather the inevitable political storms, the Cuban leaders responded by putting Cuba effectively on a war footing on 29 August 1990, with the 'Special Period in Peacetime' (Período Especial en Tiempo de Paz), an emergency programme to save oil (by 30 to 50 per cent), cut the working week and lay off thousands (on 60 per cent of normal wages), and reduce all services except health and education.

From 1993, an unprecedented reform programme was launched, largely intensifying the 1980s measures. Firstly, Cubans were at last allowed to earn or receive US dollars, helping daily survival, circulating much-needed hard currency, and undermining the burgeoning black market. Secondly, foreign investment (already encouraged) was actively courted and given greater freedom. Thirdly, petty trading and services (eliminated in 1968) were partially legalised in September 1993 as the *cuenta propia* sector, which, by 1995, soared to 208,000 *cuentapropistas* nationally, falling to 170,000 by 1997, by when 53 per cent of the 66,300 new jobs created were non-governmental (Azicri 2000: 146), showing the success in

179

formalising the informal and fillings gaps, especially the private restaurants (*paladares*). Finally, state farms were turned into cooperatives in 1993, farmers being again allowed, from 1994, to sell some of their produce on the Mercado Libre Campesino (the *agromercados*) at higher prices than the ration-book *bodegas*. With sugar declining, tourism now became the immediate source of foreign exchange, with investment given greater freedom in the sector; by 1996, a million tourists were arriving annually, approaching two million by 2001. Hence, by 1995, growth returned, thereafter continuing annually.

However, the sequence of collapse, reform and recovery profoundly affected society, creating new inequalities between the dollar and peso economies, the latter concentrated especially in health, education and sugar, and (given their lack of émigré relatives) in the black population. The characteristic sense of community and collective endeavour was also affected, replaced increasingly by a more individualistic survivalism, Cubans relying increasingly on family networks and the informal economy. This in turn meant political challenges, especially in August 1994, when unprecedented disturbances in Centro Habana led to the decision to allow the disaffected to leave, most characteristically on rafts (*balsas*) in an exodus of some 35,000 *balseros*.

However, 1994 proved to be not the end of the system but its nadir, as post-1992 political adjustments began to take effect, such as the introduction of younger politicians into the leadership (notably Carlos Lage, as economic reform supremo and effectively prime minister, and Roberto Robaina, then as foreign minister), the introduction of direct elections to, and permanent standing commissions in, the National Assembly, and the creation, in 1990–3, of a new representative layer, the indirectly elected *barrio*-level Consejos Populares (Popular Councils), which, filling a gap between the street-level CDRs and the *municipio*-level Poder Popular, had, by the end of the decade, begun to acquire an identity of their own. These changes had immediate electoral effects, participation rates rising from a record low in 1992 to 99.6 per cent and 98.35 per cent in the February 1993 and January 1998 national elections (Azicri 2000: 116).

Finally, attempts were made to broaden political involvement by reviving the CDRs and giving the CTC trade union confederation space to reflect more critical positions, through its newspaper *Trabajadores* and workplace assemblies, *parlamentos obreros*. Dialogue was broached in 1994 with émigré groups and in 1996 with the Catholic Church, and even with Clinton Adminstration in Washington; the latter, however, ended abruptly in February 1996 when Cuban air defences predictably shot down two Cuban-American piloted jets which deliberately penetrated Cuban airspace; the result was the Helms-Burton Act which tightened the embargo yet again. This put the Cuban government on the defensive, with a renewed sense of siege and alert, reinforced by a spate of hotel bombings in Havana in July 1997.

In 1998, however, the broadening process resumed, when thousands welcomed

Pope John Paul II, less as a religious leader (whose politics few accepted and whose authority few acknowledged) than celebrating Cuba's return from the cold. This mood was then reinforced from November 1999 with the six-month campaign for the return of six-year old Elián González from Miami, with daily rallies, marches, propaganda, media debates and publications involving thousands all over Cuba, often stimulated by family memories of the early 1960s experiences, which saw families divided and children being taken away from their parents in the famous or infamous Peter Pan Program, in which some 14,000 middle-class children were flown out of Cuba to Florida in 1960–2 (Triay 1999: 10).

This campaign proved seminal in several respects. The first was the return of mobilisation as a basic, characteristic form of politics to generate support, cement unity and reinforce nationalism and collective pride, reviving existing mechanisms such as the CDRs, the FEU and the UJC, and creating new ones too. For, from 1959, the public demonstration has often been as much about 'belonging' as the result of pressure, about participation regardless of discontent. Hence, the often perfunctory and sporadic attendance at CDR meetings or involvement in the monthly Sunday-morning street-tidying have become a periodic swearing of allegiance to a collective entity, peer pressure alone not explaining the huge turnouts at ritual rallies, since most *habaneros* 'attend' rather than actively participate, often identifying with *barrio* or workplace. Indeed, many 'attend' marginally, leaving during the speeches, without incurring peer disapproval, having 'registered' their attendance. Moreover, many who do not attend follow the rally on radio or television at full volume, perhaps also making a statement, especially as rallies such as the May Day event are now actually as much national as socialist celebrations. The new post-Elián mechanism, the Tribunas Abiertas, fits this pattern: weekly rallies held in a different *municipio* each Saturday with national television coverage, high-profile public speakers and a topical theme, they are significant in offering an opportunity for each locality to involve its residents, since, with national publicity, no *municipio* wishes to fail to hold its own.

A second effect of the Elián campaign was to bring youth to the fore. Since the campaign was led and carried out by the young, it raised the profile and legitimacy of the UJC and FEU and their leaders, Otto Rivero and Hassan Pérez, respectively, and, after years of relative and perhaps increasing marginality, brought into the fold a potentially disaffected youth. This then generated, from summer 2001, a new education campaign, which, echoing the urgency and the mechanisms of the 1960s, sought to spread the previously selective universities to every *municipio* and to train, in *escuelas de emergencia*, thousands of new young social workers, nurses, primary teachers and *instructores de arte*.

Retrospectively, this whole experience from 1999 has been labelled the *Batalla de Ideas* (Battle of Ideas), reflecting the new impulse for participation and commitment and seeking to fortify ideological resolve against the pressure from individualisation and social division, and against the corrosive effects of the dollar and tourism.

The new post-2000 Bush Administration, however, brought new challenges and threats, and, with the 11 September World Trade Center attacks, a new discourse of 'rogue states' and 'axis of evil', which, with unusually enthusiastic support from some EU states, partially isolated Cuba again. In a context of unilateral armed action in Afghanistan and Iraq and unprecedented US involvement in Cuba, supporting domestic opposition activists, the Cuban mood again became defensive, suggesting a possible retrenchment and new 'siege', which had a specific outcome in spring 2003 in a wave of arrests.

The Período Especial and Havana

The whole post-1989 crisis affected Havana badly. With supplies breaking down and lacking easy access to rural provision, the daily battle to survive became hard and demoralising, exacerbated by widespread pilfering of limited *libreta* supplies and the collapse of the transport network, which, for a city dependent on the huge daily movement of population to and from work, was disastrous. For *habaneros*, days were long as they struggled to make ends meet and spent hours waiting for the pitifully few overcrowded buses or *camellos* (specially converted heavy-duty 'lorry-buses') or trying to flag down the even fewer cars, or resorted to the bicycle, which now transformed the city visibly (Cuba importing about a million by 1995, mostly to Havana). Such days were then followed by nights without power and without even the respite of television entertainment for more than a few hours.

Hence, discontent was more noticeable in Havana, producing spoiled ballots and abstentions double the national level in the 1992 municipal elections (Azicri 2000: 116) and especially in the August 1994 disturbances. Indeed, what was remarkable was that this discontent took so long to emerge, given that the new shortages and demoralisation followed decades of neglect of Havana.

Equally, the subsequent reforms affected Havana more than most. Six hundred of Cuba's 1,500 *paladares* in 1999 were in Havana (Azicri 2000: 97), as were the majority of those benefiting from tourism, the new *cuenta propia* sector and remittances from Miami. Hence, as the dollar economy thrived, Havana began to recover. Conversely, however, Havana also included many of those left out of the recovery, those working in health and education, and those in the traditionally blacker districts of Habana Vieja, Centro Habana and Cerro who lacked remittances from Florida-based relatives. Thus, while Havana saw, on the one hand, a tolerated and relatively well-off informal sector, there was also a greater level of discontent and atomisation.

This fragmentation arose as the already weaker sense of community disintegrated in the face of an individual search for survival; the greater the informal sector and ordinary Cubans' access to it, the weaker 'community' became. Moreover, Havana saw collective values and social cement undermined by a particular increase in petty crime and *jineterismo* (the new illegal hustling and trading activities geared to tourism), prostitutes reaching an estimated 6,000 in Havana by 1995, all leading to public concern being expressed in *Juventud Rebelde*, at the 1996 CTC congress and in other mass organisations (Azicri 2000: 78), and finally to a widespread clampdown in January 1997, when many illegal immigrants were returned to their places of origin in the provinces.

The issue of *jineterismo* is contentious, inside and outside Cuba, some seeing it as symptomatic of a failed system and of a state collapse in the face of a growing civil society and others viewing it more positively, as a space for the young and the marginal to acquire peer prestige and resources to alleviate community poverty (Campa 2000: 163–4). However, *jineterismo* has certainly changed the face of Havana, creating a recurrence of unwelcome images of sex-tourism.

However, this is the illegal side of a whole social shift, involving both the (legal) phenomenon of qualified Cubans moving from the peso economy to the dollar economy to work as taxi-drivers or tourism workers and also the question of migration. For the same problem that produced a new emigration in 1990–4 also accelerated movement towards Havana, average annual immigration rising to a total of 55,000 recent arrivals by 1996 (Segre et al. 1997: 222; Azicri 2000: 148; Fuente 2000: 449); by the late 1990s, 505,700 *habaneros* (over one in five) were immigrants, increasingly resented by the native population (pejoratively calling them *palestinos*). Moreover, while this has been quantitatively offset by the 20,000 who leave annually (Segre et al. 1997: 169), skilled labour has generally been replaced by less skilled, increasing densities in already crowded areas. Hence, the authorities acted in May 1997, stipulating population limits and restricting housing to legal immigrants only, leading to 92,000 applications to register legally (Fuente 2000: 449), 150 immediate evictions, and 218,000 irregularities in out of 1,000,350 dwellings investigated in 1997 (Azicri 2000: 148–9).

Yet, curiously, housing and construction have also, in Havana, seen surprising evidence of a new drive to encourage and capitalise on collective endeavour, especially in strategies to address these long-neglected problems. In 1990 a new Plan prioritised the most deteriorated areas and emphasised repair and restoration via decentralised job-creation schemes, using traditional techniques rather than prefabrication, stressing recycling and local involvement in planning. The latter, based on the idea of *talleres* (piloted in 1988 in some *barrios*), used professional architects and planners to work with local residents who, in greater enforced idleness, could in theory refurbish their own dwellings and communities, boosted by the now legal opportunity to rent accommodation to tourists.

This effort has, however, largely been overshadowed by the higher-profile project to reconstruct Habana Vieja. Here, in a move which defied expectations

Figure 12 The restoration of Habana Vieja: the impressive Plaza Vieja

and indicated the project's political and cultural significance, in October 1993 (in the depths of the economic crisis), the most ambitious phase of the existing strategy began, with Decreto Ley 143. This was the compact whereby the government allowed Eusebio Leal's Oficina to reinvest in further reconstruction any tourism-generated income within Habana Vieja, in exchange for a commitment to 'social projects' (the restoration of the *municipio*'s worst housing) alongside restoration of prestigious buildings. In December 1994 (only months after the *balsero* crisis) the Plan Maestro (para la Revitalización Integral de la Habana Vieja) appeared, establishing the operation as a vast commercial, artistic and archaeological-historical project, which is, simultaneously, and self-evidently a declaration of national cultural identity on a scale which few could have predicted in the 1980s. For large areas of Habana Vieja have since become reconstruction sites, employing some 7,000 people, and the project's main commercial arm, the Habaguanex enterprise, oversees the commercialisation of the reconstructed sites and operates with relative autonomy within the *municipio*, being one of the few enterprises enabling foreign capital to invest in property.

Yet it is the impact on residents' living conditions and on the development of skills and the arts which has been most consistently impressive. On housing, the Plan has kept its part in the 1993 bargain, moving residents into purpose-built accommodation while *solares* are reconstructed as impressively as the monumental buildings and increasing employment opportunity and collective self-belief. The impact on skills has been enormous, the focus on artisan rather than artistic activity generating a network of training establishments to rival ISA in the arts, notably the 1992 Escuela Taller Gaspar Melchior de Jovellanos, training specifically for work in the Empresa de Restauración de Monumentos or the Constructora Puerto de Carenas (Plan Maestro 2002: 61). Hence, the project has both created opportunity for young Cubans at a time of shortage and boosted a critical element in Havana's cultural landscape, namely artisan activity, which, from the late 1980s, tended to be limited to small-scale production for the tourist market, producing artefacts for conventional tastes. Now, however, artisan skills have been developed more broadly for social use, in construction-related trades on a larger stage and with greater opportunity for prestige, purpose and a sense of belonging.

Indeed, one of the evident effects of reconstruction has been to redefine space in a city which, previously, lacked it meaningfully; in a narrow sense, this has meant providing new and restored spaces for the arts, the conversion of the San Francisco de Asis church into a performing base for the Camerata Romeu, the annual Encuentro Callejero de Danza Contemporánea (Street Festival of Contemporary Dance: Plan Maestro 2002: 60–1), or simply providing space for street performers, such as the ubiquitous musicians, sketch artists and the

Figure 13 The Iglesia de San Francisco restored as a concert venue

Figure 14 *Gigantes* in Habana Vieja: the adaptation of the carnivalesque to tourist dollars

colourful carnivalesque *payasos gigantes* ('giant clowns'), all geared to enter-
taining dollar-spending tourists but also providing opportunities.

More broadly, however, it has opened up social spaces for recreation and cultural expression. Before 1989, the issue of public space was perhaps less urgent
than it later became, since *habaneros* were always able to escape to the many green
spaces available in the newer areas or to spaces like the huge Parque Lenin south
of the city or the accessible beaches to the east. The Special Period, however, made
it a matter of urgency, as power cuts made crowded apartments into unventilated
hells and as reduced television and radio entertainment forced *habaneros* to escape
the home but without transport to travel far. For the population of Centro Habana
and Habana Vieja, the most readily available space became the Malecón which,
having always been fundamental to their social life, for tranquility, recreation, collective identification or protest, now became a bedroom for those fleeing the

Figure 15 Street musicians in the restored Habana Vieja, by the Lonja del Comercio

Figure 16 The creation of green spaces as an integral part of the restoration of Habana Vieja

suffocation of their apartments. In every respect, the Malecón thus became the social and cultural 'lungs' of those areas, relieving much unrest and complaint. Now, Havana's restoration has stressed space as much as residence, creating parks, gardens and squares for general use, both relieving pressure and creating public space for arts that hitherto were out of the public gaze.

The question of restoration naturally returns us to the issue of cultural identity. For the shift of Havana from neglect to protagonism has been attributable to many factors: the persuasive efforts of historians in the Oficina del Historiador, the awareness of other reconstruction projects (e.g. post-1944 Warsaw), and the realisation after 1979 that Habana Vieja was both an embarrassing eyesore and a potential source of dollar revenue and that Havana in fact could be 'marketed' to sustain that restoration. Indeed, just when the Cuban state depended increasingly on such revenue to sustain national provision, the 1993 compact was either brave or longsighted.

There were, however, other motives. Firstly, the 1990s saw such a fundamental reassessment of so much in the Revolution that the role of Havana was inevitably re-examined. Indeed, the 'errors' which were being 'rectified' from 1986 had to include the old policy of urban neglect. Hence, the deeper cause was the shift of authority back to Havana. Secondly, in the 1990s, all Cubans were exhorted to find mechanisms to solve their own problems (and *inventar* and *resolver* acquired multiple meanings). This inevitably involved a recognition that Havana should be a source of pride and not shame, that the deteriorating housing should be addressed

Figure 17 The restoration of Habana Vieja: the curious fusion of tourist-oriented manifestations of globalisation and socialism

by both urgent state action and popular participation, using residents as subjects and not objects of their own conditions. Certainly the shift towards *talleres* and residential accommodation reflected this priority. Finally, the late 1990s also saw greater collective confidence, which inevitably spilled over into attitudes towards Havana, collective pride focusing on its condition as something to be corrected, on its historic sites as a heritage to be valued as 'Cuban', and on the potential of the whole space as a major pole of attraction.

In this respect, Havana may constitute an unusual case in the global pattern of 'heritage'. On the one hand, its experience fits the pattern: 'any discussion of sub-national heritage at the regional or local scale … must continually refer to the national scale which these complete or challenge' (Graham, Ashcroft and Tunbridge 2000: 183–4). For the Havana project clearly did start as part of a national project (based on experiences like post-1945 Warsaw) to reconstruct a narrative of nation, then gradually becoming more local. In Havana as elsewhere, heritage then became 'the principal instrument for shaping distinctive local representation of space … exploited for external promotion as well as strengthening the identification of inhabitants with their localities' (Graham et al. 2000: 204). However, the local appropriation of the whole Havana project is perhaps unusual, 'heritage' here having become more than consumption or even production (or reproduction), to move into the area of significant social experiment, both in its impact on local and national skills and self-esteem but also in its emphasis on social use and on the collectivity of benefit and operation.

Hence, in searching for a national cultural identity, Cuba's political and cultural leaders did actually find an eloquent expression in the whole restoration project, which revealingly fused the artistic and the artisan, the elite cultural community and the local popular communities, creating a space in which the elusive identity might be forged.

The Evolution and Rediscovery of a Havana Culture

As we have seen, by 1989, the Havana elite/vanguard cultural community was at perhaps its lowest ebb since the early 1960s, feeling marginalised, disheartened and disoriented by changes in attitudes, and increasingly separated from the popular roots which had once attracted it.

Obviously, with economic collapse, all familiar spaces and opportunities disappeared further, worsening an existing problem. Newspapers and magazines were seriously reduced in frequency and size (*Juventud Rebelde* and *Trabajadores* becoming weeklies) and book production was limited to textbooks, closing the spaces of the previous fifteen years with little prospect of revival. Ballet was obliged to rely on taped music in rehearsals and even performances, because of the unavailability of musicians and reliable instruments. The cultural community's

Figure 18 *Azoteas* (flat roofs) in Havana: the ideal gathering site during the worst of the Special Period

traditional haunts disappeared as scarcity of goods, electricity and transport limited movement and collective activity, one effect being to restore the flat roof (*azotea*) as a cultural space; while ordinary *habaneros* had long colonised these spaces seeking fresh air, recreation, rendezvous, meetings or noisy celebration, writers and musicians now also began to use them for rehearsals or informal literature readings.

Another effect was to restore UNEAC's hegemony as a gathering space. After years of being regarded as the place where the 'official' elite gathered and defined itself, with a certain hierarchy of acceptability, the headquarters now became the only place where supplies could be guaranteed, films and videos watched, books bought for pesos and conversation with others in the community be guaranteed, usually at the outdoor Café Hurón Azul.

As well as gathering spaces, performing spaces also diminished. Although, officially, Havana in 1992 boasted 18 theatres, 80 cinemas, 26 *centros de cultura*, 29 galleries, 37 museums and 25 libraries (Segre et al. 1997: 280), many scarcely functioned without their public and some closed. Equally, opportunities for travel, both abroad and in Cuba, disappeared, and the atmosphere of shortage threatened to reduce the horizons of an already self-absorbed cultural community.

In this context, only three strategies seemed appropriate: retreat into individualistic passivity, escape into emigration or the pursuit of hard currency, all combining to make Cuban culture into 'un archipiélago' of individualism and changing cultural concerns: 'Lo cierto es que hoy el arte más joven y la nueva literatura cubana omiten la identificación revolucionaria' ('It is now true that the newest Cuban art and literature ignore any sense of identification with the revolution': Vázquez Montalbán 1998: 359–60). All three strategies, indeed, were especially followed by Havana's visual and plastic artists, who, as we have seen, were already beginning to depart from the collective, resulting in some conflict in 1989–0.

In 1989 the Ministry of Culture designated the Castillo de la Real Fuerza a special exhibition space for contemporary art, as part of a desire to settle artists' fears of an oppressive orthodoxy. However, in 1989 one such exhibition was abruptly closed because of some ambiguous depictions of Castro by the independently minded ISA teacher René Francisco Rodríguez and Eduardo Ponjuán; the exhibition was reopened but the Deputy Minister Marcia Leiseca was dismissed, leading to a collective protest and the emigration of some artists in 1990–1. Others, however, and especially the younger ISA graduates saw this as a challenge and opportunity to occupy the vacated space (Brock 2001: 10).

A number of developments now began to flourish, especially Rodríguez's group Galería DUPP (Desarrollo de una Pragmática Pedagogía – 'Development for a Pragmatic Pedagogy'), aiming to encourage 'collaborative artmaking' and to explore connections between art and daily life as a workshop for ISA students and graduates (Brock 2001: 10);[1] inspired by the work of Ana Mendieta (a painter who, taken while young to the United States, returned to Cuba in the 1980s to reclaim her cultural heritage and work (Camnitzer 2003: 335), it also took art beyond the gallery, as in the 1990 'Casa Nacional' exhibition in a housing block, where students decorated an apartment (Valdés Figueroa 2001: 18). Other experiments signalled the generation's arrival, notably an exhibition at the Echevarría baseball stadium, or the 1990 Objeto Esculturado exhibition at the Casa de Desarrollo de las Artes Visuales (including Angel Delgado's notorious defecation on a copy of *Granma*, leading to six months' imprisonment), Tania Bruguera's collaborative 1993–4 'Memorias de la posguerra', a 'simulacrum of a newspaper' as art (Valdés Figueroa 2001: 18), or the 1994 creation of Espacio Aglutinador by Sandra Ceballos and Ezequiel Suárcz.

Essentially, therefore, rather than being conflictive and challenging as some saw it, this generation was actually negotiating its space in a new environment (Acosta 2001: 23), created by the crisis and reassessment and the opportunities brought by access to the dollar earnings abroad or from tourism. With the Bienal becoming an international shop-window for Cuban art, artists in Havana (more than elsewhere in Cuba) suddenly found opportunities and challenges at the centre of a new trade, an unfamiliar position which occasionally led to conflict (as with Suárez's provocative words 'institutions are shit' in a March 1994 exhibition at Galería 23 y 12), but was mostly seeking to push back the boundaries and to parody rather than rebel,[2] or to inject 'chaos into the ritual order of the social sphere or the art world' (Valdés Figueroa 2001: 21) and develop a deliberately non-representational and even sceptical or cynical art (Mosquera 2001: 13).

Perhaps inevitably, recent tendencies, new opportunities and official reactions all led to a gradual withdrawal from public art towards individualism (Valdés Figueroa 2001: 17). Suárez for example reacted to prohibition by exhibiting in his own private space, and others began to isolate themselves more from the collective, seeking recognition less from the Cuban public than commercially abroad or from each other.

One problem here was, of course, the mixed messages emanating from a cultural hierarchy that encouraged Havana's artists to earn dollars individually on the overseas and tourist market but continued to expect a collectivity which was steadily being eroded; this tension, along with the blossoming opportunities for hard currency earnings led inevitably to a willingness to operate on a soon booming illegal market, making artists even more suspect and resented. Moreover, this boom had significant side-effects in that the growing demand in the United States for new Cuban art generated a crop of thefts of works of art (subsequently sold illegally abroad) and even counterfeits (Gomez 1996: 77–9). Hence, in at least one cultural form, the 1990s crisis and adjustment significantly reshaped approaches and attitudes and created a disintegrating individualism, professionalising artists in unforeseen ways and threatening to remove them from the supposed 'national project'.

However, two other cultural forms, theatre and film, seem to have grasped the challenges differently. The Havana theatre of 1990–3, for example, confronted the new context with an experimental verve that recalled the 1960s, notably Víctor Varela's Brook-influenced 'sacred' spectacle, *La opera ciega* (1991) and *Segismundo el Marqués* (1993) (Muguercia 1995: 120). Certainly, despite shortages and travel difficulties, Havana's established theatres evidently thrive, especially the García Lorca, the more experimental Brecht, the Nacional (including its musical space, the Café Cantante) and the Hubert de Blanck, the Guiñol. In the new Nuevo Vedado-based Teatro Buendía, Eugenio Barba's Grotowski-influenced Odin Teatret has been especially remarkable, in using the physical challenges of the Special Period to become peripatetic, performing in the Brecht or the Mella but also in the Hospital Psiquiátrico and ISA, (Martínez Tabares 2002: 34–6), and thus echoing the 1960s ideas and the proselytising drive of the visual arts' Galería Rondante, which, in the early 2000s took their cue from the Teatro Escambray to tour Cuba with a collection of forty reproductions (half of them Cuban), challenging Havana artists' evolving isolationism (Acosta 2001: 24).

Theatre, of course, with its innate responsiveness and largely dedicated audiences, can afford to respond imaginatively without risk, since it is still perceived as a minority activity. That is not true, however, of cinema, whose relevance to ordinary *habaneros* increased after 1990 as television was reduced, although ICAIC did suffer from the shortages as well, its output falling from its 1980s peak to six documentaries and two feature films a year (Soles 2000: 126), with only four films in 1996 (García Borrero 2001: 380).

However, in a less predictable political climate, but with debates about the Revolution's 'essence', the generally freer rein given to the arts allowed cinema both a space and a duty to tackle controversial issues and a duty to be financially successful abroad, through greater creativity; in other words, echoing the 1960s, to both entertain and teach. Hence the mid-1990s' 'climate of ideological ambivalence' (Campa 2000: 132) saw the ambiguous *Alicia en el Pueblo de Maravillas* (1990) and the 1995 *Guantanamera* incur official disapproval, the former being closed after a popular reception and the latter being criticised by Castro himself (until Prieto, then Minister of Culture, publicly forced him to rethink); the former's irony was simply too challenging for the time, compared to the gentler tongue-in-cheek *Sala de Espera* (2000), which resembled Gutiérrez Alea's 1966 masterpiece *Muerte de un Burócrata*, and the subtlety of *Suite Habana* (2003), whose ambivalence and focus on the human appealed to ordinary *habaneros* and authorities alike. However, Gutiérrez Alea's *Fresa y Chocolate* (1994), openly tackling homosexuality, was a defining moment; screened during the worst crisis years, it stimulated discussion beyond the cinema, reflecting a new willingness to debate and be recognised abroad, becoming the first Cuban film nominated for an Oscar.

For the economic challenge forced ICAIC to earn its way on the dollar market. It responded by trying to increase access to foreign markets (which, even before 1989, had amounted to three-quarters of ICAIC's earnings: Soles 2000: 126), and to other sources; for example, in 1993, it rented out space, actors and technical expertise to foreign productions, earnings from this equalling foreign sales (Soles 2000: 126). This all pushed ICAIC, combining the search for income with the search for identity, towards Afro-Cuban music, whose overseas appeal had grown and which now represented part of the 'essence' which everyone was seeking with added urgency. Once again, ICAIC found itself at the forefront of Cuban developments, its finger on a very much beating pulse.

This search for the collective 'soul', however, was not so evident in the Havana literary world after 1990, as the 1980s' effects combined with new difficulties, new challenges and a new individualisation to fragment the Havana writing community. Instead, until the mid-1990s, writers ploughed an increasingly lonely furrow or sought publication and appreciation abroad, the latter option leading some to criticise writers who direct their writing towards an outside commercial market and away from a Cuban readership, often seeming to confirm Cuban stereotypes of political repression, economic hardship, dissidence and even sex (Lightfoot 2002: 82). Perhaps significantly, this has come at a time of increasing concern

Figure 19 Street booksellers in the Plaza de Armas

among cultural and educational authorities that generational changes, popular culture and shortages have combined to make Cubans, and especially the young, read less, sufficiently for the 1988 Biblioteca Nacional's Programa Nacional to be reinforced (Fowler 2002: 243).

Eventually, economic recovery and a rearrangement of Havana's cultural configurations and spaces saw new opportunities emerge and a new, if cautious, confidence, especially after Prieto's appointment as Minister of Culture, which generated a new enthusiasm among a hitherto fearful community. New gathering sites developed, stimulated by access to the dollar, such as the *cafetería* of the Palacio del Segundo Cabo on the Plaza de Armas, which, with its unusual double-currency bookshop, became a critical information point when the usual information flows were scarce or inefficient. The period also saw a revival of the hotels' role in offering cultural space; the Hotel Inglaterra, for example, has resurrected its former *tertulia* role by hosting poetry readings, lectures, book launches, its Café Louvre consciously emulating the old Acera del Louvre, its decorative ceramic table-tops giving artists an opportunity for exhibition.

The new environment also meant a new importance for the book launch (*presentación*). Once a formulaic and routine event, this has now become a key part of Havana's cultural processes of production and promotion, offering valuable publicity in the following day's media and an unusual opportunity for readers to purchase a new book cheaply, since newly launched books are sold for pesos immediately after the *presentación* but for dollars thereafter. Furthermore, the *presentación* gives the cultural elite an opportunity to identify itself collectively and, above all, make contact with political leaders, more high-profile *presentaciones* being often attended by the latter, who, either key cultural players or politicians with no obvious connection with the book or author, signify by their attendance a revealing wish to be associated with culture and to maintain links with the cultural elite. Hence, while the Special Period created problems for individuals within the Havana cultural community, it also made that same community more, rather than less, important politically, echoing the early 1960s, where leading writers had access to a political vanguard that wished to be associated with them but where individual writers often felt challenged, isolated or disoriented. Now, while the writing community may be less cohesive, the profile afforded to Cuban writing abroad has made it equally important to register that link publicly.

The differing responses to the challenges by different cultural forms raises again the relevance of 'popular culture', for several factors combined after 1990 to change perspectives on the question. The first was the simple fact that the Special Period's material difficulties changed cultural, social, economic and political habits. While, on the one hand, ordinary *habaneros* followed a more individualistic route to survival and reliance on new networks, they were also forced to look to their own local communities for support, recreation and expression. One outcome was the revival of local Casas de Cultura, but another was the creation of the Casas Comunitarias by the Consejos Populares, designed to refocus and encourage communal activity and identity. Hence, by default rather than design, a new sense of local community emerged, with artists focusing on their own *barrios* for the first time rather than gathering with fellow 'professionals' centrally in protected spaces and also with local residents seeking local expression. Indeed, this has also emerged within Havana as a whole, for relative isolation from the provinces and the outside world obliged *habaneros* to focus on their own heritage and context, combining a very local *barrio* pride with a pride in the city.

The second cause of the new attention to popular culture has been the impact of the dollar, which has seriously challenged previous criteria for judging culture and entertainment. As we have seen, at various points in the Revolution's trajectory, the differences between these two concepts were problematic, culture being seen as serious and an aspirational part of the social and political revolution, but entertainment being seen at best as consisting of folkloric relics to be rescued and at worst either a lowest common denominator of taste (to be challenged and improved) or pure recreational escapism. Now, in the Special Period, the issue was brought into the open, especially with the decisions on how scarce resources were spent: on strengthening political support through didactic material or on assuaging discontent with escapist recreation.

However, this leads on to the fact that the whole post-1990 ideological reassessment has also focused on the need to recognise, rescue and reassert a 'national identity', a drive which has logically affected culture, given the international popularity of Cuban music. At its simplest, this has arisen from an awareness that, to preserve the Revolution at a time of challenge and globalisation, building a sense of national identity was essential; yet the two concepts, Revolution and 'nation', have never been far from each other, so the new emphasis also made historical sense.

The final factor has been empirical: that most Cubans were forced 'back to basics' in all senses, retreating to either previous positions or to identities with which they could identify and to which they could belong (community, *barrio*, church, Revolution, Party). Hence, the sophisticated arguments of earlier decades were reduced to what was possible and salvageable, meaning that the 'popular' in Havana culture has largely been evident in four areas: television, sport, a new prestige for the traditional and a new youth identity.

Before 1989, television's appeal in Havana had been little different to elsewhere, with musical entertainment, feature films, the *telenovela* or sport being the most popular elements; hence, as horizons closed, these remained the mainstay of programming, along with politics and education. However, as travel difficulties and reduced offerings increasingly forced *habaneros* to retreat into their homes for the more enclosed social activity of television-viewing, the *telenovela* developed a special place: in common with the rest of Latin America, these tend to be fantasies about the rich or costume dramas, and, usually screened three times a week (after 9 p.m.) and usually Latin American, these have now become enormously popular, even forcing official functions not to compete with their scheduling.

Given sport's established role at the heart of both questions of national identity and Cuban working-class culture, the 1990s' shortages and traumas presented real challenges, especially with the political decision, at the start of the crisis, to continue hosting the 1992 Pan American Games, the strategy being presented as a triumph of collective will against the odds, including the construction of the 167,000–capacity Complejo Panamericano, with its 1,206 facilities (Segre et al. 1997: 280).

Baseball, as ever, was the most affected. On the one hand, Cuba predictably won the first Olympic baseball gold medal at the 1992 Games (defeating the United States in the semi-final), repeating the success in 1996, but the combined effects of economic crisis and US baseball's financial predations meant an increasing haemorrhage of player defections, affecting the sport badly. Although, among Cubans, this produced both disappointment and a secret pride, it also resulted in unprecedented defeats, notably by the United States in the 2000 Olympics (reversed in 2004 to the Cubans' relief). Yet baseball retains its special place among Cubans, the most curious manifestation of which is the daily *tertulia* or

Figure 20 The power of baseball: a *peña* in full swing in its usual locale in the Parque Central

peña, the informal gathering in various places in the city to *discutir la pelota* (debate the game), especially in the Parque Central and on the corner of 23 and 12 in Vedado, by the Esquina Caliente café, where fans gather regularly from morning to night to argue passionately and seemingly aggressively about strategies, players and games in an effective ritualisation of involvement, almost as baseball's daily religious gathering.

Prestige for traditional culture has emerged especially in the evolution of a new sense of the 'living' folkloric. One example is the revival of traditions such as *carnaval*, which, after declining in the 1980s, has seen a marked improvement in organisation and display, as responsibility has shifted back from the mass organisations to the *barrios*, producing more imaginative *comparsas* and costumes (Feliú Herrera 1998: 59). Even the May Day rally now partly uses the folkloric, with the inclusion of choral singing and Cuban music being the norm.

Mostly, however, this folkloric revival has resulted in response to foreign tastes and appreciation. For, just as a Venezuelan appreciation of the *son* revived Cuban interest in the 1980s, so too has the Buena Vista Social Club-generated popularity led to a rescue of older styles and their exponents, notably the Vieja Trova Santiaguera, Afro-Cuba All Stars or Son de Cuba, and Compay Segundo and Rubén González. At one level this seems to confirm traditional patterns of external acceptability determining internal prestige; indeed, this music is often limited to Havana tourist locales. Yet there is more to it than cultural dependence, for the new emphasis also reflects a conscious attempt to find the common ground between cultural communities, to resolve the post-1959 debate over cultural democratisation (between bringing art down to the people and bringing the people up to art) by fusing the 'people's art' and acknowledging it, rather than ignoring it or trying to formalise it. Hence, this development is both about manifestations of *cubanidad* and about acceptable forms of art, as in the periodic *peñas* at UNEAC's Hurón Azul, with *rumbas*, *boleros* and other traditional dance forms for Cubans and not tourists, or with the Conjunto Folklórico's Saturday afternoon performances at the Gran Palenque bar of the Teatro Trianón.

There is also another factor at play: given that the post-1959 drive for professionalisation and education meant that recognised performers, artists and musicians were expected to have graduated from the ISA or other specialist schools, today's emphasis on traditional music not only provides graduates with employment and access to the dollar but has also created a generation aware of those traditions and willing to develop idiosyncratic and improvised versions of them.

The third aspect of the 'popular culture' question has been the continuation of the trend towards a 'youth culture', building on late 1980s' developments, which tentatively challenged established norms. Here, the Argentine rock singer Fito Páez proved significant, his high-profile concerts stimulating an emerging Cuban rock world to experiment, especially Santiago Feliú, Carlos Varela, Gerardo Alfonso, Iván Letour and the groups Habana Oculta and Athanai (Rodríguez Quintana 2001: 91). Although Havana radio had publicised these developments (especially Radio Ciudad de la Habana's 'Disco Ciudad'), television now began to publicise them too. From these roots new varieties of Cuban youth music emerged in the late 1990s, especially driven by the popularity of NG La Banda and from a greater willingness to improvise, use sexually and politically explicit lyrics and express the new mood of self-confidence, producing groups such as Charanga Habanera (whose rebelliousness at a Havana Youth Festival led to a six-month ban from public stages in 1997–8), Manolín el Médico de la Salsa, Bamboleo (Roy 2002: 174–5), and, later, the grunge-influenced music of Garage H.

Yet it was fusion (of imported and indigenous forms) rather than challenge that was significant, as in the 1997 BMG Ariola compilation of Havana music, *Habana Abierta*, and the 'Cubanisation' of the largely New York-originating *salsa* in the form of *timba*, returning to *salsa*'s street and percussive roots. In 1997, Formell assembled his vast Dream Team Cuba-Timba Cubana of musicians from different generations, to challenge the market-driven preference for traditional Cuban music (Roy 2002: 181). Reflecting this development, a much greater 'official' attention has been paid to youth music and the previously denied 'youth culture'. One example is the strengthening of the Asociación Hermanos Saíz, the organisation specifically promoting culture among and by the young, which, in the early 1990s, sponsored rock concerts at the Casa on Avenida del Puerto, and, later, regular rock, rap and hip-hop events at the Madriguera, in the Quinta de los Molinos park (Lightfoot 2002: 210).

The political motivation is clear: the need to include youth at a time of crisis and potential disaffection, which was so evident after 1999. As a result, despite official nervousness, 1994 saw the start of attempts to follow developments rather than suppress them, most notably with the new toleration of informal 'social spaces', such as the boisterous Vedado corner at 23 and 12, where the coincidence of bars, cafés and clubs make it a popular youth gathering site, and in the tolerance and even encouragement of rap.

Interestingly, while rap in Havana tends to emulate its American 'parent' in style, it is generally much less deliberately aggressive (Campa 2000: 160) and its tone of criticism is muted and nuanced rather than hostile, a result no doubt of the general tolerance from as early as 1991, when the Casas de Cultura in 10 de Octubre and Mónaco organised concerts, and when both radio and television accommodated the new music. In 1992–94, Hermanos Saíz also opened La Piragua, an open-air venue on the Malecón, and, after 1994, the new space available on Carlos III created a genuine 'movement', leading to the first festival in 1995 (Fernandes 2003: 580). Indeed, the movement is broad enough to generate sub-divisions, between the purist 'underground' and the more commercially oriented performers (Fernandes 2003: 582), especially those appearing regularly at what had effectively become the national rap centre in the Alamar housing estates, based on the local Casa de Cultura and the amphitheatre (Lightfoot 2002: 212).

The result challenges outside assumptions about conflict between a monolithic and gerontocratic state and youth rebellion, for it is clear that the state and the rap movement (and the underlying desire for self-expression which the latter represents among Havana's more marginalised black youth) have managed not simply to coexist pragmatically, but, rather, to create a form of constant negotiation which sees rap as the latest in a long heritage of authentic cultural expression and sees the state as facilitating that development (Fernandes 2003: 603–4). Indeed, while the state is still clearly engaging in its post-1961 cultural gate-keeping and boundary-setting role, it seems now to be doing so more by negotiation than by clumsy diktat. Strangely, therefore, it may be in the unlikely world of rap – unlikely because of its echoes of the uncomfortably assimilated ideas of 'Black Power' in the 1960s, because of its association with the United States, and because of its perceived association with aggression and conflict – that yet another stone in the search for a cultural identity has been laid. It is also telling that this development has come not in Vedado (the traditional heart of the Havana elite intellectual and cultural community) but among the more disadvantaged black youth and in the unlikely and previously discouraging setting of Habana del Este. Clearly, in all respects, the rethinking of so many aspects of the Revolution which the 1990s crisis induced has also affected the definition of the elite cultural community in Havana; the drive for informality has, simply, meant a redrawing of the boundaries of that community.

Case Study: the Casas de Cultura

Background[3]

As we have seen, in the late 1980s, several underlying problems in the Casas de Cultura had surfaced, especially the growing tensions between professionals and *aficionados*. While, in the 1960s, prestige had belonged to the *instructores*, the Revolution's cultural 'shock troops', by the late 1980s, on the basis of the education successes, the new opportunities and efforts, the professionals had replaced the *instructores*, who now felt more marginalised. This problem was then compounded by the Ministerio de Cultura's 1988 decision to adopt the notion of *doble perfil* (double role), arguing that, because there were so many artistic professionals, the *instructores* (redolent of a past era) could be replaced by professionals playing a double role, as performers and as teachers. The decision resulted in fierce debates inside the Ministerio, professionals resenting this utilitarian role and rad-

Figure 21 *Aficionado* paintings on display at a local Casa de Cultura (in Regla)

Figure 22 The entrance to a Casa de Cultura (Regla)

icals rejecting the abandonment of a basic strand the 1960s cultural revolution. However, by 1991, with UNEAC's support, all the *escuelas de instructores* and *talleres* had been closed, breaking the organic link between the Casas, the artistic vanguard and the community.

That decision was, of course, followed by the post-1991 economic crisis, removing any chance of correcting its effects and forcing the professionals and the ex-*instructores* to sell their art and skills in the marketplace in order to survive. Hence, with neither *escuelas de instructores* nor the space for an effective *doble perfil* to be realised, the Casas declined in support, resources and prestige, reflected by its national coordination by the low-profile Centro Nacional para el Trabajo Cultural con la Comunidad, from 1991 (later the equally powerless Centro Nacional de Cultura Comunitaria).

The 1991 change, however, had one significant effect. Effectively an emergency response to austerity, the new structure reflected a decision to bring into the Casas all aspects of an unprecedentedly broad definition of 'culture' (including homeopathy, organic gardening, medicinal plants and so on), obviously seeking to use the Casas to foment a new culture of basic survival. While this made economic and social sense, it effectively marginalised conventional definitions of culture, since *arte y literatura* was only one of eleven defined cultural forms.

Meanwhile, crisis led many professional and ex-*instructor* artists to leave the state sector to earn money either in the tourist-oriented dollar-based cultural marketplace in Cuba or by selling their cultural products abroad, in musical groups, selling paintings and so on. This totally new experience also, of course, helped resolve the old inability of either the *instructores* or the *aficionados* to be considered as professionals because of their lack of specialist training; now they had de facto become professionals. However, their departure had an adverse effect on the Casas, since those who remained (associated with the less commercialisable theatre, choral singing and writing) became increasingly demoralised, and the Casas lacked new blood to revive them.

However, as was often the case in the Special Period, the changes also produced some surprising benefits, especially the new recognition of 'popular culture', hitherto relegated to either the status of folkloric curiosity or to a commodity geared to a (then) small tourist sector.

Finally in August 2001, long after the economic recovery had begun, Castro, in a move unnoticed abroad, re-established the *escuelas de instructores de arte* as one strand in the new nationwide educational campaign, thus both offering desperately needed new blood for the Casas and restoring political prestige to them and the *instructores*, confirmed by the upgrading of the national body to the more powerful Consejo Nacional de Casas de Cultura, now under a Presidente. While these new Escuelas aimed to recover the function, prestige and ethos of the 1960s bodies, they also decided not to reject any of the 1990s changes, and thus to include popular culture in their curriculum and activities and in the simultaneously reopened *talleres*.

Casa de Cultura 'Flora', Marianao[4]

Marianao is in one sense an unusual choice to study the operation and profile of a Casa de Cultura, given its historical association with culture, and especially the plastic arts, housing as it does the Escuela de Arte San Alejandro and having been home to artists such as Pogolotti, Lam and Portocarrero (Lam painting his famous *Jungla* there) and Alicia Alonso and José Lezama Lima. However, with only one Casa (for the *municipio*'s 138,000 inhabitants) and with a range of social groups, cultures, labour patterns and housing, it is typical in other senses. Lying now west of the Almendares and south of Miramar (since, in the 1970s, it lost its access to the coast and acquired a slice of countryside and Havana's only sugar-mill), Marianao used to be a mix of workers' housing, shanties and overspill middle-class housing, with a reputation for lawlessness; now, although the shanties have disappeared and the mix is greater, something of the old reputation has still stuck.

The Marianao Casa de Cultura was inaugurated on 28 February 1981. A *Granma* article on 12 March, recording its foundation under Juan Carlos García, talked of its integration of *grupos aficionados*, its lack of equipment and furniture, and its appeal for new music, theatre, dance and art groups (17, 60: 3). However, of the 3,000 enrolment forms distributed in the *municipio*, some 500 had already been completed, indicating a good response and likely level of participation. At that time, the Casa already housed a Sala de Teatro, small library, *salón de danza*, music and art rooms, and a courtyard for relaxation, as well as a *librería social* (recreation library) in the entrance hall. As well as a Wednesday lecture programme each week, the focus was very much on the *municipio*'s 39,000 children, with weekend programmes for them and with a desire to provide facilities for those who lacked them in their homes or schools.

The Casa de Cultura is located in the heart of the *municipio*, close to the Poder Popular buildings and the Galería Wilfredo Lam, on the main street (the old *camino real*, royal highway). In keeping with the national pattern, the Mariano Casa is housed in a grand 1861 building that has been variously a house, a school and finally (before becoming the Casa) a funeral parlour. Also, again in common with all Casas, it carries a name, *Flora*; usually this is designed to give each Casa a unique character or cachet by association with the individual after whom it is named, but, in Marianao's case, the Casa took the title of the huge mural adorning the wall at the side of the entrance, which Portocarrero painted specially. The building, fronted by a typical colonnade to shade the pavement and set it back from the street, begins with the spacious entrance hall (with the usual desk and attendant by the door, under the *Flora* mural). This then leads into a long and high room, the Sala Cascabel: on the right are a string of arches and narrow stairs leading down to a series of workshop rooms; ahead at the far end of the hall the visitor is greeted by another Portocarrero mural (like *Flora*, badly in need of restoration, after the ravages of street pollution and damp) and on the left by an array of paintings, the regular monthly exhibition of the work of the Casa's groups of *aficionados* (the *grupos de expresión libre*, free expression groups), as well as the entrance to a number of offices and rehearsal rooms. Left of the entrance hall is a separate exhibition space, opening to the street and open daily to the public between 8.30 a.m. and 6.00 p.m.; at the time of the visit, a collection of local professional and *aficionado* paintings was displayed here, variations on the theme of a Lam painting of a chair. Next to this, accessible via a separate entrance from the street, lies a vast echoing dance hall, bordered by thirty-foot high columns which set it off from the *patio* at the back; this is for dances, dance troupe rehearsals and for dance classes requiring ample space.

It is clear that the Casa hosts an impressive but typical range of activities, for different levels of ability and purpose, and for different age groups. During the visit, for example, one of the downstairs rooms housed an art *taller* for children, one of the several weekly activities and classes run by the Casa's nine *instructores* and technicians; here one *instructor* was training about twelve children, of ages between four and twelve, all of them working on hugely imaginative and often remarkable creations. Each year about five or six *taller* students go on to the San Alejandro. At the end of the Sala beneath the mural, a small group of children (aged between five and seventeen) was rehearsing a choral round, although, apparently all are training as soloists; their accompaniment was given by their instructor, playing on a piano whose broken leg emphasised the Casa's essence: excellence of quality, poverty of resource. In one of the rooms to the left of the Sala, in fact in the ballet rehearsal room, an unexpected activity was taking place: a rehearsal by a local *mariachi* group (the Mariachi Real Jalisco de Cuba), the result of the enthusiasm of a local *aficionado* but now an impressive group of thirteen musicians and one (female) singer, a mixture of teenagers and much older artists, all practising together daily and performing around Havana. Evidently the group represents the classic Cuban evolution from pure *aficionado* enthusiasm and quality to semi-professional expertise.

Finally, during that visit, the dance hall was the base for the activities of one of the Casa's highlights, the Afro-Cuban dance group Okan-toni, one of Marianao's best-known troupes and already winners of several national prizes. Consisting of about twenty dancers, drummers and singers, the group has clearly already graduated beyond the level of pure *aficionado* to a high level of expertise and semi-professionalism, on the basis of practice between 2.00 p.m. and 8.00 p.m. each afternoon. During the visit, there was a spectacular, but scarcely impromptu, performance of the group's repertoire, which was wide, complex and thorough, ranging through a number of traditional white and Afro-Cuban dances (the *zapateo*-based *campesino*, the *garinga*, the stately *danzón*, a *chachachá* more sensual, exciting and risqué than any European or North American version), and a series of Yoruba dances, all exuberant, energetic, noisy and sensual. There were also a very Africanised *bolero*, an erotic illustration of *pregones*, and an especially sensual *rumbero*, the whole performance being rounded off by examples of contemporary 'fusion' music, apparently influenced by North American models, redolent of Michael Jackson but given a clearly Cuban sensuality and beat, then by a traditional *chancleta* dance, in which the staged competition between male and female dancers was achieved to the deafening noise of the stamping sandals on the tiled floor and of the battery of drums, culminating in the *conga*-style *comparsa*, the traditional end-of-carnival collective dance. Even though the whole performance was undoubtedly staged, it still reflected the quality and nature of the Casa's activity, the richness of the traditions that are the group's resources, the dedication, energy and enthusiasm of the *aficionados*, the attainable levels of quality, and, above all, the organic nature of the group, being clearly based in the *municipio*, despite its growing fame, but also whose performances and rehearsals are evidently open to the public to drop in off the street and watch. The group is also organic in one other less obvious but not atypical way, in that the organiser had a somewhat delinquent past before founding the group some ten years ago and training as an *instructor de arte*, seeing the activity as a means of rehabilitating other local potentially delinquent youths.

In addition to the above catalogue of activities (witnessed by chance), the Casa also houses other music groups, including a rap group, and possesses no fewer than six separate theatre groups and classes: the more classically oriented twenty-year-old Jácara group, the more adventurous Tres Tristes Teatristas, the experimental theatre-dance group Teatro X, two groups based in the nearby Instituto Superior Jose Antonio Echevarría, Los Magos and the *declamación*-focused group Los Caracoles, and one therapeutic group specially for the disabled. As for literary activity, that is carried out in the Casa del Escritor, a less impressive and more utilitarian annexe some way along the same street, closed the day of the visit.

The Casa's organisation is not untypical. With some twenty-five *técnicos de arte* (i.e. *instructores*) and sixteen support, managerial and administrative staff (making forty-one in all), and being open all day and every day, with rehearsal rooms bookable by bona fide local groups, the range of activities which it sponsors, leads or teaches is wide. In addition, with its system of annual prizes in all areas (generally being objects related and appropriate to the specific art form), the Casa fits the normal Cuban pattern of competition and reward. Its objectives are also clearly part of a traditional and evolving pattern. All of those interviewed agreed that, before the Special Period, the Casa was typically top-down in organisation and direction, but that, after 1990, the necessary reassessment of approaches (in the light of shortages which contributed to physical deterioration) led to a more participatory approach and a wider range of activities and appeal. Indeed, this change has led in Marianao, as in all *municipios*, to a more organic link to local mass organisations and the community, but also a devolution of some of the activities briefly attributed to the Casa in the time of shortages. In particular, the Casa has a series of agreements with all Marianao's major mass organisations for the provision of facilities, sponsoring of prizes and activities, and for decision-making, since the ideas for new developments are always channelled through these organisations rather than coming from isolated individuals, as well as through the five-year plans developed by each Consejo Popular in the *municipio* (there being three in Marianao, as all over Cuba, one for each *barrio*).

As for devolution, that refers above all to the creation of the local *casas comunitarias*: these have been set up below the *municipio* level, almost as the cultural arm of the *barrio*-based Consejo Popular. It is now these *casas* which, besides organising ceramics workshops, also house the wide range of less artistic activities which were foisted on the Casas de Cultura in the early 1990s. However, the Casa is also increasingly involved in the nationwide environmental programme of *talleres de transformación integral* ('workshops for environmental change'). Indeed, it is evident that the emphasis locally, if not nationally, is shifting towards a greater focus on community work, not least with the old, schools, disabled groups and even the cultural rehabilitation of prisoners. In this respect the Casa's activity seems to reflect what all those involved stressed was one of their main purposes, namely to be a site for communal action, especially for local *aficionados* and developing and 'rescuing' local traditions.

However, on the evidence of this one Casa de Cultura, the local purpose has shifted somewhat in recent years, blurring the old distinctions between *aficionados* and professionals, since it is clear that the Casa serves as a seed-bed for cultural talent as well as a site for action and belonging. While this was explicitly not their purpose when they were created, the Casa is clearly a critical cultural site in the Havana of today, not least as the place where at least two cultural communities fuse and overlap – the professional community of established artists (locally and nationally) and the local cultural community in all its manifestations. Indeed, the Casa seems to be the site where fusion takes place creatively, where one can move from one to the other, thus serving a valuable function in Havana's cultural evolution and in establishing, defining and defending a cultural identity, locally, regionally and even nationally. Once again, the redrawing of boundaries around the elite cultural community, a process that at one level has led artists to seek expression in the dollar market, has meant a blurring of distinctions and, at its most creative, a positive fusion at the edges. This is important as it means that, unlike in previous periods, those boundaries have not been drawn at the centre but determined locally at the edges.

Notes

1. These especially included Beverley Mojena, Ruslán Torres, Joan Capote, Iván Capote, Alexander Morales, Wilfredo Prieto, Inti Hernández, Juan Rivero, David Sardiñas and Oscar Moreno Anais.
2. This is suggested by Stephen Wilkinson, in a paper presented in London in July 2002.
3. For much of what follows, I am indebted to Fernando Rojas and Sara Lamerán Echevarría (of the Consejo Nacional de Casas de Cultura) and the staff of the Marianao Casa de Cultura 'Flora'.
4. The research on Marianao was carried out on 14 January 2003, supplemented by subsequent questions to the officials and participants.

Conclusion: Havana as Chiaroscuro

At the start of this study, its one purpose was made clear: to be a focused history of two or more cultural communities of one city (Havana) during a specific period (the twentieth century), all through the prism of the question of national identity. These five layers of specificity have, throughout, determined the selection of material, the arguments and the focus, but with what results?

One pattern that has emerged has been the usefulness of the terms which were outlined at the start, such as 'cultural community', cultural spaces, patronage and overlap. Certainly we have seen that, for most if not all of the period studied, at least one definable community did exist, often as a small, introverted but outwardly oriented community, often isolated from its cultural 'hinterland' and mostly preferring to seek inspiration, recognition and models from the cultural 'poles' abroad. Yet we have also seen how that same community was used, from 1902 and (albeit less so) from 1959, as a critical element in the necessary process of nation-building, often seeking that role itself but not necessarily enjoying a social or political prestige commensurate with it. For, although it was always and necessarily critical to that process (because the usual mechanisms of constitution-building, political structures and rituals are insufficient without the input of historiography and culture to express the national narratives and the forms in which the community should be imagined), the sequence of colonialism and neocolonialism, and the Revolution in search of its ideological identity after 1959 meant a subsidiary role for the would-be cultural arbiters, either subordinate to the dictates of external and externally oriented power or subordinate to an evolving agenda of participation and grass roots revolution. As we have seen, therefore, in this context spaces have been vital to survival, self-definition, internal authority and external prestige, as has been patronage.

Before 1959, both types of patron, entrepreneurs and mentors, were necessary for the several processes of cultural formation and identification, as indicated by the 1934–58 years when the former tended to be absent, leading to some cultural drift and a vacuum, saved only by the existence of a few mentors. After 1959, however, neither type was either evident or even necessary, because the new revolutionary state, as it emerged, began to adopt the former's role, providing opportunities, direction, prestige and even access to power, and above all gate-keeping through all its mechanisms. However, the lack of any clear mentors meant two processes: attempts by some to claim that role for themselves (notably *Lunes*) and a multipolarity of criteria and definitions, compounded by the de facto cultural democratisation which began almost from the outset. This, of course, highlights a key point about cultural patronage, namely that, as with any patronage system, while clients need patrons (leading to cultural dependency and disorientation when patrons are absent), so too do patrons need clients; hence, when cultural clients go elsewhere for their prestige, recognition and guidance, the result is the isolation of the patron. This seems to have happened in Havana after 1961, when the would-be patrons of *Lunes* found that their potential 'clients' were in fact developing their own cultural practice empirically and leaving them isolated, at a time when, believing they had access to power and were central to the collective task of revolutionary nation-rebuilding, they in fact discovered that they were marginal to the real political direction of the Revolution and also, more worryingly, marginal to the processes of cultural revolution. It was this discovery, as much as any Stalinism or 'Communist dialectics', that drove many to leave and which continued to mark their writing and creative work in exile, namely that they did not count in Cuba or, more importantly, in Havana.

Equally, this study has perhaps identified the usefulness of the concept of cultural overlap, taking us away from the idea of influence and towards a recognition of a more complex process of appropriation, borrowing and *sui generis* evolution. We have seen that, until the 1920s, the pattern of that overlap in Havana tended to be one-way, with resources and producers 'leaving' Havana for the world 'poles', either physically or conceptually, but that, as fractures appeared in the neo-colonial system (in 1920 and again in 1929–33), that process was challenged if not changed, the 1920 crisis producing a cultural vanguard (using the same mechanisms as those it challenged) and the 1930s crisis leading to the entry of more popular forms, some welcomed but others resisted. Equally, the 1959 fracture generated a change in the pattern, initially echoing the post-1902 (or more accurately post-1910) process, but gradually reversing the traditional cultural 'flow' and discovering new 'poles' (in eastern Europe, in Latin America and, more haphazardly, in Cuba itself).

This also indicates the usefulness of the study's focus on the Havana middle class, as the area where national cultural identity was originally sought or defined, as the ideological battleground in that search, and as the potential bridge between cultural elites and the popular. Whereas, before 1929, that class tended to aspire upwards to notions of cultural prestige and outwards towards Spain for models, between 1930 and 1958 it tended much more to identify with the popular, seeing it either as entertainment, a commodity to consume, or as an imitation of the North American, rather than European, pole. Hence, the departure of that class after 1960 meant a fundamental transformation of the whole question of cultural identity, evident in locations such as Vedado and the University, but also discernible in a range of manifestations and patterns.

As we have seen, this centrality is because the question of a cultural identity has, in Havana at least, been about belonging to a community of which one feels an organic part; before 1959, this was never easy to achieve, given social divisions, neocolonialism and the scattering of the elite and vanguard cultural communities. After 1959, however, especially as the potentially discordant elements left, it became a matter of locating, appreciating and incorporating all the population in some form or other, changing the debates about the meaning of popular culture, cultural democratisation and revolution, the three rarely synonymous with each other.

In this context it is worth pointing out that, over recent decades, the question of the 'formal' elite cultural community and its relationship with the other 'informal' communities – the Other for the mainstream – has changed fundamentally. As we have seen, before 1959, the tendency was for the 'informal' to be the 'popular', either rejected structurally and excluded, or, increasingly, incorporated into the cultural products of the formal community in a search for novelty, authenticity or identity, although tending to incorporate the folkloric manifestations of that 'informality' and reject the 'entertainment' offerings from outside the defined boundaries. After 1959, of course, as the state increasingly became the arbiter of cultural criteria and as cultural democratisation proceeded by accident and by design, the nature of 'informality' changed. While the folklorically 'popular' and even, at times, the 'informal' as entertainment were increasingly absorbed into the cultural mainstream as officially defined and stipulated, this meant that 'informality' became less a question of the popular (as opposed to the prestigious 'high' forms) than a question of political or cultural dissent. In a process which increasingly left little room for such informality, this meant that those dissenting (for whatever reason) had only two options, other than compliance. The first was to take the well-trodden path into exile (since all cultural exile is at one level a form of cultural informality, in operating beyond the defined boundaries), which, unlike pre-1959 exile, tended to remove their cultural influence inside Cuba, no matter how successfully they then achieved recognition within the accepted external poles. The second was to go underground, to engage in a form of cultural guerrilla warfare, the cultural dimension to the economic informality and illegality which became the norm for so many Cubans as the system evolved. However, this second alternative really only offered possibilities for short periods, those engaging in this activity being either coopted into the mainstream or being suppressed or ejected from the island in one form or another; one illustration of the latter was the fate of

Arenas's brief deliberately provocative challenge before 1980, which resulted in his emigration.

After the 1990s crisis, however, the spaces for such informality increased dramatically, allowing (and even encouraging) both an economic informality and a cultural informality. Hence, while the processes of democratisation have made the old 'informal' (the popular) part of a newly broadened mainstream, the role of the new Other, the culturally 'informal', has been filled by writers, musicians and artists who have plied their trade outside the formal boundaries of criteria, operation and performance, with little reference to the gate-keepers of old, state or individual cultural leaders. That is a dramatic change in the nature of the Havana cultural community, making the community's necessary boundaries no longer those between 'high' formal and 'popular' informal but, rather, between a new formality (fusing elite and popular) and a new dissident informality. The relevance here is that it is essentially within the former formality that the search for cultural identity has been carried out in the last decade or so, the latter informality largely ignoring that search and replacing it by an individual search for survival or self-advancement.

This, then, returns us to the question of the debates about the meaning of popular culture. In these debates, the experiences since 1902 had seen several possibilities aired and even implemented. During the Republic, they often focused, variously, on the need to bring the people to culture, through education, or, from the 1930s, to bring culture *from* the people, incorporating elements of the popular into the aesthetically prestigious or fashionable. After 1959, both approaches were again evident, depending on the period, the priorities or, indeed, the personnel and the institution, but, increasingly, debates tended to gravitate towards two different approaches, namely taking culture *to* the people (or *for* the people), in various campaigns designed to educate, enlighten and proselytise, and also eventually encouraging culture *by* the people. Certainly it was this latter approach and process which were so evident in the *aficionados* and *instructores* movements and in the creation of the Casas de Cultura, manifestations whose heyday came at two particular moments of confusion and dynamism, in the early 1960s and then in the 1980s (when the dynamism of 'prestigious' culture was at its lowest ebb), but which lost authority and meaning as the dramatic changes after 1990 suddenly undermined the patterns built up since 1959 but also 'freed' cultural producers to act in the market. However, just as culture in Havana was again, in many forms and genres, becoming individualised and losing its revolutionary zeal and its need to identify with a 'cultural identity', the revival of the movements signalled both a political need to reinvigorate that search and to respond to grass roots demands for cultural participation.

If true, then what this means is that the study's theme – the identification between a 'Cuban cultural identity' and Havana – seems to have discovered a significant answer in two unexpected areas. At various points in this history, we have seen how the Havana elite or vanguard has occasionally been at the forefront of the national search for identity, how the Havana middle class has been the prime Cuban site for popularisation, but also, alternatively, how that same elite, vanguard and middle class have acted as the mechanisms for cultural colonialism. In that sense, therefore, Havana has tended to figure in this history as protagonist or villain of the drama. However, at no stage was it really possible to identify a specifically Havana culture within that history, other than the processes within the elite or vanguard cultural communities (always located in Havana, acting within the city's confines and spaces, and occasionally having access to the central poles of political authority), or, alternatively, within the emerging popular communities, where religious practices and dance forms, in particular, began to develop a life of their own that was different from their earlier, rural or African, forms.

One of the underlying problems, throughout this study, and throughout the Cuban search itself, has of course been the difficulty of knowing what exactly 'cultural identity' is or should be. Indeed, at the start of the book, we saw the difficulties of defining 'culture' itself, making 'identity' even more problematic. However, what was suggested then, and has become evident as this history has been traced, is that such a 'cultural identity' is not just about 'belonging' but about collective self-confidence, about a community (a nation or, in this case, a city) feeling good about itself and feeling that it *is* a community, and identifiably so, and thus being able to approach others with a sense of confidence and without fears of domination or inferiority. Of course, once again, the difficulty lies in knowing how to judge, recognise or trust that self-confidence; certainly, even during the frenetic phase of 'cultural decolonisation' in the mid-1960s, the vehemence of the rejection of outside models meant a lack of self-confidence, however necessary that rejection at the time. Some cultural manifestations allow us to glimpse that, such as sport or music or dance, but one can still never be sure that this pride results from self-recognition or pleasure at external recognition.

Hence the answer may lie in the realisation that, if a political identity is seen as a way of acting collectively and an ideological identity as a shared way of thinking the collective, then a cultural identity is a collective way of being or a collective way of recreating (in all senses). If that is so, then one knows more clearly what evidence to seek: perhaps in the levels of cultural activity, or in the inclusion of Cuban cultural forms in a wider 'canon', or in the appreciation of Cuban cultural products (even preferring these when others are available), or in the fusion of imported and home-grown forms into an organic *sui generis* form.

However, these are still problematic, since they perpetuate the questions of influence and of inside/outside dichotomies. Moreover, we can see this repeating patterns familiar in the rest of Latin America, where a normative process of identification seems to have evolved in many countries. Usually this process has started with an increasingly self-confident production of cultural forms according to the criteria of imported models. It has then passed through some level of recognition and appreciation by the external cultural poles and through the self-conscious incorporation of elements seen to be indigenous, perhaps reflecting a search for roots or allowing the possibility of external recognition through a supposed authenticity, through a self-conscious exoticisation of one's own culture. This 'discovery' has often, then, led essentially colonised consumers to buy native products or accord prestige to local forms, perhaps breaking down distinctions between 'high' and 'popular' culture. Indeed, it is often precisely here, in the dynamics of such as fusion, that one might recognise the depth and success of the process of cultural identification, and certainly within the extent to which the colonised cultural community and its producers have appropriated the forms, visions and criteria of the metropolis, adapted them and even either re-exported them – perhaps as the voice of the periphery or the 'other' – or developed them for internal consumption, appreciation and organic development. Such a process can be seen, on occasions, as a challenge to established prestige and to imported hierarchies. If so, then it is often here that one encounters the conscious, angry rejection of the colonising world's culture, the 'fighting phase', the expression as 'a harsh style, full of images ... a vigorous style, alive with rhythms, struck through and through with bursting life ... full of colour too, bronzed, sun-baked and violent' (Fanon 1970: 177–9).

This process is all too recognisable throughout Latin America, and in Cuba too, within which the notion of fusion has often been critical, not least with the exaltation of *mestizaje* or Fernando Ortiz's famous metaphor (in his 1939 lecture 'Los factores humanos de la cubanidad') of the Cuban character and culture as the gastronomic 'fusion' of the *ajiaco* stew (Suárez 1996: 9), notions that stress 'fusion' as a necessarily beneficial and positive synthesis in a linear process of development. However, those intellectuals in Latin America, for example, who have in the past exalted fusion have often been the very people, groups or classes who have had the most to gain from the acceptance of the idea, being those who bridge two cultures or belong to none, those who are accepted neither by the external poles nor by their own cultural hinterland. Yet no fusions are genuinely equal, not least in the context of colonialism, and the pursuit of cultural fusion as cultural identity is probably the colonised society's equivalent of the Holy Grail – idealised but non-existent.

Instead, one truth that this study seems to have thrown up in the cultural experience of Havana is that the answer lies not so much in fusion as in three key areas: confidence, self-identification and participation. The first is, of course, a matter of quiet confidence, above all (rather than defiant self-affirmation), in not seeing others as threats, masters or paradigms and in measuring culture by one's own criteria as well as others'. In this sense, therefore, one might suggest that a cultural identity emerges when a community acknowledges what it is and not what others wish it to be, what it would like to be nor simply the opposite of what it rejects, not as a contingent historical fusion but a culture of the here and now. It is therefore 'never just a matter of ownership, of borrowing and lending … but rather of appropriations, common experiences, and inter-dependencies of all kinds among different cultures' (Said 1993: 261–2).

In Havana, this has had one very clear manifestation: the whole project to restore and reconstruct the city, but especially Habana Vieja, a genuine moment and process of self-discovery and quiet confidence, perhaps indeed the moment when Havana's different cultural communities and the Cuban state acknowledged their mutual identification. This is all the more so because of the nature of that process, for, as we have seen, the essentially participatory element that has been characteristic has been part of the whole process of cultural democratisation since 1959 but especially revived since the late 1990s.

Here, the key elements of the search for identity have perhaps been the questions of flexibility and dialogue. For we have seen how some cultural forms have, by their nature, been more able to reflect and express moments of tension or emotion, or the questions of identity, notably theatre (on occasions), poster art, and, of course, dance and song. Yet it is less in the form than the process that real flexibility is found, in the extent to which people participate in the creation of their own culture, which is, indeed, one of the real ways in which this cultural history of Havana has finally had its latest denouement, in the ideas, processes and implications of the Casas de Cultura (making the chapter 4 case study so central to the study). It is important, moreover, because the Casas are by no means unique to Havana but part of a national network and process, which means that Havana is now discovering its own cultural identity in several ways (including restoration and reconstruction, a youth culture and even the individualistic development of some of the arts), with a fundamental element being the local Casa. For, while allowing the local population to identify culturally with its immediate environment and community, the Casas are, at the same time and even for the first time, making Havana at one with the rest of the country, no better and no worse, no longer the 'problem' or the 'solution'.

The Casas therefore have relevance in two other recurrent themes of this study. The first is that they seem perhaps to offer some potential for filling that other overlap, between the 'upper circuit' (represented by the Havana elite community) and the 'lower circuit' of popular culture. The second is that they perhaps refer back usefully to Arnold's phrase about 'sweetness and light'. For the evidence seems to be that, as well as Havana providing us with ample proof of the importance of both qualities, the focus and purpose of the Casas are exactly what Arnold intended then, namely 'sweetness' as beauty and 'light' as education. For the eventual Cuban, and *habanero*, comfort with culture being both entertainment (recreation) and beauty (re-creation) seems to have merged, in the Casas, with the long-held belief within the cultural and political elites and vanguards in the liberating possibilities of education. In that sense, Havana is both the mosaic identified at the start and a *chiaroscuro*, in which light and shade do not necessarily mean what they immediately seem to and in which the two act upon each other creatively.

Bibliography

Acosta, L. (2001), 'Interinfluencias y confluencias en la música popular de Cuba y de los Estados Unidos, in Hernández, R. and Coatsworth, J. H. (eds), *Culturas Encontradas*: *Cuba y los Estados Unidos*, Havana: Centro Juan Marinello/ Cambridge, Mass.: Centro de Estudios Latinoamericanos David Rockefeller, University of Harvard 33–51.

Adorno, T. (1991), *The Culture Industry. Selected Essays on Mass Culture*, London & New York, Routledge.

Alvarez, I. (1987), 'Once notas sobre el proceso editorial, ideológico y artístico de la novela de la Revolución', *Letras Cubanas*, No. 6, octubre-diciembre: 153–65.

Anderson, B. (1991), *Imagined Communities. Reflection on the Origin and Spread of Nationalism*, London and New York: Verso.

Aragón, U. de (2002), 'El papel del intelectual en la República de Cuba', *La Gaceta de Cuba*, Havana, No. 3, mayo-junio: 10–14.

Armas, R. de, Cairo Ballester, A., and Torres-Cuevas, E. (1984), *Historia de la Universidad de La Habana, 1930–1978*, Havana: Editorial de Ciencias Sociales.

Arnold, M. (1995), *Culture and Anarchy and Other Writings*, Cambridge, New York and Oakleigh: Cambridge University Press.

Aufderheide, P. (1989), 'Cuba vision: three decades of Cuban film', in Brenner, P., LeoGrande, W., Rich, D. and Siegel, D. (eds), *The Cuba Reader. The Making of a Revolutionary Society*, New York: Grove Press, 498–506.

Azicri, M. (2000), *Cuba Today and Tomorrow. Reinventing Socialism*, Gainesville: University Press of Florida.

Barcia Zequeira, M. (2000), *Una Sociedad en Crisis*: *La Habana a Finales del Siglo XIX*, Havana: Editorial de Ciencias Sociales.

—— and Torres-Cuevas, E. (1994), 'El Debilitamiento de las Relaciones Sociales Esclavistas. Del Reformismo Liberal a la Revolución Independentista', in Instituto de Historia, *Historia de Cuba. Tomo I, La Colonia*: *Evolución Socioeconómica y Formación Nacional. De los Orígenes hasta 1867*, Havana: Editora Política: 405–64.

Barquet, J.J. (1992), *Consagración de La Habana. (Las Peculiaridades del Grupo Orígenes en el Proceso Cultural Cubano)*, Coral Gables: Iberian Studies Institute, University of Miami.

Benítez Rojo, A. (1996), *The Repeating Island. The Caribbean and the Postmodern Perspective*, Durham NC & London: Duke University Press.

Bhabha, H.K. (1998), *The Location of Culture*, London & New York: Routledge.

Black, G. Dopico (1989), 'The limits of expresión: intellectual freedom in postrevolutionary Cuba', *Cuban Studies*, Vol. 19: 107–44.

Bode Hernández, G. (1997), *Décimas Rescatadas del Aire y del Olvido*, Havana: Fundación Fernando Ortiz.

Brock, H. (2001), 'Remembering why', in Brock, H (ed.), *Art Cuba. The New Generation*, New York: Harry N. Abrams, Inc., 7–11.

Brock, L. and Cunningham, O. (2001), 'Los afroamericanos, los cubanos y el béisbol', in Hernández, R. and Coatsworth, J. H. (eds), *Culturas Encontradas: Cuba y los Estados Unidos*, Havana: Centro Juan Marinello/Cambridge, Mass.: Centro de Estudios Latinoamericanos David Rockefeller, University of Harvard: 203–28.

Cabrera Infante, G. (1994), *Mea Cuba*, London: Faber and Faber.

Cairo, A. (1978), *El Grupo Minorista y su Tiempo*, Havana: Editorial de Ciencias Sociales.

Camnitzer, L. (2003), *New Art of Cuba*, Revised Edition, Austin: University of Texas Press.

Campa, R. de la (2000), *Cuba on my Mind. Journeys to a Severed Nation*, London and New York: Verso.

Campuzano, L. (2001), 'La revolución Casa de las Américas, 1960–1995', in Fornet, A. and Campuzano, L., *La Revista Casa de las Américas: un Proyecto Continental*, Havana: Centro Juan Marinello, 30–70.

Carpentier, A. (1982), *La Ciudad de las Columnas*, Havana: Letras Cubanas.

Carpentier, A. (1988), *La Música en Cuba*, Havana: Editorial Letras Cubanas.

Casal, L. (1971), 'Literature and society', in Mesa-Lago, C. (ed.), *Revolutionary Change in Cuba,* Pittsburgh: University of Pittsburgh Press, 447–69.

Castro Ruz, F. (1980), 'Palabras a los Intelectuales', in Varios, *Revolución, Letras, Arte*, Havana: Editorial Letras Cubanas, 7–30.

Chanan, M. (1985), *The Cuban Image: Cinema and Cultural Politics in Cuba*, London: British Film Institute.

Chió, E. (1981), 'Ecos de una vieja Plaza', *Revolución y Cultura*, Havana, No. 107, Julio: 62–6.

Cid, J. (1986), 'La telenovela seriada en la Cuba pre-revolucionaria: algunas consideraciones', *Universidad de La Habana*, Havana, No. 227, enero–abril (mayo y junio): 359–65.

Cirules, E. (1999), *El Imperio de la Habana*, Havana: Editorial Letras Cubanas.

Clytus, J. (1970), *Black Man in Red Cuba*, Coral Gables: University of Miami.

Costales, A. (1978), 'De la música de hoy', *Universidad de La Habana*, No. 209, julio–diciembre: 79–85.

Cristóbal, A. (1995), 'Precisiones sobre nación e identidad', *Temas*, No. 2, abril–junio: 103–10.

Dear, M. and Flusty, S. (1999), 'The postmodern urban condition', in Featherstone, M. and Lash, S. (eds), *Spaces of Culture. City, Nation, World*, London; Thousand Oaks; New Delhi: Sage Publications, 64–85.

Deschamps Chapeaux, P. (1970), *El Negro en la Economía Habanera del Siglo XIX*, Havana: Ediciones UNEAC.

Desnoes, E. (1967), 'El último verano', in Desnoes, E., *Punto de Vista*, Havana: Instituto del Libro, 37–58.

Díaz, C. (1994), *La Nueva Trova*, Havana: Editorial Letras Cubanas.

Eagleton, T. (2000), *The Idea of Culture*, Oxford: Blackwell Publishing.

Eguren, G. (1986), *La Fidelísima Habana*, Havana: Editorial Letras Cubanas.

Eligio, A. (Tonel) (2001), 'Culture and society in the work of Cuban artists', in Brock, H. (ed.), *Art Cuba. The New Generation*, New York: Harry N. Abrams, Inc., 31–2.

Elliott, J.H. (1963), *Imperial Spain, 1469–1716*, London: Edward Arnold.

Esquenazi Pérez, M. (1999), 'Música popular tradicional', in Centro Juan Marinello, *Cultura Popular Tradicional Cubana*, Havana: Centro Juan Marinello, Centro de Antropología, 161–74.

Eyerman, R. (1999), 'Moving culture', in Featherstone, M., and Lash, S. (eds), *Spaces of Culture. City, Nation, World*, London; Thousand Oaks; New Delhi: Sage Publications, 116–37.

Fanon, F. (1970), *The Wretched of the Eaith*, Hardmondsworth, Penguin.

Featherstone, M., and Lash, S. (eds) (1999), *Spaces of Culture. City, Nation, World*, London; Thousand Oaks; New Delhi: Sage Publications.

Feliú Herrera, V. (1998), 'Carnavales', in Colectivo de Autores (1998), *Fiestas Populares Tradicionales Cubanas*, Havana: Centro Juan Marinello, 51–60.

—— (1999), 'Fiestas Populares Tradicionales', in Centro Juan Marinello, *Cultura Popular Tradicional Cubana*, Havana: Centro Juan Marinello, Centro de Antropología, 151–60.

Fernandes, S. (2003), 'Fear of a black nation: local rappers, transnational crossings, and state power in contemporary Cuba, *Anthropology Quarterly*, Vol. 76, No. 4, Fall: 575–608.

Fernández Retamar, Roberto (1982), 'Al final del coloquio sobre literatura cubana, 1959–1981', *Casa de las Américas* (Havana), Año XXII, No. 131, marzo–abril: 48–55.

Ferrer, A. (1999), *Insurgent Cuba. Race, Nation and Revolution, 1868–1898*, Chapel Hill, NC and London: University of North Carolina Press.

Fornet, A. (1980), 'El intelectual en la Revolución', in Varios, *Revolución, Letras, Arte*, Havana: Editorial Letras Cubanas, pp. 315–25.

—— (1982), *Cine, Literatura, Sociedad*, Havana: Editorial Letras Cubanas.

—— (2002), *El Libro en Cuba*, Havana: Editorial Letras Cubanas.

Fowler, V. (2002), 'El promotor: una variación post-Feria', in Ubieta Gómez, E (ed.), *Vivir y Pensar en Cuba. 16 Ensayistas Cubanos Nacidos con la Revolución Reflexionan sobre el Destino de su País*, Havana: Centro de Estudios Martianos, 236–47.

Franco, J. (2002), *The Decline and Fall of the Lettered City. Latin America in the Cold War*, Cambridge, Mass. & London: Harvard University Press.

Frank, A.G. (1972), *Lumpenbourgeoisie and Lumpendevelopment. Dependence, Class and Politics in Latin America*, New York & London: Monthly Review Press.

Freire, P. (1972), *Pedagogy of the Oppressed*, Harmondsworth: Penguin Books.

Fuente, A. de la (2000), *Una Nación para Todos: Raza, Desigualdad y Política en Cuba, 1900–2000*, Madrid: Editorial Colibrí.

García, M. (ed.) (1980), *Diccionario de la Literatura Cubana*, Vol. 1, Havana: Editorial Letras Cubanas.

García Alonso, M. (2002): *Identidad Cultural e Investigación. Hacia los Pasos Una Vez Perdidos*, Havana: Centro Juan Marinello.

—— and Baeza, C. (1996), *Modelo Teórico para la Identidad Cultural*, Havana: Centro Juan Marinello.

García Borrero, J.A. (2001), *Guía Crítica del Cine Cubano de Ficción*, Havana: Editorial Arte y Literatura.

García Canclini, N. (2001), *Culturas Híbridas. Estrategias para Entrar y Salir de la Modernidad*, Barcelona & Mexico: Paidós.

Gomez, E.M. (1996), 'Cuban Art: Crisis in Confidence', *Art and Antiques*, Vol. 19, April: 77–79.

González, H. (1989), 'Algunas tesis sobre las raíces de nuestra música sinfónica', in Cairo, A., Vol. 5, 421–41.

González, J.A. (2003), *Cronología del Teatro Dramático Habanero, 1936–1960*, Havana: Centro Juan Marinello.

González Echevarría, R. (1999), *The Pride of Havana. A History of Cuban Baseball*, New York: Oxford University Press.

Goodman, W. (1986), *Un Artista en Cuba*, Havana: Editorial Letras Cubanas.

Graham, B., Ashcroft, G.J. and Tunbridge, J.E. (eds) (20000, *A Geography of Heritage. Power, Culture and Economy*, London: Arnold.

Gruzinski, S. (2002), *The Mestizo Mind. The Intellectual Dynamics of Colonization and Globalization*, New York & London: Routledge.

Guevara, E. (1968), 'Man and Socialism in Cuba', in Gerassi, J. (ed.), *Venceremos: The Speeches and Writings of Ernesto Che Guevara*, New York: Macmillan, 387–400.

Helg, A. (1995), *Our Rightful Share. The Afro-Cuban Struggle for Equality, 1886–1912*, Chapel Hill, NC: University of North Carolina Press.

Henríquez Ureña, M. (1967a), *Panorama Histórico de la Literatura Cubana*, Vol. 1, Havana: Edición Revolucionaria.

—— (1967b), *Panorama Histórico de la Literatura Cubana*, Vol. 2, Havana: Edición Revolucionaria.

Hernández Otero, R.L. (2002), *Sociedad Cultural Nuestro Tiempo. Resistencia y Acción*, Havana: Editorial Letras Cubanas.

Hobsbawm, E. and Ranger, T. (eds) (1995), *The Invention of Tradition*, Cambridge, New York, Melbourne: Cambridge University Press.

Index on Censorhip (1972), 'Cuba, Revolution and the Intellectual: the Strange Case of Heberto Padilla, *Index on Censorship*, 1, No. 2, Summer: 65–134.

Johnson, J.J. (1964), *The Military and Society in Latin America*, Stanford: Stanford University Press.

Johnson, S. (2001), *The Social Transformation of Eighteenth-Century Cuba*, Gainesville: University of Florida Press.

Jorge Gómez, E. (1981), *Canciones de la Nueva Trova*, Havana: Editorial Letras Cubanas.

Juan, A. de (1996), 'La belleza de todos los días. Notas sobre diseño gráfico cubano contemporáneo', in Vega, J. (ed.) (1996), *El Cartel Cubano de Cine*, Havana: Editorial Letras Cubanas, 20–36.

Kapcia, A. (2000), *Cuba. Island of Dreams*, Oxford: Berg Publishers.

Keuthe, A. (1986), *Cuba, 1753–1815. Crown, Military and Society*, Knoxville: University of Tennessee Press.

Leal, E. (1981), 'Par hacer realidad los sueños', *Revolución y Cultura*, No. 107, julio, p. 9.

Leal, E. (1986), *Regresar en el Tiempo*, Havana: Editorial Letras Cubanas.

Leal, R. (1982), *La Selva Oscura. De los Bufos a la Neocolonia (Historia del Teatro Cubano de 1868 a 1902)*, Havana: Editorial Arte y Literatura.

Le Riverend, A. (ed.) (1984), *Diccionario de la Literatura Cubana*, Vol. II, Havana: Editorial Letras Cubanas.

Le Riverend Brusone, J. (1960), *La Habana (Biografía de una Provincia)*, Havana: Academia de Historia de Cuba.

Levinson, S.L. (1989), 'Talking about Cuban Culture: a reporter's notebook', in Brenner, P., LeoGrande, W., Rich, D. and Siegel, D. (eds), *The Cuba Reader: The Making of a Revolutionary Society*, New York: Grove Press, 487–98.

Lezama Lima, J. (1989), 'La narrativa de Ramón Meza', in Cairo Ballester, A., *Letras. Cultura en Cuba*, Vol. 4, Havana: Editorial Pueblo y Educación, 223–8.

Lightfoot, C. (2002), *Havana, a Cultural and Literary Companion*, Oxford: Signal Books.

Linares, M. (2001), 'La música cubana de la República', *Temas*, Nos 24–5, enero–junio: 132–7.

Linger, E. and Coatsworth, J. (eds), *Cuban Transitions at the Millennium*, Largo, Md.: International Development Options.

Llanes, L. (1993), *1898–1921: La Transformación de La Habana a través de la Arquitectura*, Havana: Editorial Letras Cubanas.

López, O.L. (2002), *La Radio en Cuba*, Havana: Editorial Letras Cubanas.

Lorenzo Fuentes, J., and Díaz Martínez, M. (1994), 'The Cuban writer', *Cuban Studies*, Vol. 24: 143–53.

Lumsden, I. (1966), *Machos, Maricones and Gays. Cuba and Homosexuality*, Philadelphia: Temple University Press.

Martín-Barbero, J. (1998), *De los Medios a las Mediaciones: Comunicación, Cultura y Hegemonía*, Mexico City: Ediciones G.Gili.

Martínez Carmenate, U. (2002), *García Lorca y Cuba: Todas las Aguas*, Havana: Centro Juan Marinello.

Martínez Tabares, V. (2002), 'Memoria y sentidos del espectador', *Revolución y Cultura*, Epoca IV, No. 3, julio–septiembre: 34–9.

Matas, J. (1971), 'Theater and cinematography', in Mesa-Lago, C. (ed.), *Revolutionary Change in Cuba,* Pittsburgh: University of Pittsburgh Press, 427–45.

Merino, L. (1989a), 'Apuntes para un estudio de la Academia San Alejandro', in Cairo Ballester, A. (ed.), *Letras. Cultura en Cuba*, Vol. 4, Havana: Editorial Pueblo y Educación, 223–8.

—— (1989b), 'La vanguardia plástica en Cuba', in Cairo Ballester, A. (ed.), *Letras. Cultura en Cuba*, Vol. 5, Havana: Editorial Pueblo y Educación, 393–405.

—— (2002), 'Aquel cambio del siglo', *Gaceta de Cuba*, No. 3, mayo–junio: 26–31.

Merino Acosta, L. (2001), 'La ruta de una huella', in Hernández, R. and Coatsworth, J.H. (eds), *Culturas Encontradas: Cuba y los Estados Unidos*, Havana: Centro Juan Marinello/Cambridge, Mass.: Centro de Estudios Latinoamericanos David Rockefeller, University of Harvard, 75–83.

Miller, N. (1999), *In the Shadow of the State. Intellectuals and the Quest for National Identity in Twentieth-Century Spanish America*, London: Verso.

Moreno Fraginals, M. (1977), *El Ingenio*, Vol. 1, Havana: no publisher.

Mosquera, G. (2001), 'New Cuban Art Y2K', in Brock, H. (ed.), *Art Cuba. The New Generation*, New York: Harry N. Abrams, Inc., 13–15.

Muguercia, M. (1995), 'El teatro cubano tras las utopías', *Temas*, No. 2, abril–junio: 116–22.

Núñez Machín, A. (1974), *Rubén Martínez Villena*, Havana: Editorial de Ciencias Sociales.

Olson, J. D. and Olson, J.E. (1995), *Cuban-Americans. From Trauma to Triumph*, New York: Twayne Publishers.

Ortiz, F. (1924), *La Decadencia Cubana*, Havana: Junta Cubana de Renovación Nacional.

Ortiz, R. (2000), 'Popular culture, modernity and nation', in Schelling, V. (ed.), *Through the Kaleidoscope. The Experience of Modernity in Latin America*, London: Verso: 127–47.

Otero, L. (1999), *Llover sobre Mojado. Memorias de un Intelectual Cubano (1957–1997)*, Mexico: Planeta.

Padrón Nodarse, F. (1997), 'Música a toda pantalla', *Temas*, No. 10, abril–junio: 100–7.

Paths of Culture in Cuba (1971), Havana: Political Editions (Editora Política).

Pavez Ojeda, J. (2003), *El Vedado 1850–1940. De Monte a Reparto*, Havana: Centro Juan Marinello.

Pérez, E. (1991), 'Cuban culture in the 1980s' in Tulchin, J.S., and Hernández, R. (eds), *Cuba and the United Status*: *Will the Cold War in the Caribbean End?*, Boulder, Col.: Lynne Rienner Publishers, 33–6.

Pérez, L. (1999), *On Becoming Cuban*: *Identity, Nationality and Culture*, New York: Ecco Press.

Pérez Sarduy, P. (1983), 'An Infant in English breeches: what really happened in Cuba', *Red Letters,* No. 15, summer-autumn: 24–34.

Pichardo, H. (1977), *Documentos de la Historia de Cuba*, Vol. I, Havana: Editorial de Ciencias Sociales.

Plan Maestro (2002), *Desafío de una Utopía*: *una Estrategia Integral para la Gestión de Salvaguardia de La Habana Vieja*, Havana: Oficina del Historiador de la Ciudad de La Habana.

Pogolotti, G. (1996), 'El cartel cinematográfico: arte y crónica de nuestro tiempo', in Vega, J. (ed.), *El Cartel Cubano de Cine*, Havana: Editorial Letras Cubanas, 49–51.

—— (2001), 'Para una geografía del teatro', *Temas*, Número Extraordinario 24–5, enero–julio: 144–7.

Poumier, M. (1975), *Apuntes sobre la Vida Cotidiana en Cuba en 1898*, Havana: Editorial de Ciencias Sociales.

Portuondo Zúñiga, O. (1994), 'La Consolidación de la Socicdad Criolla (1700–1765)', in Instituto de Historia, *Historia de Cuba. Tomo I, La Colonia*: *Evolucion Socioeconómica y Formación Nacional. De los Orígenes hasta 1867*, Havana: Editora Política, 180–224.

Puig Samper Mulero, M.A, and Naranjo Orovio, C. (2001), 'La acogida del exilio español en Cuba: Fernando Ortiz y la Institución Hispanocubana de Cultura', *Ibero-Americana Pragensia*, Supplementum 9: 199–213.

Pym, A. (1993), 'The Problem of Sovereignty in Regimes of European Literary Transfer', *New Comparison*, No. 15, Spring: 137–46.

Quiza Moreno, R. (2000), 'Fernando Ortiz, los intelectuales y el dilemma del nacionalismo en la República (1902–1930)', *Temas*, No. 22–3, julio–diciembre: 46–54.

Rey Betancourt, E. and García del Pino, C. (1994), 'Conquista y Colonización de la Isla de Cuba (1492–1553)', in Instituto de Historia de Cuba, *Historia de Cuba. Tomo I, La Colonia: Evolucion Socioeconómica y Formación Nacional. De los Orígenes hasta 1867*, Havana: Editora Política, 58–106.

Río Prado, E. (2002), *La Venus de Bronce. Hacia una Historia de la Zarzuela Cubana*, Boulder, Colorado: Society of Spanish and Spanish American Studies.

Rivero, A. (1981), 'El continuo reto al tiempo', *Revolución y Cultura*, Havana, No. 107, Julio: 34–8.

Robinson, A.G (1970), *Cuba. Old and New*, Westport, Conn.: Negro Universities Press (originally Longman's Green and Company: New York. 1915).

Rodríguez Quintana, A. (2001), 'Crudo: el rock cubano de los noventa', *Encuentro de la Cultura Cubana*, No. 20, primavera: 90–6.

Rostow, W.W. (1962), *The Stages of Economic Growth. A non-Communist Manifesto*, Cambridge: Cambridge University Press.

Rowe, W. and Schelling, V. (1996), *Memory and Modernity. Popular Culture in Latin America*, London & New York: Verso.

Roy, M. (2002), *Cuban Music*, translated by Denise Asfar and Gabriel Asfar, Princeton: Markus Wiener Publishers; and London: Latin America Bureau.

Said, E. (1993), *Culture and Imperialism*, London: Vintage.

—— (1995), *Orientalism. Western Conceptions of the Orient*, London: Penguin Books.

Sainz, E. (2000), 'Apuntes para una historia de la poesía de la República', *Temas*, No. 22–3, julio–diciembre: 113–23.

Sánchez Eppler, B. (1986), *Habits of Poetry; Habits of Resurrection. The Presence of Juan Ramón Jiménez in the Work of Eugenio Florit, José Lezama Lima and Cintio Vitier*, London: Tamesis Books.

Sánchez Martínez, G. (1989), 'Comienzos del arte escenográfico en Cuba', Cairo Ballester, A., *Letras. Cultura en Cuba*, Vol. 4, Havana: Editorial Pueblo y Educación, 395–408.

Santos, M. (1979), *The Shared Space*, London: Methuen.

Santos Gracia, C., and Armas Rigal, N. (2002), *Danzas Populares Tradicionales Cubanas*, Havana: Centro Juan Marinello.

Sarló, B. (2000), 'The modern city: Buenos Aires, the peripheral metropolis', in Schelling, V. (ed.), *Through the Kaleidoscope. The Experience of Modernity in Latin America*, London: Verso: 108–23.

Segre, R., Coyula, M., and Scarpaci, J.L. (1997), *Havana. Two Faces of the Antillean Metropolis*, Chichester: John Wiley & Sons.

Sellera, N. (2001), 'El melodrama en el cine cubano de la República', *Temas*, No. 24–5, enero–junio: 138–43.

Smorkaloff, P.M. (1987), *Literatura y Edición de Libros. La Cultura Literaria y el Proceso Social en Cuba*, Havana: Editorial Letras Cubanas.

—— (1997), *Readers and Writers in Cuba: a Social History of Print Cultura, 1830–1990s*, New York and London: Garland Publishing Inc.

Soles, D. (2000), 'The Cuban film industry between the rock and a hard place', in Linger, E., and Coatsworth, J. (eds), *Cuban Transitions at the Millennium*, Largo, Md.: International Development Options, 123–36.

Sorhegui D'Mares, A., and De la Fuente, A. (1994a), 'El Surgimiento de la Sociedad Criolla de Cuba (1553–1608)', in Instituto de Historia, *Historia de Cuba. Tomo I, La Colonia: Evolución Socioeconómica y Formación Nacional. De los Orígenes hasta 1867*, Havana: Editora Política, 107–38.

—— (1994b), 'La Organización de la Sociedad Criolla (1608–1699)', in Instituto de Historia, *Historia de Cuba. Tomo I, La Colonia: Evolución Socioeconómica y Formación Nacional. De los Orígenes hasta 1867*, Havana: Editora Política, 139–79.

Suárez, N. (ed.) (1996), *Fernando Ortiz y la Cubanidad*, Havana: Fundación Fernando Ortiz/Ediciones Unión.

Torre, C. de la (1995), 'Conciencia de *mismisidad*: identidad y cultura cubana', *Temas*, No. 2, abril–junio, Havana: 111–15.

Torrents, N. (1989), *La Habana*, Barcelona: Ediciones Destino.

Torres-Cuevas, E. (1994a), 'La Sociedad Esclavista y sus Contradicciones', in Instituto de Historia, *Historia de Cuba. Tomo I, La Colonia: Evolucion Socioeconómica y Formación Nacional. De los Orígenes hasta 1867*, Havana: Editora Política, 265–313.

—— (1994b), 'De la Ilustración Reformista al Reformismo Liberal', in Instituto de Historia, *Historia de Cuba. Tomo I, La Colonia: Evolucion Socioeconómica y Formación Nacional. De los Orígenes hasta 1867*, Havana: Editora Política, 314–59.

Triay, V.A. (1999), *Fleeing Castro. Operation Peter Pan and the Cuba Children's Program*, Gainesville: University Press of Florida.

Trujillo, M. (1996), 'El cartel: lo útil y lo bello', in Vega, J. (ed.) *El Cartel Cubano de Cine*, Havana: Editorial Letras Cubanas, 37–48.

Ubieta Gómez, E. (1993), *Ensayos de Identidad*, Havana: Editorial Letras Cubanas.

Valdés Figueroa, E. (2001), 'Trajectories of a rumor. Cuban art in the postwar period', in Brock, H. (ed.), *Art Cuba. The New Generation*, New York: Harry N. Abrams, Inc., 17–23.

Vega, J. (ed.) (1996). *El Cartel Cubano de Cine*, Havana: Editorial Letras Cubanas.

Villalba Garrido, E. (1993), *Cuba y el Turismo*, Havana: Editorial de Ciencias Sociales.

Vitier, C. (1975), *Ese Sol del Mundo Moral. Para una Historia de la Eticidad Cubana*, Mexico, Madrid, Buenos Aires: Siglo XXI Editores.

——, García Marruz, F. and Friol, R. (1990), *La Literatura en el Papel Periódico de la Habana, 1790–1805*, Havana: Editorial Letras Cubanas.

Weiss, J.A. (1985), 'The emergence of popular culture', in Halebsky, S. and Kirk, J. (eds), *Cuba: Twenty-Five Years of Revolution, 1959–1984*, New York, Westport, Conn. & London: Praeger, 117–33.

West Durán, A. (2000), 'Cuba: música, anhelo y sociedad', *Temas*, No. 22–3, julio–diciembre: 124–31.

Williams, R. (1975), *Culture and Society. 1780–1950*, Harmondsworth: Penguin Books.

Wright, A. (1988), 'Intellectuals of an Unheroic Period of Cuban History, 1913–1923. The *Cuba Contemporánea* Group', *Bulletin of Latin American Research*, Vol. 7, No. 1, 1988: 109–22.

Yglesias, J. (1968), *In the Fist of the Revolution. Life in Castro's Cuba*, Harmondsworth: Penguin Books.

Zaldívar, A. (2002), 'El intellectual, la nación y la política en Cuba republicana', *La Gaceta de Cuba*, No. 3, mayo–junio: 15–20.

Bohemia Editions Cited

Año II, No 10, 5 March 1911

Año II. No 11, 12 March 1911

Año II, No 12, 19 March 1911

Vol. XII, No 10, 6 March 1921

Vol. XII, No 11, 13 March 1921

Vol. XII, No 12, 20 March 1921

Vol. XII, No 13, 27 March 1921

Año 23, Vol. XXIII, No 3, 15 March 1931

Año 23, Vol. XXIII, No 4, 22 March 1931

Año 23, Vol. XXIII, No 5, 29 March 1931

Año 33, Vol. 33, No 9, 2 March 1941

Año 33, Vol. 33, No 10, 9 March 1941

Año 33, Vol. 33, No 11, 16 March 1941

Año 33, Vol. 33, No 12, 23 March 1941

Año 33, Vol. 33, No 13, 30 March 1941

Año 43, No 9, 4 March 1951

Año 43, No 10, 11 March 1951

Año 43, No 11, 18 March 1951

Año 43, No 12, 25 March 1951
Año 53, No 10, 5 March 1961
Año 53, No 11, 12 March 1961
Año 53, No 12, 19 March 1961
Año 53, No 13, 26 March 1961
Año 58, No 9, 4 March 1966
Año 58, No 10, 11 March 1966
Año 58, No 11, 18 March 1966
Año 58, No 12, 25 March 1966
Año 63, No 10, 5 March 1971
Año 63, No 11, 12 March 1971
Año 63, No 12, 19 March 1971
Año 63, No 13, 26 March 1971

Granma editions cited

Año 12, No 59, 11 March 1976
Año 12, No 61, 13 March 1976
Año 12, No 62, 15 March 1976
Año 12, No 64, 17 March 1976
Año 12, No 65, 18 March 1976
Año 12, No 66, 19 March 1976
Año 12, No 67, 20 March 1976
Año 12, No 68, 22 March 1976
Año 17, No 50, 1 March 1981
Año 17, No 51, 2 March 1981
Año 17, No 52, 3 March 1981
Año 17, No 60, 12 March 1981
Año 17, No 64, 17 March 1981
Año 17, No 65, 18 March 1981
Año 17, No 66, 19 March 1981
Año 17, No 67, 20 March 1981
Año 17, No 74, 28 March 1981
Año 17, No 75, 30 March 1981
Año 22, No 56, 8 March 1986
Año 22, No 60, 13 March 1986
Año 22, No 63, 17 March 1986
Año 22, No 64, 18 March 1986
Año 22, No 66, 20 March 1986
Año 22, No 74, 29 March 1986

Index

ABC terrorism (1930–3) 62–3, 66, 78
Academia Municipal de Artes Dramáticas 94, 101
Academia Nacional de Artes y Letras 71, 72, 84
advertising
  films 86
  magazine 110, 112, 113, 115, 169, 170
aficionados, movimiento de artistas 104, 147, 156, 160, 163, 164–5, 210
  grupos de expresión libre 203–4, 206
  and professionals/professionalism 200, 202, 206
  see also Casas de Cultura
Africa
  cultural traditions 29, 35–6, 50–1, 59, 75, 82, 138, 163
  dance forms/music 35, 51, 57, 204, 211
  and slavery and forcd labour 4, 27, 33
Afro-Cuban culture 42–3, 79, 123
  Abakuá 29, 42
  communities 43
  and Cuban cultural identity 165–6
  music/dance 42, 52, 83, 114, 147, 162, 193, 204
  mythology/folklore 95–6, 100, 147
  popular 147
  religion 69, 152
  see also santería
agriculture 27, 28, 32–3, 65, 121
  see also sugar industry
American cultural influences 52, 59
American occupation/intervention (1906–9) 58, 61–2, 64, 65
  effect on Cuban culture 69–79
Anderson, Benedict 15
  see also 'imagined communities'
architecture/architects 77, 153
  influences 90
  styles 2, 38, 67–8, 69, 90, 100
Arnold, Matthew 24

art/artists 9, 49, 81
  graphic 143–4
  new (1970s/'80s) 144, 149, 158, 160–1
  painting/painters 77, 81, 109
  poster art 143–4, 160
  and Revolution 144–5
  schools 99, 128, 160, 161, 198
  sculpture/sculptors 100
  surrealism 100
  see also visual and plastic arts
Auténticos (Authentic Cuban Revolutionary Party) 63, 90, 106
authenticity 6, 7, 11, 21, 209, 212
Azcárate, Nicolás de 45, 48, 53–4

barrios 37
Batista, Fulgencio 63, 64, 89, 90, 91–2, 106
Bay of Pigs (*Playa Girón*) invasion 120, 127
Biblioteca Nacional 58, 71, 129, 194
Bienal de La Habana 158, 191
black communities 65
  cabildos 2, 32, 34, 35, 42
  discrimination/repression 29, 37, 52, 65
  freed slaves 29, 34, 37, 42
  marginalisation 62, 65, 68
  population 28, 29
  sociedades de color 29, 43
  syncretism 29, 35
black culture 47, 65, 72, 79
  dance forms 85
  music 35, 42, 43, 52, 57
  see also Afro-Cuban culture; *santería*
Bohemia 15, 24, 73, 78, 130, 168–9
  advertising 110, 112, 113, 115, 169, 170
  agony pages 113–14
  cultural coverage 109, 110, 112–13, 115, 117, 169–72
  political focus 108, 115, 169
  readership 108, 110, 112, 113, 114, 116
  sensationalism 114, 115
  social focus 114, 115, 116

society column 108–9, 110, 111
syndicated American material 95, 115,
    116–17, 169
women's interests 109, 110, 170
bookshops 40, 99, 165, 175, 194
bourgeoisie 15, 56, 67–8, 94, 110, 127, 154
British occupation (1762) 27–8
effect on Cuban economy 36–7
bullfighting 34, 59

cabildos (councils) 2, 32, 34, 35, 42
see also black communities
Cabrera Infante, Guillermo 98, 104, 131,
    136, 139, 140, 141
Caimán Barbudo 138, 146, 155
Campeche district 33, 60
canción protesta 147
see also Nueva Trova
carnaval/carnivals 35, 57, 85, 108, 109, 197
car ownership 91
Carpentier, Alejo 77, 78, 83, 92, 129, 131,
    132, 134
drama 172, 174
exile 76, 93, 99
Carteles 76, 78, 95
Casa de las Américas *129*, 130, 132, 133,
    157, 158, 160
and external cultural policy 132
and new cinema 143
protest song gathering 146
see also cultural spaces
Casal, Julián del 53, 54, 79
Casas de Cultura 24, 156, 160, 164, 195
case study: 'Flora', Marianao 202–6
caso Padilla 153–4
Castro, Fidel 64, 120, 124, 202
Palabras a los Intelectuales 108, 133–4,
    135, 136, 158–9
Catholicism 33, 91, 127–8, 152
CDRs (Committees for the Defence of the
    Revolution) 119, 120, 122, 126, 151, 161,
    180, 181
Cecilia Valdés 49
see also Villaverde
centralisation 126
Centro Habana 67, 89, 142, 180, 182, 186
Cerro 39, 56, 67, 94, 106, 150, 164, 182
Cervantes, Ignacio 50, 52, 54
Chinese
community 43, 127
immigrant workers 28, 43, 127
Ciclón 98, 131
cinema 67–8, 86–7, 104, 192–3
Bohemia case study 111, 112, 114–15

poster art 143–4
Revolution and new cinema 142–3
see also film industry
CNC (Consejo Nacional de Cultura) 129,
    132, 133, 141
authority/dominance 134–5, 153, 155, 167
and 'Cubanisation' 145
homosexuality strictures 139, 156
coffee houses 45
coffee industry 27, 28, 36
colonialism 2–3, 28, 70
Communists 66, 78
Party membership and status 124
see also PCC (Cuban Communist Party);
    PSP (Partido Socialista Popular)
communities
fusion and overlap 58, 206
gay 136, 139, 156
imagined 7, 16, 52
see also black; cultural
comparsa 85
concert halls 49
corruption 61–2, 63
and crime 91
costumbrista/*costumbrismo* 46, 47, 57, 79,
    99, 100
Council for Mutual Economic Assistance
    (CMEA or Comecon) 123
counter-elites 14, 47, 53, 75, 92–3, 166
repression 75–6, 77, 98
countryside (*campo*) 120, 121, 126, 149
Covarrubias, Francisco 50
crime 61–2, 91
gangster violence 63, 89
criollismo
cultural identity 43, 52
music 57
criollos 28–9, 34, 40, 46–7
cultural identity 43, 52
and exile 37
politicisation 30–1
sugar elite 52–3
Cuba Contemporánea 19, 73, 73–4, 84
Cuba Libre 59, 64–5
Cuban culture 51, 197
Americanisation 1, 31, 59, 69, 90
influences 11–12, 40–1, 58, 59, 67–8, 107,
    129, 192
intellectual development 23, 37
PM affair 132–4
role of Havana culture 22–3
Spanish elements/influences 74–5, 78–9
traditional 16, 35–6, 42, 83, 85, 146, 165,
    197–8

see also Afro-Cuban culture; emigration;
   popular culture
Cuban economy 36–7, 63–4
   boom/poverty divisions 63–4
   commerce 27, 42
   crises 62, 63, 88, 108
   and dollar market 192, 195, 206
   recoveries 149–50, 194, 202
   reforms (1972–6) 122–3
   strategies 120–1
   and USSR 120–1, 122–3, 124
   see also sugar industry
cubanía 32, 65
cubanía rebelde 65, 125
cubanía revolucionaria 119
cubanidad (Cuban-ness) 28, 31–2, 45, 57–8,
   98, 107, 112
   defining 45, 79
   search for 46–7
Cuban national/cultural identity 5, 18–19,
   20, 25, 73, 164
Cuban Revolutionary Party (Partido
   Revolucionario Cubano: PRC) 30–1
Cuban-Soviet relations 120–1, 124, 125
Cuentos Contemporáneos (1927 anthology)
   99
cultural boundaries 92, 101, 130, 132, 167,
   192, 206
cultural colonialism 79, 211
cultural community(ies) 13–14, 57, 79, 95
   boundaries 13, 14, 32, 70, 71, 85, 92
   elite 14, 16, 47, 52, 88, 93–5, 107, 156,
      166–7, 189, 200
   fragmentation 4, 92, 97, 104–5, 182, 193
   frontier 13, 22
   gate-keeping 40, 71, 72, 92, 118, 166–7,
      199, 208, 210
   in Havana 128–9, 148–9, 156, 159,
      189–90, 200
   social boundaries 85, 206, 209, 210
cultural decolonisation 138, 139, 211
cultural democratisation 132, 135, 142, 145,
   198, 208, 209, 213
   debate over 198, 209
definition and meaning 160–1
   and mass culture 165
   and Revolution 145, 164
   and theatre 142
cultural development 17–18, 35–6
   groupings/layers 73, 92–3
   and self confidence 20–1
cultural elite 10, 14, 16, 22, 53, 95, 116,
   195, 208
   emigration and exile 48, 53, 70, 76, 93, 99

gate-keeping role 14, 71–2, 92, 117–18,
   166–7, 199, 208, 210
   in Havana 22, 34, 47, 49, 53, 57, 117,
   148, 208
   marginalisation by social elite 70–1, 92
   nature of 22
   and patronage 70
   and political elite 166, 195
   and prizes 94
   self-confidence/self-perception 57, 113
   and the theatre 49
   and *vanguardista* 75–7, 84, 116, 118,
   148–9
cultural identity 9, 23, 75, 84, 165–6
   artificiality 19
   debates 75, 78
   Havana's role 24, 88, 107, 164, 167, 168
   and heritage 17, 74–5
   and music 164
   and national identity 7–8, 12, 14, 16–17,
   18, 23, 117, 148
   Republican 84
   search for 5–6, 8, 23, 28, 59, 80, 117, 125,
   161, 189, 199, 210, 211, 213
   and self-confidence 19, 25
cultural institutions, and prize-giving 72
cultural overlap concept 12–13, 16, 17, 18,
   23, 167, 207, 208
   and Casas 213
   and fusion 58, 206
   see also dual circuits
cultural prizes 71, 72, 84, 92, 94, 154, 167,
   172
   see also literary prizes; music/dance
   prizes
cultural revolution 128, 131, 142, 149, 201,
   208
   definition and meaning 147, 153–4, 162
   and mass culture 154
   PM affair 132–4
   quinquenio gris effect 154–6
   Saturday debates 133–4
cultural self-confidence 19–21, 25, 52, 75,
   79, 100, 113, 198
cultural spaces 54, 58, 159–60, 190–2, 207
   Casa de las Américas 130, 135, 160
   cities as 22, 23
   exhibition spaces 191
   flat roofs 190
   gathering sites 190, 194, 199
   hotels 45, 145, 194
   newspapers, magazines and journals 59,
   73–4, 79
   Republican 81, 93

UNEAC building 135, 190
culture 9–10, 21, 79
  definition and meaning 7, 10
  evolution 91–107
  mass 10, 154, 165
  prize-giving 72, 94
  quinquenio effect 154–6
  schools 128, 135, 156, 164, 198, 203, 206
  workshops 101, 102, 164, 205
  see also popular culture

dance(s) 105, 147, 204
  ballet 82, 100, 147, 189
  as cultural nationalism 85
  danzón 41, 51, 57, 85, 173, 204
  forms 35, 57, 59
  mambo 16, 106, 107
  popular 51, 85
  public 41, 42
  rumba 16, 56, 57, 86, 163, 170, 198
  salsa 163, 198
  schools 41, 49, 82
  son 16, 85–6, 103, 163, 175, 197
De Blanck, Hubert 54
decadencia concept 74–5
defence
  city walls and fortress 33, 39
  fortification programme 38
  militias 37
  see also CDRs
degeneration 63, 89
Del Monte, Domingo 45
the Depression 23
Diario de la Marina 75, 78, 80, 81, 130
dual circuits model 12–13, 16, 23, 46, 96,
  167, 213
  and cultural overlaps 16, 17, 18, 23, 167,
  206, 213

Edelman, Jean Frédéric 51
education 8, 31, 44, 46, 74
  cultural 161, 167, 173, 176
  development and expansion 41–2, 123,
  149–50
  and elite status 34–5
  institutions 51, 129
  and literacy 36
  programmes/systems 31, 38, 74, 103, 123,
  181, 202
  reforms 43–5, 77, 128–9
  see also schools and lyceums; University
  of Havana
Ejército Libertador (Liberation Army) 31
Ejército Rebelde (Rebel Army) 64

elites
  hierarchies and status 34–5, 40–1
  and immigration 69
  political 14, 92, 157, 166, 214
  see also cultural elite; social elite
emigration
  effect on Cuban culture 48, 53, 159
  Mariel exodus 122, 124, 150, 151, 156,
  157–8
entertainment 29, 30, 41, 93, 195, 209,
  213–14
  and art 83, 84, 100, 101
  cinema 117, 142
  during the Revolution 145, 146, 147–8,
  165, 170–1
  light reading 55
  musical 117, 172–3, 196
  nightclubs 91
  and radio 101, 186
  television 182, 186, 196
Escuela de Arte de San Alejandro 40

FAR (Fuerzas Armadas Revolucionarias)
  121, 122
Fernández de Castro, José A. 73, 78, 80,
  118
Fernández Retamar, Roberto 93, 98, 130,
  134, 158, 160
festivals 35, 159, 163, 172, 175, 185, 198,
  199
El Fígaro 72, 73
film industry 59, 86, 88, 103, 174, 192
  American films 87, 111, 175
  Cuban films 87, 103–4, 110, 112, 133,
  142–3, 172, 173, 175, 193
  and cultural revolution 142
  as cultural space 159
  documentaries/feature 103, 143, 159, 193
  El Mégano 104
  film-makers 87, 98, 103–4, 128, 132, 135,
  143
  ICAIC 142–3, 159, 173, 176
  PM affair 132–4
  political power 104, 159
  reviews 111, 112, 116, 169, 171
  television effects 173
  see also cinema
First Republic 23
Fornaris, José 46, 47, 54
freemasonry 37
French styles and influences 40–1, 54, 143

Gaceta de Cuba 134, 135
Gaceta del Caribe 95

gallegos (Spanish immigrants) 30, 33–4, 42, 43, 68–9
gambling 32, 34, 40, 56, 67, 87, 88, 89, 91
García Buchaca, Edith 95, 132, 133, 135
García Caturla, Alejandro 81, 82, 83, 174
García Espinosa, Julio 104, 128, 143
García Lorca, Federico 79, 80, 96, 101, 114
Gattorno, Antonio 81
Gómez de Avellaneda, Gertrudis 53
Gottschalk, Louis Moreau 51–2
Granma 24, 168, 202
  case study 172–6
  cinema 173, 174–5, 176
  culture coverage 172–3, 174–5, 175–6
  television 172, 176
Gran Teatro (Tacón) 49, 50, 52, 66, 147
Grau San Martín, Ramón 62–3, 106
Grupo Minorista 19, 76, 76–7, 78, 79, 80
Guerra Chiquita (1879–80) 30
Guerra Grande (1868–78) 29–30, 37, 50, 52–3
Guevara, Alfredo 98, 104, 132, 133, 135, 142, 172
Guevara, Che (Ernesto) 64, 122, 124, 135, 138
  cultural school foundation 128
Guillén, Nicolás 79, 80, 93, 95, 96, 134, 139
Gutiérrez Alea, Tomás 98, 104, 142, 143, 159, 193

Habana Vieja 58, 68, 69
  and cultural identity 168
  population 66–7
  restoration 183–8, 213
Hart, Armando 155–7
Havana Bay 1, 2, 39, 67
Havana city
  commercial centre 33, 38, 89
  cultural identity 164, 167, 168
  design and planning 33, 90
  division between *intramuros* and *extramuros* 33, 34
  dockyard 32
  early history 4–5, 32–6
  economic and political evolution 65–6, 88–9
  fleet system/trading port 5, 27, 32
  and immigration 183
  infrastructure 32, 36, 39, 40, 58, 89
  population figures 4–5, 32, 34, 38–9, 42, 66–7, 89
  private sector disappearance 126
  and Revolution 128, 149–52, 181
  Revolutionary transformation (1959–71) 125–8
  spatial/social development 33–4, 38–43, 66–9, 149–53
  and Special Period 186, 190, 193, 195, 196
  suburbs 67, 89
  uniqueness 2–4
  white-black divisions 34
  as World Heritage Site 168
  see also Afro-Cuban culture; black communities; culture;immigrants/ immigration
Havana cultural elites 22, 34, 47, 49, 53, 57, 117, 148, 208
  influences 51, 52, 129
  role within national culture 22–3, 24
Havana culture, of 'sweetness and light' 24–5, 213–14
Havana Yacht Club 41, 55, 69, 79, 90–1
health issues 40, 179, 180
  reforms 123
Henríquez Ureña, Max 59, 72, 73, 77, 84
  and anthology 96
  collection 93
Heredia, José María de 48, 54
Hermanos Saíz, Brigada de 147, 153, 158, 198, 199
Hispanism 74, 78
homosexuality and gay community 136, 139, 156
hospitals 33, 40, 43, 126, 192
hotels 40, 67, 90
  as cultural spaces 45, 145, 194
  nationalisation 145
housing
  conditions 66–7, 90
  development 89–90, 149–50, 150–1
  effects of Urban Reform Laws (1959–60) 126–7
  overcrowding 68, 149
  squatter settlements 68, 90, 127

ICAIC (Instituto Cubano de Artes e Industrias Cinematográficas) 130
  cultural identity search 162–3
  and dollar market 193
  and domestic cultural policy 132
identification
  cultural belonging 166, 206
  and Hispanic culture 78
  process 6, 13–14, 19–20
  sense of belonging 1, 6, 9, 13, 16, 105, 149, 151, 152, 181, 185, 206, 211

immigrants/immigration 28, 33–4, 75, 152
  African slaves 33–4
  Chinese 43
  and housing conditions 68
  Jews (*polacos*) 69
  and politics 37–8
  Spanish (*gallegos*) 30, 33–4, 42, 43, 68–9
INDER (Instituto Nacional de Deportes
  Educación Física y Recreación) 148
industrialisation 88, 120, 121, 126
infrastructure
  transport system 39, 40
  water-supply system 32
INRA (land reform agency: 1959) 121, 122,
  138
Institución Hispanocubana de Cultura 93–4
institutions 42, 53, 93–4, 137, 157
  cultural influences 53–4
  development 43–5, 58–9
  Republican 71, 81, 92, 93
Instituto Cubano del Libro 137, 157
Instituto Superior de Arte 127
instructores movement 135–6, 142, 156,
  164, 181, 200–1, 202, 203, 205, 210
insurrection (1930–3) 62, 64, 66, 140
intellectuals 45, 73
  and *caso Padilla* 153–4
  and Cuban culture 23, 37
  political exile/exodus 136, 156, 157–8
  and *vanguardismo* 75–6
internationalism 123, 144

Jiménez, Juan Ramón 80, 94, 96–7, 98
journalists/journalism 43, 53
  prizes 94
journals 45, 46, 51, 55, 73, 93, 97
  see also magazines
26 July Movement 120, 126, 130, 176

Lam, Wilfredo 97, 100, 138, 202, 203
land grants 32
Latin America
  culture 10–11, 12, 13, 138–9, 167
  middle class 14–15
Leal, Eusebio 168, 184
Lecuona, Ernesto 81, 82, 84, 105, 116
leisure complexes 90
Lezama Lima, José 54, 96, 97, 98, 132, 134,
  136, 141, 153, 155, 202
libraries 44, 51, 87, 203
  1960s' expansion 123–4
  public 71, 93, 94, 130, 156, 190
literacy 36, 55
  lectura 38

Literacy Campaign (1961) 22, 119–20, 126,
  135, 151, 165
  enrollment of educators 120
literary prizes 44, 45–7, 53, 76, 78, 92, 130,
  134–6
  drama 84, 102, 142
  poetry 47, 81
  short story and novel 70, 94, 99, 139, 155
literature 36, 47, 96, 156–7, 205
  and black culture 43
  and *Bohemia* case study 111, 112, 114,
    116
  during Special Period 193–4
  narrative genres 80–1
  and Revolution 139–40, 155–6
  Romanticism 48, 98
  short story 99, 140, 155
  talleres literarios 154, 160, 164–5, 183,
    189, 201, 202, 205
  writers/writing 70, 81, 93, 96, 131–2, 160
  see also novels/novelists; poets/poetry
Lizaso, Félix 71, 78, 80, 92, 94
lo cubano: search for 97–8, 99–100
Lorenzo Luaces, Joaquín 47
loyalism 28, 29, 74
Lunes de Revolución 108, 131–2, 136, 138,
  139, 140, 148, 208
  Castro's criticism 133–4
  crisis and closure 108, 135, 137
Lyceum Lawn Tennis Club 90, 93

Machado, Gerardo 62, 66, 67, 86, 87
magazines 96, 189
  cultural focus 108
  as cultural space 73
  general-interest 95
  and the Grupo Minorista 78
  poetry 78
  and prizes 72
  sports 55, 59
  women 55
Malecón esplanade 58
mambises 31
Manzano, Juan Francisco 47, 48
Marianao 42, 67, 68, 73, 87, 99, 174
  Casa de Cultura 202–6
Martí, José 30–1, 45, 51, 53–4, 65, 79
  Centro de Estudios Martianos 156
Martínez Villena, Rubén 77
Marxism 12, 64, 125
Matanzas 28, 56
  culture 47–8, 57, 70, 76, 86, 117, 163
  unrest 29, 37
Mediodía 95

Méndez Capote, Renée 72, 92, 101
mestizaje 12
Meza, Ramón 53, 54
middle classes
  in 1950s 91
  and cultural identity 52, 208–9
  definition 15–16
  development 42
  and immigration 69
  petite bourgeoisie 15
Milanés, Pablo 46, 48, 49, 146, 147, 163
Ministry of Culture (1976) 155
minorismo concept 77
Miramar 58, 67, 68, 69, 89, 90, 91, 202
Missile Crisis (1962) 121, 126
modernismo 53, 54, 67, 79–80
modernity 12, 166
El Mundo 73, 130
Museo Nacional de Bellas Artes 24
musical theatre 49–50, 54, 55, 83, 102
  sainetes (musical comedy) 50, 56, 100
  see also see also *teatro bufo*; *zarzuela*
music/dance prizes 86, 176, 204, 205
music/musicians 77, 100, 105
  academies/achools/societies 35, 41, 51,
    100, 147, 162, 163, 198
  Afro-Cuban 52, 83, 114, 162, 193, 204
  avant-garde/*vanguardia* 82–3
  band music 54
  and *Bohemia* case study 109, 110, 113
  classical 81–2, 100, 106, 162, 176
  composers 82, 98–9, 162
  concerts/concert halls 41, 49, 81
  criollista 57
  Cuban 51, 54
  opera 49–50, 51, 54, 82
  orchestras 81–2, 100
  and Revolution 145–6, 162
  sacred 35
  societies 51
  see also dance; musical theatre; popular
    music

national culture 22–3, 24, 89
national identity 5–21
  artificiality and authenticity 6–7, 11–12,
    19–20
  and *Cuba Libre* 65, 125
  cubanía revolucionaria 119
  and Havana community 167–8
  Latin American 130
  political 9
  and prestige 16–17
  and sport 196

  see also cultural identity
nationalisation, Revolutionary Offensive
  (1968) 122
nationalism 31, 59, 69–70
  cultural 85, 168
  and Second Republic 91–2
  siboneyismo movement 47
negrismo 76, 79, 80, 95, 105, 148
neocolonialism 2–3, 62
newspapers 46, 47, 55, 72–3, 189
Noticias de Hoy 95, 104, 130
novels/novelists 49, 53, 54, 55, 70–1, 80
  detective genre 155
  and Revolution 140–1
  and social realism 99
Nuestro Tiempo 98, 102, 104, 107, 131
Nueva Trova movement 147, 163, 175

Oficina del Historiador de la Ciudad de La
  Habana 94, 168, 188
Oriente 62, 64
Orígenes 19, 89, 97–8, 107, 131, 136
  establishment 97
ORI (Organizaciones Revolucionarias
  Integradas) 120
Ortiz, Fernando 7, 71, 72, 76, 77
  and Cuban culture 74–5, 94, 96
  lectures 73, 74, 212
Ortodoxos (Cuban People's Party) 63

Padilla, Heberto 139
pan-Hispanism 74–5
Partido del Pueblo Cubano (Cuban People's
  Party) *see* Ortodoxos
Partido Independiente de Color (PIC) 62,
  65
Partido Revolucionario Cubano-Auténtico
  (Authentic Cuban Revolutionary Party)
  see Auténticos
patronage system 61, 64, 65, 70, 71
patron-entrepreneurs 45, 51–2, 76
  during the Republic 72, 96
  lack in 1870s–'90s 54
  and Revolution 130–1
patron-mentors 43, 53, 71–2, 97, 165, 207,
  208
PCC (Cuban Communist Party) 62, 63,
  121–2
People's Power (Poder Popular) 123
Pita Rodríguez, Félix 80, 93, 95, 101, 102,
  112, 140, 171
Plácido (Gabriel de la Concepción Valdés)
  47, 48
Platt Amendment (1901) 31, 61, 63, 64

La Poesía Moderna en Cuba, 1882–1925
    (Lizaso and de Castro) 80
poets/poetry 45, 47, 48, 53, 54
    and *Bohemia* case study 109, 110, 112,
        114
    during the Republic 70, 79–80, 93, 155
    lo cubano search 97–8, 99–100
    negrista 97
    'Primera Promoción'/Segunda
        Promocións' 140
    and Revolution 139–40
    styles 80
Pogolotti, Marcelo 81, 100, 202
politics
    corruption and instability 61–2
    and dissidence 76–7
    new (post-1934) 89
    Poder Popular system 150–1, 157
    progressive 63
    rebels/Rebel Army 64–5, 70, 120–1, 125,
        128, 131
    and Revolution 121–2, 126
    and working class 37–8
popular culture 9, 10, 11, 14, 47, 202
    in *Bohemia* case study 109, 111, 114–15
    debates 198, 209–10
    décima 36, 48, 57, 85, 103, 105, 174
    folklorism 10, 85, 148, 165–6, 174, 195,
        197, 202, 209
    and radio 101, 103, 198
    relevance debate 195
    trovadores 85, 103, 105, 174
popular music
    American influence 105–6, 145
    décima 36, 48, 57, 85, 103, 105, 174
    filin 106, 145
    'Guantanamera' 106
    jazz 83, 103, 105, 145, 162
    mambo 16–17, 106, 107
    protest songs 146
    punto 105, 106
    rock groups 145–6, 164, 198
    salsa 163, 198
    son 16, 85–6, 103, 163, 175, 197
    Western youth music 146, 163, 168, 198
population 4–5, 32, 38, 90, 152
    black community 28, 29, 31
    Chinese 28
    Cuba 4–5, 27–8, 38, 86
    of Cuba 4–5, 27–8, 38
    Havana 4–5, 32, 34, 38–9, 42, 66–7, 89
    slave 27–8, 42
    Spanish immigrant 30
    Vedado 67

populism 15, 63, 89, 135, 154
Portocarrero, René 97, 100, 202, 203
Portuondo, José Antonio 93, 95
poverty 64, 67, 68, 91, 97
printing industry 36, 40, 46
prose 99, 102
    development 48–9
    writers 47
prostitution/sex industry 32, 40, 64, 67, 68,
        91
    elimination campaign 127
proyectismo 48
PSP (Partido Socialista Popular) 63, 107,
        120, 121, 126
publishing industry 74, 77, 97, 134
    book launches 194–5
    book production 189
    book-shop based 55
    death 73, 93, 94
    expansion 141, 157
    houses 98–9, 131, 136, 137
    non-literary publications 55
    reorganisation/nationalisation 129, 144
El Puente publishing house 136–8
Punta 33, 60
PURS (Unified Party of the Socialist
        Revolution) 121

Quevedo, Miguel Angel 107

radicalism/radicalisation 62, 63, 65–6, 77,
        119, 122
radio 86, 87, 103
    and *Bohemia* case study 112–13, 114–15
    drama/playwrights 101
    groups/Big Bands 105
    Radio Diez Mil 103, 105, 106
    radionovela 101, 103
Ramos, José Antonio 73, 84, 92
reading(s) 24, 55, 153, 175, 193
    Campaña Popular de Lectura 165
    lectura 38
    Literacy Campaign 22, 135, 165, 170, 194
    poetry/public 96, 153, 164, 171, 174, 175,
        190, 194
Real Sociedad Económica de Amigos del
    País 37, 49
rebels
    Ejército Rebelde (Rebel Army) 64–5, 85,
        121
    Ejército Libertador (Liberation Army) 31
    massacre (1912) 62
Rectification strategy 124, 150, 158, 166
religion(s) 40, 152

in black culture 42, 43
and *Bohemia* case study 108, 110,
  111–12, 115
syncretism 29, 35
and white-black division/relations 34
see also santería
repression 70, 170
of black communities 29, 37, 52, 65
and counter-elite 75–6, 77, 98
of human rights 158
Machadato 77
political 193
the Republic 23, 61–4, 91
governing class 70
Revista Bimestre Cubana 44, 45, 46, 72, 73,
  95
Revista de Avance 80
revolution (1933) 64–5, 66, 89
Revolution (1959) 3, 22, 23, 24, 64, 134
1970s/'80s 149–68
agrarianism 126
Constitution 123
cultural policy 128, 133, 154
economic strategies 120–2
health reforms 123–4
historical overview 119–25
institutionalisation 123–4, 134
nationalisation 122
politics 121–2
socio-economic effects 119–20, 123–4
Revolutionary Offensive (1968) 122, 126,
  127, 145
Rodríguez, Silvio 147, 163
Rodríguez Feo, José 93, 97, 98
Roig, Gonzalo 81, 84, 87
Roig de Leuchsenring, Emilio 73, 74, 76,
  79, 94, 95
Roldán, Amadeo 76, 82, 83, 116
Roosevelt's New Deal 63, 108
Ruiz, Espadero Nicolás 51, 52

sacarocracia 40
santería 2, 29, 42, 69, 91, 123, 127, 147–8,
  152
Santiago de Cuba 3, 4, 32, 35, 36, 64
Santos, Milton 12
Saumell Robredo, Manuel 51
schools and lyceums 43, 44, 126
private 41, 91, 114
public systems 41–2
self-confidence 162
collective 160, 174, 211
cultural 19–21, 25, 52, 75, 79, 100, 113,
  198

self-identification 6, 13–14, 212
separatists 28–9, 31, 37, 43
shopping malls/stores 89, 90
siboneyismo 47, 52, 54, 59, 82
slaves/slavery
abolition 28, 29–30, 45
imports 27, 28
population 27–8, 42
trade 28
unrest 37
Social 72, 77, 78–9, 93
social development
patterns and hierarchies 40–1
Revolution's improvements 120
sense of community 40–1, 52–3
social elites 41, 70–1, 90–1, 92–3
clubs 53, 69, 90–1
and cultural elites 70–1, 92
social issues
inequalities 61, 62
racial discrimination 127
Socialist Bloc collapse 3
Sociedad de Estudios Afrocubanos 95
Sociedad de Folklore Cubano 72, 75, 94,
  148
Sociedad Económica de Amigos del País
  43–4, *44*, 75
Sociedad Patriótica de La Habana 44, 49
Sociedad Pro-Arte Música or Musical 81–2,
  84, 100
Sociedad Teatro Pro-Cubano 84
Spanish-American War (1898) 31
Spanish colonialism in Cuba
administration 27, 42
culture 35–6
historical overview 27–32
social development 33–4
Spanish immigrants/exiles 30, 33–4, 42, 61,
  101
Spanish influences/traditions 67, 69
Special Period (1990s) 3, 189–200, 202, 205
sport 55, 87, 148, 166, 196
baseball 56–7, 69, 87, 106–7, 148, 166,
  196–7
and *Bohemia* case study 113, 114, 115
clubs 41, 43, 55, 56, 69, 79, 87, 90, 93
Pan American Games 152, 196
racecourse 67
Stalinism 133, 138, 139, 208
sugar industry
decline 62, 88, 122
expansion 28, 36
harvests (*zafras*) 30, 119, 122, 126, 128,
  149, 151, 171

Matanzas cultural community 47
sugar mills (*ingenios*) 32, 38

Tacón, Miguel (Spanish Governor) 38, 39, 49
Taller Experimental de Gráfica 144
teatro bufo 50–1, 55–6, 83–4, 100, 141
television 91, 131, 196, 198
  telenovela 103, 176, 196
tertulias (cultural gatherings) 45–6, 47, 54, 58, 73, 130, 131
  hotel roles 194
  peripatetic 76–7
theatre(s) 36, 41, 49, 55–6, 59, 101, 192–3
  actors 50, 56
  attendances 103
  beginnings 36, 41, 49
  and *Bohemia* case study 110–11
  Chinese 102
  European influences 84
  experimentation 161–2
  mambí 51
  playwrights 84, 100
  political drama 101, 102
  puppet 102–3
  and Revolution 141–2
  schools and workshops 101–2, 141
  Teatro Alhambra 54, 55, 56, 83
  see also musical theatre
tobacco industry 36
  cigar and cigarette manufacturing 36
  crops (*vegas*) 32–3, 38
  factories 67
tourism 63–4, 67, 68, 90
  boom years 88–9, 90
  collapse (1959–71) 125–6, 145
  recovery (1970s) 150
trade/trading
  commercial centre 38
  and development of middle classes 42
trade unions 38, 42, 43, 62, 65, 91, 165

UMAP camps (Military Units to Aid Production) 136
UNEAC (Unión Nacional de Escritores y Artistas de Cuba) 134–5, 190

Unión 134
University of Havana 31, 34–5, 42, 58, 77, 100
  presses 157
  students/courses 65, 104
urbanisation 66, 85–6, 91, 111, 127, 188
urban planning 127
Urban Reform Laws (1959–60) 126–7
US-Cuba relationship 61, 62, 63, 119, 120, 125
  Bay of Pigs (Playa Girón) invasion 120, 127
  ideological war 158
USSR
  Cuban-Soviet economic relations 124
  Gorbachev's reform process 124, 150
  Socialist Bloc collapse 3, 179
  Stalinism 133, 138, 139, 208

vanguardia 76, 78, 84–5, 104
vanguardismo 77, 78, 81, 98, 99–100, 105
vanguardista 75, 79
Varela, Félix 45
Varona, Enrique José 53, 58, 59, 71, 73
Vedado 69, 199
  development 39–40, 67, 89, 90
Vermay, Jean Baptiste 49
Villarte, Gáspar 54
Villaverde, Cirilo 48
Villoch, Federico 55, 83
visual and plastic arts 81, 99–100, 162
  and *Bohemia* case study 109, 110, 112

Welles, Sumner (US ambassador) 62–3
Williams, Raymond 7
women
  and culture 72
  prohibitions on female labour 40
working class
  culture 42, 196
  emergence and expansion 61, 91

youth culture 151–2, 163–4, 168, 198–9, 213
  rap movement 199–200

zarzuela 50, 100